Landmarks in Australian Intellectual Property Law

Edited by Andrew T Kenyon, Megan Richardson and Sam Ricketson

This authoritative text provides a picture of how Australian intellectual property law has developed as a distinctly Australian body of law during the century since Federation. The book takes a selection of key intellectual property law cases and tells their stories, situating each case in its social context, as well as providing factual details about the arguments made in each case and the evidence adduced. *Landmarks in Australian Intellectual Property Law* offers a closer legal analysis of selected cases, many of which have been central to the framing of Australian intellectual property law. It provides a fuller sense of each case as revealing and influencing wider understandings and practices.

Landmarks in Australian Intellectual Property Law is a valuable resource for academics, researchers, practitioners and judges in Australia and throughout the common law world.

Andrew T Kenyon is Professor and Director, Centre for Media and Communications Law, Melbourne Law School, University of Melbourne.

Megan Richardson is Professor and Deputy Director, Centre for Media and Communications Law, Melbourne Law School, University of Melbourne.

Sam Ricketson is Professor of Law, Melbourne Law School, University of Melbourne.

Landmarks in Australian Intellectual Property Law

Edited by
Andrew T Kenyon
Megan Richardson
Sam Ricketson

Shaftesbury Road, Cambridge CB2 8EA, United Kingdom

One Liberty Plaza, 20th Floor, New York, NY 10006, USA

477 Williamstown Road, Port Melbourne, VIC 3207, Australia

314–321, 3rd Floor, Plot 3, Splendor Forum, Jasola District Centre, New Delhi – 110025, India

103 Penang Road, #05–06/07, Visioncrest Commercial, Singapore 238467

Cambridge University Press is part of Cambridge University Press & Assessment, a department of the University of Cambridge.

We share the University's mission to contribute to society through the pursuit of education, learning and research at the highest international levels of excellence.

www.cambridge.org
Information on this title: www.cambridge.org/9780521516860

© Cambridge University Press & Assessment 2009
The moral rights of the authors have been asserted.

This publication is in copyright. Subject to statutory exception and to the provisions of relevant collective licensing agreements, no reproduction of any part may take place without the written permission of Cambridge University Press & Assessment.

First published 2009

Cover design by Modern Art Production Group

A catalogue record for this publication is available from the British Library

Library of Congress Cataloging-in-Publication data
National Library of Australia Cataloguing in Publication data
  Kenyon, Andrew T.
  Landmarks in Australian intellectual property law / Andrew
  T. Kenyon, Megan Richardson, Sam Ricketson.
  9780521516860 (hbk.)
  Includes index.
  Bibliography.
  Intellectual property–Australia.
  Intangible property–Australia.
  Richardson, Megan.
  Ricketson, Sam.
346.94048

ISBN   978-0-521-51686-0   Hardback

Reproduction and communication for educational purposes
The Australian *Copyright Act 1968* (the Act) allows a maximum of one chapter or 10% of the pages of this work, whichever is the greater, to be reproduced and/or communicated by any educational institution for its educational purposes provided that the educational institution (or the body that administers it) has given a remuneration notice to Copyright Agency Limited (CAL) under the Act.

For details of the CAL licence for educational institutions contact:

Copyright Agency Limited
Level 15, 233 Castlereagh Street
Sydney NSW 2000
Telephone: (02) 9394 7600
Facsimile: (02) 9394 7601
E-mail: info@copyright.com.au

Reproduction and communication for other purposes
Except as permitted under the Act (for example a fair dealing for the purposes of study, research, criticism or review) no part of this publication may be reproduced, stored in a retrieval system, communicated or transmitted in any form or by any means without prior written permission. All inquiries should be made to the publisher at the address above.

Cambridge University Press & Assessment has no responsibility for the persistence or accuracy of URLs for external or third-party internet websites referred to in this publication and does not guarantee that any content on such websites is, or will remain, accurate or appropriate.

Contents

List of Contributors   *page* vii
Table of Cases   x
Table of Statutes and Regulations   xvi

Situating intellectual property law: introducing landmark Australian
cases   xviii
Andrew T Kenyon, Megan Richardson and Sam Ricketson

1 *Potter v Broken Hill*: misuse of precedent in cross-border IP litigation   1
Richard Garnett

2 The *Union Label* case: an early Australian IP story   15
Sam Ricketson

3 RPM for RPM: *National Phonograph Company of Australia
v Menck*   37
Peter Heerey and Nicole Malone

4 Horses and the law: the enduring legacy of *Victoria Park Racing*   53
Jill McKeough

5 We have never been modern: the High Court's decision in *National
Research Development Corporation v Commissioner of Patents*   73
Stephen Hubicki and Brad Sherman

6 Of vice-chancellors and authors: *UNSW v Moorhouse*   97
Sam Ricketson and David Catterns

7 *Foster v Mountford*: cultural confidentiality in a changing Australia   110
Christoph Antons

8 *Cadbury Schweppes v Pub Squash*: what is all the fizz about?   126
Mark Davison

vi CONTENTS

9 The *Firmagroup* case: trigger for designs law reform 142
Janice Luck

10 Larger than life in the Australian cinema: *Pacific Dunlop v Hogan* 160
Megan Richardson

11 *O Fortuna*! On the vagaries of litigation and the story of musical debasement in Australia 171
Elizabeth Adeney

12 The protection of *At the Waterhole* by John Bulun Bulun: Aboriginal art and the recognition of private and communal rights 191
Colin Golvan

13 The grapes of wrath: the Coonawarra dispute, geographical indications and international trade 209
Matthew Rimmer

14 Waiting for the 'Billy'® to boil: the *Waltzing Matilda* case 233
Leanne Wiseman and Matthew Hall

15 The *Panel* case 251
Melissa De Zwart

Index 267

Contributors

ELIZABETH ADENEY is Senior Lecturer in the School of Law at Deakin University, Melbourne. She holds the Mollie Holman Doctoral Medal 2004 Award from Monash University, and her publications include the book *The Moral Rights of Authors and Performers*.

CHRISTOPH ANTONS is Professor of Comparative Law and Director of the Centre for Comparative Law and Development Studies in Asia and the Pacific at the University of Wollongong. He is also an Australian Research Council QEII Fellow and an adjunct fellow of the Max Planck Institute for Intellectual Property, Competition and Tax Law in Munich.

DAVID CATTERNS QC practises at the New South Wales Bar, specialising in intellectual property, administrative law and appellate advocacy.

MARK DAVISON is Professor of Law in the Faculty of Law, Monash University. His publications include the book *The Legal Protection of Databases* (Cambridge University Press) and he is the co-author of the third edition of *Shanahan's Australian Law of Trade Mark and Passing Off*.

MELISSA DE ZWART is Senior Lecturer in the Faculty of Law, Monash University, where she teaches and researches in copyright law and new media. She has published extensively on issues of copyright and moral rights.

RICHARD GARNETT is Professor of Law at Melbourne Law School, University of Melbourne. He researches in conflict of laws, international dispute resolution and electronic commerce. He has wide experience in legal practice and has been a member of the Australian delegation to the Hague Conference on Private International Law (Jurisdiction and Judgments Convention).

COLIN GOLVAN SC is a member of the Victorian Bar and practises predominantly in intellectual property, trade practices and defamation. His publications include the books *Copyright Law and Practice*, and *Words and Law*.

viii CONTRIBUTORS

MATTHEW HALL is a partner in Swaab Attorneys, Sydney, and acts for the Waltzing Matilda Centre, Queensland. He lectures on the commercialisation of intellectual property at postgraduate level at the Australian National University and is the chair of the advisory board of the Australian Centre for Intellectual Property in Agriculture.

THE HON PETER HEEREY is a Judge of the Federal Court of Australia, who also holds the appointments of President of the Defence Force Discipline Appeals Tribunal, Deputy President of the Australian Competition Tribunal and Presidential Member of the Administrative Appeals Tribunal.

STEPHEN HUBICKI is Research Fellow at the Australian Centre for Intellectual Property in Agriculture at the TC Beirne School of Law, University of Queensland. His research focuses on patent issues in biotechnology.

ANDREW T KENYON is Professor and Director of the Centre for Media and Communications Law at Melbourne Law School, University of Melbourne. He researches in comparative media and communications law, including defamation, privacy and copyright. He is the editor of the international refereed journal, the *Media & Arts Law Review*, and a participant in the Australian Research Council Cultural Research Network.

JANICE LUCK is Senior Lecturer at Melbourne Law School, University of Melbourne, and has taught intellectual property law in the Melbourne Law Masters for many years. She is also a Consultant at Phillips Fox DLA lawyers and has been a member of the Intellectual Property Committee of the Law Council of Australia since 1985.

JILL McKEOUGH is a Professor of Law and Dean of the Faculty of Law, University of Technology, Sydney. She has written and taught primarily in intellectual property as well as torts, commercial law, legal system and legal history. She is currently on the board of the Arts Law Centre of Australia and is a member of the Law Council of Australia's Intellectual Property Committee.

NICOLE MALONE is a solicitor at Baker & McKenzie in Melbourne and a former Associate to Justice Peter Heerey. During 2007 and 2008 she has been based at St Catherine's College, University of Oxford, while undertaking study towards the BCL.

MEGAN RICHARDSON is Professor and Deputy Director of the Centre for Media and Communications Law at the Melbourne Law School, University of Melbourne. Particular areas of academic interest and expertise are in the fields of intellectual property and privacy. Her publications include the co-edited collection (with Andrew Kenyon), *New Dimensions in Privacy Law: International and Comparative Perspectives* (Cambridge University Press, 2006).

SAM RICKETSON is Professor of Law at Melbourne Law School, University of Melbourne, a member of the Victorian Bar and a Commissioner of the Victorian Law Reform Commission. He has written extensively in intellectual property law and conflicts of law and is a former member of the Commonwealth Copyright Tribunal and former president of the Intellectual Property Society of Australia and New Zealand.

MATTHEW RIMMER is Senior Lecturer and Associate Director of the Australian Centre for Intellectual Property in Agriculture at the ANU College of Law, Australian National University. His publications include *Digital Copyright and the Consumer Revolution: Hands off my iPod* and *Intellectual Property and Biotechnology: Biological Inventions*.

BRAD SHERMAN is Professor and Director of the Australian Centre for Intellectual Property in Agriculture at the TC Beirne School of Law, University of Queensland. Recent publications include 'Copyright Protection for Indigenous Creations: Issues for the Future' [2008] *Intellectual Property Journal*, forthcoming (with Leanne Wiseman).

LEANNE WISEMAN is Associate Professor and Associate Director, Australian Centre for Intellectual Property in Agriculture, Griffith Law School, Griffith University. She researches primarily in intellectual property law and has published in the fields of intellectual property, contract and company law. Her publications include *Intellectual Property Law in Australia* (Cambridge University Press, 2008, with A Monotti and M Davison).

Table of Cases

Aboriginal Sacred Sites Protection Authority v Maurice 120
Adams v Burks 41–2
Amalgamated Society of Engineers v Adelaide Steamship Co Ltd 33
Anaesthetic Supplies Pty Ltd v Rescare Ltd 95
Andrew Cash & Co Investments Pty Ltd v Porter and Ors 54
Applicant 'A' v Minister for Immigration and Ethnic Affairs 190
Atkinson Footwear Ltd v Hodgskin International Services Ltd 9
Attorney-General v Guardian Newspapers Ltd (No. 2) 71
Attorney-General for Victoria v City of Melbourne 39
Attorney-General of NSW v Brewery Employees' Union xx, xxiii, 21–36
Australasian Performing Right Association Ltd v Canterbury-Bankstown League Club Ltd 101
Australian Broadcasting Corporation v Lenah Game Meats Pty Ltd 69–70, 119, 122–3
Australian Broadcasting Commission v Parish et al 64
Autodesk Inc and Anor v Dyason and Ors 54
Badische Anilin und Soda Fabrik v Isler 42
Baltimore Orioles Inc v Major League Baseball Players Association 65
Bauman v Fussell 200
Baxendale's Vineyard Pty Ltd v The Geographical Indications Committee 229
Beringer Blass v Geographical Indications Committee xx, xxii, 210–25
Betts v Willmott 43
Boulton and Watt v Bull 86, 87, 91
Breen v Williams 124
British Mutoscope and Biograph Co Ltd v Homer 42
British South Africa Company v Companhia de Mocambique 4, 7
Brooks v Religious Tract Society 200
Bulun Bulun v R & T Textiles Pty Ltd xx, xxii, 124, 191–207, 222
Cadbury Schweppes Pty Ltd v Pub Squash Co Ltd xx, 127–40
Campbell v MGN Ltd 68, 71
Campomar Sociedad Limitada v Nike International 66–7
Catnic Components Ltd v Hill and Smith Ltd 90
CBC Distribution & Marketing Inc v Major League Baseball Advanced Media, LP 62
Cementation Co's Application 88
Cheney Bros v Doris Silk Corp 67
Chicago NL Club v Sky Box on Waveland 67
Coe v Commonwealth 206
Coin Controls Ltd v Suzo International (UK) Ltd 9
Colonial Bank of Australasia Ltd v Marshall 39

TABLE OF CASES xi

Comite Interprofessionel du Vin de Champagne v NL Burton Pty Ltd 213
Commercial Solvents v Synthetic Product 83
Commission of the European Communities v Federal Republic of Germany 232
Commissioner of Patents v Microcell 80
Commonwealth v John Fairfax & Sons 119
Commonwealth v Tasmania 35
Computer Edge Pty Ltd v Apple Computer Inc 197
Consorzio del Proscuitto de Parma v Asda 232
Coonawarra case *see also Beringer Blass v Geographical Indications Committee*
*Coonawarra Penola Wine Industry Association and Geographical Indications
    Committee* 210, 220
Crane v Price 87
David Murray v Big Pictures (UK) Ltd 71
Davis v The Commonwealth 35
Desktop Marketing Systems Pty Ltd v Telstra Corporation Ltd 54
Diamond v Chakrabarty 95
Diethelm & Co Ltd v Bradley 6
Donoghue v Stevenson 59
Douglas v Hello! Ltd 70–1
Dunlop Rubber Co Ltd v Golf Ball Development Ltd 146
Eastern Microwave Inc v Double Day Sports Inc 65
Elton and Leda Chemical's Application 88, 91
Engineers case *see Amalgamated Society of Engineers v Adelaide Steamship Co Ltd*
Erven Warnink BV v J Townend & Sons (Hull) Ltd 135
Esquel Enterprises v Tal Apparel 10–11
Ettore v Philco Television Broadcasting 65
*Federal Republic of Germany and Kingdom of Denmark v Commission of the European
    Communities* 232
Feist Publications Inc v Rural Telephone Co Inc 53, 62, 67
'Feta Cheese' case *see Federal Republic of Germany and Kingdom of Denmark v
    Commission of the European Communities*
Firmagroup designs case *see Firmagroup Australia Pty Ltd v Byrne & Davidson Doors
    (Vic) Pty Ltd*
Firmagroup Australia Pty Ltd v Byrne Davidson Doors (Vic) Pty Ltd **xx–xxiii**, 142
Football League Ltd v Littlewoods Pools Ltd 197
Foster v Mountford & Rigby Ltd **xx, xxi, xxiii**, 110–25, 203
Fraser v Evans 119
Funk Bros Seed Co v Kalo Inoculant 84, 85
Gartside v Outram 119
Gauthier v Pro-Football Inc 65
GEC's Application 88
Geographical Indications (Olive Oil 'Kalamata') 232
Gillette Safety Razor Co Ltd v AW Gamage Ltd 42
Gionfriddo v Major League Baseball 62
Girgis v Flaherty 11
Glyn v Weston Feature Film Co 102
Grain Pool of Western Australia v Commonwealth 35
'Grand Padano cheese' case *see Ravil v Bellon*
Grant v Commissioner of Patents 91, 94

xii TABLE OF CASES

Griffin v Isaacs 158
Hanfstaengl v Empire Palace 201
Hatton v Keane 197–200
Hawkes & Son (London) Ltd v Paramount Film Service Ltd 200
Heap v Hartley 43
Henderson v Radio Corporation Pty Ltd 60–1, 135, 169
Hepworth Manufacturing Company Ltd v Ryott 161
Hicks v Ruddock 13
Hickton's Patent Syndicate v Patents and Machine Improvements Co 82
Hogan v Koala Dundee Pty Ltd 139, 166, 169, 202
Hogan v Pacific Dunlop Ltd 136, 163, 202
Hornblower v Boulton 87
Hosking v Runting 123
Hosokawa Micron International Inc v Fortune 143, 152
Hotton v Arthur 197
In re The Apollinaris Co's Trade Marks 27
Incandescent Gas Light v Brogden 42
Incandescent Gas Light v Cantelo 42–4
International News Service v Associated Press 58–60, 66–7, 140
Interstate Parcel Express Co v Time-Life International 44
J Bollinger v Costa Brava Wine Co Ltd 135, 139, 213
Jewler's Circular Pub Co v Keystone Pub Co 53
John Pfeiffer Pty Ltd v Rogerson 5, 14
Johnson-Kennedy Radio Corp v Chicago
Jones v The Commonwealth (No. 2) 33
Joos v Commissioner of Patents 73, 95
Kestos Ltd v Kempat Ltd 149
Kevi A/S v Suspa-Verein UK Ltd 145
King Valley Vignerons Inc v Geographical Indications Committee 227–8
King v Murray and Anor 54
Kiren-Amgen v Board of Regents of University of Washington 94
KK Sony Computer Entertainment v Van Veen 10–11
Koowarta v Bjelke-Peterson 35, 190
Lamb v Evans 197
Lane Fox v Kensington and Knightsbridge Electric Lighting 82
LB (Plastics) Ltd v Swish Products Ltd 200
Leegin Creative Leather Products Inc v PSKS Inc 46
Lenard's Application 93, 94
Lerose Ltd v Hawick Jersey International Ltd 201
Loeb v Turner 65, 67
Lomas v Winton Shire Council xx, xxii, 234–49
Lucasfilms Ltd v Ainsworth 10
Macintosh v Dun 39
Macrae Knitting Mills Ltd v Lowes Ltd 143
Madison Square Garden Corp v Universal Pictures, Co 59, 65
Maeder v Busch 88, 90, 91, 94
Malleys Ltd v JW Tomlin Pty Ltd 145–6
McGruther v Pitcher 42
McNaghten v Paterson 39

TABLE OF CASES   xiii

Meyers Taylor Pty Ltd v Vicarr Industries Ltd 52
Milpurrurru v Indofurn Pty Ltd 192, 222
Moody v Tree 150
Moorgate Tobacco Ltd v Philip Morris Ltd (No.2) xxi, 66, 139
Moorhouse and Angus and Robertson (Publishers) Pty Ltd v University of New South Wales 99
Morris Communications Corp v PGA Tour Inc 63–4
Murray v King 54
National Basketball Association v Motorola Inc 59, 62–3, 67
National Collegiate Athletic Association v Board of Regents of the University of Oklahoma 65
National Exhibition v Fass 65
National Exhibition v Teleflash 65
National Phonograph Company of Australia Ltd v Menck xx–xxiii, 37–52
National Research Development Corporation v Commissioner of Patents xxi, xxiii, 73–96
Network Ten Pty Ltd v TCN Channel Nine Pty Ltd 251, 252
Nine Films Television v Ninox Television Ltd 255
Nine Network Australia Pty Ltd v Australian Broadcasting Corporation 255
Nine Network Australia Pty Ltd v IceTV Pty Ltd 255
Nintendo Co Ltd v Centronics Systems Pty Ltd 35
NV Philips' Gloeilampenfabrieken's Application 93, 94
Pacific Dunlop Ltd v Hogan xx, 136, 160–70, 203
Panel case *see TCN Channel Nine v Network Ten*
'Parma Ham' case *see Consorzio del Proscuitto de Parma v Asda*
Pearce v Ove Arup Partnership Ltd 10
Pedersen v Young 5
Petrotimor v The Commonwealth of Australia 13
Pfeiffer case *see John Pfeiffer Pty Ltd v Rogerson*
Pittsburg Athletic Co v KQV Broadcasting Co 65, 67–8
Polyaire Pty Ltd v K-Aire Pty Ltd 143, 146
Post Newsweek Stations-Connecticut Publishing Ins Inc v Travellers Ins Co 65
Potter v Broken Hill Pty Co Ltd xx, xxiii, 1–14
Powell v Birmingham Vinegar Brewery Co 27
Prince Albert v Strange 116
Pub Squash case *see Cadbury Schweppes Pty Ltd v Pub Squash*
Queensland Wire Industries Pty Ltd v Broken Hill Pty Co Ltd 52
R Griggs Group Pty Ltd v Evans 10
R v Sparrow 124
R v Wheeler 87, 91
Rantzen's Application 88
Ravil v Bellon 232
Re AF's Application 79, 80
Re Amalgamated Services Pty Ltd and the New South Wales Rugby Football League 64
Re Australian Cricket Board, PBL Marketing Pty Ltd, World Series Cricket Pty Ltd and Publishing and Broadcasting Ltd 64
Re BA's Application 80
Re Bayer's Design 150
Re Brisbane TV Ltd 64
Re Brislan; Ex parte Williams 33

xiv TABLE OF CASES

Re Interlego AG and Lego Australia Pty Ltd v Croner Trading Pty Ltd 9
Re South Queensland Broadcasting Pty Ltd 64
Re Sykes and Co's Trade Mark 31
Re The Warumungu Land Claim 120
Re Universal Telecasters Queensland Ltd 64
Re Wolanski's Registered Design 149
Regie Nationale des Usines Renault v Zhang 6, 13
RHF's Application 93, 94
Robertson v Lewis 197, 198
Rudolph Mayer Pictures Inc v Pathe News Inc 59, 65
Schmidt v Won 13
Schott Musik International GmbH Co v Colossal Records of Australia Pty Ltd xx, xxiii, 172–89
Shantou Commercial Development Co v P & O Swire Containers Ltd 11
Société Anonyme des Manufactures de Glaces v Tilghman's Patent Sand Blast Co 43
South West Broadcasting Co v Oil Centre Broadcasting 65
Southey v Sherwood 102
Special Effects Ltd v L'Oreal SA 243
Spiliada Maritime Corp v Cansulex 11
Standard Oil Development Corp's Application 79
Strickland v Rocla Concrete Pipes Ltd 35
Taco Co (Aust) Inc v Taco Bell Pty Ltd 136
Taddy & Co v Sterious & Co 42
TCN Channel Nine Pty Ltd v Network Ten Pty Ltd xx, xxii, 251–66
TCN Channel Nine Pty Ltd v Network Ten Pty Ltd (No. 2) 252
Te Runanga o Wharekauri Rehohu Inc v Attorney-General 124
The King v Burgess; Ex parte Henry 35
Thomas A Edison Ltd v Stockdale 44
TR Flanagan Smash Repairs Pty Ltd and Anor v Jones 54
Tritech Technology Pty Ltd v Gordon 9
Twentieth Century Sporting Club v Transradio Press Service Inc 59, 65
Tyburn Productions Ltd v Conan Doyle 9
Underhill v Hernandez 4, 7
Union Label case see *Attorney-General of NSW v Brewery Employees' Union*
United States v Arnold, Schwinn & Co 47
United States v National Football League 65
Universal Music Australia Pty Ltd v Sharman License Holdings Ltd 109
University of London Press Ltd v University Tutorial Press Ltd 197
University of New South Wales v Moorhouse xx, xxiii
Venus Adult Shops Pty Ltd v Fraserside Holdings Ltd 97–109
Victoria Park Racing and Recreation Grounds Company Ltd v Taylor xx–xxiii, 53–68, 139, 140
Voth v Manildra Flour Mills Pty Ltd 6, 11
Wainwright v Home Office 71
Wakim, Re; Ex parte McNally 5
Walter v Lane 196
Waltzing Matilda case see *Lomas v Winton Shire Council*
Waltzing Matilda Centre Ltd v Jolly Swagman Pty Ltd 246

Ward v Western Australia 121
Weitmann v Katies Ltd 165
Wik Peoples v Queensland 206
Winton Shire Council v Lomas 234, 235, 239
WT4'WV Inc v National Football League 65
Zacchini v Scripps-Howard Broadcasting Co 65

Table of Statutes and Regulations

Acts Interpretation Act 1901 (Cth)
  s 15AB **184**
*America's Cup Yacht Race (Special
  Arrangements) Act* 1986 (WA) **65**
*Australian Bicentennial Authority Act
  1988* (Cth) **35**
Australian Constitution s 51(xviii) **3,
  135**
*Australian Formula One Grand Prix Act
  1984* (SA) **65**
Australian Grand Prix Act 1995
  (Vic) **64–5**
*Australian Wine and Brandy Corporation
  Act 1980* (Cth) **210, 215–16, 222,
  229**
  s 3(1) **215**
  s 4 **215**
  s 40C **215**
  s 40D(2) **216**
  s 40E **216**
  s 40F **216**
  s 40N **216**
  s 40P **216**
  s 40Q(1) **217**
  s 40T(1) **216**
  s 40ZC **216**
*Australian Wine and Brandy Corporation
  Regulations 1981* **216–18, 222,
  227–9**
Broadcasting and Television Act 1942
  (Cth) **60, 64**
Broadcasting Services Act 1992
  (Cth) **254**
  s 115 **254**
Business Names Act 1962 (Vic) s 5 **134**
Civil Law (Wrongs) Act 2002 (ACT) **13**
  s 220 **13**
Commonwealth Games Act 1982
  (Qld) **65**

Copyright Act 1968 **98, 99, 172, 192,
  204, 257–8**
  s 10(1) **183, 257**
  s 14(1)(a) **200**
  s 25(4)(a) **258, 259**
  s 30 **183**
  s 31 **183**
  s 32 (2) **192, 200**
  s 36 **103, 182**
  s 39A **108–9**
  s 40 **100, 101, 103**
  s 41A **257**
  s 49 **100**
  s 50 **100**
  s 53A **108**
  s 53B **108**
  s 55 **181, 183**
  s 55(2) **172**
  s 87 **256, 257, 259, 260**
  s 101 **260**
  s 103AA **257**
  s 103A **256**
  s 103B **256**
*Copyright Amendment (Moral Rights)
  Act 2000* s3, Sch 1 Item 1A
  188
Copyright, Designs and Patents Act 1988
  (Cth) s 80(2)(b) **185**
Corporations Regulations 2001 **244**
Designs Act 1906 (Cth) **143–6, 150,
  151–7**
  s 4 **144**
  s 18 **151**
  s 30 **145**
  s 30(1) **144**
Designs Act 2003 (Cth) **153**
  s 5 **153**
  s 15 **154**
  s 16 **154**

xvi

s 19 154, 155, 156
s 71(1)(a) 153
Designs Amendment Act 1981
(Cth) 151–2
Fine Arts Copyright Act 1862 (UK) 201
Human Rights Act 1998 (UK) 71, 123
Income Tax Assessment Act 1936
(Cth) 162
Div IOBA 162
Jurisdiction of Courts (Cross-vesting) Act
1987 (NSW) 5, 12
s 4(3) 5
Jurisdiction of Courts (Foreign Land) Act
1989 (NSW) 12
s 3 12
s 4 12
Patents Act 1903 (Cth) 41
Patents Act 1990 (Cth) 51, 158
Patents Amendment (Innovation Patents)
Act 2000 (Cth) 158
s 7(4) 159
s 18(1A) 159
Patents Designs and Trade Marks Act
1883 (UK) 144
Privy Council (Limitations of Appeals) Act
1968 (Cth) 127
Registered Designs Act 1949 (UK)
s 7(1) 144
Restrictive Trade Practices Act 1971
(Cth) 44, 45
s 66 44, 45

Statute of Monopolies, s 6 86, 89–91,
94–5
Supreme Court Act 1970 (NSW)
134
Trade Mark Regulations 1995
Sch 2(f) 243
Trade Marks Act 1905 (Cth) xxi, 15, 22,
66, 234
Part VII 22–4, 29
s 18 245
s 43 239–41
s 58 239–41
s 60 239, 241
Trade Marks Act 1955 (Cth) 135
Trade Marks Act 1995 (Cth)
s 39(2) 243
s 42(b) 216
s 43 239, 240, 241
s 44 241
s 58 234, 239, 240
s 60 239, 241
s 129 133
s 197 241
Trade Practices Act 1974 (Cth) 45,
51, 66, 126, 157, 169, 192,
202
s 2 51
s 48 45, 46, 50
s 52 136, 164, 165
s 52(1) 136
s 53 164

Situating intellectual property law: introducing landmark Australian cases

Andrew T Kenyon, Megan Richardson and Sam Ricketson

That law and social conditions are inexorably intertwined is shown by the fact that the first inventions granted patents in Australia, under the then state Acts, included a windlass, an improved method of manufacturing charcoal, improvements in the construction of timber and iron bridges, and improvements in the manufacture of pipes.[1] Nor is it surprising that the Australian colonies would be among the first in the world to introduce modern-style patent, designs, trade marks and copyright regimes, and also among the first to use them. As Barton Hack notes, the second half of the 19th century was a period of great development in Australia, especially in Victoria and especially during the long boom years of the 1870s and 1880s:

> The stump-jump plough was invented by RB Smith in 1876, the commercial shearing machine by Savage and Wolseley in 1877, telephone exchanges were opened in Melbourne and Brisbane in 1880 and in Sydney in 1881, superphosphate was available by the eighties, the Melbourne International Exhibition was held in its new building in 1880–1881, Melbourne and Sydney were finally linked by rail in 1883, HV McKay demonstrated his combine harvester in 1884, Melbourne's first cable tram ran in 1885, a state system of education was established in NSW in 1883, the Working Man's College (later the RMIT) was inaugurated in 1887 (Sydney University had opened in 1852 and Melbourne University in 1855), the Broken Hill lode was discovered in 1883 and mining commenced in 1885, and between 1871 and 1891 the population of Sydney increased from 137 586 to 383 333 and that of Melbourne from 206 780 to 490 896. The rapid industrialization was of course achieved at a social cost, but the changes caused by technological advancement could not be reversed.[2]

Even at this early stage, however, the influence of imported legal models was evident with both state legislation and case law following closely the precedents of the 'mother country'. In part, the influence may be attributed to the effects of

---

1 South Australian Private Act No. 1 of 1848; South Australian Private Act No. 2 of 1850; Victorian Patent No. 1, 1854; Queensland Patent No. 1, 1860. See also B Hack, 'A History of the Patent Profession in Colonial Australia', paper presented at the Annual Conference of The Institute of Patent Attorneys of Australia, Brisbane, Queensland, 29–31 March 1984; and Victorian patent indexes, 1854 to 1904, held at the State Library of Victoria.
2 Hack, ibid., pp. 47–8.

xviii

British colonialism in the Australian states, as one of us has pointed out in another context.[3] But it may also have been a response to the tension universally found within intellectual property law between the particular territorial concerns of sovereign states and the essentially non-territorially confined character of the subject-matter – whose physical boundaries, if any can be ascertained, may vary over time and are certainly not dictated by considerations of where state borders start and finish. The response was found in a high level of symmetry in state-based legal standards, followed by an eventual move to a supra-state level, once Australian federalism made Commonwealth legislation on intellectual property a feasible option. Now, the tension has been transferred to the international arena, and we can again observe the symmetry of national law standards and foresee the possibility of fully internationalised standards as well. But a question that remains is how much such harmonised and internationalised intellectual property standards can take into account the exigencies of social circumstances, which may vary according to time and place. As shown by the cases discussed in this volume, the answer is a surprising amount when it comes down to actual issues being debated in courts. And this becomes particularly apparent when the story of the case is told and integrated with the legal analysis, our chosen methodology. Or, as Matthew Rimmer puts it in his chapter, the *petite histoire* is a useful way of understanding this reality.

The case studies are placed in chronological order from earliest to latest in time, not simply as a matter of convenience. If anything, we suggest, Australian courts have over years become more openly socially aware in their decisions, exploring opportunities for solutions to be found to problems that are not merely legal within the scope allowed by the statute or precedent in the case of equitable and common law actions. That trend, of course, also influences the ways in which chapters engage in their storytelling, with greater opportunity to broaden doctrinal analysis into contextual understanding for decisions from more recent decades. Already, in the late 1950s, we see the High Court referring in *NRDC v Commissioner of Patents* to the

> remarkable advantage, indeed to the lay mind a sensational advantage [of the applicant's invention for a process of applying weedkiller to crops] ... [lying in] the cultivation of the soil for the production of its fruits' as crucial to answering the essential question of whether the claimed invention was 'a proper subject of letters patent'.[4]

Stephen Hubicki and Brad Sherman note that the language demonstrates 'the widespread cultural appeal that technological control over nature has exerted in the modern era', especially since World War II. Sixteen years later, as Sam Ricketson and David Catterns observe, the High Court's extension of authorisation in copyright law to the provision of photocopiers in a university library in

---

3 See S Ricketson, 'The Future of Australian Intellectual Property Law Reform and Administration' (1992) 3 *Australian Intellectual Property Journal* 3, 9–11 (the context there being a discussion of British influences on post-federation Commonwealth legislation).
4 *National Research Development Corporation v Commissioner of Patents* (1959) 102 CLR 252, 277; 1A IPR 63, 75.

XX SITUATING INTELLECTUAL PROPERTY LAW

University of New South Wales v Moorhouse[5] represented an imaginative but logical response to the culture then prevalent within Australian universities of treating copyright as irrelevant to educational concerns. Australia's highest courts may have eschewed social referencing in *Cadbury Schweppes v Pub Squash*[6] and *Firmagroup v B & D Doors*[7] in the 1980s (and although the *Pub Squash* case may be put aside as a Privy Council decision, Mark Davison questions whether the High Court would have taken a markedly different approach), but by then the lower courts were taking on a more significant role. The Aboriginal folklore and art cases of *Foster v Mountford & Rigby*[8] and *Bulun Bulun v R & T Textiles*[9] show modern Australian courts seeking to accommodate traditional cultural values in their decisions. References to the values and customs of modern society can be found in judicial comments about the audience's response to the *Crocodile Dundee* film and character in the case of *Pacific Dunlop v Hogan*.[10] And, according to Elizabeth Adeney, the Full Federal Court's refusal to find that a popular techno dance version debased Carl Orff's *O Fortuna* chorus in *Schott Musik v Colossal Records*[11] displays an Australian unwillingness to make negative value judgments about (derivative) creativity – although she adds that this may have to change in an era of Berne Convention compliance on moral rights.

There are cases still where judges appear unable to find a satisfactory solution to a matter of social concern within the established parameters of the law (as in *Lomas v Winton Shire Council*[12] and its 'Waltzing Matilda' trade mark registrations), or they fail to find a consensus on how social policies might be accommodated within legal standards (as with the different judgments on fair dealing for criticism or review and news reporting in the *Panel* case, *TCN Channel Nine v Network Ten*[13]), or resolve only the narrow 'legal' issue before them while leaving broader ones open (as in the Coonawarra wine label case, *Beringer Blass v Geographical Indications Committee*[14]). But they seem ready to acknowledge at least that the cases have a social dimension. In contrast, *Potter v BHP*,[15] *Attorney-General of NSW v Brewery Employees' Union* (*Union Label* case)[16] and *National Phonograph Co v Menck*[17] at the turn of the 20th century, and even *Victoria Park Racing v Taylor*[18] in the late 1930s, were almost entirely black-letter law in their

---

5 (1975) 133 CLR 1.
6 *Cadbury Schweppes Pty Ltd v Pub Squash Co Ltd* [1981] RPC 429.
7 *Firmagroup Australia Pty Ltd v Byrne & Davison Doors (Vic) Pty Ltd* (1987) 9 IPR 353.
8 *Foster and Others v Mountford and Rigby Ltd* (1976) 14 ALR 71.
9 *Bulun Bulun and Another v R & T Textiles Pty Ltd* (1998) 41 IPR 513.
10 *Hogan and Others v Pacific Dunlop Ltd* (1988) 12 IPR 225 and (on appeal) *Pacific Dunlop Ltd v Hogan and Others* (1989) 14 IPR 398.
11 *Schott Musik International GMBH & Co and Others v Colossal Records of Australia Pty Ltd and Others* (1997) 38 IPR 1.
12 *Lomas v Winton Shire Council and the Waltzing Matilda Centre Ltd* (2003) AIPC 35,165.
13 *TCN Channel Nine Pty Ltd v Network Ten Pty Ltd* (2002) 65 IPR 112.
14 *Beringer Blass Wine Estates Ltd v Geographical Indications Committee* (2002) 125 FCR 155.
15 *Potter v Broken Hill Pty Co Ltd* (1906) 3 CLR 479.
16 *Attorney-General (NSW) v Brewery Employees of NSW* (1908) 6 CLR 469.
17 *National Phonograph Company of Australia Ltd v Menck* (1908) 7 CLR 481 and (on appeal) [1911] AC 336.
18 *Victoria Park Racing & Recreation Grounds Co Ltd v Taylor* (1937) 58 CLR 479; 1A IPR 308.

reasoning – with the notable exception of the later-to-be influential dissent of Higgins J in *Union Label*.[19]

As close inquiry into those cases show, however, the first two involved fascinating stories of political controversy (*Potter* an early case of states' rights with respect to an invention patented in New South Wales before federation, and *Union Label* involving a dispute over original versus more progressivist interpretations of the intellectual property power under the Commonwealth Constitution, in the face of new 'union label' provisions inserted into the *Trade Marks Act 1905* (Cth) by the then Labor Government), while *Menck* presaged modern economic debates about the extent to which intellectual property rights holders should be free to exploit their market power by seeking to control an industry. Moreover, as Jill McKeough's discussion of *Victoria Park* makes clear, the case was not just about the High Court's treatment of legal arguments relating to copyright, nuisance, privacy and unfair competition. It was at heart a story of an ingenious broadcaster profiting from a neighbour's ability to overlook the spectacle of races being conducted on a commercially operated racetrack. Yet, with the possible exception of Latham J's passing comment that the plaintiff could have built a higher fence (for economists a signal of a cheaper cost avoidance analysis),[20] there is little mention of broader policy issues in the leading judgments in the case, which were rather framed around judicial statements about the settled boundaries of existing law.

The inevitable conclusion is that a court's readiness to address the social dimension of law depends, at least in part, on the attitude judges have to their role. Although it has been said in an earlier *Landmarks* book that '[u]ndoubtedly the High Court in its present composition is signalling a retreat from the Mason era of judicial activism',[21] we might wonder whether this is especially a feature of Australian intellectual property decisions or whether the experience has rather been one of gradual expansion of the judicial role over the hundred and more years since the High Court was established.

True, it was in the Mason era that Deane J said in *Moorgate Tobacco v Philip Morris*[22] that courts should be prepared to adopt a flexible approach to existing forms of action within their purview to 'meet new situations and circumstances' in preference to adopting torts of uncertain definition and parameters[23] (curiously, this was but three years before a similarly constituted High Court gave one of its most conservative and uninspiring judgments in the *Firmagroup* designs case,[24] leaving the reform agenda here squarely with the legislature). By contrast, as

---

19 See *Grain Pool of Western Australia v Commonwealth* (2000) 46 IPR 515.
20 (1937) 58 CLR 479, 494; 1A IPR 308, 310.
21 HP Lee, 'The Implied Freedom of Political Communication' in HP Lee and G Winterton (eds.), *Australian Constitutional Landmarks*, Cambridge University Press, Cambridge, 2003, p. 405.
22 *Moorgate Tobacco Co Ltd v Philip Morris Ltd (No. 2)* (1984) 156 CLR 414.
23 See especially ibid., p. 445.
24 (1987) 9 IPR 353. Three of the five judges – Wilson, Deane and Dawson JJ – were on both panels, *Firmagroup* having also Brennan and Gaudron JJ (neither of whom are known for their conservatism) and *Moorgate Tobacco* having also (the normally conservative) Gibbs CJ as well as Mason J.

xxii SITUATING INTELLECTUAL PROPERTY LAW

McKeough points out with respect to *Victoria Park*,[25] no such flexibility was evidenced in that case when the High Court declined to find any intellectual property or other basis for granting exclusive rights over the spectacle of races being carried out in the plaintiff's grounds.

But already by the end of the 1950s, Hubicki and Sherman observe, incremental adaptation of legal standards was a feature of the Dixon court in *NRDC*.[26] More recently, various members of the (in some respects) Dixon-like contemporary High Court have not eschewed Deane J's statement of 'preferred legal method' but instead have endorsed it as a way forward for the court, making it clear that Deane J's language of 'situations and circumstances' must include not only new technologies and trading practices but social practices and values as well.[27] That such broadening out might lead to judicial uncertainty and even anxiety cannot be denied. For instance, the differences that emerged in the *Panel* case, the apparent inability to resolve more than the narrow issues in *Beringer* and the abject failure to protect the folkloric status of Banjo Paterson's much loved national song in the *Waltzing Matilda* case do not just result in less clear and stable legal precedents (as those having to deal with the cases may complain), but reveal courts grappling with their own realisation of their limited abilities to address all the social aspects of the case before them.

The challenges for judges are even greater where social practices and values may be highly localised and vary over time. Nevertheless, we suggest, the benefits of an 'anthropological' approach can still be immense. The particular case studies we have selected are designed to show that, at least in some circumstances – those involving mining, union marks, crop farming, the spectacle of horse racing, pubs, cars, crocodile hunters who run tourist operations on the side, Aboriginal stories and art, Coonawarra wines and Australian folk songs, for instance – there is a distinctly Australian flavour. Some of them, especially *Foster v Mountford*,[28] *Bulun Bulun*[29] and *Beringer*[30] show the inklings of a more narrowly localised flavour as well. Moreover, while many of our cases may be seen as especially about rural Australia, there are also some fascinating urban tales as well: the location of *Menck*[31] in Nicholson Street at the border between Fitzroy and Carlton in Melbourne shows the significance in 1908 of small inner-suburban businesses in Australian life;[32] *Firmagroup*,[33] with its back-story of a garage door handle-lock, shows the popularity of the commuting suburb 80 years later; the techno

---

25 (1937) 58 CLR 479; 1A IPR 308.
26 (1959) 102 CLR 252; 1A IPR 63.
27 See for instance *Australian Broadcasting Corporation v Lenah Game Meats Pty Ltd* (2001) 208 CLR 199, 250; (2002) 54 IPR 161, 192 (Gummow and Hayne JJ), and for an earlier signal of Gummow J's endorsement of this approach, the beginning of his judgment in *Hogan v Pacific Dunlop* (1988) 12 IPR 225.
28 (1976) 14 ALR 71.
29 (1998) 41 IPR 513.
30 (2002) 125 FCR 155.
31 (1908) 7 CLR 481; [1911] AC 336.
32 An urban setting revelled in Fergus Hume's classic crime novel, *The Mystery of a Hansom Cab*, published by Hume in Melbourne in 1886, and in Great Britain by the Hansom Cab Publishing Co in 1887.
33 (1987) 9 IPR 353.

dance remix of Orff's *O Fortuna* chorus, which featured in the *Schott* case,[34] was popular at rave parties in the early 1990s;[35] *Crocodile Dundee*[36] is as much a story about successful Australian film-making by citified entrepreneurs as it is about a fictional crocodile hunter in the Northern Territory; and *The Panel*,[37] with its sophisticated mash-ups of Channel 9 content, was a wildly popular Australian television program in the predominantly urbanised sub-40 Australian demographic. Taken together, the facts of the cases, ranging over the century after the first Australian Act, give a picture of a varied and complex Australia. Accordingly, they invite a variety of possible multilayered responses from commentators, whether of a more doctrinal or scholarly kind, as reflected in this book, which includes diverse contributions from the judiciary, legal practice and academia.

For this reason, if no other, the essays are worth reading. But we also suggest that understanding the stories aids an understanding of their role in the development of intellectual property law in Australia, and sometimes other areas of law as well (particularly at the contestable boundary with privacy, an issue that features in several of the chapters, most notably *Victoria Park*[38] and *Foster v Mountford*[39]). Some cases undoubtedly have cast a longer shadow over the law than others, and their shadow may extend beyond the shores of Australia. *Victoria Park*,[40] *NRDC*[41] and *Moorhouse*[42] come especially to mind and, as a result, we predict their chapters will be read especially carefully. But one reason for their longevity comes from a certain universal quality to their circumstances, despite their highly localised character in other respects – with digital and genetic innovation, the phenomenal business of sport, and internet-based music sharing presenting 21st-century parallels to the race-going, crop spraying and student photocopying of the 1930s, 50s and 80s. Other cases are more interesting in the changes they initiated, as for instance *Menck*[43] and *Firmagroup*,[44] which prompted a degree of legislative takeover of issues initially left to courts, and *Union Label*,[45] which prompted a different approach to Constitution-reading in more recent times. Finally, and most subtly, it will be seen that some of the cases have, somewhat anomalously, served as precedents long after the particular conditions that led to their being ceased to exist. The most obvious example is the earliest case in the collection, *Potter v BHP*,[46] which has become a

---

34 (1997) 38 IPR 1.
35 And still is, according to our informal consultations.
36 *Hogan v Pacific Dunlop* (1988) 12 IPR 225 and (on appeal) *Pacific Dunlop v Hogan* (1989) 14 IPR 398.
37 The program featured not only in *TCN Channel Nine Pty Ltd v Network Ten Pty Ltd* (2002) 65 IPR 112 but also (on the issue of what constitutes a broadcast) *Network Ten Pty Ltd v TCN Channel Nine Pty Ltd* (2004) 59 IPR 1 and *TCN Channel Nine Pty Ltd v Network Ten Pty Ltd (No. 2)* (2005) 65 IPR 571.
38 (1937) 58 CLR 479; 1A IPR 308.
39 (1976) 14 ALR 71.
40 (1937) 58 CLR 479; 1A IPR 308.
41 (1959) 102 CLR 252; 1A IPR 63.
42 (1975) 133 CLR 1.
43 (1908) 7 CLR 481 and (on appeal) [1911] AC 336.
44 (1987) 9 IPR 353.
45 (1908) 6 CLR 469.
46 (1906) 3 CLR 479.

Commonwealth precedent on the territoriality of intellectual property jurisdiction, and whose continuing force, as Richard Garnett points out, is at odds with a world of multi-territorial communications. This case surely is an example of what the legal realist Guido Calabresi has called 'legal obsolescence'.[47]

****

There are undoubtedly many cases that might qualify as Australian intellectual property 'landmarks' in a purely legal sense that have not been included in this volume. But there are plenty of excellent other sources of discussion about these, no doubt with more to come. This volume sets out, rather, to frame Australian intellectual property cases that tell us something not just about the development of intellectual property law in Australia, but also about the situation of intellectual property law – and intellectual property itself – in the economic and broader social fabric of our society. It finds its initial inspiration in an American collection, *Intellectual Property Stories*.[48] We are grateful to the editors of that book for their helpful advice on our project. We are also grateful to the editors of Cambridge University Press and anonymous referees for their support and guidance, and we particularly thank our commissioning editor, Zoe Hamilton, for her unstinting enthusiasm. Acknowledgment must be given to Bella Li, of the Melbourne Law School's Centre for Media and Communications Law, for her excellent editorial and research support in transforming this collection of chapters into a complete, consistent and coherent book. Our colleagues David Brennan, John Waugh and Robin Wright provided cheerful advice and assistance at various points along the way; their help is much appreciated. Above all, we are grateful to our distinguished authors for their significant contributions to a broader understanding of intellectual property judicial decision-making in Australia and, in particular, for their unwavering commitment to participation in the project notwithstanding the many other calls on their time.

---

47 G Calabresi, *A Common Law for the Age of Statutes*, Harvard University Press, Boston, 1982, p. 2 (although talking about statutes in referring to 'laws ... governing us that would not and could not be enacted today', analogous reasoning applies to the common law in a strongly precedent-based system).
48 J Ginsburg and R Cooper Dreyfuss (eds.), *Intellectual Property Stories*, Foundation Press, Thompson West, New York, 2006.

1

Potter v Broken Hill: misuse of precedent in cross-border IP litigation

Richard Garnett

Introduction

The case of *Potter v Broken Hill*[1] is a highly appropriate one for inclusion in this work on intellectual property 'landmarks' for a number of reasons. First, the background story and facts of the case are interesting: an individual invents a process which has a significant impact on mining operations to the present day and then seeks to protect his invention by launching a David and Goliath–type suit against one of Australia's (even in 1905) largest corporations. Secondly, the case reveals much about early post-federation Australia and the degree to which the states still considered themselves separate and distinct entities from one another. Thirdly, the decision of the High Court of Australia itself established a precedent which was to restrict the capacity of intellectual property rights holders throughout the British Commonwealth to obtain redress for cross-border infringements for almost 100 years.

As will be argued below, much of the impact of the *Potter* case is largely due to an overbroad interpretation of its actual decision by later courts and the tendency to blindly follow the case as a matter of precedent rather than undertaking any serious policy analysis of the question of enforcing foreign intellectual property rights. What is also worth noting is that, given the altered legal and constitutional regime in Australia, *Potter* is a case which could not arise on the same facts today.

---

1 *Potter v Broken Hill Pty Co Ltd* (1906) 3 CLR 479.

2   LANDMARKS IN AUSTRALIAN IP LAW

The *Potter* case: factual background[2]

Charles Vincent Potter, an analytical chemist by occupation, was born in England in 1859. He arrived in Victoria, Australia, in 1885 and became a consulting chemist and brewer. After securing a number of Victorian patents for a variety of products, he began work on a process for treating sulphide ores which were being mined at Broken Hill in New South Wales. In 1901 Potter invented a process for 'flotation' of sulphide ores whereby the ores were separated from valuable metals using hot acid. The effect of this process was that metals such as zinc, lead and silver could be more easily and effectively extracted. He obtained patents for this process in both New South Wales and Victoria. The Block 14 Company at Broken Hill adopted Potter's process and between 1903 and 1905 extracted increased quantities of zinc.

However, around 1902, Potter discovered that Guillaume Delprat, general manager of the BHP mine at Broken Hill, had obtained patents for a very similar process and this led Potter to sue BHP for infringement of both his Victorian and New South Wales patents in the Supreme Court of Victoria. While the High Court, on appeal, proceeded to strike out his action in relation to the New South Wales patent,[3] Potter was allowed to proceed with the claim for infringement of his Victorian patent. Unfortunately for Potter, this case was also unsuccessful, with the Supreme Court finding his patent invalid for lack of utility.[4]

In 1907 Potter and BHP reached a settlement, with the company agreeing to adopt aspects of his invention in what became known as the Delprat–Potter process. The use of this process proved highly successful in zinc extraction at Broken Hill and was later purchased by the Zinc Corporation. Flotation continues to be used worldwide today for the extraction of metals from sulphide ore and has even been described as 'Australia's greatest contribution to world technology'.[5] Perhaps not surprisingly, Potter's work continues to be discussed in current academic literature on mineral science.[6] Unfortunately for Potter personally, while he received royalties for his invention, he died in debt in Melbourne in 1908. Potter may yet be another example of a person whose greatness has only been fully recognised in posterity.

---

2 I rely heavily here on the description of Potter's life in the *Australian Dictionary of Biography* (online edn), available at http://www.adb.online.anu.edu.au/biogs/A110271b.htm.
3 (1906) 3 CLR 479.
4 *Potter v Broken Hill Pty Co Ltd* (1907) 13 Argus Law Reports (CN) 3b.
5 Australian Academy of Technological Sciences and Engineering, *Technology in Australia 1788–1988* (online edn, 2001), p. 633, available at http://www.austehc.unimelb.edu.au/tia/633.html.
6 See, for example, ME Clark, I Brake, BJ Huls, BE Smith and M Yu, 'Creating Value through Application of Flotation Science and Technology' (2006) 19 *Minerals Engineering* 758.

The *Potter* case: the legal landscape in 1906

State patent laws

As noted above, in 1901 Potter acquired patents in both New South Wales and Victoria for his flotation process. The issue of timing here is important as the federation of Australia had occurred in the same year, with the new federal parliament given power to enact laws with respect to patents of inventions under the Constitution.[7] However, as there was no federal legislation on patents until 1903, pre-federation state laws continued to operate. Interestingly therefore, had Potter applied for his patent only two years later there would have been no longer any separate state registrations, only a single federal monopoly. Consequently, the great jurisdictional problem lying at the heart of the *Potter* litigation – that is, the capacity of a Victorian court to adjudicate a matter involving a New South Wales patent – could not have arisen. Instead, the Victorian court would have been able to deal directly with the merits of the case, namely, whether an infringement of the patent had occurred and whether the patent had been validly granted.

This is the first of many ironies of the case: while the decision was to have a great impact on the enforcement of foreign intellectual property rights in many Commonwealth countries, it rested on pre-federation laws of Australian states which were very soon superseded.

Cross-border disputes in a federation

Another key aspect of the legal landscape operating at the time of the *Potter* case was the advent of federation five years earlier. The federal Constitution not only allocated powers to the new Commonwealth parliament and government but also included provisions which suggested a closer relationship between the states. Examples include the creation of a final appellate court on both state and federal matters (the High Court), s 92 (freedom of interstate trade) and s 118 (full faith and credit). These factors, combined with the common cultural, political and legal inheritance from the United Kingdom (all Australian states inherited the English common law), may have suggested that in the new federation, conflicts of law and jurisdiction between Australian states should rarely arise, and if they did occur, they should be dealt with in a manner consistent with the needs of a single, unified nation.

Curiously, though, a strong theme that runs through the High Court judgments in *Potter* is the degree to which all members of the court treated the Australian states as *foreign countries* in their relations to one another. While the English common law rules of private international law (jurisdiction and choice of law)

---

7 Australian Constitution s 51(xviii).

4   LANDMARKS IN AUSTRALIAN IP LAW

were developed and intended to apply to disputes with foreign nation states, the High Court applied them automatically to the Australian federal context without any query as to their appropriateness or need for modification. A similar point was made by Castles when he noted that in the 19th century there had been a 'general disinclination on the part of Australian courts to take into account special local conditions in deciding whether the general principles of [English] unenacted law should apply'.[8]

To show the absurdity of this approach, the leading English case relied upon in *Potter* was *British South Africa Company v Companhia de Mocambique*,[9] which concerned a highly politically sensitive dispute involving lands in Africa between two colonial empires. Similarly, the United States decision referred to with approval, *Underhill v Hernandez*,[10] concerned a tort arising from an armed revolution in South America. Such exotic transnational disputes seem very remote from the relatively mundane granting of a patent by administrative officers in New South Wales.

Yet, quite apart from unthinkingly applying the above international cases to the Australian domestic context, the court in *Potter* explicitly noted the foreignness of the Australian states as between themselves:

> This case must therefore, in my opinion, be considered on precisely the same basis as if the patent in question had been granted by the government of the French Republic or of the United States of America.[11]

> The states of the Commonwealth are separate in this respect, that they have separate powers, distinct and operating upon different territories and rights. They are so distinct from each other that the aspect in which their respective exercise of power is to be regarded is not that of municipal but that of international law.[12]

> It has been conceded throughout the argument that, for the purposes of the question now under consideration, the several states of Australia stand towards each other in the position of foreign states.[13]

The approach of the High Court in *Potter* in assuming that the English common law private international law rules applied to interstate disputes within Australia had the effect of establishing an unfortunate orthodoxy in Australian law which lasted for many years. Rules of private international law designed to resolve conflicts between the laws and jurisdictions of foreign states necessarily place limitations on the degree to which foreign institutions can be admitted in the forum court. These restrictions exist to protect local sovereignty and also

---

8 A Castles, 'The Reception and Status of English Law in Australia' (1963) 2 *Adelaide Law Review* 1, 9.
9 [1893] AC 602.
10 168 US 250 (1897).
11 (1906) 3 CLR 479, 495 (Griffith CJ).
12 ibid., p. 505 (Barton J).
13 ibid., p. 510 (O'Connor J).

because such laws are likely to be very different to local rules and so difficult to apply. Yet within a politically, culturally and linguistically homogenous federation like Australia, conflicts of laws can only arise upon one state statutorily deviating from the uniform common law (or two states having conflicting statutes).[14] Arguably, therefore, a different methodology for applying (or not applying) interstate law should govern. Indeed in *Potter* the oddity of adopting the traditional private international law approach was compounded by the fact that the Victorian and New South Wales patent statutes in force at the time were effectively identical and so there was no 'true conflict' of laws for the court to resolve.[15] A'Beckett J, in his dissenting judgment in the Supreme Court of Victoria in *Potter*, seemed to appreciate this point:

> In the case before us the defendant was bound to observe the obligation imposed by the New South Wales patent in New South Wales. It was under no similar obligation in Victoria, but that would not prevent a Victorian court from affording redress for the wrong committed in New South Wales if our court would, as it undoubtedly would, redress a wrong of the same character committed in Victoria.[16]

Unfortunately Australian courts in the 20th century generally followed the approach of the High Court in *Potter* and applied private international law rules to interstate cases without great reflection. So for example, almost 60 years after the *Potter* decision, one High Court judge could still say: 'the States are separate countries in private international law, and are to be so regarded in relation to one another'.[17]

It was not until the late 20th century that this 'transplant' approach was seriously challenged. In 1987 the Commonwealth and states enacted 'cross-vesting' legislation which conferred the subject-matter jurisdiction of all superior state and federal courts on each other to prevent gaps in jurisdiction arising.[18] While the conferral of state jurisdiction on federal courts was subsequently held to be unconstitutional,[19] the vesting of state jurisdiction in other state courts has survived. In 1992 a national jurisdiction for service of process and recognition of interstate judgments was established,[20] and in 2000 the High Court recognised for the first time a separate body of private international law rules for interstate and intranational disputes, one uniquely influenced by the text and structure of the federal Constitution.[21]

---

14 Australian Law Reform Commission, *Choice of Law*, Report No. 58, 1992, para. 5.2.
15 Compare *Patents Act 1890* (Vic) with *Patents Act 1899* (NSW).
16 *Potter v Broken Hill Pty Co Ltd* [1905] VLR 612, 634–5.
17 *Pedersen v Young* (1964) 110 CLR 162, 170 (Windeyer J).
18 See, for example, *Jurisdiction of Courts (Cross-vesting) Act 1987* (NSW) s 4(3).
19 *Re Wakim; Ex parte McNally* (1999) 198 CLR 511.
20 *Service and Execution of Process Act 1992* (Cth).
21 *John Pfeiffer Pty Ltd v Rogerson* (2000) 203 CLR 503.

6 LANDMARKS IN AUSTRALIAN IP LAW

The *Potter* case: intellectual property and jurisdiction

The *Potter* decision

With these observations in mind it is now necessary to examine the *Potter* case in detail. As noted above Potter, after having discovered Delprat's competing process, brought an action in Victoria against BHP for infringement of both his Victorian and New South Wales patents. Specifically, Potter sought an injunction to restrain the defendant from infringing his New South Wales patent in its mines in New South Wales and damages for infringement so far incurred. In its defence BHP denied infringement of both of Potter's patents and argued that such patents were, in any event, invalid. BHP also alleged that Potter's action in respect of his New South Wales patent was not justiciable in Victoria.

The Supreme Court of Victoria held by a majority of two to one that the action in respect of the New South Wales patent could not proceed and this decision was unanimously upheld by a three-member High Court.

Before examining the judgments of the High Court a procedural point should be noted. Potter sued BHP in Victoria most likely because the company was incorporated and registered there under the local companies legislation. Because Potter had also filed suit for infringement of a Victorian as well as a New South Wales patent, it was no doubt convenient for him to consolidate both actions in the one Victorian proceeding inasmuch as they arose out of similar facts. While Potter could presumably have sued BHP in separate proceedings in New South Wales in relation to the New South Wales patent, this would have required him to show that BHP was amenable to the jurisdiction of that state's courts. In addition, the bringing of such separate and further proceedings in New South Wales would have imposed a highly onerous costs burden on Potter as an individual litigant suing what was, even then, a major national corporation. While today courts are very mindful of procedural burdens in cross-border litigation, especially where individuals are suing large transnational corporations,[22] such concerns do not appear in the reasoning of the judges of the High Court in *Potter*.

The court ultimately found that Potter's action for infringement in New South Wales of a patent registered in that state was not justiciable in Victoria because the substantial question in the case was the validity of the patent. Although Potter himself had made no allegation regarding validity in his pleadings, the defendant had raised validity in its defence, which made this issue a critical question for the court to determine.

---

22 See, for example, *Regie National des Usines Renault v Zhang* (2002) 210 CLR 491 and *Diethelm & Co Ltd v Bradley* [1995] ATPR 41-388 (NSWSC), where Australian courts refused to stay personal injury actions brought against foreign corporate defendants on the ground that the Australian court in each case was not a 'clearly inappropriate forum' under the test in *Voth v Manildra Flour Mills Pty Ltd* (1990) 171 CLR 538. In both cases, the court felt that the Australian plaintiffs would suffer a denial of justice if forced to sue abroad, in *Diethelm* specifically because the plaintiff would be unable to join all its defendants in one proceeding.

The three judges of the High Court did, however, reach this result by two distinct, although related, paths. Griffiths CJ relied on the principle in the *Mocambique* case[23] to the effect that a question relating to the validity of a patent is analogous to a determination as to the title or possession of foreign land, an issue which is beyond the subject-matter jurisdiction of an Australian court. Crucial to his application of the *Mocambique* rule is the conclusion that patents for inventions are a form of 'immovable property' (with land being the paradigm example).

In the view of Griffith CJ:

> as the patent right is the creation of the State the title to it must devolve, as in the case of land, according to the laws imposed by the State. [A patent also] has no effective operation beyond the territory of the State under whose laws it is granted and exercised.[24]

The effect of a patent being classified as an 'immovable' is that it is regarded as closely associated with the territory of its creation and so is treated as a 'local' right, the validity of which must be adjudicated in the place of grant. Neither of the other High Court judges in *Potter* (Barton and O'Connor JJ) adopted this line of reasoning.

Griffith CJ relied on a further principle to deny justiciability of the action: the act of state doctrine. This doctrine provides that the court will not adjudicate upon the acts of a foreign state performed within the state's own territory.[25] Here the grant of a monopoly, even though made by administrative authorities rather then the executive government, amounted to an unreviewable act of state. The two other High Court judges in *Potter*, Barton[26] and O'Connor JJ,[27] relied solely on the act of state doctrine to deny justiciability of the action, O'Connor J noting that for one state to rule on a monopoly granted by another would violate 'the principles of international law which ... recognise that the courts of a country will not inquire into the validity of the acts of a foreign state'.[28]

What should be noted at this point is the very limited nature of the court's decision: that the validity of a foreign statutory patent is not justiciable in the forum. The reasoning of the court should also be noted: only one judge concluded that the action was barred because foreign patents were 'immovables', while all three relied on the act of state doctrine as the basis of non-justiciability. Commentators have generally supported this limited reading of the *Potter* decision.[29] So

---

23 [1893] AC 602.
24 (1906) 3 CLR 479, 494.
25 *Underhill v Hernandez* 168 US 250 (1897).
26 (1906) 3 CLR 479, 504–5.
27 ibid.
28 ibid., p. 510.
29 See, for example, J Fawcett and P Torremans, *Intellectual Property and Private International Law*, Oxford University Press, Oxford, 1998, p. 284; L Bently, *Interpretation of Copyright Rules: The Role of the Interpreter – The Creation Function* (2005), available via http://www.cipil.law.cam.ac.uk/. But compare R Arnold, 'Cross-border Enforcement: The Latest Chapter' (1999) 4 *Intellectual Property Quarterly* 389, 408 ('the better view is that statutory intellectual property rights are immovables ... in Griffith CJ's words').

8 LANDMARKS IN AUSTRALIAN IP LAW

interpreted, the decision is defensible on at least two grounds. First, a court may understandably feel uncomfortable in reviewing the act of a foreign government on its territory because of the perceived intrusion upon the sovereignty of that state. That said though, a decision of an administrative official to grant a patent is unlikely to be as politically sensitive as determining the borders of lands between colonial empires or the legality of acts during a revolution and so the 'act of state' argument as applied to intellectual property should not be taken too far.[30]

The second, stronger argument in support of the High Court decision is the question of effectiveness of any orders made: in the case of any findings as to the validity of the patent, the compliance and cooperation of the administrative authorities in the country of grant will obviously be crucial and may therefore require a determination by a local court.

An interesting question which arises is whether the High Court would have allowed Potter's action to proceed had the pleadings been limited to the issue of infringement with no question of validity of the patent raised. Although the three judgments are not absolutely clear on the point, the judges' repeated emphasis on their inability to review the 'validity' of the acts of a foreign state except where validity arises only 'incidentally' in the litigation suggests that a 'pure' infringement case may have been admissible. Although the court gives no example of an 'incidental' exception, an example may arise in an action for breach of licence or a suit for infringement where the court, as an implicit condition of giving relief to the plaintiff, assumes that the registered right was validly granted. If, however, validity is raised as a distinct pleading in the defence or counterclaim, then *Potter* would apply to bar jurisdiction.

Strictly speaking also, the act of state doctrine would not seem to be engaged in an infringement suit since such a claim necessarily focuses on the acts of the *parties* rather than any decision by a *government* authority. A similar point can also be made of intellectual property rights which are not based on registration, such as copyright, passing off and trade secrets. In all such cases there should be no objection to ruling upon either the *validity or infringement* of such rights since no foreign act of state is involved other than the operation of the law conferring such a right.

Moreover, giving a very wide interpretation to the *Potter* exclusion on enforcement of foreign intellectual property rights imposes an unreasonable burden on rights holders. In a world of increasingly global technology, infringement of rights can often occur simultaneously in many countries. Plaintiff rights holders therefore may wish to sue for multiple infringements, but obviously this will be impractical and unwieldy if separate actions have to be brought in each country of infringement. The need to consolidate infringement actions in one proceeding in one forum is therefore crucial in providing effective intellectual property

---

30 See further R Garnett, 'Foreign States in Australian Courts' (2005) 29 *Melbourne University Law Review* 704, 718–19 for an argument that the act of state doctrine can in fact produce results which are antithetical to the notion of respect for the sovereignty of other states.

protection and, to the extent that *Potter* limits this capacity, it must be confined as far as possible.

The interpretation of *Potter* in later cases

Unfortunately in later cases (at least until recently) the apparent limitation of the *Potter* decision to questions of validity of registered rights was not appreciated and significantly wider interpretations of its scope were made. For example, in some cases courts have declared that *Potter* stands for the proposition that foreign statutory intellectual property rights in general are not justiciable.[31] The reasoning underlying this view is that because all such rights are immovables, any action in relation to such rights, whether relating to ownership, infringement or validity, is necessarily 'local' and so barred. This approach is reminiscent of that of Griffith CJ in *Potter* and had the effect in one case that the court declined to hear an action seeking a declaration as to rights under US copyright in England.[32]

In other cases courts have taken the position that *Potter* denies jurisdiction to hear foreign *patent infringement* claims.[33] While in none of these cases was this conclusion critical to the court's decision, it is significant that in one of the authorities, an application for an injunction to restrain infringement of a foreign copyright was refused.[34]

By contrast, one current member of the High Court of Australia appears to have accurately interpreted the decision: '[*Potter*] says no more than that the grant of a patent is an act of sovereignty behind which the courts of another state will not go'.[35]

Similarly, in a number of more recent decisions from England, New Zealand and Hong Kong there has been a reassessment of the rule in *Potter* to provide for more liberal enforcement of foreign intellectual property rights. The impetus for this reappraisal appears, in part, to have come from European developments.

The current position in European law under the Brussels I Regulation[36] appears to be consistent with the suggested interpretation of *Potter* above. The regulation applies where the defendant is domiciled in a member state of the European Union with such state being the presumptive place of personal jurisdiction.[37] However, under Art 22(4) of the regulation the courts of the member state of registration are granted *exclusive* jurisdiction in respect of actions concerning

---

31 *Tyburn Productions Ltd v Conan Doyle* (1990) 19 IPR 455; *Coin Controls Ltd v Suzo International (UK) Ltd* [1997] 3 All ER 45, 52.
32 *Tyburn Productions Ltd v Conan Doyle* (1990) 19 IPR 455.
33 *Atkinson Footwear Ltd v Hodgskin International Services Ltd* (1994) 31 IPR 186, 190; *Tritech Technology Pty Ltd v Gordon* (2000) 48 IPR 52, 58.
34 *Atkinson Footwear Ltd v Hodgskin International Services Ltd* (1994) 31 IPR 186.
35 *Re Interlego AG and Lego Australia Pty Ltd v Croner Trading Pty Ltd* (1992) 25 IPR 65, 98 (Gummow J) (with whom Black CJ and Lockhart J agreed).
36 Council Regulation (EC) No. 44/2001 of 22 December 2000 on Jurisdiction and the Enforcement of Judgments in Civil and Commercial Matters (Brussels I Regulation).
37 Article 2.

the validity of registered rights such as patents and trademarks. This provision applies where the question of validity arises either in proceedings to invalidate the right or as a defence to an infringement action.[38] It follows therefore, under EU law, that where an action involving foreign intellectual property rights arises other than one concerning the validity of registered rights, it may proceed in a court other than the country of grant (assuming that the rules of personal jurisdiction are otherwise satisfied).

Consequently, where the defendant is domiciled in an EU member state and the regulation applies, the rules of national private international law (including, in England, *Potter*) are not applicable. Yet interestingly, it was in exactly such a case, involving an action to enforce intellectual property rights under the law of another EU country, that an English court consciously sought to redefine the scope of *Potter*, presumably in contemplation of non-EU cases in the future.

Pearce v Ove Arup[39] involved an action in England for infringement of a Dutch copyright. After finding that the claim was justiciable in the forum under the almost identical predecessor to the regulation,[40] the court, obiter, also proceeded to reject the earlier mentioned wide interpretation of *Potter*. Significantly, Roch LJ stated that nothing in *Potter* requires justiciability to be denied over any proceedings concerned with the validity of unregistered rights. Indeed such a conclusion 'has [no] place in a rational scheme of jurisprudence'.[41] In the court's view, therefore, *Potter* has no operation outside the field of registered rights.

Significantly, in the later English case of *R Griggs Group v Evans*[42] (which concerned the validity of an assignment of foreign, non-EU copyrights) the court went even further, declaring that not only is *Potter* irrelevant to copyright cases but it also has no application to cases of 'pure' infringement more generally. Such cases would presumably be those involving registered rights where validity arises no more than 'incidentally' as opposed to when validity is squarely raised as a distinct pleading in the defence or counterclaim.

Next, there is the New Zealand case of *KK Sony Computer Entertainment v Van Veen*,[43] which was a suit for infringement of both local and foreign copyrights. In that decision the court, strongly persuaded by the *Pearce* decision, agreed that the *Potter* case must be confined to cases where title or validity is put in issue.[44] Consequently, there was no bar to an action for breach of foreign copyright proceeding.

Finally, there is the Hong Kong decision in *Esquel Enterprises v Tal Apparel*,[45] where the court followed the *Pearce* and *Griggs* cases in holding that an action for

---

38 *Gesellschaft fur Antriebstechnik mBH & Co KG v Lamellen und Kupplungsbau Beteiligungs KG* Case C-4/03 13 July 2006 (European Court of Justice).
39 *Pearce v Ove Arup Partnership Ltd* [2000] Ch 403.
40 Convention on Jurisdiction and the Enforcement of Judgments in Civil and Commercial Matters, opened for signature 27 September 1968 (entered into force 1 February 1973).
41 [2000] Ch 403, 436. See also, very recently, to the same effect: *Lucasfilms Ltd v Ainsworth* [2008] EWHC 1878 (Ch).
42 *R Griggs Group Pty Ltd v Evans* [2005] Ch 153.
43 (2006) 71 IPR 179.
44 ibid., para. 21.
45 *Esquel Enterprises Ltd v Tal Apparel Ltd* [2006] HKCU 184.

infringement of foreign patents could be determined in Hong Kong. The court nevertheless, in its discretion, declined to hear the claims, for reasons further discussed below.

It is important to note, though, that the courts in the *Sony* and *Esquel* cases did advert to a further possible obstacle in a case of enforcement of foreign intellectual property rights: *personal* jurisdiction over the defendant. There will of course be no problem of personal jurisdiction over such a party where the defendant is present for service in the forum. In such a case, assuming *Potter* is given the suggested restricted interpretation above, the infringer can be sued in relation to any rights, local or foreign, provided that validity of a registered right is not raised as a principal issue. This was the outcome in *Sony*. However, the *Sony* court was much less certain about the position where the defendant was resident outside the jurisdiction and would have to be served with process under the statutory rules for service out. In this situation, in most Commonwealth countries, the plaintiff rights holder will have to show either an infringement within the forum or damage suffered there to establish personal jurisdiction. It is by no means obvious that an infringement of a foreign intellectual property right will satisfy either test: indeed the territorial limitation in most intellectual property statutes requires an infringement in the place where the rights were granted, which would obviously preclude a showing of an infringement in the forum. The plaintiff would therefore be forced to fall back on the damage ground for service out, which admittedly has been very broadly interpreted in Australia to include any loss of business or financial harm to the plaintiff in the forum.[46]

The Hong Kong court in the *Esquel* case also identified another possible jurisdictional obstacle for plaintiffs. While service out of the jurisdiction requires establishment of one of the two connecting factors mentioned above, a defendant in a common law country may also argue that the court in its discretion should decline to exercise jurisdiction on the ground that the local court is an inappropriate forum. While in Australia this is a difficult test for defendants to satisfy since they must show that the Australian court is a 'clearly inappropriate forum',[47] in other Commonwealth countries a stay will be granted if a foreign court is shown to be 'more appropriate'.[48] In the *Esquel* case the court found that even though an action for infringement of foreign patent was not barred by *Mocambique* or *Potter*, the existence of such a claim will nevertheless be a weighty factor in showing that the country of registration is the more appropriate forum.[49]

---

46 *Girgis v Flaherty* (1985) 4 NSWLR 248, 266 (McHugh JA). Note that in the Supreme Court of Victoria a practice has developed whereby it is possible to 'tack on' claims not supported by the rules for service out where the plaintiff can show that at least one plea falls within the rules. Applying this view, a claim for infringement of a foreign intellectual property right could be validly joined to a plea for infringement of a local right. See *Shantou Commercial Development Co v P & O Swire Containers Ltd* [1999] VSC 347.
47 *Voth v Manildra Flour Mills Pty Ltd* (1990) 171 CLR 538.
48 *Spiliada Maritime Corp v Cansulex* [1987] 1 AC 460.
49 Note though that in that case there were also claims for defamation which occurred outside the forum and so the case as a whole had few links with Hong Kong.

12   LANDMARKS IN AUSTRALIAN IP LAW

So, it should be remembered that, even if a court takes a narrow view of the *Potter* restriction on enforcing foreign intellectual property rights, in the case of a defendant resident outside the jurisdiction, there are still the hurdles of personal jurisdiction and appropriate forum to overcome.

A final point to note is that the American Law Institute has recently published a set of Principles for cross-border intellectual property adjudication.[50] In the Principles there is only one bar imposed on a party suing to enforce foreign intellectual property rights: where a declaration of invalidity is sought in respect of a registered right in one country or registered rights in more than one country. In the first case the court of the country of registration has exclusive jurisdiction,[51] while in the second jurisdiction is exclusively reserved to the defendant's country of residence.[52] This approach is consistent with that under EU law and the limited interpretation of *Potter* proposed above.

The current relevance of *Potter* in Australian law

The current status of *Potter* in Australia in the context of foreign intellectual property rights remains ambiguous, given the few cases in which the issue has arisen and the lack of uniformity in those cases regarding the decision's scope. Indeed, the New South Wales Law Reform Commission in its 1988 report titled *Jurisdiction of Local Courts over Foreign Land*[53] seemed to suggest that *Potter* had no current relevance at all in Australian law on the question of enforcement of foreign intellectual property rights. In its report the commission said that 'the effect of the decision in *Potter*'s case has been rendered virtually obsolete by the [enactment of federal patent legislation] and the international conventions relating to patents to which Australia is a party'.[54] Such a view fails to appreciate that the *Potter* principle has continued to apply in respect of actions to enforce *non-Australian* registered intellectual property rights; the 'international conventions ... to which Australia is a party' have not altered this position.

The 1988 report led to legislation in New South Wales that abolished the *Mocambique* rule, replacing it with a discretionary test for the exercise of jurisdiction in cases where title to foreign land is involved.[55] While this legislation is obviously significant for New South Wales, its provisions may also apply throughout Australia on the basis that s 4(3) of the cross-vesting legislation referred to above[56] confers subject-matter jurisdiction of the New South Wales courts on all other superior state courts in Australia. Hence, if the abolition of *Mocambique* in

---

50 The American Law Institute, *Intellectual Property: Principles Governing Jurisdiction, Choice of Law and Judgments in Transnational Disputes*, American Law Institute Publishers, St Paul, MN, 2008 (Principles). For a further discussion of the Principles see R Garnett, 'An Overview of Choice of Law, Jurisdiction and Foreign Judgment Enforcement in IP Disputes' (2006) 11 *Media and Arts Law Review* 341.
51 Principles, op. cit., s 213(2), p. 84.
52 ibid. s 213(2), p. 84.
53 Report No. 63, 1988.
54 ibid., para. 2.20.
55 *Jurisdiction of Courts (Foreign Land) Act 1989* (NSW) ss 3 and 4.
56 See, for example, *Jurisdiction of Courts (Cross-vesting) Act 1987* (NSW).

Australia has had the effect of expanding the jurisdiction of New South Wales courts, then such 'expansion' may be enjoyed by other state courts as well. The correctness of this view has been left open by a judge of the Victorian Court of Appeal,[57] but it creates at least a possibility that the *Potter* bar on enforcing foreign intellectual property rights has been lifted throughout Australia.

The key question to consider, therefore, is whether the legislation overrules *Potter*. Section 3 of the Act provides that 'the jurisdiction of any court is not excluded or limited merely because the proceedings relate to or may otherwise concern land or immovable property in NSW'. While the reference to 'immovable property' here may include intellectual property rights, following the analysis of Griffith CJ in *Potter* and Vinelott J in *Tyburn*, it is clear from the New South Wales Law Reform Commission's report that the drafters were concerned only with land, not intellectual property. In any event, the basis of the reasoning of the other members of the High Court in *Potter* (and Griffith CJ in the alternative) was not the immovable analogy but the act of state doctrine, as noted above. The act of state doctrine is not referred to in the New South Wales legislation and remains good law in Australia.[58] On this view, therefore, *Potter* remains unaffected by the New South Wales legislation.

A similar conclusion can be drawn about the legislation of the Australian Capital Territory which gives a court of the territory the power to adjudicate on matters concerning 'land or other immovable property outside the ACT', provided that no question of 'title to or right to possession of' such property is involved.[59] A key difference between this statute and the New South Wales enactment appears to be that questions of validity of rights to foreign land or other immovable property would continue to be excluded from adjudication, which would be consistent with the narrow view of *Potter* proposed above. However, again, the lack of any reference to intellectual property or the act of state doctrine in the explanatory materials arguably means that the legislation has no effect at all on actions in respect of foreign intellectual property rights.

Perhaps it is appropriate to leave the last word on the current status of *Potter* in Australian law to the High Court, which, after all, was originally responsible for the decision and, given the doctrine of precedent, is the only Australian tribunal which can reject it or seriously modify its scope. In this regard, in *Regie Nationale des Usines Renault v Zhang*[60] a majority of the court said: 'We would also reserve for further consideration in an appropriate case the *Mocambique* rule and the standing of *Potter v Broken Hill*.'[61]

It is unclear whether this statement suggests a willingness to confine the scope of the *Potter* principle as the English, New Zealand and Hong Kong courts have done or reject the rule altogether. However, change is needed: in a world of

---

57 *Schmidt v Won* [1998] 3 VR 435, 448 (Ormiston JA).
58 *Petrotimor v The Commonwealth of Australia* (2003) 126 FCR 354; *Hicks v Ruddock* [2007] FCA 299, para. 19.
59 *Civil Law (Wrongs) Act 2002* (ACT) s 220.
60 (2002) 210 CLR 491.
61 ibid., p. 520 (Gleeson CJ, Gaudron, McHugh, Gummow and Hayne JJ).

increasingly multi-territorial communications and infringements, greater flexibility and scope for enforcement of intellectual property rights across borders is essential. *Potter* has acted as an obstacle to this process by denying plaintiffs (including Potter himself) the right to consolidate actions for infringements of both local and foreign rights in one proceeding and requiring them instead to seek redress in each country where their rights are granted. Such an approach is both cumbersome and costly and would likely deter most individual litigants. While the *Potter* bar may be supported where a substantial question is raised as to the validity of registered rights, it is much less acceptable where non-registered rights are involved or the action is purely for infringement.

In addition, it may be argued that because the plaintiff must still satisfy the ordinary rules of personal jurisdiction and appropriate forum in any suit, it is unreasonably onerous on that party to impose a further jurisdictional burden. The High Court showed in the *Pfeiffer* case[62] that it was possible to overturn another unfortunate legacy of *Potter* – the unthinking application of English common law private international law rules to interstate disputes within Australia – and so now it is time for it to address the foreign intellectual property rights restriction.

It would be an unfortunate irony indeed if the inventor responsible for 'Australia's greatest contribution to world technology'[63] had also lent his name to a legal doctrine which undermined the capacity of other intellectual property rights holders to seek effective redress for cross-border infringement.

---

62 *John Pfeiffer Pty Ltd v Rogerson* (2000) 203 CLR 503.
63 See text at n. 5 above.

2

The *Union Label* case: an early Australian IP story

Sam Ricketson

Introduction

We have just recently come out of a federal election in which the terms 'unionist' and 'union power' were freely thrown around by the now defeated Coalition Government in response to the challenge of the resurgent Labor Party; '70 per cent of a Labor cabinet will be ex-unionists' was one of the Coalition's campaign themes. It is interesting, then, to find similar rhetoric, used by non-Labor politicians more than a century ago, in the most unexpected context of trade marks law.

The source of concern was to be found in provisions of Pt VII of the new trade marks bill, which sought to provide for registration of a new class of marks, to be called 'workers' marks' – marks that could be registered and used to indicate that goods were made by 'an individual Australian worker or association of Australian workers'[1] (i.e., a trade union). It was an offence for any person to apply the mark to goods not produced by that worker or association, although unlike trade marks in respect of goods, these marks were only to be applied by or with the authority of the employer for whom the goods were produced.[2] Passed after a great deal of rancorous parliamentary debate, the new provisions remained in force for less than two years before they were declared invalid by the High Court. During this time, only two workers' marks were actually applied for and registered: one for the Tailoresses Union of New South Wales,[3] and the second, the subject of the

---

1 *Trade Marks Act 1905* (Cth) s 74(1).
2 ibid., s 74.
3 *Australian Official Journal of Trade Marks*, Vol. II, 19 July 1907, p. 708. For a representation of the mark, see p. 611.

Figure 2.1 Registered mark of Brewery Employees' Union of New South Wales

High Court challenge, for the Brewery Employees' Union of New South Wales.[4] The 'story' of this case is therefore one that reverberates far beyond the narrow confines of trade mark law doctrine.

The origins of the workers' mark provisions

The first decade of the 20th century was a busy one for the newly elected members of the Commonwealth parliament. If the preceding decade had been devoted to negotiating and devising the federal compact, the first sessions of the new federal parliament were concerned with passing the legislation necessary to give effect to this and the new federation that had come into being on 1 January 1901. Members and senators were concerned with legislating for many of the diverse subject-matter listed under s 51 of the Constitution: conciliation and arbitration, customs and defence, immigration, industry preservation, the establishment of the High Court, crimes and evidence, acts interpretation, to mention only a few. Under s 51(xviii), patents, designs and copyright were early candidates for attention, together with trade marks.

Political parties and groupings were far more fluid than today, and there was a succession of governments in the first decade. Most of these were minority administrations dependent for support from some other grouping of members. There was less 'spin' than today, as the main means of dissemination of information was through the newspapers, and the only means of relatively fast transport between the former colonies to the new, temporary federal capital in Melbourne was by train or ship. Political debate was as vigorous as now, and often highly

---

[4] *Australian Official Journal of Trade Marks*, Vol. 1, 16 November 1906, p. 207. See Figure 2.1 above.

personal. State differences were still keenly felt, which is hardly surprising, but this only serves to underline the enormity of the federal achievement. And many of the founding fathers (there were no women) now sat in the Senate or the House of Representatives: in 1904, these included Deakin, Reid, Lyne, Forrest, Quick and Inglis. Barton and O'Connor had only just departed to become justices of the High Court; Higgins and Isaacs, soon to be appointed as the fourth and fifth members respectively of that court, were active members of the lower house. Political creeds were divided between protectionists and free traders, Millsean liberals and conservatives, but Labor members had been elected from the very start, and had, in fact, formed a short-lived minority government under John Christian Watson in mid-1904.

It was the Watson Government that introduced the first Commonwealth trade marks bill although it is possible that it had been drafted by the previous Deakin Liberal Government. It appears that this bill made no specific reference to workers' marks, and was a close copy of a bill then before the UK parliament and drafted by Fletcher Moulton QC, the doyen of the English trade marks bar. In the Senate, however, George Pearce from Western Australia[5] queried whether it would be possible for groups of workers to register marks to indicate their connection with goods on which they had worked. He indicated that this was already the case in Western Australia. It appeared, however, that such registrations had to be done by proxy, in that the unions could not register marks in their own name, and as he later explained to the Senate:

> The label must be registered in the name of some other manufacturer, who agrees to give authority to other manufacturers to use it.[6]

Specific provisions for workers' marks were then added to the bill by the Senate in committee, but by the time it returned to the parliament there was a new government (Reid's) and it met a more hostile reaction, with an attempt being made to remove the provisions. The language of class and the struggle between capital and labour is all too evident in the speech of one opponent (Senator Lt-Col Gould from New South Wales):

> The object can only be to prevent non-unionists from earning a livelihood. It is the same old game. The intention is to put into the hands of a certain class the power to dominate everybody else. Of course, it may have the opposite effect. People may say that there is too much trade union domination, and that they will not buy goods which have a union mark upon them. But it is absolutely unfair that we should attempt to denominate goods as made by union or non-union labour.[7]

Senator Pearce, in more moderate but perhaps no less forceful tones, stated the object of the provisions as follows:

---

5 A minister in later Labor governments, and then, after crossing the floor with Hughes, of successive Nationalist and UAP governments.

6 Commonwealth of Australia, *Parliamentary Debates*, Senate, 30 November 1904, p. 7298 (George Pearce). Two examples of such registrations that were given by Senator Pearce were the Bootmakers Union and the Tailors' Union of Kalgoorlie.

7 *Parliamentary Debates*, ibid., pp. 7282–3 (Lt-Col Gould).

18   LANDMARKS IN AUSTRALIAN IP LAW

to provide that goods shall be manufactured under proper conditions. We take it that union conditions are proper conditions, and will guarantee to the public that goods bearing a union label have been made by persons working for fair pay and under fair conditions. Honourable senators must be aware that a union label can be of value to the union only if the public look for it, and if members of the public entering a shop say, 'We want boots with the union label'. If unions attempt to use these labels in a tyrannical fashion, the result will be that a great body of the public who are not unionists will say, 'We decline to be parties to these tyrannical measures, and will refrain from buying goods with these union labels on them.' In those circumstances, the very fact that a union label is placed on goods instead of being an inducement would be a deterrent to people to buy them, and the union registering the label would be the greatest sufferer.[8]

Parliament went into recess for six months after this (a reflection of the time involved for members to travel home from Melbourne), and shortly after its resumption in June 1905, the Reid Government fell and a Deakin coalition, supported by Labor, came into office. The incoming Attorney-General was Isaac Isaacs,[9] who took on board the ambitious legislative agenda of the new government with his usual energy and vigour. This included reintroduction of the trade marks bill, together with redrafted provisions for workers' marks, as part of the Deakin Government's amorphous 'New Protection' policy which ensured, among other things, continued support from the Labor Party.[10]

Passage of the bill was far from easy, with the bulk of the debates being centred on the workers' marks provisions. In fact, a review of the Commonwealth parliamentary debates for sessions in late 1905 shows that discussions of the bill in committee in both houses extended over more than 500 pages and took place on more than 10 sitting days.[11] Isaacs' second reading speech reads like an opening address in court where he reviews carefully all the arguments in favour of the new (and redrafted) provisions, finding support for them in English

---

8 ibid., p. 7597.

9 An excellent biography of Isaacs is Z Cowen, *Isaac Isaacs*, Oxford University Press, Melbourne, 1967. For a shorter account by Cowen, see the *Australian Dictionary of Biography* (online edn), entry for 'Sir Isaac Isaacs, 1855–1948', available at http://www.adb.online.anu.edu.au/biogs/A090439b.htm. According to Cowen, Isaacs was instrumental in bringing down the Reid Government and obtaining Labor support for a Deakin government: 'While never a supporter of socialism, Isaacs saw the virtues of trade union organization, the justice of the demand for fair and reasonable wages and working conditions, and the need for state intervention to bring them about. He was especially aware of the threat to protectionist policies, and scathing in his attacks on Reid.'

10 See generally J La Nauze, *Alfred Deakin: A Biography*, Melbourne University Press, Melbourne, 1965, pp. 412–13 and Cowen, ibid., pp. 101–4.

11 See Commonwealth of Australia, *Parliamentary Debates*, 27 July 1905, p. 281 (Isaac Isaacs' second reading speech); Commonwealth of Australia, *Parliamentary Debates*, 2 August 1905, pp. 501–9 (Isaac Isaacs' second reading speech cont); Commonwealth of Australia, *Parliamentary Debates*, 3 August 1905, pp. 581–610 (Isaac Isaacs' second reading speech cont); Commonwealth of Australia, *Parliamentary Debates*, 8 August 1905, pp. 669–728 (debate); Commonwealth of Australia, *Parliamentary Debates*, pp. 752–84 (debate cont); Commonwealth of Australia, *Parliamentary Debates*, 14 November 1905, pp. 5031–41 (in committee); Commonwealth of Australia, *Parliamentary Debates*, 15 November 1905, pp. 5168–219 (in committee); Commonwealth of Australia, *Parliamentary Debates*, 28 November 1905, pp. 5851–900 (in committee); Commonwealth of Australia, *Parliamentary Debates*, 30 November 1905, pp. 6072–184 (in committee); Commonwealth of Australia, *Parliamentary Debates*, 15 December 1905, pp. 6188–257 (in committee). The Senate debates are to be found in Commonwealth of Australia, *Parliamentary Debates*, Senate, 6 December 1905, pp. 6257–59, 6377–81; Commonwealth of Australia, *Parliamentary Debates*, Senate, 7 December 1905, pp. 6399–423; Commonwealth of Australia, *Parliamentary Debates*, Senate, 8 December 1905, pp. 6530–65.

and American trade marks law. In the UK, the Sheffield Cutlers' marks were cited as a precedent, while in a number of US states reference was made to specific union marks legislation (particularly in the garments industries). Isaacs argued that such a mark was consistent with the notion of a 'trade mark' as it had been developed in the common law and in statute in the mother country, and that it was therefore within the new power over trade marks contained in s 51(xviii) of the Constitution.

> A trade union label is exactly analogous to every other trade mark which is placed on commodities offered for sale. If a man vends pure sugar or milk, he has a right to put a mark on his goods to indicate that fact; if goods be made by a certain process, the manufacturer has a right to inform the public of it; and if goods be made by union labour, the manufacturer also has a right to say so. Then, again, if unions be allowed to select a label that will be an indication to the world at large that the goods on which it is placed are the workmanship of members of a union, they have a right to use that label.

The debates are notable for their highly coloured and contentious language, with personal attacks particularly directed against Isaacs, while the tensions over the role of the union movement are patent. Petitions from all sides, union and employer groups alike, were tabled, but the bill was finally passed with the workers' mark provisions, together with a further, rather odd new Part that was inserted by Isaacs in the last moments of the debates. This was for a 'Commonwealth trade mark', the purpose of which was to 'certify that goods bearing the mark had been made in Australia under conditions regarded by the parliament as fair and reasonable'.[12] It appears that, in the heat of battle over the workers' marks provisions, little attention was paid to this new Part,[13] and there is only passing comment on it in the debates.

The provisions of the new Part

There can be no doubt that the provisions of Pt VII (ss 74–77) broke into new territory so far as statutory formulations of the term 'trade mark' were concerned. Their operation, however, was quite confined.

Thus, s 75(1) provided for the registration of a 'workers' trade mark' by a 'worker or association'. The term 'worker' was undefined, and 'association' received only inclusive interpretation, embracing 'any number of associations acting together, and in such case the members of the association shall be the members of the association acting together' (s 74(3)). The right conferred by registration was carefully circumscribed, being the entitlement to institute legal proceedings to prevent and recover damages for 'any contravention of *this* Part in respect of that trade mark' (s 75(1)). More specifically, it was provided that

---

12 Cowen, op. cit., p. 102.
13 ibid. This Part (Pt VIII) remained in the *Trade Marks Act 1905*, unchallenged, unrepealed and apparently unused until the final repeal of the 1905 Act by the *Trade Marks Act 1955*.

20   LANDMARKS IN AUSTRALIAN IP LAW

such marks were incapable of assignment (s 75(3)) and none of the substantive Parts of the Act applying to trade marks in general[14] were to apply to workers' trade marks (s 75(4)).

The prohibitions in relation to workers' trade marks were contained in s 74 as follows:

(1) No person shall –
  (a) falsely apply to any goods for the purpose of trade or sale; or
  (b) knowingly sell or expose for sale, or have in his possession for sale or for any purpose of trade or manufacture, any goods to which there is falsely applied; or
  (c) knowingly import into Australia any goods not produced in Australia, to which there is applied a mark which is a distinctive device, design, symbol, or label registered by any individual Australian worker or association of Australian workers corporate or unincorporate for the purpose of indicating that articles to which it is applied are the exclusive production of the worker or of members of the association (and which mark is hereby declared to be a workers' trade mark), or any mark substantially identical with a registered workers' trade mark, or so nearly resembling it as to be likely to deceive.
(2) The workers' trade mark is falsely applied unless in truth –
  (a) the goods to which it is applied are exclusively the production of the worker or of members of the association; or
  (b) the goods to which it is applied are in part but not exclusively the production of the worker or of members of the association, and the mark is applied in such a manner as clearly to indicate that its application does not refer to, describe, or designate the parts of the goods not being the production of the worker or of members of the association; and
  (c) the mark is applied to the goods (being goods produced in Australia) by the employer for whom they are produced, or, with the authority of the employer by the worker or a member of the association registering the mark.
(3) In this section –
  (a) 'Association' includes any number of associations acting together, and in such case the members of the 'association' shall be the members of the associations which are acting together;
  (b) 'Production' means production, manufacture, workmanship, preparation or product of labour;
  (c) 'Produced' has a meaning corresponding with 'production.'
  (d) Penalty: Fifty pounds, in addition to any liability to forfeiture provided by law.

Provision was also made against the registration of a workers' trade mark if it was 'substantially identical with any registered trade mark within the meaning of this Act or so nearly resembles it as to be likely to deceive' (s 75(5)). Furthermore, in a carefully extended olive branch to those fearful that the new provisions might enlarge the lawful range of trade union activities, it was provided that nothing in this Part was to be construed so as to make lawful for any person or association of persons to do anything that would have been previously unlawful (s 76). A curious final provision stipulated that the new Part did not apply to any primary

---

14 These were Pts III (Registrable Trade Marks), IV (Registration of Trade Marks), V (Assignment of Trade Marks) and VI (The Register of Trade Marks).

products of the agricultural, viticultural (including wine-making), horticultural, dairying (including butter-making and cheese-making) or pastoral industries (s 77). Quite separate, then, from any larger question of constitutional invalidity, it was therefore arguable that the Brewery Union Employees' registered mark for 'Beer, Porter (in Bottles, Cases &Barrels), Malt in Bags & Tanks, Mineral, Aerated Waters, Cordials, Hop Beer, Ginger Beer (in Bottles, Cases & Barrels)'[15] fell outside the scope of Pt VII in any event (unless it was to be said that 'beer', 'porter', and so on are not primary products, but secondary or processed products).

In sum, the provisions of Pt VII were something of an oddity by comparison with previous trade marks legislation (at least in Australia). While their union provenance was, of course, quite explicit, their practical impact on employers was carefully limited, and it was possible to characterise them as a kind of consumer protection measure – what we might describe today as a special kind of certification mark. And, if we are all agreed – employees and employers alike – that the avoidance of 'sweated labour' conditions is desirable, how could anyone rationally oppose such measures directed at drawing the attention of consumers to the fact that goods had been made by union (and 'non-sweated') labour? This point, indeed, was made somewhat ingenuously in the following description of the provisions by Higgins J, one of the dissentients in the subsequent High Court challenge:

> the 'workers' trade mark' is a mark which may be registered by a worker or a workers' union (or other association) to show that the goods marked are the workmanship of members of the union; and it is to be the property of the union. But the mark is not to be applied to any goods without the sanction of the owner of the goods. It is to be used by the owner of the goods for the purposes of his trade, as it is believed that many people will prefer to buy goods which bear a mark such as this, a mark which is a guarantee that the goods have not been produced by 'sweated' labour. The mark is, in short, a device to enable the public, if they so desire, to discourage 'sweating' of human beings – to give to purchasers the opportunity of carrying out the moral duty which 'Parson Lot' (Charles Kingsley) inculcated sixty years ago, in burning words, in his pamphlet, 'Cheap clothes and nasty.' The mark is legal even without the Act; so that even if there were no Part VII at all, such a mark could be applied to the goods by the owner of the goods or with his consent. Without any legislation at all this mark could be used by the owner of the goods for the purposes of his trade, for the purpose of attracting purchasers who are in sympathy with the objects of unions. But Part VII is necessary for the purpose of punishing a manufacturer who untruthfully applies the mark to his goods. If Part VII is void, that penalty cannot be enforced, and the manufacturer cannot be restrained by the union from applying it to his goods untruthfully. The plaintiffs' contention is, in short, that the Federal Parliament has no power to punish the untruthful application of a workers' mark to goods.[16]

For trade mark purists, let alone employers, the provisions of Pt VII were potentially more troubling, as was reflected in the speed with which a challenge to the constitutional validity of the provisions was mounted.

---

15 *Australian Official Journal of Trade Marks*, 16 November 1906, Vol. 1, No. 13.
16 *Attorney-General for NSW v Brewery Employees' Union of NSW* (*Union Label* case) (1908) 6 CLR 469, 599–600.

The constitutional challenge

Despite the parliamentary furore, there was hardly a flood of applications by workers and unions to register marks under Pt VII. As noted at the outset of this chapter, by the time of the High Court case only two had progressed to registration: those of the Tailoresses Union of New South Wales and the Brewery Employees' Union of New South Wales. By contrast, there were thousands of applications to register 'traditional' marks: the new Act came into force on 2 July 1906 and the first issue of the *Australian Official Journal of Trade Marks*[17] reported the details of 266 applications received on that date, with a note that Applications 267 to 758 were also received on that day and would be published in the next issue.[18] By the end of 1906, 3208 applications had been filed.[19] The new Trade Marks Office in Melbourne (also the Patent and Designs Office) had, in addition, the carriage of applications that were made or still in train under the various state trade marks acts.

Nonetheless, a constitutional challenge to remove the threat posed by Pt VII was rapidly mounted, albeit that this may seem to have been unnecessary in purely practical terms. Even within this short time, however, the composition of the High Court had changed. Less than a year after the passage of the *Trade Marks Act 1905*, both Isaacs and Higgins[20] were appointed to the High Court bench, two more radical additions to the founding (and more conservative) trio of Griffith,[21] Barton[22] and O'Connor.[23] Isaacs's tenure of the office of Attorney-General had been relatively short but eventful, while Higgins had served even more briefly as Attorney-General in the Watson Government. Despite his sponsorship of the trade marks bill, however, Isaacs saw no reason why he should not sit on any constitutional challenges to enactments that he had drafted or sponsored in his parliamentary capacity, including that mounted by the New South Wales brewery employers the following year. Such disregard for possible conflicts was not unusual for Isaacs: even as Commonwealth Attorney-General, he had continued to accept private briefs and had conducted a large practice at

---

17 24 August 1906, Vol. 1, No. 1.
18 ibid., p. 11.
19 *Australian Official Journal of Trade Marks*, 28 December 1906, Vol. 1, No. 19, pp. 290–1.
20 See further J Rickard, *HB Higgins: The Rebel as Judge*, George Allen & Unwin, Sydney, 1984.
21 See further the *Australian Dictionary of Biography* (online edn), entry for 'Sir Samuel Walker Griffith, 1845–1920', available at http://www.adb.online.anu.edu.au/biogs/A090113b.htm. Griffith had been Premier and Chief Justice of Queensland, as well as a prominent participant in the federation debates.
22 See further *Australian Dictionary of Biography* (online edn), entry for 'Sir Edmund Barton, 1849–1920', available at http://www.adb.online.anu.edu.au/biogs/A070202b.htm. Barton had been a member of the New South Wales parliament, Attorney-General and a leading proponent for federation; he was the first Prime Minister of the new commonwealth in 1901, and, despite a reputation as a relaxed, even convivial, and undisciplined political leader, he was subsequently regarded as a good and careful judge.
23 See further *Australian Dictionary of Biography* (online edn), entry for 'Richard Edward O'Connor, 1851–1912', available at http://www.adb.online.anu.edu.au/biogs/A110062b.htm. O'Connor was also a colonial and early Commonwealth politician, serving under Barton until his appointment to the High Court in 1903. A point of commonality between Griffith, Barton and O'Connor, reflected in their harmonious relations in judgment writing, may have been that, as Griffith later claimed, their 'minds ran in similar grooves', perhaps due to 'early training at our common University of Sydney'. Higgins and Isaacs, by contrast, came from a more radical alma mater in the south (The University of Melbourne). More important, however, may have been the close links between Griffith, Barton and O'Connor in the federation debates of the 1890s.

THE *UNION LABEL* CASE 23

the bar.[24] Indeed, it seems that there may have been a financial necessity to do so as ministerial salaries were limited, and, in the absence of a private income, many members had to pursue their private professional or business interests to maintain themselves.[25]

The bringing of the challenge came quickly after enactment: at the relation of several brewery companies,[26] the Attorney-General of New South Wales instituted a suit in the High Court against the union and Registrar of Trade Marks for the following orders:

1. a declaration that the registration of the worker's mark by the Brewery Employees' Union of NSW was null and void in so far as the provisions of Pt VII of the Act pursuant to which it was registered were beyond the powers of the Commonwealth Parliament and also 'inasmuch as the mark so registered never was a trade mark';

2. a further declaration that the provisions of Pt VII were null and void, inasmuch as they were beyond power;

3. an order removing the said mark from the register; and

4. a declaration that the registrar had no authority or power to keep a register of workers' trade marks, and an injunction restraining him from so doing.

The parties were represented by an array of notable legal and political identities from the Victorian, New South Wales and South Australian bars: the breweries by Edward Mitchell KC from Melbourne[27] and Patrick Glynn from South Australia[28] (with Lamb);[29] the union by WA Holman[30] and DR Hall,[31]

---

24 Cowen, *ADB* entry, op. cit. n. 9, notes that, even as Attorney-General, Isaacs had continued to conduct one of the largest private practices at the Victorian Bar: 'While holding office as attorney-general, Isaacs maintained a large private practice; when criticized in parliament he defended his conduct with characteristic vehemence. According to Garran: 'Isaacs' capacity for work was amazing. By day he carried on the biggest practice of the Victorian Bar; by night he did full justice to the duties of Attorney-General'. They would work on a draft of legislation which Garran would leave with the government printer about midnight: in the morning Garran might find the draft redone, Isaacs having had second thoughts and recovered the bill from the printer's office. Between 1901 and 1906 Isaacs appeared as leader in well over one hundred reported cases in the Victorian Supreme Court and in twenty-five in the High Court. Their range was very wide, including some of constitutional importance; he also argued will, trust and administration matters, liability to land tax, mining law, and matters of statutory construction.'

25 This appears to have been an issue for O'Connor, who had to leave his busy practice in Sydney for months while attending to ministerial business in Melbourne in 1901–03: see *ADB* entry for RE O'Connor.

26 The principal of these was Tooth and Company Ltd, now part of CUB.

27 *Australian Dictionary of Biography* (online edn), entry for 'Sir Edward Fancourt Mitchell, 1855–1941', available at http://www.adb.online.anu.edu.au/biogs/A100517b.htm, and one of the pre-eminent High Court barristers of the first decade and a half of the court's existence.

28 Another leading member of the pre-federation conventions, a founding member of the Commonwealth parliament, and subsequently Attorney-General, Minister for External Affairs and Minister for Home Affairs: see further *Australian Dictionary of Biography* (online edn), entry for 'Patrick Glynn, 1855–1931', available at http://www.adb.online.anu.edu.au/biogs/A0900296.htm.

29 Unfortunately, not further identified.

30 Subsequently Labor (and then Nationalist) Premier of New South Wales: see further *Australian Dictionary of Biography* (online edn), entry for 'William Arthur Holman, 1871–1934', available at http://www.adb.online.anu.edu.au/biogs/A90346b.htm.

31 Another Labor politician (state and Commonwealth) and later Attorney-General of New South Wales, a close colleague of Holman's both at the bar and in politics: see further *Australian Dictionary of Biography* (online edn), entry for 'DR Hall, 1874–1945', available at http://www.adb.online.anu.edu.au/biogs/A090153b.htm.

24   LANDMARKS IN AUSTRALIAN IP LAW

and the registrar by Duffy KC[32] from Melbourne and Cullen KC[33] (with Bavin)[34] from Sydney. In crude terms, there were two parties (the union and the registrar) supporting the validity of Pt VII, with one party (the breweries) advancing the case against. As will be seen, this made no difference to the outcome.

The hearing occupied 11 days, commencing on 30 March 1908 and concluding on 11 April – a lengthy proceeding by contemporary standards. By contrast, the court's decision was delivered, after a reasonably short period, on 8 August 1908. Within less than three years of its enactment, Pt VII was declared invalid and became just a footnote in Australian trade mark history, its demise not even noted in the *Official Journal*.[35]

The court's decision

Given the politics of the matter, it is not surprising to find the High Court split between a majority comprising the original trinity (Griffith CJ, Barton and O'Connor JJ) and a minority comprising the two Victorian radicals (Isaacs and Higgins JJ). The decisions of the justices (all five delivered separate judgments), however, reveal significant insights into the history and rationales for trade mark protection, and are a vivid illustration of the erudition and breadth of learning to be found in the early High Court.

The majority judgments

The majority[36] found that Pt VII was beyond power and was therefore invalid, on the basis that a workers' mark did not come within the concept of a trade

---

32 Later Sir Charles Gavan Duffy, justice and then Chief Justice of the High Court of Australia: *Australian Dictionary of Biography* (online edn), entry for 'Charles Gavan Duffy, 1852–1936', available at http://www.adb.online.anu.edu.au/biogs/A080377b.htm.

33 A prominent Sydney silk and academic (at one point Acting Dean of the Sydney Law School) and later Chief Justice of New South Wales: *Australian Dictionary of Biography* (online edn), entry for 'Sir William Portus Cullen, 1855–1935', available at http://www.adb.online.anu.edu.au/biogs/A090029b.htm.

34 Like Holman and Hall, another aspiring lawyer-politician, later to be become Premier of New South Wales and Supreme Court justice, and also Barton J's first associate: see further *Australian Dictionary of Biography* (online edn), entry for 'Sir Thomas Rainsford Bavin, 1874–1941', available at http://www.adb.online.anu.edu.au/biogs/A070213b.htm.

35 Thus, the issue of the *Official Journal* after the date of the decision (14 August 1908, Vol. 3, No. 33) makes no reference to the High Court's decision, although it notes the adherence of the Commonwealth to the Paris Convention for the Protection of Industrial Property was to take effect as from 5 August 1907. Coincidentally, among the trade marks listed for acceptance on that date was one for 'Higgin's Fine Salt' (along with applications for 'The Dreadnought Hosiery', 'Red Cross' and 'Zesto'). Formal legislative burial of Pt VII did not occur until the *Trade Marks Act 1912* (Cth) ss 3 and 24 repealed the provisions.

36 As noted above, this comprised Griffith, Barton and O'Connor, each of whom delivered judgments. In the case of Barton, it is interesting to note that he was now beginning to give separate judgments, rather than just concurring with Griffith. There had been criticism of him for this during his first three years on the court, with observers attributing his readiness to concur to his general laziness: see the *ADB* entry for Barton. It appears though that Barton was far from lazy in performing his judicial duties, and became a far more regular judgment writer from 1906 (in general, siding with Griffith and O'Connor, whose early death in 1912 caused Barton great personal distress): see further the entry for Barton by Geoffrey Bolton and John Williams in T Blackshield, M Coper and G Williams (eds.), *The Oxford Companion to the High Court of Australia*, Oxford University Press, South Melbourne, 2001, pp. 53–6.

mark. In their view, in determining the scope of the power under s 51(xviii), it was necessary to ascertain the meaning which the term 'trade mark' bore in 1900, the time at which the Constitution was enacted. This, in turn, involved a careful consideration of the statutory and non-statutory law concerning trade marks which had developed both in the UK and the Australian colonies prior to this date. In the light of this examination, the majority concluded that in 1900, the word 'trade mark', whether it was to be regarded as a term of art or as a word used in popular language, did not denote every kind of mark which might be used in trade, but, in Griffith CJ's words:

> meant a mark which is the visible symbol of a particular kind of incorporeal or industrial property consisting in the right of a person engaged in trade to distinguish by a special mark goods in which he deals, or with which he has dealt, from the goods of other persons.[37]

This involved 'five distinct elements' (with which Barton and O'Connor JJ in substance agreed):

(1) A right which is in the nature of property;
(2) The owner of the right must be a person, natural or artificial, engaged in trade;
(3) The right is appurtenant or incident to the dealing with goods in the course of his trade;
(4) The owner has such an independent dominion over the goods to which the mark is to be affixed as to entitle him to affix it to them . . .
(5) The mark distinguishes the goods as having been dealt with by some particular person or persons engaged in trade . . .[38]

Applying these criteria, the majority concluded that the workers' mark did not come within the meaning of 'trade mark'. Thus, it could not be said that the right to prevent others from using a workers' mark conferred a right of property in the exclusive use of that mark. Again, although individual workers could engage in trade, this could not be said of an association of workers such as a trade union. Furthermore, at no stage did the union have such an independent dominion over the goods to which the mark was to be affixed as to entitle it to do so on its own behalf. While the union might perhaps stipulate that no persons other than union members should be employed in the production of the goods, the mark was still applied by or with the authority of the employer and this was an 'entirely different concept from the right of dominion involved in the concept of a trade mark'. Finally, the workers' mark did not in fact purport to distinguish the goods to which it was affixed as being those of a particular trader but merely indicated that certain persons, in other words, unionists, had been engaged in the production of the trader's goods.[39] O'Connor J pithily described this gap in relation to the brewery employees' mark in the following terms:

---

37 (1908) 6 CLR 469, 512–13.
38 ibid., pp. 513 (Griffiths CJ), 525 (Barton J) and 540 (O'Connor J).
39 ibid., pp. 513–17 (Griffiths CJ).

The different breweries of New South Wales, for instance, each selling its own manufacture, are, it must be assumed, in competition for the favour of the public. But the workers' trade mark in no way aids the public to distinguish one set of goods from another. Every brewer employing union labour may use the mark. Its use distinguishes those who do not from those who do employ union labour. But amongst those who employ union labour there is no distinction of goods or of manufacture. Indeed, it is no part of the object of the mark or its application to make any such distinction. Its object simply is to distinguish the breweries in which union labour is employed from those in which union labour is not employed, just as a mark might be used to distinguish goods made in Australia or by white labour from those made abroad or by coloured labour.

But that is not the kind of 'distinctiveness' in a mark which enables the public to distinguish the goods with which one person or corporation has had a business connection, using that phrase in the sense which I have explained, from those with which another person or corporation have had a business connection of a like kind. The mark is wanting, therefore, in the second essential, that of 'distinctiveness,' which is inseparable from the very nature of a trade mark as known to the law at the time when the Constitution was passed. No doubt, the sections under consideration provide that the 'device, design,' etc., shall be 'distinctive,' but in the context that can mean nothing more than 'distinctive' within the limits fixed by the Statute. And, as I have pointed out, it is impossible that the mark as created can have any 'distinctiveness' in the sense in which the law understands that expression.[40]

This led inexorably to the conclusion:

The more the matter is examined the plainer does it become that the whole nature and purpose of the workers' trade mark is different from that of the ordinary trade mark as known to the law. The latter originated in its use by traders for trade purposes, and has for its sole object the benefit and interest of the trader in competition with other traders. It has no other purpose to serve, and it has won its recognition as a necessary incident of trade for the benefit and protection of traders and of the purchasing public. The workers' trade mark is not an incident of the business in which it is used; its object is not the benefit of the manufacturer who uses it, nor does the benefit to the workman who has taken part in the manufacture arise directly from the use of the mark in the business – his benefit is the indirect gain which may come to him by advancement of the interest of his union generally. In my opinion, therefore, the workers' trade mark is wanting in the essential characteristics of a trade mark within the meaning of pl. xviii of sec. 51 of the *Constitution*, and the Commonwealth Parliament in enacting the provisions of Part VII of the *Trade Marks Act* has exceeded the powers conferred upon it by that sub-section.[41]

Further arguments that the provisions of Pt VII might be upheld as within the trade and commerce power were rejected, as there was nothing in the provisions to confine them exclusively to interstate trade or trade with other countries.[42]

Finally, none of the majority justices were prepared to accept preliminary or threshold arguments to the effect that the breweries were not 'persons aggrieved'

---

40 ibid., pp. 543–4.
41 ibid., p. 545.
42 ibid., p. 547 (O'Connor J).

by the registration of the brewery employees' trade mark. While taking pains to assert that the court would not 'entertain a question brought before it merely to satisfy those whose political views prompt them to struggle to remove an enactment that offends them',[43] the members of the majority concluded that the very presence of such a registration affected the breweries' freedom of trade:

> It is said that the registration of the mark in question and its use by other rival traders would not have any such prejudicial effect, since the plaintiffs themselves might acquire the right to use it. But, since they could only do so by the exclusive employment of members of the defendant Union, it is plain that they are interfered with to this extent – that they are no longer free to compete with rival traders on the same terms as before. They must either use or abstain from using the mark. The user or non-user are of equal significance. They are, therefore, obliged to inform their customers that they do or do not exclusively employ persons who are members of the defendant Union, and this information may be of great importance in the opinion of a large class of persons to whom they look for custom. It was suggested that such an interference is so trivial that the Court should disregard it, which seems a singular argument to use in a case in which the right to the mark has been so long and so strenuously contested. In my opinion, this interference with freedom is substantial, and is, unless authorized by some positive law, unlawful and actionable. To use the words of Holt CJ in *Ashby v White* [Raym (Ld), 938, at p. 955]: – 'A damage is not merely pecuniary, but an injury imports a damage, when a man is thereby hindered of his right'; of which he gives many illustrations. I think, further, that the injury is a particular injury to every person whose freedom is so interfered with, and that every such person may maintain an action for an injunction to restrain the interference.[44]

The minority judgments

As might be expected, the minority viewed the 'workers' trade mark' as containing all the essential characteristics of a 'trade mark' as understood at the time of enactment of the Constitution, in that it was unnecessary that a mark should indicate the particular trade origin of the goods to which it was attached. Isaacs J's judgment is of particular interest in view of his association with the drafting and parliamentary adoption of the trade marks bill; it is dismissive, even dogmatically so, of the plaintiffs' claims for standing.[45] On the substantive issue of constitutional validity, his judgment drew heavily on, and repeated, the

---

43 ibid., p. 519 (Barton J).
44 ibid., p. 498 (Griffith CJ); pp. 519–20 (Barton J); and pp. 549–53 (O'Connor J). This seems quite in line with UK authorities such as *Powell v Birmingham Vinegar Brewery Co* [1894] AC 8, and *In re The Apollinaris Co's Trade Marks* (1891) 2 Ch 186, 225.
45 (1908) 6 CLR 469, 553–7. Isaacs J, however, towards the end of his judgment (at 586) does make express reference to his 'former parliamentary connection with the Statute', stating that he has been more than 'ordinarily solicitous to re-examine the challenged provisions *ab initio*, and have endeavoured to follow in detail the various objections raised to their legality and to state explicitly the reasons on which my judgment is based'.

28   LANDMARKS IN AUSTRALIAN IP LAW

same arguments he had advanced in his second reading speech.[46] His 'governing principle' here was as follows:

> To ascertain the really essential characteristics of a trade mark it is necessary to distinguish what is merely occasional, though frequent, and to strip the expression of everything that is not absolutely fundamental. If we find some attribute universally attaching to the idea in all circumstances, that attribute is probably indispensable; but if any feature, however usual its presence may be, is not invariably existent, if trade marks, well recognized and established and enforceable by English law, can be found without that feature, it cannot, I apprehend, be asserted that the fundamental concept includes the variable feature. The power of legislation is with respect to *trade marks,* that is, trade marks in the fullest sense, and not merely usual or ordinary trade marks. The fundamental concept once ascertained, the power is unlimited. I shall consider the various points in order, one by one.[47]

And consider them he did, in a carefully constructed forensic exercise intended to strip down the concept of a trade mark to its central core. In particular, he sought to show, in detail, why such elements as ownership or dominion over the goods and exclusive ownership of the mark were not essential characteristics of a trade mark.[48] Extensive references were made to both UK and US decisions that exemplified these points, in an attempt to show that the workers' marks provisions were simply part of a continuum of Anglo-American law in this area. In a somewhat rhetorical style, he stated that if the state courts and parliaments could deal with such matters (with particular reference here to US state legislation on workers' marks), it would be odd if the grant of power to the Commonwealth to legislate with respect to trade marks should not extend to them:

> It is said that the States alone can do this. If so it would, as I think, be not only a restriction of the constitutional grant of power and a shortening of federal jurisdiction which might be required to effectually deal with the subject of trade marks, but also a commingling of powers assumedly equal, creating possibly conflicting provisions, and leading very probably to confusion in different States, on the one subject of trade marks. This is the very result, it seems to me, that the Constitution, by placing this power in a single hand for the guidance of the whole people, intended to avert.[49]

Higgins J's judgment is perhaps the more persuasive, and reflective of his developing approach to constitutional interpretation:[50] even if the meaning of 'trade mark' in 1900 was not so wide as to include the workers' mark, the Constitution had conferred on the federal parliament full power to make laws on the whole

---

46 Cowen (*ADB* online entry) notes that Isaacs always had a marked reluctance to change his arguments once formulated: 'The style of his speaking and of his judgments, however, was often rhetorical and verbose. More objectionable was his appalling certainty, his unshakeable conviction of the rightness of his opinion and his utter inability to see merit in any other view. He was unwilling to confess error in those cases where he simply had to reverse course and retreat from a position dogmatically stated and wrong. Reading his judgments sometimes leaves a sense that a result has been achieved by a trick, by sleight of hand. He never ceased to be a committed advocate ...'.
47 (1908) 6 CLR 469, 560.
48 ibid., p. 560ff.
49 ibid., p. 587.
50 Although it must be said that it still reflects the argumentative style of the advocate who has only recently made the transition to the bench: see the various passages extracted in the principal text above.

THE *UNION LABEL* CASE   29

subject of 'trade marks', that is, to say what marks should be enforceable and what should not. Thus, Pt VII of the 1905 Act did not transgress the power conferred on the parliament 'to make laws with respect to ... trade marks', the meaning of the expression in 1900 giving the 'centre, not the circumference, of the power'.[51] The present case, of course, involved only a challenge to the Commonwealth's power to legislate with respect to workers' marks: it was not disputed by the plaintiffs that the former colonies and present states could have enacted such laws. To Higgins J, if this were so, then it was a 'flaw in the Constitution'. He went on to say:

> if the plaintiffs' argument be successful, we shall have as a result a position which must be confusing and baneful to traders and to the public – we shall have seven different bodies of law makers in Australia laying down laws as to marks used for trade purposes.[52]

Like Isaacs J, Higgins J contended that the workers' marks, in any event, fell within the scope of a 'trade mark' as understood in 1900, having regard here to broader non-legal understandings of the term, as well as to the special protection historically given to 'guild marks' in the UK (in particular, those of the Cutlers' Company now protected as 'Sheffield marks' under the UK Act of 1905[53]) and the protection given to union marks in various US states.[54] In the case of the Cutlers' marks, the analogy to a workers' mark was close: every apprentice, after serving his term, was entitled to get a mark and to be made a freeman of the company.[55] These marks were personal property and assignable or transmissible in gross.

> In short, the only attributes that I can find to be common to these words in all their varying uses, the only essential *differentia* from other marks is this – the marks must be used to identify the commodities with some person or body of persons and for the purpose of attracting trade; and these attributes are all found in this 'workers' trade mark.'[56]

---

51 (1908) 6 CLR 469, 610.

52 ibid., p. 601. In this regard, Higgins J referred also to provisions in the *Trade Marks Act 1905* (UK) which provided for 'certification marks' to be registered by associations under s 62, which were not part of UK law in 1900, and which, therefore, on a strict interpretation would not have been within the scope of the term 'trade mark' in 1900.

53 The Cutlers' Company was incorporated in 1623 by Act 21 Jac 1, c 31. For a brief history of 'Sheffield marks', see TA Blanco White and R Jacob, *Kerly's Law of Trade Marks and Trade Names*, 10th edn, Sweet & Maxwell, 1972, chap. 6. This material appears to have been deleted from later editions, but was contained in the second edition (1901) which was available to, and cited by, the various members of the High Court in the *Union Label* case. Other special marks of this kind were marks for gold and silver smiths which were the subject of legislation dating back to 1423: 2 Hen 6, c 17. Under a later statute, 13 Geo 3, c 52 (1772), it was provided that, among the markings to be applied gold and silver was 'the mark of the worker or maker which shall be the first letters of his Christian and surname' (the others being the marks of the company, the symbol of a lion passant and the year): s 4.

54 In argument, Holman had referred to state Acts giving trade unions the right to register trade marks that had been passed prior to 1900 in California (as early as 1889), Minnesota, Georgia, Indiana and Colorado: (1908) 6 CLR 469, 483.

55 ibid., p. 608.

56 ibid.

30   LANDMARKS IN AUSTRALIAN IP LAW

As to the various statutory US precedents, Higgins J noted that these had all occurred before 1900, observing that these statutes actually referred to workers' marks as 'trade marks':

> I suppose it will not be contended that we are not to take into consideration the English language as used in America – the country where most of those who use the English language live. Probably, as our Constitution is contained in a British Act, if the British meaning were in conflict with the American meaning, that meaning should be adopted which the language would bear as coming from a British legislature in preference to the meaning which it would bear as coming from an American legislature. But this is not a case of conflict; and we are entitled, I think, to take into account the use of the English language wherever that language is heard – even if the sound have the *timbre* of a gramophone.[57]

Quite apart from these considerations, Higgins J argued that, even if the workers' marks fell outside the scope of 'trade mark' as understood in 1900, they still came properly within the general ambit of the power to legislate with respect to that subject-matter in s 51(xviii):

> What is committed to the Federal Parliament is not the *class* of things called trade marks, but the whole *subject* of trade marks. No doubt, we are to ascertain the meaning of 'trade marks' as in 1900. But having ascertained that meaning, we have then to find the extent of the power to deal with the subject of trade marks – or, what is the same thing, to find the meaning of the 'power to make laws with respect to trade marks.' The usage in 1900 gives us the central type; it does not give us the circumference of the power. To find the circumference of the power, we take as a centre the thing named – trade marks – with the meaning as in 1900; but it is a mistake to treat the centre as the radius.[58]

More memorably, Higgins J lays down his approach to constitutional interpretation in the following trenchant terms:

> The plaintiffs in their argument treat the power of the Federal Parliament to make laws with respect to trade marks as if it were a power to make laws with respect to cattle. In such a case, if a beast does not come under the term 'cattle,' as understood in 1900, there is no power, it is said, to make any laws about it. But I am clearly of opinion that this narrow doctrine propounded by the plaintiffs is, in construing a constitutional power to make laws, unwarrantable and absolutely wrong. In the first place, there is a vital distinction arising from the nature of the subject. Cattle are concrete, physical objects, and the boundaries of the class are fixed by external nature; whereas 'trade marks' are artificial products of society, and dependent upon the will of society. The class 'cattle' cannot well be extended by man; the class 'trade marks' can be extended. Power to make laws as to any class of rights involves a power to alter those rights, to define those rights, to limit those rights, to extend those rights, and to extend the class of those who may enjoy those rights. In the same clause of sec. 51, power is given to make laws with respect to 'copyrights' (rights of multiplying copies of books, etc.); with respect to 'patents' (rights to make or sell inventions); and with respect to 'trade

---

57 ibid., p. 609.
58 ibid., p. 610. In a peculiarly Australian reference, Higgins J subsequently goes on to refer the outer limits of the trade mark power as the 'ring fence': ibid., p. 613.

marks' (rights to use marks for the purposes of trade). The power to make laws 'with respect to' these rights, involves a power to declare what shall be the subject of such rights. In the second place, although we are to interpret the words of the Constitution on the same principles of interpretation as we apply to any ordinary law, these very principles of interpretation compel us to take into account the nature and scope of the Act that we are interpreting – to remember that *it is a Constitution, a mechanism under which laws are to be made, and not a mere Act which declares what the law is to be.*[59]

Several comments can be made about the historical and comparative precedents cited in support by the dissentients:

1. In relation to the issue of whether the trade mark owner should have ownership or dominion over the goods to which the mark is applied, it is noteworthy that some of the authorities referred to here actually concerned the provision of services and were what we would now regard as 'service marks'. For example, *Re Sykes and Co's Trade Mark*[60] concerned the activities of calico bleachers who bleached materials for manufacturers and applied their mark to the inside of the first fold of each parcel of calico, with the manufacturer's mark then being applied to the outside. More generally, it was clear that the common law and equity were ready to protect marks used in businesses and in relation to indicia that would not have qualified for registration under either the UK or Australian statutes, including such things as the get-up of goods.[61]

2. The Cutlers' Company and other similar marks, strongly relied on by Isaacs and Higgins JJ as precursors of the workers' mark, were equally readily distinguished by the majority as 'having their origin in local conditions or relating only to special trades', and therefore 'in their nature and incidents entirely different from ordinary trade marks . . .'.[62] It could hardly be supposed that the framers of s 51(xviii) of the Constitution 'had in mind when the sub-clause was enacted "trade marks" as generally known and recognized in commerce, and protected by the conventions of all mercantile nations, and not some special and local variety of mark used only in England'.[63]

3. The statutory protection that had been given to workers' marks in various states in the US, such as California and Minnesota, could be used on either side of the argument. To the minority, these were simply illustrations of the expansive concept of a 'trade mark'. To the more sceptical critics, such

---

59 ibid., p. 613.

60 (1880) 43 LT 626, referred to by Isaacs J in the *Union Label* case: (1908) 6 CLR 469, 561.

61 All of the judges quoted various authorities to this effect, and it is also clear from a perusal of the coverage given to such matters in contemporary text books, such as DM Kerly, *The Law of Trade-Marks, Trade-Names, and Merchandise Marks: With Chapters on Trade Secrets and Trade Libel, and a Full Collection of Statutes*, 2nd edn, Sweet & Maxwell, London, 1901; and LB Sebastian, *The Law of Trade Marks and Their Registration and Matters Connected Therewith*, 4th edn, Stevens and Sons, London, 1899.

62 (1908) 6 CLR 469, 537 (O'Connor J).

63 ibid. An interesting point, considering that all members of the court had participated, to different degrees, in the various pre-federation conventions.

as Barton[64] and O'Connor JJ,[65] these enactments proved the opposite: such special legislation was clearly necessary because workers' marks otherwise did not come within the scope of that concept. Furthermore, it was accepted by all sides that, in the absence of such statutory provisions, US courts had typically refused to protect workers' marks.[66] There was also a marked division of opinion between the members of the majority and minority (all arguably themselves 'framers of the Constitution') as to whether they (the framers) would have had regard to the existence of workers' marks laws in the US in formulating the trade marks power in s 51(xviii). In Higgins J's view:

> it is not a violent assumption to suppose that the framers of our Constitution and the British Parliament know something of the long controversy as to the union label in the Courts and in the legislatures of the United States, and meant to give the Australian Parliament full power, under the head of 'trade marks,' to deal with the whole subject as it saw fit – power as full as each State of the Union had, as each Australian Colony had, as the British Parliament had . . .[67]

Such knowledge and prescience, however, was denied by Barton J:

> that legislation, in my opinion, cannot, even apart from its many variances, be supposed to have been known to and to have been in the minds of the framers of the Australian Constitution. Where a part of the Constitution of the United States has been judicially interpreted and an identical or manifestly equivalent form of expression has been adopted in the Australian Constitution, the words of the former and the meaning judicially given them are of much importance, at any rate in weighing the reasons for the interpretations cited. But this is a different matter. The United States Constitution contains no provision similar to that of our sec. 51(xviii.) Besides, if the framers of the Constitution knew of the Statutes, they knew of the decisions, and knew that the great bulk of American authority was to the effect that trade marks do not include union labels.[68]

The wider issue faced by the High Court

It will be seen that the problem facing the High Court here is the same one that has confronted that court on numerous other occasions, namely, how is it to interpret the scope of a head of power conferred on the Commonwealth parliament by an instrument enacted in 1900? While the majority held that the meaning of the terms used in that instrument were to be 'ascertained by their signification in 1900', Griffiths CJ nonetheless recognised that 'with advancing civilization new developments, now unthought of, may arise with respect

---

64 ibid., pp. 529–30.
65 ibid., p. 536.
66 ibid., p. 529 (Barton J); p. 536 (O'Connor J, referring to the decision of the Massachussetts court in *Werner v Brayton* 152 Mas 101); and pp. 577–81 (Isaacs J examining and distinguishing various US authorities).
67 ibid., p. 609.
68 ibid., p. 530.

to many subject-matters' and that as long as these new developments related to the same subject-matter the powers of parliament would continue to extend to them. On the other hand, parliament was not entitled to 'enlarge its powers by calling a matter with which it is not competent to deal by the name of something else which is within its competence'.[69] On this view, the heads of power enumerated in s 51 were not to be interpreted restrictively: provided that the same essential object or function covered by the head in question is being fulfilled, it should not matter how this is done.[70] At the same time, it should be noted that the differences between the majority and minority judges reflected a marked philosophical division between them over the proper approach to the interpretation of the provisions of the newly minted Commonwealth Constitution. In particular, a powerful factor impelling the majority to a narrower view of the scope of s 51(xviii) was the doctrine of reserved state powers which had been formulated in earlier decisions of the court, pursuant to which 'some heads of Commonwealth legislative power were given a narrow interpretation to avoid undue encroachment on the reserved powers of state power'.[71] This self-limiting doctrine of constitutional interpretation was to continue for another 12 years after the *Union Label* case until it was overthrown in the *Engineers'* case[72] by a differently constituted High Court in which Isaacs and Higgins JJ were now in the majority.

Questions of constitutional interpretation aside, there was also a real fault line of substance between the majority and minority in relation to the proper function of trade mark protection: the separation between ownership of the mark and ownership of the goods to which it was applied was one thing, but more significant, in the final analysis, was the connection indicated by the mark. In the majority's view, the association of the worker with the goods was too transient or ephemeral for the purposes of a trade mark. Thus, the latter was not a certification that particular things had happened to goods or that particular persons had worked upon them: it was a proprietary right that indicated that at some time the trade mark owner had had dominion over the goods, howsoever transient. As O'Connor J makes clear in the passage quoted above, the nature and purpose of the workers' mark was quite different from that of the 'ordinary trade mark known to the law'. To repeat his Honour's words:

> The workers' trade mark is not an incident of the business in which it is used; its object is not the benefit of the manufacturer who uses it, nor does the benefit to the workman who has taken part in the manufacture arise directly from the use of the mark in the business – his benefit is the indirect gain which may come to him by advancement of the interest of his union generally. In my opinion, therefore, the workers' trade mark is

69 ibid., p. 501.
70 See, for example, cases concerning the scope of the posts and telegraphs power under s 51(v) of the Constitution: *Re Brislan; Ex parte Williams* (1935) 54 CLR 262 (FC, HC); *Jones v The Commonwealth (No. 2)* (1965) 112 CLR 206 (FC, HC).
71 K Booker, entry on 'Reserved state powers' in Blackshield et al, op. cit., pp. 601–2, and see further the judgment of Kirby J in *Grain Pool of Western Australia v Commonwealth* (2002) 202 CLR 479, para. 108ff.
72 *Amalgamated Society of Engineers v Adelaide Steamship Co Ltd* (1920) 28 CLR 129.

34 LANDMARKS IN AUSTRALIAN IP LAW

wanting in the essential characteristics of a trade mark within the meaning of pl. xviii. of sec. 51 of the Constitution.[73]

Implications of the decision

The dry legal argument of the court tends to obscure the intense political debates that had accompanied the adoption of the workers' marks provisions – the members of the majority were at pains to observe that they were simply interpreting the Constitution without regard to 'its own notions of what it is expedient that the Constitution should contain or the parliament should enact'.[74] But the political context cannot be disregarded, nor can the 'chilling' effect of the decision on the future development of Australian intellectual property law. In the case of trade marks, it was to be almost 70 years before the Commonwealth government felt confident enough to legislate for the protection of service marks,[75] although the latter probably met the criteria of the majority in the *Union Label* case in any event. In their view, the essential feature of a trade mark was that it indicated the trade origin of the goods to which it was applied. This was not true of a worker's mark, the object of which, at most, was to indicate that certain persons had worked in the production of a particular trader's goods. On the other hand, a mark in respect of services does indicate the trade origin of those services, the only difference being that the subject-matter is services rather than goods. Thus, the arguments in favour of extending the trade marks power under s 51 (xviii) were stronger than those in favour of workers' marks. In addition, it can be argued that, prior to 1900, even if statutory trade mark protection in respect of services did not exist, trade marks in respect of services were protected equally with those in respect of goods by the common law and equity courts.[76]

Subsequent developments in constitutional interpretation by the High Court, particularly after the overthrow of the doctrine of reserved state powers, now

---

73 (1908) 6 CLR 469, 545.

74 ibid., p. 500 (Griffith CJ). And, it must be said, both Isaacs and Higgins JJ in their judgments still adopted the role of advocates for their previous parliamentary and political positions.

75 See, for example, the doubts expressed by the Dean Committee in 1954 which described the *Union Label* case as imposing a 'serious handicap upon any reform of the law', noting that 'whereas other countries have been free to extend the definition of 'trade mark', we are not'. See Dean Committee, Commonwealth of Australia, *Report of the Committee Appointed by the Attorney-General of the Commonwealth (Senator the Honourable JA Spicer, QC) to Consider What Alterations are Desirable to the Trade Marks Law of the Commonwealth*, 1954, para. 10. Note also that the committee did not believe in any event that, at that time, extension of registered trade marks protection to services was warranted: see paras. 38–41. It does not appear that the Knowles Committee of 1938 (the predecessor to the Dean Committee and the report of which is appended to Dean) considered the issue of service marks or other extensions to registered trade mark protection, apart from noting the restrictive effect of the *Union Label* case in removing the workers' mark provisions of Pt VII of the 1905 Act: Knowles Committee, para. 9.

76 At the same time, if legislation with respect to service marks could not be supported under s 51(xviii), the external affairs power in s 51(xxix) might provide a suitable basis, because Art 6 sexies of the Paris Convention for the Protection of Industrial Property to which Australia is a signatory provides for their protection. While this need not be by way of a registration system, it is highly likely that legislation to this effect can still be justified under s 51(xxix).

THE *UNION LABEL* CASE   35

render the *Union Label* case largely a matter of historical interest: consider, for instance, the High Court's more expansive approach to the interpretation of s 51(xviii) in such cases as *Nintendo Co Ltd v Centronics Systems Pty Ltd*[77] and, in particular, *Grain Pool of Western Australia v Commonwealth*,[78] in which the dissenting view of Higgins J was explicitly approved.[79] In other areas too, such as corporations, external affairs, and communications,[80] the court has liberated these powers from their 1900 shackles, and has augmented the Commonwealth parliament's powers in a way that would have been quite unexpected, if not shocking, to the carefully nuanced approach of the founding trinity of Griffith CJ, Barton and O'Connor JJ.[81] On the other hand, even given the most expanded view of the scope of s 51(xviii), it is unlikely that the decision of the High Court in *Davis v The Commonwealth*[82] in relation to the *Australian Bicentennial Authority Act 1988* (Cth) would have been any different. (In that case, among other things, the High Court held that s 51(xviii) could not sustain provisions in that Act that sought to protect 'common words and expressions having no capacity to distinguish the Authority or the activities in which it engages or which it promotes'.[83])

Quite apart from the constitutional perspective, the story of the *Union Label* case still resonates strongly today, raising the following wider issues of political and social concern:

1. The clash of labour and capital, in particular the strong conflict over the place of union power, with the workers' mark legislation being seen as playing a crucial part in the economic nationalist policies of early Commonwealth governments.

2. The ready and well-informed reference that was made by all parties, both in parliament and in the court, to legislative models to be found in other common law jurisdictions, such as California and other American states, as well as to judicial decisions from those places.

---

77 (1994) 181 CLR 134.
78 (2000) 202 CLR 479.
79 ibid., paras. 19 and 20 (Gleeson CJ, Gaudron, McHugh, Gummow, Hayne and Callinan JJ).
80 See further *The King v Burgess; Ex parte Henry* (1936) 55 CLR 608 (FC, HC); *Strickland v Rocla Concrete Pipes Ltd* (1971) 124 CLR 468; *Koowarta v Bjelke-Peterson* (1982) 56 ALJR 625 (FC, HC); *Commonwealth v Tasmania* (1983) 158 CLR 1.
81 In this regard, see the separate judgment of Kirby J in the *Grain Pools* case in which his Honour examines the judgments in the *Union Label* case in some detail, noting that one of the circumstances explaining the more restricted approach of the majority in tying the interpretation of s 51 (xviii) to 1900 as the 'terminus' was the doctrine of the implied reserve powers of the States: see *Grain Pool of Western Australia v Commonwealth* (2002) 202 CLR 479, para. 108, and see further Booker, op. cit.
82 (1988) 63 ALJR 35.
83 ibid., p. 40 (Mason CJ, Deane and Gaudron JJ). The judges took the view that such provisions would not be sustained under either the majority or minority views in the *Union Label* case. In consequence, protection of such kinds of words and expressions under state legislation would appear to be justifiable, so long as such enactments do not stray into the protection of 'trade marks'. See, for example, the limited protection extended under Victorian law to certain descriptive and geographic expressions by the *Australian Grand Prix Act 1994* (Vic) ss 3 (definition of 'grand prix insignia') and 21(1)(j) (power of Australian Grand Prix Corporation to 'restrict, control and make charges for the use of grand prix insignia'), and under the *Commonwealth Games Arrangements Act 2001* (Vic) ss 3 and 56K (protection, now repealed, for 'Commonwealth Games references').

36   LANDMARKS IN AUSTRALIAN IP LAW

3.   The emerging and central role of the High Court as interpreter of the new Commonwealth Constitution.

Some lesser, but interesting, *Leitmotiven* are also evident:

4.   The notion of conflict of interest, in particular that of judicial independence, as exemplified by the readiness of Isaacs J to sit in judgment on legislation for which he previously had had carriage as Commonwealth Attorney-General. It is hard to believe that this would occur today,[84] but, as much as Isaacs attracted controversy throughout his career, it does not appear that he was criticised specifically in this regard. Things have changed, and Isaacs J was by no means the last former Commonwealth Attorney-General to be appointed to the High Court.[85]

5.   The continuity and intimacy of relations between those involved in the foundation of the new Commonwealth. As noted above, both justices and counsel had been, or were still, participants in the broader political and legislative sphere, and there is no doubt that each saw himself as an active participant in the shaping of the new federal system. A fight over trade marks was only a small, but significant, part of that fledgling but emerging system of governance.

---

84 One more recent instance is that of Dawson J who did not sit in *Hematite Petroleum Pty Ltd v Victoria* (1983) 151 CLR 599, because he had previously given advice to the Victorian government on the likely result of the matter in his capacity as Solicitor-General: see further the entry for 'Disqualification of Justices' in Blackshield et al, op. cit., p. 215.

85 The other two examples are Sir John Latham in 1934 and Lionel Murphy in 1975. Neither of these ceased entirely to abandon their previous political positions in their subsequent judicial careers: see further their entries in the *Australian Dictionary of Biography*, online version, as well as in Blackshield et al, op. cit. HV Evatt was an instance of a former justice moving into politics and subsequent high office.

3

RPM for RPM: *National Phonograph Company of Australia v Menck*

Peter Heerey and Nicole Malone*

Introduction

One of the earliest decisions of the Privy Council on appeal from the High Court, *National Phonograph Company of Australia v Menck*,[1] exemplifies the tension between intellectual property and competition law – although in the past, that being a foreign country, they saw things differently then.

On the north-eastern corner of the intersection of Nicholson and Johnson Streets, in the inner Melbourne suburb of Fitzroy, there stands a large service station. To the east lies the main Iberian enclave of multicultural Melbourne, with Spanish restaurants and grocery stores. To the south, across Johnson Street, is the Tankerville Hotel, with the now ubiquitous poker machines.

Exactly a century ago on that north-eastern corner, at 232 Nicholson Street, one Walter T Menck conducted a business at which he sold Edison phonographs and records.

Thomas Alva Edison invented the phonograph in 1877 by accident while working on an instrument for transcribing telegrams.[2] The Edison phonograph and its associated records and blanks were the subject of some of the earliest patents granted by the new Commonwealth of Australia, being numbers 2108, 2109 and 2110, granted on 6 December 1904.[3] Subsequently the patents were

---

* We gratefully acknowledge the assistance of Richard York, Economic Analyst for the Australian Competition Tribunal.
1 *National Phonograph Company of Australia Ltd v Menck* (1908) 7 CLR 481.
2 DJ Steffen, *From Edison to Marconi: The First Thirty Years of Recorded Music*, McFarland & Co, Inc, Jefferson, NC, 2005, p. 24.
3 *National Phonograph Company of Australia v Menck* (1908) 7 CLR 481, 482.

38 LANDMARKS IN AUSTRALIAN IP LAW

assigned to a New South Wales company, the National Phonograph Company of Australia.[4]

The early recorded songs were a mix of vaudeville, marches (Edison's first cylinder was 'Semper Fidelis' played by the US Marine Corps Band), opera and popular tunes such as 'Bill Bailey, Won't You Please Come Home' (1902) and 'Give My Regards to Broadway' (1904). During the course of the litigation with which we are concerned, there was 'Shine on Harvest Moon' (1908) and the immortal Irving Berlin's first great hit, 'Alexander's Ragtime Band' (1911). Jazz came a little later with the original Dixieland Jazz Band and King Oliver's Creole Jazz Band. Ragtime, dominated by Scott Joplin, predated jazz, but like classical music, and unlike jazz, was distributed through sheet music rather than live recordings.

The first decade of the 20th century was a peaceful time. Memories of the Boer War were receding and World War I was far over the horizon. Edward VII, dubbed 'the Peacemaker', found the statesmanship of the *Entente Cordiale* and the delights of Paris equally congenial.

The British Empire was at its apogee. In 1907 its supreme bard, Rudyard Kipling, became the first writer in English to win the Nobel Prize for literature.

Although then and for decades thereafter an unequivocal part of the Empire, Australia was enjoying its first decade as a nation. A metaphor for this dawning sense of identity might be found in domestic architecture. The early 1900s federation style broke away from the moral rigours of the mid-to-late Victorian era. Federation houses were characterised by freedom of expression, terracotta roofs (as opposed to slate) with decorative embellishments such as gargoyles and wyverns. Windows, frequently featuring leadlighting, were bigger and opened onto verandahs, in recognition of the demands of the Australian climate.

The case against Menck

National Phonograph engaged in what we would call today resale price maintenance (RPM).[5] It sought to prevent Menck from selling its patented products below its stipulated prices. It claimed that by doing so he was in breach of the contract under which he acquired the goods and also, independently of any contractual obligation, that he had infringed the patents. This latter, much broader, claim raised what the trial judge, Isaacs J, identified as

> a most important question as to how far the right to use a patented article is separable from the right of ownership of the article itself.[6]

---

4 ibid.
5 Readers of a certain age will recall that in the distant past, before DVDs, CDs or even cassette tapes, recorded music was sold in the form of discs differentiated by the speed at which they were meant to revolve: 33,45 or 78 revolutions per minute (RPM). This serendipity has inspired the title of the present piece.
6 (1908) 7 CLR 481, 502.

THE *MENCK* CASE   39

Before the High Court, National Phonograph failed on all issues.[7] It appealed to the Privy Council.

As far as one can tell from the Commonwealth Law Reports, *Menck* was the fifth appeal to go from the High Court to the Privy Council,[8] the second commercial appeal,[9] the first appeal in an intellectual property case (although that term did not come into use until much later), and the second appeal in which the High Court was reversed.[10]

The board was constituted by Lords MacNaghten, Atkinson, Shaw, Mersey and Robson. National Phonograph again failed on its contract case. However, their Lordships held that a patentee may, by virtue of his patent, sell his patented article accompanied by restrictive conditions which would not apply in the case of ordinary chattels. The rights of the purchaser of a patented article will be limited if there is brought home to him knowledge, at the time of the purchase, of conditions imposed upon his vendor by the patentee.[11]

The contract case

National Phonograph sold its patented products to retailers such as Menck either directly or through 'jobbers' (wholesalers). The retailer's contract, whether between retailer and jobber or between retailer and National Phonograph, provided that the goods should not be sold at less than current list prices. The retailer agreed that in the event of breaching any conditions of the contract his name would be removed from the dealers list and thereafter he would not sell, deal in or use the patented articles.

In its pleadings, National Phonograph alleged a sale by Menck at under list price to one Beckett in July 1906, the subsequent removal of Menck's name from the dealers list on 28 July 1906, and later sales to Whiting (December 1906), Campbell (February 1907) and Thomson (May 1907).[12] Further sales, the particulars of which were not known, were also alleged. Sales after removal of Menck's name from the dealers list were asserted to be wrongful, whether or not below the list price.

As the evidence unfolded before Isaacs J, some further sales were relied on. In the case of two transactions, those involving Pearson and Beckett, it was disputed

---

7 (1908) 7 CLR 481. Isaacs J sat as the trial judge. Because of the importance of the questions raised Isaacs J thought they should be considered at an appellate level. However, if judgment were given against Menck he could not, as Isaacs J put it, 'obtain the opinion of the Full Court without a severe strain on his resources, if at all'. Accordingly Isaacs J stated a case on the facts as found and reserved all questions of law for the consideration of the Full Court: (1908) 7 CLR 481, 502. The Full Court was in due course constituted by all members of the High Court: Griffith CJ, Barton, O'Connor and Higgins JJ and Isaacs J himself.

8 After *Colonial Bank of Australasia Ltd v Marshall* (1906) 4 CLR 196; *Attorney-General for Victoria v City of Melbourne* (1907) 5 CLR 257; *McNaghten v Paterson* (1907) 6 CLR 257; and *Macintosh v Dun* (1908) 6 CLR 303. For an account of one of the last Australian appeals from state Supreme Courts (appeals from the High Court having been earlier abolished) see Heerey, 'A Last Hurrah – Privy Council Days', *Victorian Bar News*, Spring 1986, p. 30.

9 The first was *Colonial Bank of Australasia Ltd v Marshall* (1906) 4 CLR 196 (customer's duty to banker).

10 The first was *Macintosh v Dun* (1908) 6 CLR 303 (defamation).

11 *National Phonograph Company of Australia Ltd v Menck* [1911] AC 336.

12 (1908) 7 CLR 481, 484.

40 LANDMARKS IN AUSTRALIAN IP LAW

whether they were 'sales' at all within the meaning of the retailer's contract. The former was an arrangement whereby Menck left goods with another authorised Edison retailer on the basis that the profit from any sale to a customer would be shared. The latter was an exchange of Edison products with another retailer.

By the time the case reached the Full High Court, National Phonograph had abandoned any of the alleged sales other than those to Pearson and Beckett. Indeed before Isaacs J, the only sale in the ordinary sense alleged to be made at under list price was that by one Kerrigan, an employee of Menck, to a Mr Pettifer, a director of National Phonograph.

Pettifer's evidence was that he went to Kerrigan's home and said he wanted to buy a phonograph. Kerrigan offered him one at less than the list price. The following evening Pettifer returned. Kerrigan became suspicious that Pettifer was not really interested in a purchase. Kerrigan threatened to hit Pettifer, who beat a hasty retreat but not before he caught a glimpse, or so he thought, of Menck hiding in a cupboard. On leaving Kerrigan's house Pettifer hid behind a hedge and observed Menck leaving the house on his bicycle. Pettifer saw Menck the next day and taxed him with responsibility for Kerrigan selling below list price. According to Pettifer, Menck admitted that Kerrigan was his employee.[13]

National Phonograph must have selected Menck for the running of a test case. That being so, it is remarkable how slender was its evidence of the fundamental allegation of selling below list price. Apart from the Pettifer imbroglio, the evidence as to the Thomson sale in May 1907 was that Thomson, who was the company secretary of National Phonograph, went to the Nicholson Street premises under the assumed name of Millar and tried to buy goods at lower than list price. Even though Menck had by this time been removed from the dealers list, Thomson could not get a reduction in price.[14] Perhaps National Phonograph saw Menck, a sole trader in working-class Fitzroy, as a pushover. In that, at least, it was mistaken.

Presumably acting on shrewd legal advice, Menck offered Pettifer an open letter to any buyer to ascertain the price at which an article had been sold. Every machine had a number, so it could be traced. Pettifer did not take advantage of the offer.[15]

Menck's argument in the Full High Court was that he was not contractually bound to National Phonograph because no consideration moved from the company. Alternatively, he contended that no instance of sales at below list price had been proved and thus removal of his name from the dealers list was wrongful and in breach of the agreement.[16]

The first argument failed. The privilege of being a dealer was an advantage or benefit to Menck and thus consideration moved from National Phonograph to him.[17] However, as to the second, the Full Court by a majority held that

---

13 Court Book for Privy Council appeal.
14 (1908) 7 CLR 481, 498.
15 ibid.
16 ibid., p. 520.
17 ibid., pp. 521 (Griffith CJ), 527 (Barton J), 527 (O'Connor J), 532 (Isaacs J) and 543 (Higgins J).

the transactions with Pearson and Beckett were not 'sales'.[18] The Privy Council agreed.[19]

The patent case – the High Court's approach on principle

The applicable statute was the *Patents Act 1903* (Cth), s 62 of which granted to the patentee 'sole privilege and authority ... to make, use, exercise and vend the invention'. As Griffith CJ pointed out, the Act did not confer a right on the patentee to put his invention into practice, this being a common law entitlement, but rather the right to forbid the use of the invention by others.[20]

National Phonograph's case was that it sold its patented goods to a limited class of persons (jobbers or retailers) subject to conditions as to prices on resale. By reselling the goods contrary to those terms Menck engaged in a *use* of their invention without National Phonograph's permission. This was an invasion of their monopoly.[21]

Griffith CJ held that to 'use the invention' meant putting the invention, that is, the idea, into practice for the purpose of bringing some new thing into existence, or effecting a physical change in some existing thing, and does not mean or include the case of making use of the product of the invention.[22]

Such an article had, in the American phrase, 'passed out of the limit of the monopoly'.[23] 'Vend', in Griffiths CJ's view, meant to put the product of the invention in the possession of the public and did not refer to any sale of the article after it had 'once, without violation of the monopoly, become part of the common stock'.[24]

Barton J agreed.[25] He pointed out that once the article had been sold by the patentee the object of the law had been attained because the patentee 'had obtained the profit which it was intended he should receive'.[26]

O'Connor[27] and Higgins JJ[28] also agreed. Isaacs J dissented.[29]

US v English authority

In the High Court there was reference to a number of US authorities, typified by *Adams v Burks* where the US Supreme Court said:

> In the essential nature of things, when the patentee, or the person having his rights, sells a machine or instrument whose sole value is in its use, he receives the consideration for

---

18 ibid., pp. 522 (Griffith CJ), 527 (Barton J) and 543 (O'Connor J); contra, Isaacs J, p. 532 and Higgins J, p. 544.
19 [1911] AC 336, 345.
20 (1908) 7 CLR 481, 508 and 510.
21 ibid., p. 508.
22 ibid., p. 511.
23 ibid.
24 ibid., p. 512. Perhaps the qualification as to not violating the monopoly might be said to beg the question.
25 ibid., p. 523.
26 ibid., p. 524.
27 ibid., pp. 527 and 531.
28 ibid., p. 543.
29 ibid., p. 536.

42   LANDMARKS IN AUSTRALIAN IP LAW

its use and he parts with the right to restrict that use. The article, in the language of the Court, passes without [outside] the limit of the monopoly. That is to say, the patentee or his assignee having in the act of sale received all the royalty or consideration which he claims for the use of his invention in that particular machine or instrument, it is open to the use of the purchaser without further restriction on account of the monopoly of the patentee.[30]

However, within the decade or so before *Menck* was heard, a line of English decisions at first instance appeared to take a different view, holding that the patentee's right of monopoly in the use of the invention could be extended to a right to control the use of the product of the invention after it had become part of the 'common stock of personal property'.[31]

The first of these authorities was *Incandescent Gas Light v Cantelo*.[32] The plaintiffs alleged infringement of their patent by contraventions of conditions that the patented articles be only used by the immediate purchaser and then only as an adjunct to other articles sold by the plaintiffs. Wills J found as a fact that the defendant had no notice of the restriction. But his Lordship thought that had there been notice the defendant would have been bound. The patentee had the sole right of using and selling the articles and might prevent anybody from dealing with them at all. The patentee therefore had the right 'to do the lesser thing', that is to say impose conditions as to use, however unreasonable or absurd.[33]

The next case, which happened to involve the same patentee, was *Incandescent Gas Light v Brogden*.[34] This time the question whether a restriction could be imposed other than by contract was squarely raised. In effect, Kennedy J applied the dictum of Wills J in the earlier *Incandescent Gas Light* case. Griffith CJ's comment was somewhat provocative:

> The point that the common law does not admit restrictions upon the right of the owner of chattels to dispose of them as he thinks fit does not seem to have been presented to the mind of the learned Judge.[35]

The subsequent English cases[36] were analysed in detail by Griffith CJ and found to be mostly obiter.[37]

---

30 17 Wall 453 (Mass, 1873), p. 456, cited in ibid., p. 510 (Griffith CJ). Other authorities cited were *Crane v Price* (1844) 1 Web Pat R 393, 413; *Bloomer v Millinger* 1 Wall 340 (Pa, 1863), 351; and *Chaffee v Boston Belting Co* 22 How 217 (Mass, 1859), 223.
31 (1908) 7 CLR 481, 512.
32 *Incandescent Gas Light Co v Cantelo* (1895) 12 RPC 262.
33 ibid., p. 264.
34 *Incandescent Gas Light Co v Brogden* (1899) 16 RPC 179.
35 (1908) 7 CLR 481, 515.
36 *British Mutoscope and Biograph Co Ltd v Homer* [1901] 1 Ch 671; *Taddy & Co v Sterious & Co* [1904] 1 Ch 354; *McGruther v Pitcher* [1904] 2 Ch 306; *Badische Anilin und Soda Fabrik v Isler* [1906] 1 Ch 605; and *Gillette Safety Razor Co Ltd v AW Gamage Ltd* (1908) 25 RPC 492.
37 (1908) 7 CLR 481, 515–18.

The Privy Council

National Phonograph's case before the Privy Council was that a patentee could sell patented goods under terms authorising only a limited right to deal therewith and that such limited licence ran with the goods and bound all persons into whose possession they might come, *irrespective of notice*.[38]

At the outset, their Lordships noted that only one of the series of allegations against Menck remained to be dealt with (the Beckett transaction). Notwithstanding the 'insubstantial extent of the questions as matters of business which have been raised by the appellants', it appeared to their Lordships that in view of the judgments below 'in which the decisions of distinguished judges of the English courts have been examined in much detail' (and, one might infer from the tone of the language, disrespectfully) it was expedient that the questions, especially those dealing with the nature and effect of a patent grant, should be 'scrutinised and dealt with'.[39]

Their Lordships identified the competing propositions: (i) a patentee can impose terms which run with the patented goods irrespective of notice or (ii) apart from contract, a patentee cannot impose any terms. These were respectively the views of the minority and majority in the High Court.

Both propositions were, in their Lordships' view, unsound.[40] It was 'perfectly possible' to reconcile the principle that ordinary (unpatented) goods may be used or disposed of by the purchaser as he thinks fit with the incidence of ownership of patented goods. In their Lordships' view 'this has been done for a long period of years in England by decisions which are consistent and sound'.[41] The principles were not novel, 'nor did they start, as might appear to be the view of the case law adopted by some of the judges in the court below, with the judgment of Wills J in the case of *Incandescent Gas Light v Cantelo*'.[42] The latter decision was anyway 'undoubtedly a leading authority in the law of England'.[43]

The key to their Lordships' reasoning is the rejection of the extreme case of National Phonograph and the insistence on the requirement of notice. A patentee, by virtue of his statutory monopoly, could make a sale accompanied by restrictive conditions which would not apply in the case of ordinary chattels. The imposition of such conditions in the case of a sale is not presumed but, on the contrary, there is a presumption that the full right of ownership is to be vested in the purchaser. However, the purchaser's rights in a patented chattel will be limited if there is brought home to him knowledge of the conditions imposed.[44]

---

38 [1911] AC 336, 339.
39 ibid., p. 342.
40 ibid., p. 346.
41 ibid., p. 348.
42 ibid., p. 349. Their Lordships found earlier authority in *Betts v Willmott* (1871) LR 6 Ch 239; *Société Anonyme des Manufactures de Glaces v Tilghman's Patent Sand Blast Co* (1883) 25 Ch D 1; and *Heap v Hartley* (1888) 5 RPC 603, 610.
43 [1911] AC 336, 350.
44 ibid., p. 353.

44   LANDMARKS IN AUSTRALIAN IP LAW

Thus Menck lost, although he had been 'acquitted of every charge of violation of contract' laid against him by the appellants and had shown that their
claim as patentees was 'extreme and unsound in law'.[45] But he took the goods
with knowledge of the conditions and could not treat himself as an unrestricted
trader.[46] A practical indication of their Lordships' sympathy for his position was
their order that the costs order in his favour in the High Court should stand.
Under the conditions upon which special leave was granted, he was entitled to
his costs of the appeal as between solicitor and client.[47]

The result was not a happy one for the High Court. The Privy Council found
that neither majority nor minority had got it right. To add insult to injury, their
Lordships made it plain that the Chief Justice had misunderstood the decisions
of 'distinguished' English judges!

The legacy of *Menck*

Since it would often not be difficult for a manufacturer of a patented article to
make a retailer (or wholesaler) aware of RPM conditions, and there were no
legislative prohibitions on RPM in Australia until 1971,[48] it might have been
thought that *Menck*-based RPM conditions would feature prominently in Australian commerce and litigation. Moreover, there are many non-price restrictions
which a patentee might want to impose on purchasers. For example, in *Cantelo*
the restrictions involved limiting use to the immediate purchaser and only as an
adjunct to other articles sold by the patentee.

Eight years after the Privy Council's decision, National Phonograph, which
by then had changed its name to Thomas A Edison Ltd, obtained an injunction
against a retailer in New Zealand who sold Edison products below list price
despite a warning from the company: *Thomas A Edison Ltd v Stockdale*.[49] In this
case the defendant was a second-hand dealer who had no contractual or other
business connection with the company.

But after *Stockdale* there is no report of an Australian or New Zealand case
citing *Menck* involving patented products. It is not until the 1970s that *Menck*
appears to be mentioned at all, and then only for the purpose of distinguishing
it in copyright litigation.[50]

Perhaps that tells us that RPM just continued to be a part of Australian business
life, its desirability accepted and its enforceability unchallenged. So we might
ask, just what are the objections to RPM, and how did it become the subject of
legislative proscription, and a per se offence at that?

---

45 ibid.
46 ibid., p. 354.
47 ibid.
48 *Restrictive Trade Practices Act 1971* (Cth) s 66.
49 *Thomas A Edison Ltd v Stockdale* [1919] NZLR 276.
50 *Interstate Parcel Express Co v Time-Life International* (1977) 138 CLR 534.

Changing attitudes to RPM

After Menck was removed from National Phonograph's dealers list he arranged for a man called Reyment to be appointed as a dealer through whom he could surreptitiously obtain supplies. In Isaac J's words, Reyment was Menck's 'dummy'; Menck had organised 'an imposition upon the company, which was deceived into giving its consent to recognise Reyment as a dealer'.[51]

But Isaacs J saw one 'redeeming feature', this being that

> apparently Menck contemplated no underhand cutting of prices, nor ever engaged in that method of business – he making no use of the position he gained by Reyment's connivance to undersell competitors who were honestly abiding by the terms of their agreements.[52]

Thus in 1908 RPM was not only lawful but, in terms of business ethics and community values, breaching RPM arrangements was on a par with downright fraud, and quite possibly worse.

RPM was first outlawed in Australia in 1971.[53] The current prohibition is contained in s 48 of the *Trade Practices Act 1974* (Cth). It is a per se prohibition, that is to say it is contravened whether or not the conduct in question results in any actual lessening of competition.[54]

When the bill for the *Trade Practices Act* was introduced in the parliament, the Minister for Secondary Industry and Supply, the Hon Kip Enderby, said:

> Restrictive trade practices have long been rife in Australia. Most of them are undesirable and have served the interests of the parties engaged in them, irrespective of whether those interests coincide with the interests of Australians generally.[55]

The minister was speaking of restrictive trade practices generally. As he pointed out, under the 1971 Act, agreements which might restrict trade were required to be registered with the Commissioner of Trade Practices, who had the exclusive right to institute legal proceedings. Since 12 360 agreements had been registered by 30 June 1974, the practical prospect of interference with the vast majority of anti-competitive agreements was slight. The 1974 Act was to change this fundamentally; anti-competitive agreements and arrangements were directly proscribed and enforcement was not limited to the regulatory authority.[56]

But interestingly for present purposes, RPM was the one form of anti-competitive conduct which had been directly prohibited by the 1971 Act. Apparently attitudes had changed sufficiently in the 60 years since *Menck* for RPM to

---

51 (1908) 7 CLR 481, 499.
52 ibid., p. 491.
53 *Restrictive Trade Practices Act 1971* (Cth) s 66.
54 However, the Australian Competition and Consumer Commission may grant an authorisation to a person to engage in conduct that constitutes or may constitute the practice of RPM: s 88(8A). The commission must be satisfied that the conduct would result in such a benefit to the public that the authorisation should be granted: s 90(8)(a)(iv). The commission's grant or refusal of authorisation may be reviewed by the Australian Competition Tribunal under Pt IX.
55 Commonwealth of Australia, *Parliamentary Debates*, House of Representatives, 25 October 1973, p. 2733.
56 The Trade Practices Commission, later the Australian Competition and Consumer Commission.

be regarded for competition law purposes as the baddest of the bad. Yet there remains today serious debate among economists about the impact of RPM on competition and efficiency, particularly with respect to the appropriateness of a per se ban.

This issue recently arose in the US Supreme Court case of *Leegin Creative Leather Products v PSKS*.[57] The court abandoned per se prohibition and adopted a rule of reason approach for RPM. In the majority judgment Kennedy J specifically referred to expert economic evidence that RPM may actually improve competition.[58]

The current law

As already mentioned, s 48 of the *Trade Practices Act* prohibits the practice of RPM. The concept is the subject of elaborate definition in Pt VIII, ss 96–100. For present purposes, however, it is sufficient to say that, broadly speaking, RPM is conduct whereby a supplier (usually a wholesaler or manufacturer) seeks to ensure that a buyer (usually a retailer) will not resell goods or services to a third party at less than a price specified by the supplier.

RPM and the retailer

A retailer may benefit from RPM. Provided the wholesale price remains the same, the retail profit level will be maintained. If there is a wholesale supplier with substantial market power in the wholesale market, the retailers will benefit from a horizontal restraint (assuming the supplier is imposing the same retail price on all retailers). It will thus be in the interests of existing retailers to ensure that suppliers impose RPM, otherwise a new retailer entrant can charge lower prices and win market share from existing retailers.

RPM and the supplier

Usually suppliers will seek to maximise their profits by increasing the sales of their own products at the expense of their competitors'. In some market conditions, a fixed retail price forces competition on the basis of factors other than price, for example on advertising or quality of associated services offered. As a result, while competition for that particular brand of product (intra-brand) is eliminated, the competition between different brands of the same (or similar) product (inter-brand) is enhanced.[59] This is because if retailers can sell a particular product at

---

57 *Leegin Creative Leather Products Inc v PSKS Inc* 127 S Ct 2705 (2007).

58 ibid., pp. 2715–16. *Leegin* was one of a batch of eight decisions, handed down on the last day of term, 28 June 2007, regarded by one observer as a 'sharp and swift ... move to the right' by the court under the 5–4 majority created by the Bush appointments of Roberts CJ and Samuel Alito J. It 'openly overturned what had been settled law ... since a 1911 Supreme Court decision': A Lewis, 'The Court: How So Few Have So Quickly Changed So Much', *New York Review of Books*, 20 December 2007, p. 58.

59 PH Clarke, *Vertical Price Fixing in Australia*, Federation Press, Sydney, 1994, p. 14; R Pitofsky, 'The Sylvania Case: Antitrust Analysis of Non-price Vertical Restrictions' (1978) 78 *Columbia Law Review* 1, 4.

THE *MENCK* CASE   47

a fixed price (and presumably at a higher profit margin than would be the case if they were competing on price), there is a motivation for the retailer to sell more of that particular brand. Consequently, the retailer tends to offer other services to encourage consumers to buy that brand, thereby increasing the number of sales (benefiting both the supplier and the retailer).

Another motivation for supplier-invoked RPM is to maintain a perceived reputation and standing in the market place that a particular product is luxurious and highly sought after.[60] In this situation, the fall in the price of a product may actually reduce sales because consumers may no longer view the product as exclusive. At the other end of the spectrum, RPM may benefit suppliers in situations where the product is often purchased on impulse (generally an inexpensive item, for example chewing gum) where it is critical to have the widest distribution to retailers in order to maximise the number of sales made.[61] The more attractive the profit margins for retailers, the greater the number of retailers who will stock the suppliers' product.

Suppliers that insist on RPM may also be using this technique in order to preserve the relationship between retailer and supplier. A retailer that is guaranteed a certain profit margin because of a fixed retail price is less likely to pressure the supplier into reducing the wholesale price. Further, with a fixed retail price the supplier has more bargaining power to ensure that its products are displayed in an area that will ensure maximum sales.[62]

RPM and mainstream economic theory

In many situations there can be a cosy, mutually beneficial, incentive for suppliers and retailers to impose RPM, resulting in higher prices for consumers. According to some economists, however, the higher prices under RPM will distort market outcomes and lead to allocative inefficiency.[63]

To illustrate, Figure 3.1 shows a standard textbook market outcome where demand and supply are in equilibrium at a price of P_0 and a quantity of goods bought and sold of Q_0. Some economists argue that, in the absence of market failures, such an outcome should represent an efficient allocation of resources. This is because the value to consumers of the last unit of the good bought and sold (as measured by the demand curve[64]) should be equal to the cost of producing it (as measured by the supply curve[65]). Hence, in equilibrium (where the demand

---

60 Pitofsky, ibid., p. 16.
61 ibid., p. 17.
62 ibid.
63 In the US, RPM is a per se violation of s 1 of the Sherman Act: *United States v Arnold, Schwinn & Co* 388 US 365 (1967), 373. One Richard A Posner, then aged 28, was leading counsel for the US Government. Since in the US students usually do not complete formal legal education until their mid-20s, the appearance of Posner, as he then was, in this major case manifested a Mozart-like precocity.
64 That is, a demand curve measures the amount consumers are willing to pay for each successive unit of a good they might purchase. In other words, it effectively measures the 'marginal valuation (MV)' of each unit of a good available for consumption.
65 A supply curve measures the minimum amount suppliers of a good must receive in order for them to be willing to supply a given unit of it. In general, a supply curve should measure the cost of supplying successive

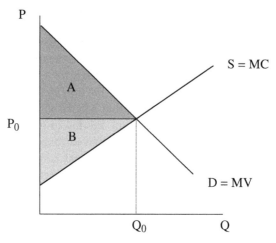

Figure 3.1 Demand and supply in equilibrium

curve intersects with the supply curve) consumers' valuation of the last unit of the good produced equals the cost of producing that good.[66]

Under RPM, an artificial price is set by the supplier in excess of that which would occur under a normal competitive market. Under this scenario, which is illustrated in Figure 3.2, a higher price set under RPM (e.g., P_1) will lead to a lesser level of goods bought and sold (i.e., Q_1). Consequently, while producer surplus may increase,[67] consumer surplus will decrease.[68] From an overall social welfare perspective,[69] the sum of producer and consumer surplus will be less than that which would occur under the competitive market outcome illustrated in Figure 3.1. In particular, a social welfare loss (or, as economists refer to it, a

---

units of a good. This is because suppliers should require that they at least recover their costs of supplying a given unit of a good before they would be willing to do so. Hence, a supply curve should measure what economists refer to as the 'marginal cost (MC)' of producing successive units of a good.

[66] This is allocatively efficient because if an additional unit of the good was bought and sold beyond the equilibrium level (i.e., Q_0 in Figure 3.1), the marginal cost of producing this additional good would be greater than the value placed on it by consumers (i.e., for this amount of output, the supply/MC curve lies above the demand/MV curve). Similarly, if a lesser amount of goods were bought and sold than in equilibrium, this too would represent an allocatively inefficient outcome because there could be more units of the good bought and sold (up to the equilibrium level) which would be valued more by consumers than their cost of production.

[67] In the case of Figure 3.2, it increases to be the sum of areas B + C. Producer surplus is the difference between the amount producers would require in order to produce a good and the actual price they receive. Given the supply curve represents the amount producers require in order to supply successive units of the good produced, it follows that producer surplus can be measured in Figure 3.1 as the area between the price they receive per unit (P_0) and the supply curve. This is represented by the shaded area B.

[68] To area A in Figure 3.2. Consumer surplus measures the difference between the price consumers pay for the units of the good they consume and their valuation of these units, that is to say the price they would be prepared to pay for the good rather than go without. Given a demand curve also represents consumers' valuation of goods consumed, the area under a demand curve measures the total valuation (in the sense above defined) from consuming units of the good. In the equilibrium outcome in Figure 3.1, consumers pay a price for each unit they consume equal to P_0. Hence, consumer surplus can be measured by the shaded area A.

[69] Social welfare is said to be measured by the sum of consumer and producer surplus. An allocatively efficient market coincides with a market outcome where the sum of consumer surplus and producer surplus is maximised.

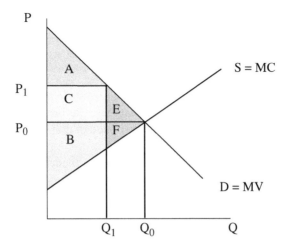

Figure 3.2 Deadweight loss under RPM

deadweight loss) will be created equal to the lost social welfare. This is measured by the shaded area E + F in Figure 3.2.[70]

Hence, under mainstream economic theory, RPM would be socially undesirable as it would lead to a lower level of social welfare and a consequent deadweight loss.

RPM and the Chicago School

Economists of the Chicago School argue that RPM should be lawful.[71] The primary reason, according to this view, is that the supplier has an interest in increasing sales, not in restricting output.[72] Posner contends that

> a manufacturer will (unilaterally) restrict distribution only in order to be more competitive. It gains nothing by reducing competition in the distribution of its product, though it may gain from redirecting that competition from price to service.[73]

If the retailer does not compete on price and is guaranteed to gain a minimum price, it will engage in non-price competition (such as advertising) that will result in a greater number of sales (i.e., inter-brand competition at the expense of intra-brand competition).[74] Posner believes that '[t]he imposition of resale price maintenance reflects a judgment on the part of the suppliers that sales will increase if the dealers of distributors compete in areas other than price'.[75]

---

70 Area E + F represents the difference between the valuation of those units of the good no longer bought and sold (i.e., $Q_0 - Q_1$) and the cost of producing these goods.
71 S Corones, *Competition Law in Australia*, 4th edn, Thomson, Sydney, 2007, p. 526.
72 ibid.
73 R Posner, 'The Next Step in the Antitrust Treatment of Restricted Distribution: Per Se Legality' (1981) 48 *University of Chicago Law Review* 6, 23.
74 Corones, op. cit., p. 527.
75 ibid.

50   LANDMARKS IN AUSTRALIAN IP LAW

A similar view was expressed by the Hilmer Committee:

> Economic theory indicates that there are circumstances in which resale price mainte-
> nance could enhance economic efficiency. For example, it may be that consumers will
> buy more of a certain good if there are associated pre-sale services, such as explanation
> of certain technical matters.[76]

However, the committee was of the view that there was insufficient evidence that
efficiency-enhancing RPM occurs frequently enough that the per se prohibition
should be removed.[77]

The mainstream argument against the Chicago theory is that in practice it
is often the case that large numbers of consumers are already familiar with
a certain product. Hence, non-price competition (such as advertising) does
not actually result in a greater demand for the service and a consequent
increase in the number of sales of the good in question (thereby creating
inefficiency).[78]

The interaction between intellectual property and competition law

If *Menck* were decided in 2007 it seems certain that the National Phonograph
Company, by fixing the retail price, would have engaged in RPM, thereby con-
travening s 48 of the *Trade Practices Act*. Further, the National Phonograph Company could not argue that their patent allowed them to impose any condition
they chose provided the retailer had notice. While s 51(3) exempts intellectual
property holders from compliance with some provisions of Pt IV of the Act, that
exception does not include s 48.

While both intellectual property and competition law seek to enhance innovation, the IPCRC Report, released in September 2001, found that the two laws
often conflict in practice.[79] Specifically, the report concluded that the divergence between intellectual property and competition law results from the grant
of market power inherent in the intellectual property right.[80] In other words, the
practical operation of intellectual property rights (granting market power) can
conflict with the objective of increasing competition in a market, which generally
decreases market power.[81]

---

76 Independent Committee of Inquiry, *National Competition Policy* (Hilmer Report), AGPS, Canberra, 1993,
p. 57.
77 Corones, op. cit., p. 529.
78 Pitofsky, op. cit., pp. 15–16.
79 Intellectual Property and Competition Review Committee (IPCRC), Parliament of Australia, *Review of
Intellectual Property Legislation under the Competition Principles Agreement*, 2001, p. 6.
80 ibid., p. 25.
81 National Competition Council (NCC), *Review of Sections 51(2) and 51(3) of the Trade Practices Act 1974
(Cth)*, 1999, pp. 160–4.

Goals of competition law

The objective of competition law, as set out in s 2 of the *Trade Practices Act*, is 'to enhance the welfare of Australians through the promotion of competition and fair trading and the provision for consumer protection'. Competition benefits consumers in two ways: it lowers prices and encourages innovation. Producers under competitive pressure will reduce their prices in order to avoid losing market share.[82] In addition, market participants also engage in non-price competition in an attempt to increase profits.[83] For example, producers may innovate in order to differentiate their products to secure greater market share,[84] thereby increasing the degree of innovation occurring in the marketplace; this also works to increase consumer wellbeing, the ultimate objective of the Act.

Goals of the intellectual property system

Similarly, intellectual property is also designed to increase innovation through the 'protection of creative effort'.[85] Benefits are provided to intellectual property holders in recognition of the fact that research and development processes carry many risks and costs with no guarantee that the investment will be profitable.[86] Further, the intellectual property system counteracts market failure arising from the 'free rider' problem.[87] This situation occurs where, for example, a producer invents a new production method only to have it quickly adopted by competitors, permitting market participants to reap the benefits of their competitors' investments while avoiding the concomitant risks.[88] Intellectual property laws are an attempt by parliament to remedy this market failure by providing rewards in the form of compensation and control. Thus, by s 13(1) of the *Patents Act 1990* (Cth) a patent gives the patentee 'exclusive rights, during the term of the patent, to exploit the invention and to authorise another person to exploit the invention'.

Practical operation of intellectual property and competition law

The common objective of encouraging innovation might well suggest that there would be little or no conflict between these two regimes. However, the tension becomes immediately apparent on consideration of the differences in the practical deployment of intellectual property and competition law.[89] For example, at

---

82 ibid.
83 J Jackson et al, *Economics*, 5th edn, McGraw-Hill, Sydney, 1998, p. 19.
84 ibid.
85 IPCRC, op. cit., p. 22; and for a particular discussion regarding copyright see W Landes and R Posner, 'An Economic Analysis of Copyright Law' (1989) 18 *The Journal of Legal Studies* 325, 326.
86 S Basen and L Raskind, 'An Introduction to the Law and Economics of Intellectual Property' (1991) 5 *Journal of Economic Perspectives* 3, 5.
87 F Hanks, 'Intellectual Property and Price Discrimination: A Challenge for Australian Competition Law' (2004) 16 *Journal of Information, Economics and Policy* 113, 115.
88 T McCarthy, 'Intellectual Property and Trade Practices Policy: Coexistence or Conflict? The American Experience' (1985) *Australian Business Law Review* 198, 201.
89 See discussion in NCC, op. cit., p. 160.

the most obvious level, patents create monopoly rights that prohibit other producers from exploiting the invention.[90] While innovative products are likely to have substitutes,[91] the patent provides market power because it enables product differentiation, that is to say the patentees' product will be different from competing products.[92] The higher the degree of market power, the greater the ability of the producer to increase the price. Moreover, the grant of market power also increases the capacity of the right holder to engage in anti-competitive conduct,[93] a concern expressed in the IPCRC Report, which described the potential for intellectual property rights 'as a mere camouflage for entering into agreements to fix prices, to divide markets and/or in other ways to monopolise supply'.[94]

Intellectual property rights promote innovation especially in works that are risky and/or require substantial capital investment.[95] But this must be contrasted with the harm to consumers that occurs when the granting of intellectual property rights gives such market power that it facilitates anti-competitive conduct. As stated in the IPCRC Report, the 'correction of one form of market failure creates another'[96] – the use of the intellectual property system to relieve the free-rider problem and to increase innovation can create anti-competitive conduct.

Moreover, there is no necessary relationship between the inventive merit of a given patent, or the amount of research and development devoted to it, and the commercial value of the legal monopoly conferred by the patent. A mere 'scintilla of inventiveness' is sufficient[97] and 'no smallness or simplicity will prevent a patent being good'.[98]

Conclusion

Menck recorded a decisive victory for intellectual property rights over competition principles, a victory that, in the specific case of RPM, endured for 60 years. Its relative obscurity is all the more remarkable.

---

90 *Patents Act 1990* (Cth), s. 13; J McKeough, 'Is Intellectual Property Different, or Are All Unhappy Monopolists Similar?' (2003) 9 *UNSW Law Journal Forum* 40, 40; and B Yu, 'Potential Competition and Contracting in Innovation' (1981) 24 *Journal of Law and Economics* 215, 215.
91 G Adams and D McLennan, 'Intellectual Property Licensing and Part IV of the Trade Practices Act: Are the TPA's Pro-competitive Provisions Anti-IP Commercialisation?' (2002) 51 *Intellectual Property Forum* 10, 14.
92 Market power reduces constraints from other competitors and consumers: *Queensland Wire Industries Pty Ltd v Broken Hill Pty Co Ltd* (1989) 167 CLR 177, 200 (Dawson J).
93 IPCRC, op. cit., p. 27.
94 ibid., p. 26.
95 McCarthy, op. cit., p. 201.
96 IPCRC, op. cit., p. 25.
97 *Meyers Taylor Pty Ltd v Vicarr Industries Ltd* (1977) 137 CLR 228, 249.
98 *Vicars, Sons & Co v Siddell* (1896) 14 RPC 105, 115.

4

Horses and the law: the enduring legacy of *Victoria Park Racing*

Jill McKeough*

Introduction

The Victoria Park Racing and Recreation Ground was a popular racecourse in Sydney in the 1930s. Built on an open fairground, the owners erected a fence around the track to ensure that only ticket buyers could watch the action or place bets on the races. The defendant, Taylor, built a tower that was used by a Mr Angles to peer over the fence and, using a telephone, broadcast descriptions of the races on radio 2UW. In *Victoria Park Racing and Recreation Grounds Company v Taylor* (*Victoria Park Racing*),[1] both the neighbour and the broadcaster were sued in nuisance and infringement of property rights by the owners of the racecourse. The High Court dismissed the suit but the minority judgment of Evatt J foreshadowed the potential problems for those mounting spectacles and events with the advent of television on the horizon.

Victoria Park Racing is still an important decision in the light of attempts to expand notions of property and control of information. The case is not only about intellectual property, as conceived in terms of creators' rights, and the extent to which rewards of entrepreneurial activity can be protected as a form of property, but property law in general. The case foreshadows some of the great debates on whether the 'sweat of the brow' leads to creation of protectable subject matter;[2] whether the common law recognises rights of privacy; and whether using baseball statistics somehow infringes on personality rights. The principles discussed are relevant, for example, to attempts by sports associations

---

* I would like to acknowledge the work of my research assistant, Katherine Giles, BA/LLB (UTS).
1 (1937) 58 CLR 479; 1A IPR 308.
2 See *Feist Publications Inc v Rural Telephone Co Inc* (1991) 20 IPR 129; *Jewler's Circular Pub Co v Keystone Pub Co* 281 F83 (CA 1922).

53

54 LANDMARKS IN AUSTRALIAN IP LAW

and various sporting leagues and codes to assert control over athlete blogging, posting photographs, podcasting (audio online), vodcasting (video online) and the use of player statistics.[3] It raises copyright issues and is frequently cited for the proposition that copyright in compilations is conferred by the exercise of skill, judgment or labour, and that this can amount to originality even where the compilation consists of existing material.[4] In addition, the case demonstrates a particular use of legal method and approach to action on the case. In declining the opportunity to formulate a property right in spectacles such as sporting events, the majority 'cautioned against the use of ... a unity of underlying principle between different causes of action when, in truth, there is none'.[5]

Judicial decisions to recognise or to refuse recognition of novel proprietary interests are influenced by more general theories about the purposes and justifications for the existence of private property. *Victoria Park Racing* is, perhaps, an 'anti-proprietarianism'[6] example of a case. In *A Philosophy of Intellectual Property*, Peter Drahos explains proprietarianism as

> a creed and an attitude which inclines its holders towards a property fundamentalism ... A person who is first connected with an object that has economic value or with an activity that produces economic value is entitled to a property right in that object or activity. The property right can be thought of as an extraction right. It is a right to extract or appropriate economic value.[7]

Drahos proposes an instrumental rather than a proprietarian approach to the law of intellectual property.[8] The proprietarian approach, he posits, is a 'property fundamentalism' that assigns property rights a fundamental and entrenched status. According to Drahos, instrumentalism in this sense refers to the idea that law is a tool that recognises the social costs of intellectual property protection, rules out the idea of property as a natural right, and displays a scepticism concerning any theory based on the idea that property is a subjective right.[9] As Drahos maintains: 'Instrumentalism would require a strongly articulated conception of the public purpose and the role of intellectual property.'[10] The apparent conservatism of the majority in *Victoria Park Racing* is based on a refusal to extrapolate doctrine to novel situations without a compelling justification.

---

3 M Geist, 'Silencing Sports Bloggers', *Mediacheck*, 7 January 2008, available at http://thetyee.ca/Mediacheck/2007/07/10/SportsBloggers/.
4 *Murray v King; King v Murray and Anor* (1983) 2 IPR 99; *Desktop Marketing Systems Pty Ltd v Telstra Corporation Ltd* (2002) 55 IPR 1; *TR Flanagan Smash Repairs Pty Ltd and Anor v Jones* (2000) 48 IPR 19; *Autodesk Inc and Anor v Dyason and Ors* (1992) 22 IPR 163; *Andrew Cash & Co Investments Pty Ltd v Porter and Ors* (1996) 36 IPR 309; *Millwell Pty Ltd v Olympic Amusements Pty Ltd* (1999) 43 IPR 32.
5 *Australian Broadcasting Corporation v Lenah Game Meats Pty Ltd* (2001) 208 CLR 199, 250; (2002) 54 IPR 161, 192 (Gummow and Hayne JJ), referring to *Moorgate Tobacco v Philip Morris* (1984) 3 IPR 545, 562 (Deane J), who was in turn discussing *Victoria Park Racing* and *International News Service v Associated Press* (1918) 248 US 215.
6 P Drahos, *A Philosophy of Intellectual Property Law*, Dartmouth, Aldershot, 1996, p. 201.
7 ibid.
8 ibid., pp. 199–200.
9 ibid., pp. 213–16.
10 ibid., p. 223.

Background to the case

Racing has been an integral part of the economy since the earliest days of the Australian colonies. Besides being a spectator sport, horse racing is also a major industry, which provides full-time or part-time work for almost 250 000 people. In addition, some 330 000 people have a direct interest as owners or members of syndicates in the 31 000 horses training in Australia.[11] All this is usually hidden, however, until an event like equine flu exposes the data to our gaze. On 28 February 2008 New South Wales was declared free of equine influenza[12], following a year of severe restrictions on the transport of horses, racing and other activities associated with horses. In 2007 equine influenza arrived in Australia (most probably from Japan) and affected Sydney first and most of all. The 'darkest day in racing history'[13] occurred when Randwick racecourse was locked down for at least three months and the Sydney Spring Racing Carnival was cancelled. There was much discussion in the press relating to the economic effects on the Australian racing industry, which is a major employer of up to 50 000 people in New South Wales alone. The loss of income to the state coffers and individual bookmakers was also 'in the hundreds of millions'.[14]

Thoroughbred horse racing is the third most-attended spectator sport in Australia, behind only Australian rules football and rugby league, with almost two million admissions to the 379 racetracks throughout Australia in 2002–03.

In the 1930s horse racing was no less important, in fact more so in the context of no television, no internet, silent movies and early closing.[15] In *Victoria Park Racing* the High Court was dealing with a case that went to the heart of the leisure activities of the time. Seven horses arrived with the First Fleet and as the Australian colonies developed, the community began to rely on fast, sound horses in order to explore the continent and provide transport. Sporting interests based around horses emerged early with unofficial racing, including over large distances,[16] and a reference to a racecourse was made in the *Sydney Gazette* in 1805, although the first official meeting took place in what is now Hyde Park in October 1810.[17]

---

11 Available at http://en.wikipedia.org/wiki/Thoroughbred_racing_in_Australia.

12 NSW Department of Primary Industries, 'Equine Influenza Conquered: Macdonald', 28 February 2008, available at http://www.dpi.nsw.gov.au/aboutus/news/recent-news/agriculture-news-releases/equine-influenza-conquered.

13 J Fife-Yeomans and R Thomas, 'The Darkest Day in Racing History', *Daily Telegraph*, 31 August 2007, available at www.news.com.au/dailytelegraph/story.

14 'Horse Flu to Hurt Economy, Warns Treasurer Costello', *Herald Sun*, 27 August 2007, available at http://www.news.com.au/heraldsun/story/0,21985,22314190–662,00.html.

15 'Early closing' was the 6pm closing of hotel bars, introduced in Australia during World War I; populous states abolished it in the 1950s and 60s. For background see, for example, http://australianscreen.com.au/titles/australia-today-lucky-strike/clip3/.

16 For example, Hawkesbury to Sydney. See J Churchill, 'NSW: The Birthplace of the Thoroughbred in Australia', *Thoroughbred Breeders New South Wales*, 3 October 2006, p. 1, available at http://www.tbnsw.com.au/aushistory.htm.

17 W Peake, 'Unregistered Proprietary Horse Racing in Sydney 1888–1942', UWS PhD thesis, chap. 1, p. 30, available at http://library.uws.edu.au/adt-NUWS.

56 LANDMARKS IN AUSTRALIAN IP LAW

All elements of the white community, including women and children, attended Sydney's first formal race meeting organised by the 73rd Regiment at the Hyde Park racecourse in October 1810, a holiday having been declared for each of the three days, which consisted entirely of heat racing. Later Hyde Park meetings included pony races – not as part of the advertised program, but in the form of impromptu challenges arranged to satisfy the desire for additional racing. This extempore organisation was to be the model for pony racing for the next 80 years.[18]

From the earliest days of the 20th century racing thrived, with clubs being formed by 'proprietary groups' of speculators from about 1900. Among these was the Associated Racing Clubs (ARC), a non-profit organisation racing under the patronage of the government and in opposition to the Australia Jockey Club (formed in 1828).[19] Races organised by the ARC were known as 'pony' meetings. Victoria Park was the base for 'pony racing' and was completed in January 1908, the last course for galloping to be constructed in metropolitan Sydney.[20] The importance of the 'proprietary courses' was the capacity to determine the type of betting and the persons who could attend; 'By building racecourses on their own land at their own expense, where racing could be conducted as seen fit, and in pursuing their own ends in determining who would be allowed to attend.'[21] Importantly the upkeep of the track could be organised by the owners. The damage done to tracks by racing meant that those on government-owned land could only host two to three meetings a year, in the absence of somebody prepared to undertake the upkeep of the track.

The first Victoria Park meeting, which the club promoted as 'the event of the year', took place on Wednesday, 15 January 1908, followed by a second meeting three days later. The completion of Victoria Park marked the end of the great era of racecourse building in Sydney. Intended to become a Sydney institution, it was used as a racecourse for less than 35 years. Victoria Park racecourse was in fact the most ambitious and most expensive project associated with the creation of a Sydney pony racecourse. James Joynton Smith, manager of Brighton and Epping racecourses, wanted a track that would rival Randwick. Smith and his companies spent an estimated £70 000 on the development of Victoria Park racecourse.[22] In fact, it could be said that '[t]he position of and the improvements to the land thus fit it for a racecourse and give its occupation a particular value'.[23]

Legal analysis

This is primarily a property case in which the full High Court considered whether to recognise or refuse recognition of a new form of proprietary interest. There

---

18 ibid.
19 Churchill, op. cit, p. 3.
20 ibid, p. 28.
21 'Sweepstake' betting, which allows more fun at more affordable odds, is a feature of 'proprietary racing' and is a whole study in itself: see ibid., pp. 29–30.
22 ibid., p. 30.
23 (1937) 58 CLR 479, 506; 1A IPR 308, 317 (Dixon J).

were three separate judgments by the majority and two separate dissenting judgments. The dissenters, Evatt and Rich JJ, found in favour of the plaintiffs by relying on the tort of nuisance. The majority, Latham CJ, Evatt and McTiernan JJ, took the view that nuisance should not be stretched to cover these particular facts and, finding it too difficult to define 'property in a spectacle'[24] in accordance with underlying legal principle, declined to give such a thing proprietary status. Infringement of copyright was also argued in use of the information concerning the names of the horses, their positions, the jockeys, and so on, but this was held by the majority not to be a literary work.[25]

In the report of the High Court case it is possible to discern a certain criticism of the pleadings at first instance in the Supreme Court of New South Wales. The majority judges seemed to be saying that they were 'not quite certain what the plaintiffs were expecting us to do although certainly the plaintiffs expect some relief'. In fact, Latham CJ was quite contemptuous of the nature of the plaintiff's argument:

> It has been argued that by the expenditure of money the plaintiff has created a spectacle, and that he therefore has what is described as a quasi-property in the spectacle which the law will protect. The vagueness of his proposition is apparent upon its face. What it really means is that there is some principle (apart from contract or confidential relationship) which prevents people in some circumstances from opening their eyes and seeing something and then describing what they see ... the mere fact that damage results to a plaintiff from such a description cannot be relied upon as a cause of action.[26]

On Latham CJ's view, labelling the subject-matter 'quasi-property' indicated that the plaintiff did not really believe a proprietary interest could subsist. The plaintiff's argument that staging of a spectacle is proprietary and that the defendants and Angles were, by their actions, interfering with that property right, was far too vague and imprecise; a spectacle can be 'property only in a metaphorical sense', any appropriateness in the metaphor would depend on the existence of the legal principle. The principle cannot be based upon such a metaphor'.[27] Furthermore, damages were impossible to assess as there was no way of knowing whether people would have bought a ticket (although the plaintiffs were seeking an injunction partly because the damage could not be calculated and there was little doubt the interference would persist).

In order to conform to a more conventional form of pleadings, the action was framed in nuisance. The majority dealt with the nuisance case fairly conventionally and easily: 'It is not shown that the broadcasting interferes with the use and enjoyment of the land or the conduct of the race meetings or the comfort or enjoyment of any of the plaintiff's patrons.'[28] In dealing with the rather novel claim of infringement of a property right, both Latham CJ and Dixon J took a fairly similar line. Latham CJ applied a more 'legalistic' approach, arguing that use of

---

24 ibid., p. 496; 1A IPR 308, 311 (Latham CJ).
25 ibid., p. 511; 1A IPR 308, 320 (Dixon J).
26 ibid., p. 496; 1A IPR 308, 311 (Latham CJ).
27 ibid., p. 497; 1A IPR 308, 312.
28 ibid., p. 523; 1A IPR 308, 328 (McTiernan J).

the term 'quasi-property' was an admission of lack of a case and not a doctrine within any known case law. Similarly, Dixon J declined to accept the American doctrine of 'quasi-property' or recognition of 'broadcast rights' in respect of the races, referring instead to the history of intellectual property rights as 'dealt with in English law as special heads of protected interest, and not under a wide generalisation'.[29]

Dixon J applied a typical 'Dixon analysis': strong on legal history and discussing the development of negligence with nuisance as an action on the case. His judgment contains an admission that the law was once more flexible so that the judges, by developing the action on the case, were able to expand the common law to accommodate new wrongs where an existing writ did not fit the bill. Nuisance itself came from an action on the case,[30] but apparently by 1937 the possibility of the law developing as it had in the past was no longer appropriate and this was too novel an action: 'the right to exclude the defendants from broadcasting a description of the occurrences they can see upon the plaintiff's land is not given by law. It is not an interest protected in law or equity'.[31] With respect to action on the case in the nature of nuisance, Dixon J said:

> The feature in which the plaintiff finds the wrong of the nuisance is the impairment or deprivation of the advantages possessed by the plaintiff's land as a racecourse by means of a non-natural and unusual use of the defendant's land ... the fact is that the substance of the plaintiff's complaint goes to interference, not with its enjoyment of the land, but with the profitable conduct of its business. If English law had followed the course of development that has recently taken place in the United States, the 'broadcasting rights' in respect of the races might have been protected as part of the quasi-property created by the enterprise, organisation and labour of the plaintiff ... But courts of equity have not in British jurisdictions thrown the protection of an injunction around all the intangible elements of value ... which may flow from the exercise by an individual of his powers and resources . . .[32]

The majority of the court relied on the dissent of Brandeis J in *International News Service v Associated Press*[33] to dismiss the notion of 'quasi-property'. This case 'has long occupied a prominent place in American legal education',[34] and been used as an example of the 'incremental power of common law reasoning'[35] as compared with the lumbering legislature's attempts to balance competing public policies. The case dealt with news gathered by International News Service from Associated Press newspapers, bulletin boards, news services and newspapers. Taking advantage of time differences between the east and west coast of the US, International News Service provided rewritten stories to newspapers on the

---

29 ibid., p. 509; 1A IPR 308, 319.
30 ibid., p. 506; 1A IPR 308, 317.
31 ibid., p. 510; 1A IPR 308, 319.
32 ibid., pp. 506–9; 1A IPR 308, 317–19.
33 (1918) 248 US 215.
34 DG Baird, 'The Story of *International News Service v Associated Press*: Property, Natural Monopoly and the Uneasy Legacy of a Concocted Controversy' in JC Ginsberg and R Cooper Dreyfuss, *Intellectual Property Stories*, Foundation Press, New York, 2006, p. 9.
35 ibid.

west coast. As International News Service had only used the facts as reported by Associated Press, and not the actual expression of these facts, Associated Press couldn't sue for copyright infringement. Despite this, the US Supreme Court granted relief based on the common law action of unfair competition due to the appropriation of labour which was 'contrary to good conscience'.[36] There was also reference made to the fact that the two parties were direct competitors.[37]

International News Service illustrates contrasting views on the nature of property rights as between 'Lockeans who believe that property comes into being as a result of labor . . . against utilitarians who insist on weighing the costs and benefits of bestowing rights and denying them'.[38] Baird points out that the 'quasi-property' right in news that the court discovered in *International News Service* 'came without any metes and bounds and proved nearly impossible to apply in later cases'.[39] In fact, Baird considers the case not properly about property at all, but about competition law; the regulation of a natural monopoly, being the large fixed costs of the network of telegraph lines which comprised the wire service, over which news travelled. The difficulties created by extrapolating *International News Service* to 'an abstract pronouncement of a grand principle that has no obvious boundaries'[40] have partly been overcome by reading the case narrowly, including in a number of cases associated with 'pure information' such as basketball statistics.[41]

The majority judgments in *Victoria Park Racing* demonstrate the utilitarian (or instrumental) approach to property. In contrast, Evatt J's judgment is perhaps the most interesting. He was prepared to find a protectable property interest in the provision of the spectacle through holding the race meeting, given that the 'inherent adaptability' of the common law would allow this action as an example of nuisance, extended using the 'fundamental principles recently summarised in the House of Lords in *Donoghue v Stevenson*'.[42] These principles were that

> The grounds of action may be as various and manifold as human errancy; and the conceptions of legal responsibility may develop in adaptation to altering social conditions and standards. The criterion of judgment must adjust and adapt itself to the changing circumstances of life. The categories of negligence are never closed.[43]

---

36 *International News Service v Associated Press* (1918) 248 US 215, 240.
37 ibid., pp. 229, 240 and 235.
38 Baird, op. cit. n. 34, p.10. See also Drahos, op. cit.
39 Baird, ibid., pp. 10–11.
40 ibid., p. 32.
41 *National Basketball Association v Motorola Inc*, 105F 3d 841 (2nd Cir 1997). See also *Rudolph Mayer Pictures Inc v Pathe News Inc*, 255NYS 1016 (App Div 1932) where photographs of a boxing match were taken from the roof of a nearby building; *Madison Square Garden Corp v Universal Pictures, Co*, 7NYS 2d 845 dealing with photographs that simulated Madison Square Garden's interior which were held to violate a property right in the arena's reputation; and *Twentieth Century Sporting Club v Transradio Press Service Inc*, 300 HYS 159 which concerned the violation of the club's terms against broadcasting a boxing match.
42 (1937) 58 CLR 479, 515; 1A IPR 308, 322.
43 *Donoghue v Stevenson* [1932] AC 562, 619 (Lord Macmillan) cited in ibid., p. 515; 1A IPR 308, 323 (Evatt J).

60 LANDMARKS IN AUSTRALIAN IP LAW

Evatt J continued:

> Here the plaintiff contends that the defendants are guilty of the tort of nuisance. It cannot point at once to a decisive precedent in its favour, but the statements of general principle in *Donoghue v Stevenson* are equally applicable to the tort of nuisance.[44]

Although the relief granted by Evatt J would have been on the basis of tort, his reasoning does seem to approach what could be called a proprietary analysis and he suggests that where people expend money to create something they have a property interest which can exclude the rest of the world from interfering with that thing, where that interference is taking away potential earnings. The defendants are 'trespassing' upon this right and reaping without sowing in a way that is 'not honest',[45] and therefore an injunction could be granted because this unlawful interference amounted to a legal wrong being committed. In his conclusion, Evatt J approved of the majority judgments in *International News Service v Associated Press*[46] which

> In my opinion ... [evidence] an appreciation of the function of law under modern conditions, and I believe that the judgment of the majority, and of Holmes J, commend themselves as exposition of principles which are not alien to English law.[47]

Evatt J's decision contemplated the ability of tort law to protect not just quasi-property rights, but also notions of privacy, as part of the 'functions of law under modern conditions'. He discussed nuisance in response to the defendant's claim that 'the law of England does not recognize any general right of privacy', saying that it was erroneous to assume that under no circumstances could systematic watching amount to a civil wrong. Evatt J also referred to Brandeis J's minority judgment in *International News Service*, which found that 'news' is not property in the strict sense and that a person who creates a spectacle does not create exclusive rights of first publication. He did not take Brandeis J's comments to mean that 'because some overlooking is permissible, all overlooking is necessarily lawful'.[48] Although television did not become available in Australia until 1956, Evatt J mentioned the development of TV and the possibility that this might be important in the future. This seems perhaps a bold prediction in 1938, but parliament subsequently had to step in to legislate for the relevant broadcaster's rights.[49]

In 1960 as Chief Justice of the Supreme Court of New South Wales Evatt CJ took a very similar approach in the case *Henderson v Radio Corporation*.[50] In this action, relief was sought based on the development of tort law – not nuisance but the tort of passing off. Evatt CJ there granted relief by finding a property interest in the reputation of the Hendersons – well-known ballroom dancers whose photograph had been used without permission on the sleeve of an

---

44 (1937) 58 CLR 479, 515; 1A IPR 308, 323 (Evatt J).
45 ibid., pp. 518–19; 1A IPR 308, 325 (Evatt J).
46 (1918) 248 US 215.
47 (1937) 58 CLR 479, 518; 1A IPR 308, 324 (Evatt J).
48 ibid.
49 *Broadcasting and Television Act 1942* (Cth); see below.
50 *Henderson v Radio Corporation Pty Ltd* [1960] SR (NSW) 576; 1A IPR 620.

album of dance music. Again, he extrapolated from tort law to protect a property interest; the reputation was property and had been appropriated, much as the defendants had done in *Victoria Park Racing*. In *Henderson* the defendants had interfered with the rights of the plaintiffs to exclude the rest of the world from using that property (their reputation) at a time when passing off still required other hurdles, including that of common field of activity.[51]

The other dissenting judge in *Victoria Park Racing*, Rich J, was prepared to give a finding in favour of the plaintiffs on the basis of the action in nuisance and principles of land law. In an analysis that was bold but clumsy, Rich J referred to 'the right of the normal use of the land by the adjoining owner' and the idea that 'defendant's rights are related to the plaintiff's rights and each owner's rights may be limited by the rights of the other'.

He argued that the defendants' act of overlooking a lawful meeting conducted by the plaintiffs on their land could constitute a 'nuisance', just like things such as vibration, smells and fumes. This example was likened to voyeurism, or 'watching and besetting', and

> the prospects of television make our present decision a very important one, and I venture to think, that the advance of that art may force the courts to recognise that protection against the complete exposure of the doings of the individual may be a right indispensable to the enjoyment of life.[52]

Rich J's analysis does not distinguish between invasion of personal privacy and damage to commercial interests.

The legacy of *Victoria Park Racing*

It is hard to believe that a single Australian case from the late 1930s would turn out to have myriad implications for contemporary life, both in Australia and internationally, especially given its (on the face of it) rather dated facts and dry reasoning. The following discussion highlights four key areas in which this classic decision is not only traditional but surprisingly modern.

Copyright in compilations and 'raw data'

Victoria Park Racing is often cited on the point of copyright in compilations, and that they require

> some original result [to] be produced. This does not mean that new or inventive ideas must be contributed. The work need show no literary or other skill or judgment, but it must originate with the author and be more than a copy of other material.[53]

This dealt with the argument in the case that the board displaying names and figures amounted to an original literary work.

---

51 See J McKeough, A Stewart and P Griffith, *Intellectual Property in Australia*, 3rd edn, Butterworths, Sydney, 2004, para. 16.17.
52 (1937) 58 CLR 479, 505; 1A IPR 308, 316 (Rich J).
53 ibid., p. 511; 1A IPR 308, 320 (Dixon J).

62   LANDMARKS IN AUSTRALIAN IP LAW

Foreshadowing recent US cases on baseball and other player statistics, the Spicer Committee discussed whether copyright exists in the names of players and their numbers. They stated:

> We are unable to see how copyright can be conferred merely in respect of the name of a player associated with his football number. It has been held that copyright may exist in various compilations such as an alphabetical list of railway stations, a list of fox-hounds and hunting dogs and lists of stock exchange prices and football fixtures. In all these cases the question of whether copyright exists depends to a large extent on the amount of labour, capital or skill expended in making the compilation. We think that the law in this regard should not be changed. It seems that the football clubs may have copyright in the lists they prepare as published in various football publications (see *Football League Ltd v Littlewoods Pools Ltd* (1959) 3 WLR 42). Such copyright, however, does not prevent a person making his own list by attending a match. In the field of copyright there is not, in our view, any way to legislate against this. Indeed, no proposal on how this could be achieved was submitted to us. We, therefore, reject the submissions in this regard.[54]

Copyright protection for compilations has been taken to extremes in attempts to prohibit use of data for 'fantasy baseball' games, as the professional sports industry tussles with the issue of who owns player statistics in fantasy league games. Big media companies such as Yahoo, ESPN and CBS operate online 'fantasy leagues' where participants create teams comprised of real baseball players. Over the course of a season, participants track statistics to judge how well players are performing. Websites provide player statistics and this information is used as the basis of 'fantasy baseball' games which are played online. In *CBC Distribution & Marketing v Major League Baseball Advanced Media*,[55] a fantasy sports games operator sued to retain the rights to produce and promote fantasy games using player statistics without having to get a licence from Advanced Media, the organisation that runs baseball's interactive division. The ruling is currently under appeal but appears to follow a more robust approach, similar to that taken in earlier cases.[56] The defendant's argument is that the raw data is information in the public domain and cannot be protected by copyright without something more. Advanced Media insists that the statistics cannot be used for commercial gain without a licence. In fact, Advanced Media has already been sued itself by a group of former players who argued that printing their names and statistics in a game program was a violation of their rights of publicity. The court held that they were historical facts and Major League Baseball had a right to use them.[57]

In *National Basketball Association v Motorola*,[58] Motorola supplied player statistics of NBA games to pagers and mobile phones while the games were

---

54 *Report of the Committee Appointed by the Attorney General of the Commonwealth to Consider What Alterations are Desirable to the Copyright Law of the Commonwealth*, AGPS, Canberra, 1959 (Spicer Report), paras. 483–4.
55 *CBC Distribution & Marketing Inc v Major League Baseball Advanced Media*, LP 443F Supp 2d 1077, 1091 (ED Mo 2006); 505F 3d 818 (8th Cir 2007), denied, Nos. 06-3357 & 06-3358 (8th Cir 26 November 2007).
56 *Feist Publications Inc v Rural Telephone Co Inc* (1991) 20 IPR 129.
57 *Gionfriddo v Major League Baseball* 94 Cal App 4th 400 (2001).
58 *National Basketball Association v Motorola Inc* 939F Supp 1071 (SDNY 1996), rev'd, 105F 3d 841 (2nd Cir 1997).

in progress. NBA sued for copyright infringement for the publishing of player statistics created by its efforts. The court held that misappropriation exists when

(i)   a plaintiff generates or gathers information at a cost;
(ii) the information is time sensitive;
(iii) a defendant's use of the information constitutes free-riding on the plaintiff's efforts;
(iv) the defendant is in direct competition with a product or service offered by the plaintiff; and
(v)   the ability of other parties to free-ride on the efforts of the plaintiff or others would so reduce the incentive to produce the product or services that its existence or quality would be substantially threatened.[59]

The NBA's action failed as Motorola was compiling its own statistics and not obtaining them from the NBA: just because the NBA organised the games did not mean that Motorola were free riders. The court held that players' names and statistics are not protected by copyright.[60]

In *Morris Communications v PGA Tour*[61] the court also considered the extent to which a promoter should be able to control the diffusion of information about a golf tournament. The PGA Tour developed a real-time system for reporting each golfer's score on a website. This information was available in the PGA Tour media centre and restrictions were placed on journalists, who were unable to use the information for a certain period of time. Journalists who didn't follow the restrictions had their credentials revoked. Morris Communications asked for permission to syndicate the results and PGA Tour declined their request and informed them that their credentials would be revoked if they did. Morris Communications filed a suit for unlawful monopilisation. PGA Tour argued that they had a property right in the real-time scores. The court held that PGA Tour had a property right in the scores, which dissolved when scores entered the public domain. The public domain was defined as the area outside the media tent, when they were made available for public consumption.[62]

> In effect, the court held that when someone expends resources to create or gather information ... that person has a property right to control that information as long as it does not become known to third parties over whom the person has no legitimate control.[63]

In both the *Motorola* and *Morris* cases the promoters were given the right to control real-time data (referred to as 'hot news') and exploit the commercial

---

59 ibid., p. 845.
60 GP Quiming, 'Playing by the Rules of Intellectual Property: Fantasy Baseball's Fight to Use Major League Baseball Players' Names and Statistics' (2006) 29 *University of Hawaii Law Review* 301; JF Williams, 'Who Owns the Back of a Baseball Card? A Baseball Player's Rights in His Performance Statistics' (2002) 23 *Cardozo Law Review* 1705; S Ross Saxer, '*Baltimore Orioles, Inc v Major League Baseball Players Association*: The Right of Publicity in Game Performances and Federal Copyright Preemption' (1989) 36 *UCLA Law Review* 861, 861.
61 *Morris Communications Corp v PGA Tour, Inc*, 117F Supp 2d 1322 (MD Fla 2000) (Morris Communications' motion for a preliminary injunction denied); *Morris Communications Corp v PGA Tour, Inc*, 235F Supp 2d 1269 (MD Fla 2002) (PGA Tour's motion for summary judgment is granted).
62 *Morris Communications Corp v PGA Tour, Inc*, 117F Supp 2d 1322 (MD Fla 2000), p. 1281.
63 GR Roberts, 'The Scope of the Exclusive Right to Control Dissemination of Real-Time Sports Event Information' (2004) 15 *Stanford Law & Policy Review* 167, 181.

64   LANDMARKS IN AUSTRALIAN IP LAW

value of this data until it became available to third parties beyond their control. Reflecting on both the cases, one commentator writes:

> The larger question raised by this entire discussion is to what extent good public policy supports giving sports event promoters the right to control the dissemination of information about their athletic contests . . . As a starting point there is always a public interest in disseminating anything of value as widely, easily, and cheaply as physically possible, whether the subject is tangible property, services, or intellectual property . . . The question is then whether there is some overriding reason why the public interest would be better served by restricting the public's access to the product.[64]

Copyright in events

There have not been too many cases concerning copyright in sporting spectacles following the definitive decision in *Victoria Park Racing*.[65] As television loomed on the horizon, however, lobbying for protection for sporting events increased. The Association for the Protection of Copyright in Sports (ACPS) lobbied the Beveridge Committee into Broadcasting (1949) for the promoter of any sporting event to be considered an author of a copyright protected work and thus able to control its reproduction. This was opposed by the British Broadcasting Corporation (BBC).[66] While property rights still cannot exist in the spectacle itself, specific rules relating to particular activities and events have emerged.

Following the lead of the Gregory Committee[67] in the UK, and the decision in *Victoria Park*, the Spicer Committee declared that a sporting spectacle was not protected by copyright, although the *Broadcasting and Television Act 1942* (Cth) was consequently enacted to protect against 'unauthorised' broadcasts.[68] Section 115 provides:

> The Commission or holder of a licence for a commercial television station shall not televise, either directly, or by means of any recording, film or other material or device or otherwise, the whole or part of a sporting event or other entertainment held in Australia, after the commencement of this section, in a place to which a charge is made for admission, if the images of the sporting event or other entertainment originate from the use of equipment outside that place.

Specific special events legislation has also been introduced, particularly when the sporting spectacle will take place in public, for example the *Australian Grand*

---

64 ibid., p. 186.
65 (1937) 58 CLR 479; 1A IPR 308; *Re South Queensland Broadcasting Pty Ltd* (1977) ATPR, 103.547; *Re Universal Telecasters Queensland Ltd* (1977) ATPR, Commission Decisions Authorizations and Notifications, 16757; *Re Brisbane TV Ltd* (1977) ATPR, Commission Decisions, Authorizations and Notifications, 16766; *Re Amalgamated Services Pty Ltd and the New South Wales Rugby Football League* (1980) ATPR, Commission Decisions, Authorizations and Notifications, 17076; *Re Australian Cricket Board, PBL Marketing Pty Ltd, World Series Cricket Pty Ltd and Publishing and Broadcasting Ltd* (1980) ATPR, Commission Decisions, Authorizations and Notifications, 17065; *Australian Broadcasting Commission v Parish et al* (1980) 40 FLR 311.
66 J-P Blais, 'The Protection of Exclusive Television Rights to Sporting Events Held in Public Venues: An Overview of the Law in Australia and Canada' (1992) 18 *Melbourne University Law Review* 503, 515.
67 *Report of the Copyright Committee*, Her Majesty's Stationary Office, London, 1952 (Gregory Report).
68 Spicer Report, op cit., para. 479. New Zealand also enacted a similar provision.

Prix Act 1995 (Vic). Section 35 states that during the race period a person must not, without consent and the payment of a fee, make a sound recording or audio recording of a Formula One event or any part of a Formula One event from a place inside or outside Albert Park for the purpose of profit or gain. Section 42B provides similar requirements for the Motor Cycle Grand Prix.[69]

The issue of broadcast rights in sporting spectacles has received a great deal of attention in the EU.[70] The rights of broadcasters to control coverage of events and other aspects of sporting or entertainment spectacles has become increasingly contested over recent years. The possibilities of the internet, which allows compilation of data such as statistics and the use of blogs, posted photographs and video, led to a series of actions, mainly in the US, to significantly restrict the use of widely available material. The National Football League recently announced significant restrictions on the use of online video clips. The league is attempting to restrict news organisations to no more than 45 seconds per day of video filmed at team facilities, including news conferences, interviews, practice sessions and the like.

One way of controlling this is to make rules that athletes, coaches and others associated with events such as the Olympics are not to blog or podcast during events. The International Olympic Committee warned athletes at the 2006 Turin Winter Olympics that they faced disqualification if they blogged during the Games.[71] These attempts to protect corporate sponsorship presumably would be difficult to enforce through the courts and rely instead on arrangements between organisations, athletes and others. Given the politically charged atmosphere of the 2008 Beijing Olympics, Australian athletes were allegedly required to sign an agreement that placed limits on what they could say in public, including the requirement that they ask permission to comment on human rights.[72] According to media reports, they were able to podcast and blog, as long as they followed rules set out by the International Olympic Committee that protect copyright,

---

69 Other examples include: *America's Cup Yacht Race (Special Arrangements) Act 1986* (WA); *Commonwealth Games Act 1982* (Qld); *Australian Formula One Grand Prix Act 1984* (SA); compare Blais, op. cit., pp. 66 and 511.

70 *Rudolph Mayer Pictures Inc v Pathe News Inc* 235 App Div 774, 255 NY Supp 1016 (1932); *National Exhibition v Teleflash* 24F Supp 488 (1936); *Twentieth Century Sporting Club v Tansradio Press Service Inc* 165 Misc 71, 300 NY Supp 159 (1937); *Pittsburg Athletic Co v KQV Broadcasting Co* 24F Supp 490 (1938); *Madison Square Garden Corp v Universal Pictures Co* 255 App Div 459, 7 NYS (2d) 845 (1938); *Johnson-Kennedy Radio Corp v Chicago Bears Football Club Inc* 97F (2d) 223 (1938); *South West Broadcasting Co v Oil Centre Broadcasting* 210 SW (2d) 230 (1948); *Gauthier v Pro-Football Inc* 304 NY 354, 107 NE (2d) 485 (1952); *United States v National Football League* 116F Supp 319 (1953); *Loeb v Turner* 257 SW (2d) 800 (1953); *National Exhibition v Fass* 133NYS (2d) 379, 136NYS (2d) 358 (1954), 143NYS (2d) 767 (1955); *Ettore v Philco Television Broadcasting* 229F (2d) 481 (1956), certiorari denied 351 US 926 (1956*)*; *Zacchini v Scripps-Howard Broadcasting Co* 433 US 562 (1977); *Post Newsweek Stations-Connecticut Publishing Ins Inc v Travellers Ins Co* 510F Supp 81 (1981); *Eastern Microwave Inc v Double Day Sports Inc* 691F (2d) 125 (1982), certiorari denied 459 US 1226; *WT4'WV Inc v National Football League* 678F (2d) 142 (1982); *National Collegiate Athletic Association v Board of Regents of the University of Oklahoma* 468 US 85 (1984*)*; *Baltimore Orioles Inc v Major League Baseball Players Association* 805F (2d) 663(1986), certiorari denied 480 US 941 (1987).

71 Geist, op. cit.

72 ABC, 'Olympic Officials to Vet Athletes' Political Comments', *ABC*, 18 March 2008, available at http://www.abc.net.au/news/stories/2008/03/18/2193465.htm.

66 LANDMARKS IN AUSTRALIAN IP LAW

confidential information and security and prevent athletes from profiting from the 'Games' name.[73]

Unfair competition

The question of allowing copyright or some other form of property right in events has at times been merged with discussion of a broader doctrine of unfair competition or misappropriation. In *Victoria Park Racing*, Dixon J referred with approval to the dissenting judgment of Brandeis J in *International News Service*, which considered relevant US and English authorities and concluded that the law did not recognise any general proprietary right in knowledge or information nor any general action for unfair competition.[74] The decision of the majority of the US Supreme Court in that case, however, has generally been taken as founding a broadly framed tort in respect of unfair competition.

Recognition of a new general tort of unfair competition was rejected by the High Court in *Moorgate Tobacco v Philip Morris*[75] where Deane J, in the course of deciding that Australian law knows no general tort of unfair competition or unfair trading, referred with approval to Dixon J's comments in *Victoria Park Racing*. Deane J (with whom all the other judges agreed) pointed out that the majority judgment in *International News Service* assumed rather than sought to establish that 'unfair competition in business' was in itself an actionable wrong, and did not establish that 'published news as distinct from copyright in its presentation or arrangement, itself constitutes property, or provides any basis for a general cause of action for unfair competition'.[76]

In *Campomar Sociedad Limitada v Nike International*,[77] the Full Court of the High Court of Australia approved Dixon J's timeless statement that

> Courts of equity have not thrown the protection of an injunction around all the intangible elements of value, that is, value in exchange, which may flow from the exercise by an individual of his powers or resources whether in the organization of a business or undertaking or the use of ingenuity, knowledge, skill or labour.[78]

The court noted that this 'should be regarded as an authoritative statement of contemporary Australian law'.[79] Given that 'wide generalisations' of unfair competition, or protecting the 'sweat of the brow' because someone has worked to produce that sweat, are not allowed in Australian law, the issue in that case was whether the *Trade Marks Act*, *Trade Practices Act* or action for passing

---

73 L Tung, 'Aussie Olympian Blogs Muzzled, Not Censored', *ZDNet*, 19 February 2008, available at http://www.zdnet.com.au/news/communications/soa/Aussie-Olympian-blogs-muzzled-not-censored/0130061791339286027,00.htm.
74 (1918) 248 US 215, 624.
75 *Moorgate Tobacco Ltd v Philip Morris Ltd (No. 2)* (1984) 156 CLR 414; 3 IPR 545.
76 ibid., p. 441; 3 IPR 545, 563.
77 *Campomar Sociedad Limitada v Nike International Ltd* (2000) 202 CLR 45.
78 (1937) 58 CLR 479, 509; 1A IPR 308, 319.
79 (2000) 202 CLR 45, 55.

off were apt to deal with two parties using the name NIKE in the market place.[80]

In the US many states have a common law tort of misappropriation 'which does not require proof of deception but is aimed at preventing commercial free riding on the efforts of others in certain defined and quite limited circumstances'.[81] It is generally conceded that these circumstances need to be more than the principle that property rights are natural rights with no easily recognised limitations, or that 'misappropriation is contrary to good conscience';[82] 'intellectual property disputes, like all legal disputes, cannot be decided merely by invoking an idea as vague as the right to reap what one sows'.[83]

Despite the invitation to discover 'quasi-property' rights in a spectacle, the broad principles of the tort of misappropriation in *International News Service* have been reluctantly applied[84] and narrowly construed since the decision was handed down. *International News Service* has become a doctrine that 'lives at the margins of intellectual property law';[85] it was initially applied unenthusiastically by the judiciary in American states,[86] although admittedly with some 'oddball cases now and then'.[87] One such case occurred when copyright in Chicago Cubs games was argued in *Chicago NL Club v Sky Box on Waveland*.[88] The Cubs sued a group of nearby property owners who were allowing people to watch games from their rooftops and charging for admission. This 'old Chicago tradition' had become a significant money-making scheme. The case settled with the rooftop owners agreeing to pay the Cubs 17 per cent of their annual profits.[89]

In *Pittsburg Athletic v KQV Broadcasting*,[90] the plaintiff was successful in preventing a live broadcast of the Pittsburg Pirates baseball game by a commentator, who was overlooking the stadium from a vantage point on a roof across the street from Forbes Field. The judge in *Pittsburg Athletic* relied heavily on and expanded

---

80 The US Supreme Court also rejected a sweat of the brow doctrine for copyright protected in *Feist Publications, Inc v Rural Telephone Service Co* 111S Ct 1282 (1991). This is discussed in JC Ginsburg, 'No "Sweat"? Copyright and Other Protection of Works of Information After *Fiest v Rural Telephone*' (1992) 92 *Columbia Law Review* 338.
81 MJ Davison, AL Monotti and L Wiseman, *Australian Intellectual Property Law*, Cambridge University Press, Sydney, 2008, p. 4. See also MJ Davison, *Legal Protection of Databases*, Cambridge University Press, Cambridge, 2003, p. 162, and *National Basketball Association v Motorola Inc* 939F Supp 1071 (SDNY 1996), rev'd, 105F 3d 841 (2nd Cir 1997).
82 (1918) 248 US 215, 240–1.
83 Baird, op. cit. n. 34, p. 63.
84 *Cheney Bros v Doris Silk Corp* 35F 2d 279 (2nd Cir, 1929).
85 Baird, op. cit. n. 34, p. 34: citing RA Posner, 'Misappropriation: A Dirge' (2003) 40 *Houston Law Review* 621.
86 Davison, op. cit. n. 81, pp.160–1. See also DG Baird, 'Common Law Intellectual Property and the Legacy of *International News Service v Associated Press*' (1983) *University of Chicago Law Review* 411.
87 Baird, op. cit. n. 34, p. 34.
88 No 02C 9105 (ND Ill).
89 T Baldas, 'Pro Sports: Technology Changes Rules of the Game', *The National Law Journal*, 4 March 2005, available at http://www.law.com/jsp/article.jsp?id=1109128216973.
90 *Pittsburg Athletic Co v KQV Broadcasting Co* 24F Supp 490 (D PA 1934). See also *Loeb v Turner* 257SW 2d 800 (1953) where the opposite decision was made. Referred to in Davison, op. cit. n. 81, pp.183–4.

68 LANDMARKS IN AUSTRALIAN IP LAW

the Supreme Court's decision in *International News Service*. The court ruled that the radio station had violated Pittsburg Athletic's property rights and engaged in unfair competition, based on the production of an event as a result of expense and effort of the plaintiff on private property, and stated:

> The plaintiffs and the defendant are using baseball news as material for profit. The Athletic Company has, at great expense, acquired and maintains a baseball park, pays the players who participate in the game, and have, as we view it, a legitimate right to capitalize on the news value of their games by selling exclusive broadcasting rights to companies which value them as affording advertising mediums for their merchandise. This right the defendant interferes with when it uses its broadcasting facilities for giving out the identical news obtained by its paid observers stationed at points outside Forbes Field for the purpose of securing information which it cannot otherwise acquire. This, in our judgment, amounts to unfair competition, and is a violation of the property rights of the plaintiffs.[91]

A tort of privacy?

In *Victoria Park Racing*, Rich J stated: 'in the absence of any authority to the contrary I hold that there is a limit to this right of overlooking and that the limit must be found in an attempt to reconcile the right of free prospect from one piece of land with the right of profitable enjoyment of another'.[92] It is arguable that in this statement, which runs together the concept of personal privacy with the rights of those conducting a business, he foreshadowed the extension of nuisance to the point where it almost amounts to a right of privacy. Even more explicitly, Evatt J stated:

> A person who creates or uses devices for the purpose of enabling the public generally to overlook or spy upon the premises of another person will generally become liable to an action of nuisance, providing appreciable damage, discomfort, or annoyance is caused.[93]

Subsequent discussion of any emerging action has tended to limit the ambit of a right to privacy in that whatever development may take place will be for the benefit of natural persons, not corporations, and despite the hint in *Victoria Park Racing* that a right of privacy for commercial information might emerge, the weight of authority favours recognition of the privacy of personal information rather than 'proprietary' information. As the 'celebrity cases' mentioned below illustrate, these considerations are most often discussed in the context of a personal/private nexus; an example is the rights of public figures to protect private information such as rehabilitation from a drug habit.[94]

---

91 24F Supp 490 (D. PA 1934) at 492.
92 (1937) 58 CLR 479, 504; 1A IPR 308, 316 (Rich J).
93 ibid., p. 521; 1A IPR 308, 326 (Evatt J).
94 *Campbell v MGN Ltd* [2004] 2 AC 457.

The New South Wales Law Reform Commission has a current reference to inquire into and report on whether existing legislation in New South Wales provides an effective framework for the protection of the privacy of an individual. Consideration of a statutory tort of privacy and the question of uniformity of legislation across Australia are also relevant to the investigation. In a Consultation Paper released in May 2007,[95] *Victoria Park Racing* was the starting point for the discussion of the development of the common law of privacy in Australia. Referring to developments in the UK, the NSWLRC stated: 'The persuasiveness of the reasoning in many of the English cases leads us to believe, however, that the solutions proposed in those cases could be adopted as part of the common law of Australia.'[96] It should be noted that discussion of the emerging tort in English cases is in the context of the UK *Human Rights Act 1998* which incorporates into English law Art 8 of the European Convention for the Protection of Human Rights and Fundamental Freedoms.[97] It is also the case that the path to a tort of privacy is not an easy one, and among the 'stumbling blocks' are Australian cases where circumspection has been exercised, for example by the Chief Justice in the High Court.[98]

It was argued in *Australian Broadcasting Corporation v Lenah Game Meats*[99] that the Australian courts had not developed 'an enforceable right to privacy' because of what generally was taken to follow from the failure of the plaintiff's appeal in *Victoria Park Racing*. In *Lenah Game Meats* the High Court of Australia declined to grant a remedy purely on the basis that information had been obtained through what might be considered 'unconscionable actions', even involving allegedly unlawful conduct. In this case the plaintiffs were attempting to prevent the ABC from broadcasting film of the process used to slaughter possums for game meat. The film had been taken by animal rights activists and it was alleged that their activities were both surreptitious and involved a trespass and break-in to plaintiff's property. The High Court found, however, that there was no information clearly of a confidential nature to protect and so the action for breach of confidence did not apply. The judges observed that the plaintiff would need to ground an action in a general tort designed to protect against invasion of privacy, and the case contains some speculation that it might be time for the common law to recognise such an action.[100]

Strong support for a tort of invasion of privacy came from Callinan J, who stated:

---

95 NSW Law Reform Commission, *Invasion of Privacy*, Consultation Paper 1, May 2007. See also Australian Law Reform Commission, *For Your Information: Australian Privacy Law and Practice*, Report 108, August 2008, para. 74.61.
96 ibid., para. 2.16.
97 Entered into force 3 June 1952.
98 See R Wacks, 'Why There Will Never Be An English Common Law Privacy Tort' in A Kenyon and M Richardson, *New Dimensions in Privacy Law*, Cambridge University Press, 2006, p. 176.
99 (2001) 208 CLR 199; (2002) 54 IPR 161.
100 See D Lindsay, 'Playing Possum? Privacy, Freedom of Speech and the Media Following *ABC v Lenah Game Meats Pty Ltd*. Part II: The Future of Australian Privacy and Free Speech Law, and Implications for the Media' (2002) 7 *Media Arts Law Review* 161.

It seems to me that, having regard to current conditions in this country, and developments of the law in other common law jurisdictions, the time is ripe for consideration whether a tort of invasion of privacy should be recognized in this country, or whether the legislatures should be left to determine whether provisions for a remedy for it should be made.[101]

Earlier in the judgment he also stated:

Even if there be no, or there is to be no, tort of intrusion of privacy as such, the law may need to devise a remedy to protect the rights of the 'owners' of a spectacle at least against unauthorized reproduction of it by broadcast, telecast or publication of photographs or other reproductions of it, under the rubric of nuisance or otherwise.[102]

In *Victoria Park Racing* Latham CJ rejected the proposition that under the head of nuisance the law recognised a right of privacy. But that is not to say the decision precludes any proposition with respect to the existence or otherwise of a tort identified as unjustified invasion of privacy. According to Gummow and Hayne JJ in *Lenah Game Meats*, 'Victoria Park does not stand in the path of the development of such a cause or action ... nothing said in these reasons should be understood as foreclosing any such debate or as indicating any particular outcome, nor should the decision in Victoria Park'.[103] However, Gleeson CJ's circumspection (praised as 'wisdom') in being very cautious about declaring the emergence of a new tort is based on 'lack of precision in the concept of privacy'.[104]

Although *Victoria Park Racing* does not necessarily stand in the way of an action for unjustified invasion of privacy, it is relevant to the distinction made by some later cases between the rights that an individual might have as compared with a corporation. The 'privacy' in *Victoria Park Racing* concerned the opposition by the plaintiff to the turning to commercial account by the defendants of the business operations of the plaintiff, where the plaintiff was a corporation.

In addition to a corporate/individual distinction relevant to notions of protection of privacy, recent cases have focused on the distinction between public/private lives and tended to confine protection to the truly 'private' aspects. A recent Australian Law Reform Commission Report on privacy[105] focused on the protection of personal information as distinct from corporate information, and in fact one recommendation is that privacy legislation be named *Privacy and Personal Information Act*.[106] It can be difficult to distinguish between the private and public lives of famous people who, in some contexts, actually court publicity. In *Douglas v Hello!*[107] two celebrities objected to publication of 'unauthorised' photos of their wedding. Sedley LJ doubted that the surreptitious obtaining of

---

101 (2001) 208 CLR 199, 328; (2002) 54 IPR 161, 255–6.
102 ibid., p. 322; (2002) 54 IPR 161, 250–1.
103 ibid., pp. 248 and 258; (2002) 54 IPR 161, 191 and 199.
104 Wacks, op. cit., p. 176.
105 Australian Law Reform Commission, *For Your Information: Australian Privacy Law and Practice*, Report 108, August 2008.
106 Ibid., Ch 5.
107 *Douglas v Hello! Ltd* [2001] 2 All ER 289.

personal information would always be protected by the action for breach of confidence even if the information was of a confidential nature. He was concerned about the requirement that an obligation of confidence should exist between the parties and, reflecting upon the artificiality of finding such a relationship in cases of snooping, paparazzi photographs or by way of found material, speculated that a more general tort of interference with privacy might be required. He said:

> What a concept of privacy does ... is accord recognition to the fact that the law has to protect not only those people whose trust has been abused but those who simply find themselves subjected to an unwanted intrusion into their personal lives. The law no longer needs to construct an artificial relationship of confidentiality between intruder and victim: it can recognise privacy itself as a legal principle drawn from the fundamental value of personal autonomy.[108]

The existence of such a tort was rejected in *Wainwright v Home Office*;[109] indeed the *Human Rights Act 1998* (UK) was there argued to pre-empt the need to develop a tort of invasion of privacy. A majority of the House of Lords in *Campbell v MGN*,[110] however, found that where private or personal information was of a confidential nature it could be protected from unauthorised publication where it had been obtained in a surreptitious fashion. This was in keeping with the broad formulation of the equitable obligation of breach of confidence by Lord Goff in *Attorney General v Guardian Newspapers*,[111] although this adherence to protecting private information as a breach of confidence rather than as a positive right to privacy is regarded as expanding the reach of the traditional action, rather than developing a new tort.[112]

Lenah Game Meats was referred to with approval by the court in *Campbell v MGN*, and Gleeson J's judgment in that case was also referred to approvingly in *David Murray v Big Pictures (UK)*.[113] In the *David Murray* case the parents of young David Murray, whose mother is the world-famous author JK Rowling, objected to the use of his photograph taken with a long-range lens by a paparazzi photographer while they were on a family outing. At trial Patten J had found that the parents were trying to establish privacy for themselves, even when in public, but on appeal it was considered relevant that they sought privacy for David, not for his mother, who had not hidden herself from the press and understood that the public was interested in her. Relying on *Campbell v MGN* but distinguishing the case on the basis that it concerned a child, the appeal court found that Art 8 of the European Convention on Human Rights, which provides the right to respect for family and private life, creates a greater onus for protection of children's interests:

> the law should indeed protect children from intrusive media attention, at any rate to the extent of holding that a child has a reasonable expectation that he or she will not

---

108 ibid., p. 320.
109 [2003] 4 All ER 969.
110 *Campbell v MGN Ltd* [2005] UKHL 61.
111 *Attorney-General v Guardian Newspapers Ltd (No. 2)* [1990] 1AC 109, 281.
112 Wacks, op. cit., p. 166.
113 *David Murray v Big Pictures (UK) Ltd* [2007] EWHC 1908 (Ch), para. 25 (Clarke MR, Laws and Thomas LLJ).

72   LANDMARKS IN AUSTRALIAN IP LAW

be targeted in order to obtain photographs in a public place for publication which the person who took or procured the taking of the photographs knew would be objected to on behalf of the child.[114]

The language of the courts is developing from use of proprietary analysis to words invoking privacy.[115] It is this fault line developing between property and privacy which means the likelihood of any action to protect 'private' information will be not be framed in terms of protecting commercial interests and is likely to be quite restricted. *Victoria Park Racing* provides an early example of the challenges of emerging technology to commercial and private interests, and illustrates the use of legal principle in consideration of this interaction.

---

114 ibid., para. 57.
115 M Richardson and L Hitchens, 'Celebrity Privacy and Benefits of Simple History' in Kenyon and Richardson, op. cit., p. 263.

5

We have never been modern: the High Court's decision in *National Research Development Corporation v Commissioner of Patents*

Stephen Hubicki and Brad Sherman

Introduction

On 17 December 1959, the High Court of Australia handed down its judgment in the decision of *National Research Development Corporation v Commissioner of Patents* (*NRDC*).[1] The decision considered the patentability of two herbicidal compositions and their uses.[2] In deciding the fate of NRDC's application, the High Court dealt with three doctrinal issues: whether the claims related to a mere new use of known substances; whether the claimed invention was a 'manner of manufacture'; and the patentability of agricultural and horticultural inventions generally.

The *NRDC* decision is widely regarded as a 'watershed' in Australia,[3] a Copernican-like moment that signalled the emergence of modern patent law. It is also seen as having established a template that has shaped Australian patent law over the course of the 20th century and beyond. There is no doubt that in certain respects this is the case. In other ways, however, the High Court decision is better seen as a classic common law decision, albeit applied to a new form of technology and by the highest court in Australia, which makes incremental changes to longstanding practices and traditions. It also can be seen as having reinforced a particular image of 'invention' – one that has recently been called into question, particularly in terms of its suitability to digital inventions. In this sense, the decision offers an important insight into some of the tensions and paradoxes that characterise modern patent law.

---

1 (1959) 102 CLR 252; 1A IPR 63.
2 Patent Application No. 10,301/55; Australian Patent No. 227457, 'Herbicidal Compositions', 16 March 1960.
3 *Joos v Commissioner of Patents* (1972) 126 CLR 611, 616 (Barwick CJ).

74 LANDMARKS IN AUSTRALIAN IP LAW

Background

The inventor of the patent in suit in *NRDC*, who inexplicably is unrecognised in the High Court's judgment, is the late Ralph Louis Wain. Regarded by many as the pre-eminent British agricultural scientist of the 20th century,[4] Wain discovered the herbicidal properties of the phenoxybutyric acids, in particular 2,4-DB (2,4-dichlorophyenoxybutyric acid) – a derivative of the notorious 2,4-D (2,4-dichlorophenoxyacetic acid) – and MCPB (2-methyl-4-chlorophenoxybutyric acid). Along with 2,4-DC (2,4-dichlorophenoxycaproic acid), 2,4-DB was the subject of the application in suit in *NRDC*. Both are synthetic compounds which mimic the activity of natural plant growth hormones. At the time of the application neither compound was new – both were disclosed in Franklin Jones' Canadian patent application for the use of 2,4-D as a herbicide in 1944,[5] if not earlier. What was novel about Wain's invention was the way it exploited the ability of different plant species to convert these compounds, which are inactive as herbicides by themselves, into 2,4-D – a potent broad-spectrum herbicide.

As was the case with 2,4-D and other hormone herbicides, recognition of the herbicidal properties of 2,4-DB and 2,4-DC was inhibited by the fact that plant hormones were initially seen as being solely concerned with enhancing plant growth. The idea that plant hormones could be used to bring about plant death could not have been further from the minds of plant physiologists who studied them during the early 20th century. Following on from the work of Ciesielski and Darwin, who described the effects of a hypothetical substance found in the tips of plants which encouraged them to grow towards light,[6] plant physiologists in the late 19th and early 20th centuries worked 'to unravel the chemical mechanisms governing plant growth and development'.[7] By 1920, plant physiologists had discovered that a light-sensitive 'growth' hormone located in the tip of seedlings controlled their growth. In 1926, Frits Went of the Botanical Institute at the University of Utrecht isolated the long-sought-after growth substance, dubbed 'auxin' after the Greek *auxein* ('to increase').[8]

The discovery of auxin helped establish the physiology of plant hormones as 'one of the most dynamic life science fields in the interwar years'.[9] According to the historian of science, Nicholas Rasmussen:

---

4 L Fowden, 'Ralph Louis Wain, CBE, 29 May 1911–14 December 2000' (2002) 48 *Biogr Mems Fell R Soc Lond* 439, 441.
5 The US patent was granted on 11 December 1945: Patent No. 2,390,941, 'Methods and Compositions for Killing Weeds' (American Chemical Paint Co).
6 A Woodward and B Bartel, 'Auxin: Regulation, Action, Interaction' (2005) 95 *Annals of Botany* 707, 707; C Darwin, *The Power of Movement in Plants*, John Murray, London, 1880; G Peterson, 'The Discovery and Development of 2,4-D' (1967) 41 *Agricultural History* 243, 243–4.
7 N Rasmussen, 'Plant Hormones in War and Peace: Science, Industry, and Government in the Development of Herbicides in 1940s America' (2001) 92 *Isis* 291, 294.
8 Woodward and Bartel, op. cit., p. 707. Auxin's chemical name is 3-indole acetic acid.
9 Rasmussen, op. cit., p. 293.

even more than genes, hormones were the interwar era's prime examples of 'master molecules' ... Knowledge of these master molecules, hormone physiologists promised, was the key to controlling growth, and other vital phenomena, artificially.[10]

Much like the nascent molecular biology of the time (and many fields of life science today), the discovery of auxin held out the possibility of control over life itself. In his keynote address to the 1945 North Central States Weed Control Conference held in St Paul, Minnesota, Erza Kraus, who would later share credit for the discovery of the herbicidal properties of synthetic plant hormones, remarked: '[My] feeling is that there is not a single thing that deals with living plants that is not eventually going to find its solution through the application of growth-regulating substances.'[11] Kraus concluded: 'I know of no single process of the living plants that cannot be brought eventually under absolute control' by plant growth-regulating substances.[12] It was even envisaged that investigation of the mechanism of hormonal growth promotion in plants 'might throw some light on human cancer'.[13]

While many of these objectives were never realised, the discovery of plant growth hormones would eventually have a dramatic impact upon modern agriculture. Shortly after auxin was isolated, scientists successfully synthesised it in the laboratory. Significantly, this synthetic auxin displayed the same activity as naturally occurring auxin. In an effort to identify the molecular structures necessary for auxin activity, plant physiologists produced a vast number of synthetic compounds of similar structure to auxin.[14] By 1940, a number of synthetic hormone products resulting from this research were commercially available, enabling nurserymen to promote the rooting of cuttings and orchardists to spray trees to prevent root drop, increase the set of fruit, and develop seedless fruits.[15]

Of the numerous compounds produced and studied by plant physiologists and agricultural scientists in this period, one compound captured their attention: the notorious 2,4-D. The circumstances surrounding the discovery of 2,4-D remain unclear – it was the subject of a number of top-secret wartime biological warfare and crop improvement programs in the UK and the US, the details of which remained secret until after the war when a number of scientists would claim credit for the discovery of its herbicidal properties. The first public suggestion of using 2,4-D as a herbicide, however, appears to have been made in a paper published in 1944.

In this paper the authors acknowledged that the idea of using synthetic plant growth hormones as herbicides was given to them by Erza Kraus, a consultant

---

10 ibid., 295. The 'plant hormone field was one of the first in which specific molecular signals governing organic growth and development were deciphered and manipulated in an effort to engineer life on an industrial scale'. N Rasmussen, 'The Forgotten Promise of Thiamin: Merck, Caltech Biologists, and Plant Hormones in a 1930s Biotechnology Project' (1999) 32 *Journal of the History of Biology* 245, 246.
11 Rasmussen, op. cit., p. 312.
12 ibid.
13 ibid., p. 301.
14 ibid., p. 295. See also Peterson, op. cit., p. 244; J Troyer, 'In the Beginning: The Multiple Discovery of the First Hormone Herbicides' (2001) 49 *Weed Science* 290, 291.
15 Rasmussen, op. cit., pp. 297–8.

76 LANDMARKS IN AUSTRALIAN IP LAW

to the US Department of Agriculture and Head of the Department of Botany at the University of Chicago.[16] This claim was (apparently) corroborated by an informal proposal drawn up by Kraus for the National Academy of Sciences' top-secret committee on biological and chemical warfare barely a week after the Japanese attack on Pearl Harbor in December 1941.[17] In the proposal, Kraus suggested that plant hormone treatments might be developed that would damage crops and vegetation useful to the enemy:

> Release of growth destroying substances ... over rice fields would be a feasible and comparatively simple means of destruction of rice crops, the staple food supply of the Japanese. Distribution of sprays or mists over enemy forests would, through killing the trees, reveal concealed military depots. These are examples of many obvious military uses of these compounds.[18]

Applied in sufficient doses, plant growth hormones would literally cause plants to grow themselves to death.[19] While Kraus later formalised his ideas in a military contract in 1942, they were not deployed by the military against an enemy until the Vietnam War (as Agent Orange, in which the active ingredients are 2,4-D and 2,4,5-T).[20]

Although 2,4-D was not used as a biological weapon for another 20-odd years, the war played an important role in the advancement of research into its use as a herbicide. In particular, it helped to overcome the conceptual barrier that had 'hindered plant biologists of the 1930s: namely the notion that plant hormones were (only) growth stimulators'.[21] The disparate claims to scientific credit for the discovery of the herbicidal properties of 2,4-D, and the consequent uncertainty surrounding the novelty of the numerous patents granted in respect of 2,4-D, ensured that the new herbicide was 'as widely, quickly and cheaply available as market forces would allow immediately after the war'.[22] By 1947, 30 different herbicides containing 2,4-D had appeared on the market.[23] The growing market also stimulated the production of new and better herbicides.

---

16 This was suggested to them in private correspondence in August 1941. P Marth and J Mitchell, '2,4-dichlorophenoxyacetic Acid as a Differential Herbicide' (1944) 106 *Botanical Gazette* 224. See also J Mitchell and C Hamner, 'Polyethylene Glycols as Carriers for Growth-Regulating Substances' (1944) 105 *Botanical Gazette* 474; C Hamner and H Tukey, 'The Herbicidal Action of 2,4-dichlorophenoxy Acid and 2,4,5-trichlorophenoxyacetic Acid on Bindweed' (1944) 100 *Science* 154; C Hamner and H Tukey, 'Selective Herbicidal Action of Midsummer and Fall Applications of 2,4-dichlorophenoxyacetic Acid' (1944) 106 *Botanical Gazette* 232.
17 Rasmussen, op. cit., p. 301.
18 ibid., p. 302. Workers at the Rothamsted Agricultural Experiment Station in the UK also suggested to the British Agricultural Research Council that 2,4-D might have importance as a wartime weapon of crop destruction. Troyer, op. cit., p. 292.
19 Ironically, rice (and other cereals) would turn out to be one of the most resilient crops to the effects of 2,4-D.
20 Rasmussen, op. cit., p. 301. The British Government apparently rejected the idea of using selective hormone herbicides to destroy crops during World War II on technical, political and moral grounds, although it subsequently deployed them in Malaya from 1951 to 1953. Troyer, op. cit., p. 294.
21 Rasmussen, op. cit., p. 313.
22 ibid., pp. 308–9.
23 Peterson, op. cit., p. 252.

By 1962, approximately 100 herbicides in 6000 different formulations had been marketed.[24]

The emergence of 2,4-D, and other hormone herbicides such as 2,4,5-T and MCPA, revolutionised agriculture and are considered to be among the greatest scientific discoveries of the 20th century.[25] The very characteristic which made 2,4-D so successful as a weed-killer – its potency – was, however, also a shortcoming. It not only killed many common weeds but also a number of important crops, such as cotton, fruit trees, vines and most vegetable crops, including peas, canola, soybeans and lupins.[26] The success of 2,4-D, as well as its shortcomings, stimulated the search for other more selective herbicides. A breakthrough in the development of new, more selective hormone herbicides was made after World War II. Percy Zimmerman and Martin Synerholm discovered that a group of homologous compounds[27] with an even number of carbon atoms in the side-chain (i.e., the butyric, caproic and octanoic acids) were active growth substances, whereas those with an odd number of carbon atoms in the side-chain (i.e., propionic, valeric and heptanoic acids) were not.[28] Zimmerman and Synerholm suggested that acids with an even number of carbon atoms in the side-chain were inactive as growth substances per se, but were converted into an active growth substance by the process of beta-oxidation, the same process responsible for the breakdown of fatty acids in the animal body.[29] While beta-oxidation was known to occur in animals, this was the first time it had been suggested that plants might utilise a similar mechanism.

In a series of 'celebrated' experiments carried out in the early 1950s,[30] Wain and his colleagues at Wye College at the University of London confirmed Zimmerman and Synerholm's results with a related class of compounds applied to flax seedlings. When Wain later expanded his investigations to include wheat, pea and tomato bio-assays, he made what he would later describe as a 'spectacular' discovery: while most of the compounds tested exhibited the expected behaviour (i.e., compounds with an even number of carbon atoms in the side-chain were active as growth substances, whereas those with an odd number were not), Wain found that in some plant species certain types of compounds did not behave as expected.[31] Rather than debunking Zimmerman and Synerholm's beta-oxidation hypothesis, however, these results suggested to Wain 'a new and fundamental

---

24 ibid.

25 Troyer, op. cit.

26 Cereal crops (wheat, maize, rice and sorghum) and grasses are resistant to 2,4-D. However, even crops that can be sprayed safely with 2,4-D can be sensitive at some stages of growth or at excessive application rates.

27 Omega-(2,4-dichlorophenoxy)carboxylic acids.

28 A homologous series is one in which successive members of the series have a regular difference in composition. For example, the alkane homologous series differs by CH_2 starting with methane (CH_4), followed by ethane (C_2H_6), propane (C_3H_8) and so on.

29 In beta-oxidation, fatty acids with an even number of carbon atoms in the side-chain are converted into an acetic acid derivative, whereas those with an odd number of carbon atoms in the side-chain are converted into phenol.

30 F Taylor, 'Obituary: Professor RL Wain', *The Independent*, 10 January 2001.

31 In particular, the 2,4,5-trichloro- and the 2,4-dichloro-5-methyl- series.

78   LANDMARKS IN AUSTRALIAN IP LAW

basis upon which selective weed control might operate'.[32] This was based on the hypothesis 'that specific [beta]-oxidase systems may be present in different plant species'.[33] More particularly, Wain proposed that it might be possible to take advantage of the differences between the beta-oxidation capabilities of different species of plants to develop selective herbicides which exploited these differences. Taking 2,4-DB (which has an even number of carbon atoms in its side-chain) as an example, plants that are sensitive to 2,4-D but do not have the specific enzymes necessary to convert 2,4-DB to 2,4-D can be safely treated with 2,4-DB. In contrast, plants which are sensitive to 2,4-D and which have the capacity to convert 2,4-DB to 2,4-D would succumb to the herbicidal effect of 2,4-D. Fortunately, many common weeds are capable of carrying out this conversion, while a number of economically important crops that are sensitive to 2,4-D, in particular leguminous fodder crops and grasses, are unable to carry out this conversion to any appreciable extent. This capacity to differentiate between the enzyme systems of different types of plants meant that a farmer could spray leguminous fodder crops and grasses indiscriminately, safe in the knowledge that the crop would be unaffected, while certain weeds would die.

Four compounds were singled out by Wain from this research and were made the subject of patent applications in both Australia and overseas. These were 2,4-DB, 2,4-DC, MCPB and MCPC.[34] The first two compounds would become the subject of the application in question in *NRDC*;[35] the latter two compounds would form the basis of a separate application. As noted above, all of these compounds were known when Wain filed his application. Thus, the compounds themselves were not and could not be claimed. Instead, Wain's Australian patent application, which was assigned to NRDC,[36] contained two distinct types of claims. The first were claims to herbicidal compositions containing 2,4-DB and 2,4-DC, their salts, esters, nitriles and amides as active ingredients (claims 4–6). The second were claims to methods of using 2,4-DB and 2,4-DC, their salts, esters, nitriles and amides to eradicate weeds from crop areas containing a growing crop selected from leguminous fodder crops of the genera *Trifolium* and *Medicago*, celery and parsnip (claim 1), and to control weeds of the type of charlock, creeping thistle, and annual nettle in lucerne (alfalfa) (claim 2) and clover (claim 3) crops.

According to a contemporary of Wain, his discovery opened 'a whole new field for weed-control research ... One can scarcely visualize the limits of the application of this principle ... I know of no area in the fields of biochemistry

---

32 R Wain, 'The Behaviour of Herbicides in the Plant in Relation to Selectivity' in L Audus (ed.), *The Physiology and Biochemistry of Herbicides*, Academic Press, London, 1964, p. 474.
33 ibid.
34 2,4-DB (2,4-dichlorophenoxybutyric acid); 2,4-DC (2,4-dichlorophenoxycaproic acid); MCPB (2-methyl-4-chlorphenoxybutyric acid); MCPC (2-methyl-4-chlorphenoxycaproic acid).
35 Patent Application No. 10,301/55; Australian Patent No. 227457, 'Herbicidal Compositions', 16 March 1960.
36 The NRDC was a statutory corporation established by the *Development of Inventions Act* in 1948 to secure the development in the public interest of inventions resulting from public research. It was consolidated with the National Enterprise Group to form the British Technology Group in 1981.

and plant physiology that offer greater promise to the researcher.'[37] Despite the significance of Wain's research, his Australian patent application received a bleak report from the Australian Patent Office. While the composition claims were not contentious, the method claims were rejected by the examiner on the basis that they merely claimed a new use of known substances and did not result in a vendible product. NRDC appealed the examiner's decision to the Deputy Commissioner who also refused the application on the authority of *Standard Oil Development Corp's Application*,[38] arguing that the method claimed did not result in any vendible product. NRDC subsequently appealed to the High Court of Australia sitting as the Patents Appeal Tribunal.

Before the High Court, the Commissioner reaffirmed the grounds of refusal raised in the Patent Office proceedings and added a further ground of refusal: namely, that agricultural and horticultural methods per se (a class of inventions to which Wain's discovery purportedly belonged) were not patentable subject-matter. In what has been lauded as a 'masterly' and 'watershed' judgment, the High Court rejected all three grounds of refusal and allowed NRDC's appeal against the Commissioner's decision to reject the method of use claims. In the following sections, we will examine the High Court's treatment of each of the grounds of refusal relied on by the Commissioner.

New use claims

The first ground of refusal considered by the High Court was the Commissioner's claim that NRDC's application was a mere new use of a known product. Here, the Commissioner's argument proceeded along two lines: first, while Wain's discovery of the differences between the capacities of different species of plants to break down certain compounds might have involved an inventive step, the mode of exploiting this discovery – that is, the use of 2,4-DB and 2,4-DC in the claimed methods – was so straightforward that it was obvious.[39] Secondly, the Commissioner alleged that Wains' discovery consisted of no more than an unpatentable abstract idea. As counsel for the Commissioner put it, 'neither in claim 1 nor in claims 2 or 3 is there any process involved. There is no process independent of the discovery itself'.[40] That is, there was no patentable new use or manufacture at all. The court rejected both arguments.

In respect of the first argument, the Commissioner relied upon what Lord Buckmaster had referred to in *Re AF's Application* as the 'old and well-established principle that the mere discovery of a new use of a particular known product is

---

37 A Crafts, 'Weed Control: Applied Botany' (1956) 43 *American Journal of Botany* 548, 553.
38 (1951) 68 RPC 114.
39 As counsel for the Commissioner argued: 'Once the discovery of the reaction between the compound of the higher members of the homologous series is made, the question remaining is simply what is the proper quantity of that compound to apply to the weed in order to produce by degradation, the acetic compound which will destroy the weed'. (1959) 102 CLR 252, 259 (McInerney QC).
40 ibid.

80   LANDMARKS IN AUSTRALIAN IP LAW

not what is meant by invention within the meaning of the Patents Acts.'[41] Lord Buckmaster elaborated upon the meaning of this principle in *Re BA's Application* when he said that 'once a substance is known, its methods of production ascertained, its characteristics and its constituents are well defined, you cannot patent the use of that for a purpose which was hitherto unknown.'[42] In *Commissioner of Patents v Microcell*[43], decided shortly before *NRDC*, the High Court affirmed these principles when it upheld the Commissioner's decision to reject an application in respect of a self-propelled rocket projector which was made up of a tube of synthetic resinous plastic material reinforced with mineral fibres. Tubular self-propelled rocket projectors and synthetic resinous plastics reinforced with mineral fibres were well known at the time of the application, as were the properties of reinforced plastic materials, which had been used in the manufacture of a wide variety of articles, in particular for their high-impact strength, lightness and high resistance to heat.

In these circumstances, the court in *Microcell* upheld the Commissioner's decision to reject the application on the basis that the alleged invention consisted of 'nothing but a claim for the use of a known material in the manufacture of known articles for the purpose of which its known properties make it suitable.'[44] The court acknowledged that while 'many valid patents are for new uses of old things', the mere fact that no-one had previously thought to use the substance in a particular way was not sufficient to confer inventiveness upon the suggestion that it could be used for a new purpose. This was particularly the case where 'no new product is obtained, no new method of manufacture is suggested, or a new one improved'.[45] In these circumstances, the High Court said that where it is manifest on the face of the specification that a patent only claims mere new use of a known product, the Commissioner not has only the power but is under a duty to reject the application.[46]

In *NRDC*, the court held that the Commissioner's reliance upon the principles outlined by Lord Buckmaster to reject Wain's application was misplaced. In responding to the Commissioner's argument that NRDC's application was not patentable on the basis of Lord Buckmaster's reasoning in *Re AF's Application* and *Re BA's Application* – namely that a mere new use of a known product was not patentable – the court emphasised, just as it had done in *Microcell*, that 'it must always be remembered how much is wrapped up' in the words 'nothing but' which appear in Lord Buckmaster's statement in *Re BA's Application*. Lord Buckmaster did not, the court explained,

> use the words without explanation: '. . . once a substance is known,' he said, 'its methods of production ascertained, its characteristics and its constituents well defined, you cannot patent the use of that for a purpose which was hitherto unknown.' And why?

---

41 (1914) 31 RPC 58.
42 (1915) 32 RPC 348, 349.
43 *Commissioner of Patents v Microcell* (1959) 102 CLR 232.
44 ibid., p. 251.
45 ibid., p. 250 (adapting *Re AF's Application* (1914) 31 RPC 58, 59).
46 ibid., p. 247.

Because in the postulated state of knowledge [about the substance] the new purpose is only analogous to the purposes for which the utility of the substance is already known; that is, the new purpose lacks the quality of inventiveness.[47]

In these circumstances, no valid patent can be granted 'unless invention is found in some new method of using the material or some new adaptation of it so as to serve the new purpose'.

In rejecting the Commissioner's argument, the court drew a distinction between two situations. The first arises where the alleged invention lies in the discovery that a particular substance can be applied in a new way. In this case there is no new knowledge about the product or substance per se; instead, the alleged invention is limited to the way in which the product is applied or used. The second situation arises where the applicant has discovered a 'hitherto unknown or unsuspected property' of a substance or product. In this situation two factors are important: first, the inventor has discovered a new or unsuspected attribute or property of the substance in question; and secondly, the inventor has suggested a way in which this discovery can be practically applied to bring about a new result or effect.

In reviewing the law in this area, the High Court suggested that the test outlined by Lord Buckmaster was not applicable in all cases. More specifically, the High Court said, in effect, that the principle outlined by Lord Buckmaster did not apply to the second situation outlined above. As the High Court stated, where

the new use that is proposed consists in taking advantage of a hitherto unknown or unsuspected property of the material, the situation is not that to which Lord Buckmaster's language refers. In that case there may be invention in the suggestion that the substance may be used to serve the new purpose; and then, provided that a practical method of so using it is disclosed and that the process comes within the concept of patent law ultimately traceable to the use in the Statute of Monopolies of the words 'manner of manufacture,' all the elements of a patentable invention are present.[48]

The High Court then applied this reasoning to the facts before them. In the court's view, the substances employed in the claimed methods of use belonged to the second scenario outlined above; they were, to borrow Hans-Jörg Rheinberger's phrase, 'epistemic things'. The essence of an epistemic thing is 'its potential for surprise, its capacity to outstrip expectations and imagination framed by the current way of thinking and doing'.[49] Epistemic things are characterised by their 'preliminarity, of what we do not yet know about them, not by virtue of what we already know about them'.[50] Wain's specification brings these qualities

---

47 (1959) 102 CLR 252, 262 (internal references omitted); 1A IPR 63, 65.
48 ibid.
49 L Daston, 'Introduction: The Coming into Being of Scientific Objects' in L Daston (ed.), *Biographies of Scientific Objects*, University of Chicago Press, Chicago, 2001, pp. 11–12.
50 HJ Rheinberger, 'A Reply to David Bloor: 'Toward a Sociology of Epistemic Things' (2005) 13 *Perspectives on Science* 406, 407. See generally HJ Rheinberger, *Towards a History of Epistemic Things: Synthesizing Proteins in the Test Tube*, Stanford University Press, Stanford, 1997.

82 LANDMARKS IN AUSTRALIAN IP LAW

of epistemicity into sharp relief. As the specifications states, the fact that the compounds employed in the claimed methods of use were effective as herbicides was

> highly surprising for on the basis of known facts and generally accepted theory one would expect them to behave in precisely the same way, i.e. to have the same plant regulant properties, as 2,4-D and its derivatives.

The 'generally accepted theory' Wain referred to is the theory that compounds in a homologous series will generally exhibit the same chemical properties. However, Wain noted that the compounds 'possess no appreciable growth regulating activity with respect to such crop plants of economic importance as clover, celery, parsnip and pea', all of which are 'severely affected' by 2,4-D and other hormone herbicides when applied at the same concentration. The reasons for this disparity were unclear and initially resulted in 2,4-DB and 2,4-DC being discarded as potential herbicides. It was not until Wain drew the link between the beta-oxidase systems in different plant species and the capacity of different plant species, in particular many common weeds, to metabolise these compounds into 2,4-D, that the herbicidal potential of the compounds was realised. Viewed in this light, the court said:

> this is not a claim which can be put aside as a claim for a new use of an old substance, true though it be that the chemicals themselves were known to science before the applicant's investigations began. It is a claim which denies that the chemicals are old substances in the sense in which the expression has been used in such cases as *Re AF's Application*; *Re BA's Application* and *Re CGR's Application*. It treats them as substances which in the relevant sense are new, that is to say as substances which formerly were known only partially and, so far as weed-killing potentialities are concerned, were unknown . . .[51]

In these circumstances, it was not necessary to show, as the Commissioner had contended, that there was invention in the way that the substance was applied. Instead, it was sufficient to show that there was inventiveness in the discovery of the new properties of the substance in question. That is, the invention belonged to the second category of case described above. Following the English Court of Appeal's decision in *Hickton's Patent Syndicate v Patents and Machine Improvements*[52], the High Court said:

> it is irrelevant, even if true, that once the discovery was made that the chemicals produce a lethal reaction when applied to the weeds and produce no such reaction when applied to the crops there was no more ingenuity required in order to show how the process might be performed. The point that matters is that a weed-killing process is claimed which is distinguished from previously known processes by a feature the suggestion of which for such a process involved a step plainly inventive.[53]

---

51 (1959) 102 CLR 252, 265 (internal references omitted); 1A IPR 63, 67.
52 *Hickton's Patent Syndicate v Patents and Machine Improvements Co* (1909) 26 RPC 339.
53 (1959) 102 CLR 252, 265; 1 A IPR 63, 67. At first blush, this seems inconsistent with *Lane Fox v Kensington and Knightsbridge Electric Lighting* (1892) 3 Ch 424 where Lindley LJ held that a method of using a known thing for a purpose for which it has never been used before will only be patentable if there is novelty in the

Once the court rejected the Commissioner's first argument, the second ground relied on by the Commissioner effectively dissipated. However, aspects of the Commissioner's argument warrant further consideration. As noted above, in addition to the argument that the claimed methods of use merely consisted of a new use of a known substance, the Commissioner put forward the alternative (albeit incongruent) argument that there was 'no process independent of the discovery itself'.[54] In particular, it was argued that the claims were 'only for a discovery of a bio-chemical reaction; there is no control of it and the result is identical with the discovery'.[55] This points to a central difficulty encountered by Wain in prosecuting his application in the Australian Patent Office, which is attributable to the nature of his discovery – namely, that his invention straddled the troublesome boundary between 'basic' research and 'applied' science. As Wain explained, 'the discovery of [the phenoxybutyric] herbicides arose from *fundamental* investigations on the breakdown of [omega]-substituted fatty acids in plants.'[56] In what has become a recurring tension in the history of biological inventions, the Commissioner argued, in effect, that Wain's discovery was closer to basic than applied science, discovery than invention. As counsel for the Commissioner argued, 'the whole process claimed is dependent on the operation of natural laws or the natural properties of the materials involved.'[57] The uncertainty surrounding the patentability of Wain's invention was exacerbated by the fact that the inventive step taken by Wain primarily resided in the discovery that different plant species are capable of converting synthetic plant hormones into active herbicides by the process of beta-oxidation. As counsel for NRDC acknowledged, the difference between this discovery and its practical embodiment was 'very small'.[58] Once the discovery had been made, all that the researchers had to do to was to carry out relatively simple empirical experiments to assess the toxicity of the compounds upon different plant species.

Counsel for NRDC, Sir Keith Aickin, responded to this argument by suggesting that there was no logical distinction between the facts in *NRDC* and in *Commercial Solvents v Synthetic Products*,[59] in which the validity of a microbiological

---

mode of using it (as distinguished from novelty of purpose), or if any new modification of the thing, or any new appliance is necessary for using it for its new purpose. In *NRDC*, the court suggested that Lindley LJ's statement should be read in the same way as it read Lord Buckmaster's decisions in *AF's Application* and *BA's Application* – that is, as applying only to things which are 'known' in the sense that their 'characteristics and properties . . . are understood'. Another interpretation of Lindley LJ's statement is that he was merely adhering to the reverse-infringement test of novelty, which, as with infringement, pays no mind to the intention of the user. So long as the mode of practically applying the discovery differs from previous ways of using the substance or thing (which the High Court appears to take for granted), then the High Court's approach causes few problems. Where this is not the case, however, the court or decision-maker will have to grapple with the same slippery issues of 'inherent anticipation' that courts in the UK must now deal with as a result of the House of Lords' endorsement of the European Patent Office's approach to novelty in *G02/88 Mobil/Friction-reducing Additive* [1990] EPOR 73.

54 (1959) 102 CLR 252, 259 (McInerney QC).
55 ibid.
56 Wain, op. cit., p. 472. As counsel for NRDC argued, 'the invention lies in observing the practical significance of the initial discovery' of the fact that specific beta-oxidase enzyme systems may be present in different plant species.
57 (1959) 102 CLR 252, 259 (McInerney QC).
58 ibid., pp. 255 and 257 (Aickin QC).
59 *Commercial Solvents Corporation v Synthetic Products Co Ltd* (1926) 43 RPC 185.

84 LANDMARKS IN AUSTRALIAN IP LAW

process for the production of acetone was upheld by Romer J.[60] In both cases, the inventor employed a natural process in order to produce a useful result. In the *Commercial Solvents* case, the inventor utilised a strain of bacteria to produce acetone by the fermentation of starch; in *NRDC*, Wain took advantage of the ability of certain species of plants to degrade certain types of chemical compounds into 2,4-D, which, in turn, produced a herbicidal effect in plant species capable of carrying out this conversion, while leaving plants without this capacity unharmed.

In a clear rebuttal of the Commissioner's argument that Wain's method of use claims were unpatentable on the basis that 'the whole process claimed was dependent on the operation of natural laws or the natural properties of the materials involved',[61] the High Court said that 'it is not decisive – it is not even helpful – to point out in such a case that beyond discovery of a scientific fact nothing has been added except the suggestion that nature, in its newly ascertained aspect, be allowed to work in its own way.' The court then approvingly referred to Frankfurter J's dissenting judgment in the US Supreme Court's decision in *Funk Bros Seed v Kalo Inoculant*:

> It only confuses the issue, however, to introduce terms such as 'the work of nature' and the 'laws of nature'. For these are vague and malleable terms infected with too much ambiguity and equivocation. Everything that happens may be deemed 'the work of nature', and any patentable composite exemplifies in its properties 'the laws of nature'. Arguments drawn from such terms for ascertaining patentability could fairly be employed to challenge almost any patent.[62]

The High Court continued:

> The truth is that the distinction between discovery and invention is not precise enough to be other than misleading in this area of discussion. There may indeed be a discovery without invention – either because the discovery is of some piece of abstract information without any suggestion of a practical application of it to a useful end, or because its application lies outside the realm of 'manufacture'.[63]

Putting the latter principle to one side, the court emphatically rejected the Commissioner's argument that the subject-matter of the claims in question was in substance a discovery, an abstract idea having no practical embodiment:

> No-one reading the specification in the present case can fail to see that what it claims is a new process for ridding crop areas of certain kinds of weeds ... There is a clear assertion of a discovery that a useful result can be obtained by doing something which the applicant's research has shown for the first time to be capable of producing that result ... Its tenor is that by an application of scientific ingenuity, combining knowledge, thought and experimentation, not only in relation to the chemicals but in relation also to the

---

60 It appears that there was no discussion of whether the claimed process was a 'manufacture', which would appear to have been taken for granted.
61 (1959) 102 CLR 252, 259 (McInerney QC).
62 *Funk Bros Seed Co v Kalo Inoculant* 333 US 127 (1948), 134–5.
63 (1959) 102 CLR 252, 264; 1A IPR 63, 66. Until the 18th century 'invention' was synonymous with 'discovery', and it was only during the 18th century that they became antonymous. Daston, op. cit., pp. 3–4.

enzyme systems of certain weeds and plants, the applicant has evolved a new and useful method of destroying weeds without harming useful vegetation amongst which they are growing.[64]

Viewed in its context, it is clear that the High Court did not, as some commentators have suggested, draw a distinction between patentable and unpatentable subject-matter based upon the degree of human intervention involved in the production of the claimed invention.[65] The court's endorsement of Frankfurter J's dissenting comments in *Funk Bros*, along with its denial of the utility of the distinction between 'discovery' and 'invention' as a basis for demarcating unpatentable from patentable subject-matter, indicate that the High Court was endeavouring to avoid the difficult metaphysical questions implicated by such distinctions. As we discuss in the next section, the way that the court attempted to transcend these delicate metaphysical questions was to emphasise a particular mode of invention which, ironically, restored the concept of manufacture to its earlier performative meaning.

Manner of manufacture

The second and, in the High Court's view, central question in the case was whether the claimed invention was a manner of manufacture.[66] The response by the High Court to this question is at once the most well known and also the most troubling aspect of the decision. In order to understand the way that the court responded to this issue, it is important to appreciate that the court was dealing with two discrete arguments made by the Commissioner. The first related to the meaning of 'manufacture'. While the Commissioner accepted that the meaning given to 'manufacture' would change over time, he argued that the term should be read literally and in accordance with the prevailing meaning of the term at the time of the decision.[67] The second issue related to the meaning of the term 'vendible product' and the role that this should play in determining patentability. This was in response to the Commissioner's argument that in order to be patentable a process or method must result in a vendible product. While the Commissioner accepted that the vendible product test was not decisive, he argued that as processes of manufacture normally result in a vendible product, in many cases it was a convenient test for determining patentability. Following the main thrust of authority in the UK, as well as Australian Patent Office practice, the Commissioner's argument reflected the view that a vendible product was only present where a method or process *resulted* in a tangible, vendible object.

---

64 (1959) 102 CLR 252, 264–5; 1A IPR 63, 67.
65 See, for example, J Pila, 'Inherent Patentability in Anglo-Australian Law: A History' (2003) 14 *Australian Intellectual Property Journal* 109; J Pila, 'Bound Futures: Patent Law and Modern Biotechnology' (2003) 9 *Boston University Journal of Science and Technology* 326.
66 (1959) 102 CLR 252, 268; 1A IPR 63, 69.
67 ibid., pp. 258 and 259.

86   LANDMARKS IN AUSTRALIAN IP LAW

In contrast, counsel for NRDC argued that there was a 'manufacture' whenever a process produced a useful physical result *in relation* to a material or tangible entity.[68]

Meaning of 'manufacture'

The court dismissed the Commissioner's first argument that 'manufacture' should be interpreted in accordance with the meaning of the term prevailing at the time of the decision. In doing so, the court warned against the attempt to place upon the term 'the fetters of an exact verbal formula'. The court said that any attempt to precisely define 'manufacture' was bound to fail. In part, this was based on the view that as the subject matter of patents was constantly evolving, the interpretation of manufacture also had to evolve accordingly.[69] It was also based on the view that manufacture

> finds a place in the present Act, not as a word intended to reduce a question of patentability to a question of verbal interpretation, but simply as the general title found in the Statute of Monopolies for the whole category under which all grants of patents which may be made in accordance with the developed principles of patent law are to be subsumed. It is therefore a mistake, and a mistake likely to lead to an incorrect conclusion, to treat the question whether a given process or product is within the definition as if that question could be restated in the form: 'Is this a manner (or kind) of manufacture?' It is a mistake which tends to limit one's thinking by reference to the idea of making tangible goods by hand or by machine, because 'manufacture' as a word of everyday speech generally conveys that idea.[70]

After warning against the attempt to reduce the inquiry to a question of strict verbal interpretation, the High Court focused on the approach that should be adopted. Instead of inquiring into the literal meaning of 'manufacture', the court said the proper question to ask was: 'Is this a proper subject of letters patent according to the principles which have been developed for the application of s 6 of the Statute of Monopolies?'[71] In a similar vein, the High Court said that the

> inquiry which the definition demands is an inquiry into the scope of the permissible subject matter of letters patent and grants of privilege protected by the section. It is an inquiry not into the meaning of a word so much as into the breadth of the concept which the law has developed by its consideration of the text and purpose of the Statute of Monopolies.[72]

---

68 The Commissioner appeared to emphasise Morton J's 'vendible product' test to resist NRDC's argument that Wain's invention was indistinguishable from the decision in *Commercial Solvents*. In both cases, the inventor employed a natural process in order to produce a useful result. In response, the Commissioner argued that the cases were distinguishable on the basis that the use of the process claimed in the *Commercial Solvents* resulted in a vendible product.
69 (1959) 102 CLR 252, 271; 1A IPR 63, 70.
70 ibid., p. 269; 1A IPR 63, 70.
71 ibid.
72 ibid. The High Court's approach to 'manufacture' recalls Eyre CJ's comment in *Boulton and Watt v Bull* (1795) 2 HBI 463, 494; 126 ER 651, that 'in my apprehension it is strictly agreeable to the *spirit and meaning* of the Statute Jac 1, that [improvements of this kind] should be encouraged.' (Emphasis added.)

In so doing, the court rejected the Commissioner's argument that 'manufacture' should be understood according to its commonly accepted definition. As we will argue below, the court also opened up a number of questions.

The meaning and role of 'vendible product'

The second issue discussed by the court when considering whether NRDC's application was patentable related to the meaning and role given to the term 'vendible product'. The immediate problem facing the court was that it was not possible to identify a consistent approach from the case law regarding the role and significance of the vendible product test. As counsel for NRDC argued,[73] in some cases patents had been granted for new processes which did not result in a vendible product, while in other cases patents had not been granted for new processes that produced a vendible product.[74] NRDC accordingly argued that the vendible product test was not decisive, a point somewhat significantly conceded by the Commissioner.[75]

In responding to this problem, the High Court noted that the introduction of the vendible product test (though not the modern idea of it) could be traced back to *Boulton and Watt v Bull* (1795)[76] where in looking at the scope of the phrase 'manner of manufacture' Heath J said that two classes of manufacture fell within the ambit of s 6. The first class includes machines, the second includes substances (such as medicines) formed by chemical and other processes,

> where the vendible substance is the thing produced, and that which operates preserve no permanent form. In the first class the machine, and in the second the substance produced, is the subject of the patent.[77]

On this view, processes were not patentable on the basis that they were not vendible.[78] Each of the four judges deciding the case wrote different opinions, however, and consequently no judgment was given. Moreover, as the court observed in *NRDC*, the expression 'vendible substance' was used by Heath J while making the now 'heretical' argument that there could not be a patent for a method. The court also noted that Heath J's interpretation had not been followed in subsequent decisions.[79] The implication was that the 'vendible substance' requirement may not have been entirely sound.

---

73 (1959) 102 CLR 252, 255.
74 The former included Boulton and Watt's patent for the process of lessening the consumption of steam, which was upheld by the House of Lords in *Hornblower v Boulton* (1799) 101 ER 1285, as well as Crane's patent for the use of anthracite instead of bituminous coal with the hot-air blast in smelting iron ore, the validity of which was upheld by the Court of Common Pleas in *Crane v Price* (1842) 1 WPC 393, a decision which was supposed to have settled, once and for all, the patentability of processes.
75 (1959) 102 CLR 252, 258 and 259.
76 (1795) 2 HBI 463, 481–2; 126 ER 651, 660–1.
77 ibid.
78 Heath J said that he approved of the term 'manufacture' in the statute 'because it precludes all nice refinements; it gives us to understand the reason of the proviso that it was introduced for the benefit of trade. That which is the subject of a patent, ought to be specified, and it ought to be that which is vendible, otherwise it cannot be a manufacture.'
79 The court referred to Abbott CJ's influential decision in *R v Wheeler* (1819) 106 ER 392.

88   LANDMARKS IN AUSTRALIAN IP LAW

The 'vendible product' requirement subsequently faded from the doctrinal landscape until it was revived by Morton J's decision in *GEC's Application*.[80] In this case, Morton J said:

> a method or process is a manufacture if it (a) results in the production of some vendible product or (b) improves or restores to its former condition a vendible product or (c) has the effect of preserving from deterioration some vendible product to which it is applied.[81]

As the High Court noted, while Morton J said that he had no intention of laying down a binding principle applicable to all cases, this is in fact what happened as Morton J's judgment subsequently came to take on a life of its own. More specifically 'Morton's rules', as they became known, were applied in a formulaic fashion by the Australian Patent Office to determine the patentability of claims for methods and processes.

As the High Court noted, however, if these principles were applied literally they would have had a narrowing effect on the law. Importantly, this would have contradicted the 'widening conception' of the notion of 'manner of manufacture' which Dixon J (as he then was) had previously identified as being 'a characteristic of the growth of patent law'.[82] The court observed that Morton J's statement had therefore 'already been found to stand as much in need as the statute itself of a generous interpretation'.[83] The court then looked at three decisions which 'substantially qualified' Morton J's proposition and, in so doing, cast doubt over this aspect of the Commissioner's case: the decisions of Evershed J in *Cementation Co's Application*[84] and *Rantzen's Application*,[85] and Lloyd-Jacob J's decision in *Elton and Leda Chemical's Application*.[86] In essence, these cases heralded a shift away from a rigid conception of 'product' as a material object produced by a process, towards a broad conception of 'product' as the action resulting from, or the effect produced by, a process.[87] These cases also decided that although it was necessary for there to be a 'product' of a process in order to test the validity of the new and useful effect promised by the inventor, it was not necessary that this product should itself be vendible.[88] Rather, the term 'vendible' should be understood as emphasising the 'trading or industrial' character of the process.[89]

---

80 (1942) 60 RPC 1.
81 ibid., p. 4.
82 *Maeder v Busch* (1937) 59 CLR 684, 706.
83 (1959) 102 CLR 252, 271; 1A IPR 63, 71.
84 (1945) 60 RPC 1.
85 (1946) 64 RPC 63.
86 [1957] RPC 267.
87 In *Rantzen's Application* (1946) 64 RPC 63, 66, Evershed J stressed that 'vendible product' should not be given a narrow or rigid construction by placing 'undue emphasis upon the material requirements of what may otherwise fairly be regarded as the outcome of a process of manufacture'.
88 *Elton and Leda Chemical's Application* [1957] RPC 267, 269.
89 *Rantzen's Application* (1946) 64 RPC 63, 66.

As the High Court noted, the effect of these decisions was to undermine the narrow reading of 'vendible product' urged by the Commissioner.[90] Summarising the effect of these decisions, the High Court said:

> It is, we think, only by understanding the word 'product' as covering every end produced, and treating the word 'vendible' as pointing only to the requirement of utility in practical affairs, that the language of Morton J's 'rule' may be accepted as wide enough to convey the broad idea which the long line of decisions on the subject has shown to be comprehended by the Statute.[91]

Adopting this broader reading of 'vendible product', the court rejected the Commissioner's argument and held that the claimed methods were a 'manner of manufacture'. As the court said, the 'view which we think is correct in the present case is that the method the subject of the relevant claims has as its end result an artificial effect falling squarely within the true concept of what must be produced by a process if it is to be held patentable.'[92] The court went on to say:

> the effect produced by the appellant's method exhibits the two essential qualities upon which 'product' and 'vendible' seem designed to insist. It is a 'product' because it consists in an artificially created state of affairs, discernible by observing over a period the growth of weeds and crops respectively on sown land on which the method has been put into practice. And the significance of the product is economic; for it provides a remarkable advantage, indeed to the lay mind a sensational advantage, for one of the most elemental activities by which man has served his material needs, the cultivation of the soil for the production of its fruits.[93]

There are a number of notable aspects about the High Court's response to the Commissioner's argument that NRDC's application was not a 'manner of manufacture' and thus unpatentable. The first relates to the role that the purposive approach plays in deciding whether a claimed invention is a manner of manufacture. Contrary to what some commentators have suggested, the High Court did not intend that the purposive approach should take on a life of its own to become the ultimate arbiter of patentable subject-matter.[94] While the approach can be seen as a response to the Commissioner's argument for a literal reading of manufacture, beyond this it is not immediately clear what role the High Court intended it should take. It is far from clear, for example, what role, if any, the court envisaged that the purpose of s 6 of the Statute of Monopolies was to play in deciding whether an alleged invention falls within the 'established ambit' of the section. Indeed, there is no reference to the 'text and purpose' of s 6 in the court's subsequent consideration of the Commissioner's argument that in order

---

90 No doubt the court was aided here by the concessions made by counsel for NRDC and the Commissioner that the vendible product test was inadequate. See (1959) 102 CLR 252, 255 (Aickin QC) and 259 (McInerney QC).
91 ibid., p. 276; 1A IPR 63, 75.
92 ibid., p. 277; 1A IPR 63, 75.
93 ibid.
94 The court's repeated references to the importance of the principles which the law has developed by its consideration of the text and purpose of s 6 of the Statute of Monopolies would be superfluous were it otherwise.

90 LANDMARKS IN AUSTRALIAN IP LAW

to satisfy the manner of manufacture requirement a method or process must result in a 'vendible product'.

As a result, it is only possible to speculate about the role that the court thought that the 'purpose of s 6' should play in the assessment of patentable subject-matter. Some insights can be gleaned, however, from certain comments made by the court. As Lord Diplock noted when talking about the use of a purposive approach to patent claim interpretation in the House of Lords' decision in *Catnic Components v Hill and Smith*,[95] 'purpose' is an open-ended and slippery term. While it is often assumed that the adoption of a purposive approach to construe patent claims necessarily leads to a more liberal interpretation, this is not necessarily the case. This is because a purposive reading could, depending on the purpose or intent of the drafter, lead to either a more expansive or a more restrictive reading of the patent claims. Indeed, in some cases, a purposive interpretation may mean that the claims are read literally. The same is true, or at least should be, of the use of 'purpose' to determine patentable subject-matter. One of the insights that can be taken from Lord Diplock's comments in *Catnic* is that there is nothing inherent in a purposive approach that necessarily means that the claims should be interpreted broadly: instead the way that the claims are interpreted depends on the intent of the author (or, more accurately, on how the court construes this authorial intent).

The same is true where the purpose of s 6 is used as a basis to decide patentable subject-matter. That is, it is possible that the approach advocated by the High Court could either limit or expand the scope of patentable subject-matter. In practice, however, this has not been the case. The reason for this is that the High Court construed the purpose of s 6 of the Statute of Monopolies as necessarily leading to a generous interpretation of the patentable subject-matter. This is reflected in the telling comment in *NRDC*, where the High Court positively cited Dixon J's comment in *Maeder v Busch* that 'a widening conception of the notion has been a characteristic of the growth of patent law'.[96] In one sense, this comment is somewhat trite: the fact that patent law has expanded to accommodate new types of technologies is not surprising. If not, the law would have stopped with the steam engine. In another sense, however, and one that is more telling in light of recent critiques about the over-extension of patent law, Dixon J's comments, and the approach of the High Court in *NRDC* more generally, highlight what could be seen as a positive and expansive approach to subject-matter and patentability. It is unlikely, for example, that a court in the 19th century – a period when patents were viewed much more suspiciously – would have construed the 'purpose of s 6' as enthusiastically as the High Court did in *NRDC*. In this sense, the High Court's judgment – much like the emergence of hormone herbicides such as those at the centre of the *NRDC* decision – is symptomatic of the assumptions which underlie the modern approaches to patentability. Both embody the widespread

---

95 *Catnic Components Ltd v Hill and Smith Ltd* [1982] RPC 183.
96 (1938) 59 CLR 684, 706.

cultural appeal that technological control over nature has exerted throughout the modern era and an unwavering confidence in science and technology, which was perhaps at its highest point immediately after World War II.[97]

Another notable aspect of the decision relates to the way in which the court shifted emphasis away from manufacture as 'thing' to the performative nature of invention. Rejecting a narrow interpretation of Morton J's 'rules', which had focussed on the substance or material produced by the claimed process, the court emphasised a different question: is the effect or phenomenon produced by the process an *artificially created* state of affairs?' According to this conception of manufacture, the 'product' resulting from the use of a claimed method or process was only relevant insofar as it enabled the new and useful effect promised by the applicant to be verified. At the same time, the emphasis upon artificial production highlights the performative nature of invention as a mode of employing art and skill to produce a result that is designed by the inventor.[98] Ironically, in order to modernise the law the High Court drew upon and reinstated a definition of 'manufacture' that had dominated patent law in the 18th and 19th centuries, but subsequently fell out of favour.[99] This is an image of invention which focuses on the performative nature of the inventive process. Rather than seeing invention solely as a tangible thing, the performative approach sees invention as a mode of action, as a process of making by art or skill. While, in emphasising the performative nature of invention, the High Court moved away from the idea of invention (or manufacture) as a thing, it was unable to detach itself from the invention in its corporeal form. The reason for this is that the law can only ever deal with the traces or results of the inventive process. As Lloyd-Jacob J said in *Elton and Leda Chemical's Application*, 'there must of necessity be some product whereby the validity of the promise can be tested';[100] that is, there must be 'physical phenomenon in which the effect, be it creation or merely alteration, may be observed'.[101] In this sense, *NRDC* highlights one of the tensions that shapes modern patent law, namely that patent law never operates exclusively with an intangible invention, but with a hybrid that constantly moves between the tangible and intangible.[102]

---

97 Rasmussen, op. cit., p. 314.

98 The original meaning of 'artificial' referred to *making* by art, while 'manufacture' referred to *making* by hand.

99 The origins of the 'artificially created state of affairs' approach can be found in the judgments of Eyre CJ in *Boulton and Watt v Bull* (1795) 2 HBI 463; 126 ER 651, and Abbott CJ in *R v Wheeler* (1819) 2 B and A 345; 106 ER 392, two cases which clearly influenced the court's approach in *NRDC*. In the former case, Eyre CJ, in what the High Court described as a 'powerful judgment', stated that 'manufacture' extends to 'new process in any art producing effects useful to the public' (p. 492, p. 661). In *R v Wheeler*, Abbott CJ said that 'something that can be made by man from the matters subjected to his art and skill, *or at the least some new mode of employing practically his art and skill*', was requisite to satisfy the term 'manufacture' (p. 350, p. 395). The emphasis is the High Court's. Traces of this approach can also be found in Dixon J's judgment in *Maeder v Busch* (1938) 59 CLR 684, where he said 'to be patentable an invention must relate to an art.'

100 [1957] RPC 267, 269.

101 This calls to mind Hacking's justification for the existence of electrons, 'as far as I'm concerned, if you can spray them then they are real'. I Hacking, *Representing and Intervening: Introductory Topics in the Philosophy of Science*, Cambridge University Press, New York, 1983, p. 23.

102 This has become clear in subsequent decisions which have attempted to apply *NRDC*. As the Full Federal Court said in *Grant v Commissioner of Patents* (2006) 234 ALR 230, 237, the question to be asked is: 'Does

92   LANDMARKS IN AUSTRALIAN IP LAW

While the members of the High Court highlighted the need to focus on the policy behind the Statute of Monopolies, they did not give any sustained consideration to the image of the invention they were operating with. Instead, the problematic and volatile idea of invention was taken as an unstated given that could be distilled from the term 'manufacture'.[103] One of the problems with *NRDC* is that it is based on a particular image of invention that is not clearly articulated and certainly not subject to much reflection. Although the High Court jettisoned the distinction between discovery and invention on the basis that it was problematic, it supplanted this bifurcation with an equally problematic distinction between the natural and the artificial. Insofar as *NRDC* replaced one seemingly intractable conceptual bifurcation with another, it left unanswered as many questions as it answered.

Agricultural and horticultural processes

The third and final objection raised by the Commissioner was that the claimed herbicidal methods were not patentable on the basis that 'agricultural or horticultural processes are, by reason of their nature, outside the limits of patentable inventions.'[104] The Commissioner's objection reflected the then-existing Patent Office practice of denying that any agricultural or horticultural process could be a 'manner of manufacture'.

While *NRDC* is often presented as marking an important turning point in the patentability of horticultural and agricultural inventions in Australia, the High Court did not directly address the standing of agricultural and horticultural inventions. Instead, it sidestepped the issue by characterising NRDC's invention as a chemical invention and not, as the Commissioner had suggested, an agricultural invention. As the court said:

> We are here concerned with a process producing its effect by means of a chemical reaction, and the ultimate weed-free, or comparatively weed-free condition of the crop-bearing land is properly described as produced by the process. The fact that the relevance of the process is to agricultural or horticultural enterprises does not in itself supply or suggest any consideration not already covered which should weigh against the conclusion that the process is a patentable invention.[105]

The strongest criticism made by the court of the proposition that agricultural or horticultural processes were not patentable inventions was that it was

> a generalization not supported by the reasons leading to the conclusions in the particular instances from which the generalization is drawn. If it means that there is some

---

the invention produce any artificial state of affairs, in the sense of a concrete, tangible, physical or observable effect.'

103 This was highlighted in the comment made by the court that 'all that is nowadays understood by [invention] as used in patent law is comprehended in "new manufactures"': (1959) 102 CLR 252, 269; 1A IPR 63, 70.

104 (1959) 102 CLR 252, 277; 1A IPR 63, 75.

105 ibid., p. 279; 1A IPR 63, 77.

consideration wrapped up in the label 'agricultural or horticultural' which necessarily takes a process outside the area of patentability even though it is a novel process and of sufficient inventiveness, the consideration is not easy to identify. There seems to be here a classic illustration of thinking in terms of the everyday concept of manufacture instead of following the lines along which, over a long period, the courts have given effect to the real purpose and operation of s 6 of the Statute of Monopolies.[106]

While these comments cast doubt over the Commissioner's third objection, there are other remarks in the decision which support the sentiment, if not the letter, of that objection. This is reflected in the fact that the High Court cast doubts over both the novelty of breeding methods and also over whether the products of those processes were patentable.[107] In particular, the court commented that it 'may be conceded . . . that if there were nothing that could properly be called a "product" of the process, even an ingenious new departure would be outside the limits of patentability.'[108] In this sense, NRDC reflects an antiquated worldview which sees plant and animal breeding, along with agricultural and horticultural practices more generally, as husbandry practices, rather than as technical or scientific practices deserving of patent protection.

In considering, albeit briefly, the standing of agricultural and horticultural inventions, the court also provided some insights into what it meant by artificiality and, hence, manufacture and invention. This is reflected in the court's comments upon the decisions in *Lenard's Application*[109] (which concerned a method of pruning to reduce mortality from disease in clove trees) and *NV Philips' Gloeilampenfabrieken's Application*[110] (which claimed a method for producing a new form of poinsettia). In both cases, the applications were rejected. Without expressing a view on the validity of those decisions, the court observed that 'both seem to depend on the view that the process in question was only one for altering the conditions of growth, so that the contemplated end result would not be a result of the process but would be "the inevitable result of that which is inherent in the plant".'[111] Later the court agreed with Morton J in *RHF's Application* that 'fruit and other growing crops, although the assistance of man may be invoked for their planting and cultivation, do not result from a process which is a "manner of manufacture".'[112] As the court added, 'however advantageously man may alter the conditions of growth, the fruit is still not produced by his action.'[113]

In this regard, the court made it clear that human intervention (or labour) was not sufficient in itself to produce a patentable invention. Instead, what was

---

106 ibid., pp. 278–9; 1A IPR 63, 76.
107 For instance, the court observed that 'it must often happen in a sphere of endeavour as old as that of primary production that a newly-devised procedure amounts to nothing more than an analogous application of age-old techniques; and where that is the case, want of novelty is a fatal objection to a patent': ibid., p. 278; 1A IPR 63, 76.
108 (1959) 102 CLR 252, 278; 1 A IPR 63, 76.
109 (1954) 71 RPC 190.
110 (1954) 71 RPC 192.
111 (1959) 102 CLR 252, 279 (citing *N v Philips*, p. 194).
112 (1944) 61 RPC 49.
113 (1959) 102 CLR 252, 278; 1A IPR 63, 76.

94   LANDMARKS IN AUSTRALIAN IP LAW

needed was that the final product was a direct product of the breeder's actions, rather than the 'inevitable result of processes inherent in the plant'. Only when this could be shown, only when the breeder was able to show that they had taken control of nature and, to borrow Roger Bacon's phrase, 'used it as an instrument', could the outcome be seen as being 'artificially created' and thus potentially patentable. Rather than intervention, the quality of 'manufacture' that was emphasised was the control or exploitation of the laws and phenomena of nature with deliberate design to produce a contemplated result.[114] Only then could it be said that the breeder has produced an 'artificially created state of affairs'.

Conclusion

NRDC is a difficult decision. In part this can be attributed to the fact that the court was dealing with a number of complex issues. These difficulties were exacerbated by the fact that the language and the concepts used were not as clear as they might have been. The problems are further compounded by the fact that the judgment is a classic common law decision which reflects the best and the worst of the 'strict and complete legalism' championed by Dixon CJ.[115]

The post-NRDC period has witnessed a further expansion of the field of patentable subject-matter, including fields which previously were unpatentable, such as methods of medical treatment.[116] This may simply be the result of the inevitable widening of the concept of 'manner of manufacture' of which Dixon J spoke in *Maeder v Busch*. There can be no doubt, however, that NRDC – at any rate, the way in which it has been applied – has facilitated this trend.[117] To return to a point raised earlier, the starting premise of many post-NRDC decisions seems to be that the encouragement of any new form of technology prima facie accords with the purpose of s 6 (however that may be defined). The problem (insofar as one arises) is how to distinguish or qualify those decisions which are seen to stand in the way of the patentability of the particular invention-at-hand. In NRDC, the court was able to do so largely without doing violence to established authorities; at all stages, the court was able to support its conclusion with existing case law. It is far from clear, however, how successful subsequent decisions have been in doing so. Armed with a vaguely defined 'text and purpose' of the Statute of Monopolies, judges less inclined to adhere to the 'strict

---

114 The same logic underlies the traditional principle that scientific principles or laws of nature per se are unpatentable.
115 *Swearing in of Sir Owen Dixon as Chief Justice* (1952) 85 CLR xi, xiv.
116 Remarkably, unlike most other jurisdictions, no superior Australian court has yet to decide the question of whether biotechnological inventions are patentable, not to mention plants and animals. In *Kiren-Amgen Inc v Board of Regents of University of Washington* (1995) 33 IPR 557, the Deputy Commissioner of Patents accepted that a claim to an isolated and purified DNA sequence was a manner of manufacture; however the point was not directly argued.
117 The decision of the Full Federal Court in *Grant v Commissioner of Patents* (2006) 69 IPR 221 is an exception to the general trend towards expansion of the boundaries of patentable subject-matter, if only because it is one of the few decisions to have relied upon NRDC to reject an application.

NRDC v COMMISSIONER OF PATENTS   95

'legalism' espoused by Dixon CJ have been able, in classic common law fashion, to manoeuvre around decisions thought to limit the patentability of particular types of subject-matter.[118]

In this respect, the effect that *NRDC* has had upon the scope of patentable subject-matter can be likened to the effect which the US Supreme Court's decision in *Diamond v Chakrabarty*[119] has had upon patentable subject-matter in the US. More particularly, *NRDC* has transferred what Rebecca Eisenberg has described as 'the burden of inertia' onto those opposing patent protection for new fields of technology to approach parliament, rather than the courts.[120] While it is accepted that not every new technology is embraced by the concept of 'manner of manufacture', there has been a subtle shift in responsibility for patrolling the boundary between patentable and unpatentable subject-matter. Historically, this was a role performed by the courts. Post-*NRDC*, this burden has fallen squarely on the shoulders of parliament. If parliament disapproves of the expansion of patentable subject-matter presided over by the courts, they are free to change the law.[121] That they have not seen fit to do so is interpreted by the courts as tacit approval of their decisions.

Despite these similarities, *NRDC* remains peculiarly Australian. *NRDC* is often presented as marking a critical juncture in Australian patent law, as heralding the emergence of a truly modern patent system. A closer reading of the case, however, shows that it reveals many of the hallmarks of pre-modern patent law.[122] Moreover, many of the supposed novelties of the decision – such as the plea to look to the purpose of s 6, as well as the particular view that the court took of vendible product – are based on earlier decisions. Even those aspects of the decision which are not usually noted, such as the change in the way the invention was viewed, were not new: instead, they merely reinstated an earlier way of thinking about the invention. The conflation of subject-matter with novelty and inventive step, which occurs constantly throughout the judgment, is also a throw back to pre-modern patent law, one that Australian patent law has yet to discard. While the judgment of the High Court in *NRDC* is nearly 50 years old,

---

118 See, for example, Barwick CJ's decision in *Joos v Commissioner of Patents* (1972) 126 CLR 611, where in dealing with the examiner's objection that methods of surgery and treating the human body were not patentable because, following *NRDC*, 'the whole subject is conceived as *essentially* non-economic', Barwick CJ said: 'the national economic interest in the product of good surgery – and therefore the advancement of its techniques – if in no other respect than the repair and rehabilitation of the members of the work force . . . may be regarded as sufficiently proximate . . . as to be capable of satisfying the economic element of an invention.' Whether or not this answers the way in which the High Court put the objection in *NRDC* – namely, that the *whole* subject is *essentially* non-economic – may well be questioned.
119 (1980) 447 US 303.
120 R Eisenberg, 'The Story of *Diamond v Chakrabarty*: Technological Change and the Subject Matter Boundaries of the Patent System' in J Ginsburg and R Cooper-Dreyfuss (eds.), *Intellectual Property Stories*, Foundation Press, New York, 2006.
121 In *Anaesthetic Supplies Pty Ltd v Rescare Ltd* (1994) 122 ALR 141, the fact that in drafting the 1990 Act parliament had chosen not to exclude methods of medical treatment from the field of patentable subject-matter was interpreted as providing implied support for the Patent Office practice of granting patents for methods of medical treatment following Barwick CJ's decision in *Joos v Commissioner of Patents* (1972) 126 CLR 611.
122 On this see B Sherman and L Bently, *The Making of Modern Intellectual Property Law*, Cambridge University Press, Cambridge,1999, pp. 2–4

it still represents many important traits of contemporary law. This is not, however, a modern, forward-looking legal regime. Rather, the decision highlights the pre-modern and backward-looking nature of Australian patent law. To the extent that *NRDC* highlights and reflects the pre-modern nature of Australian patent law, it acts as a continuing reminder of the fact that 'we have never been modern'.[123]

123 B Latour, *We Have Never Been Modern*, Harvard University Press, Cambridge, MA, 1993.

6

Of vice-chancellors and authors: *UNSW v Moorhouse*

Sam Ricketson and David Catterns

Introduction

More than 30 years after the High Court case bearing his name as respondent, the author Frank Moorhouse is still reported as having a financially precarious existence, dependent on his royalties and the occasional literary prize.[1] *UNSW v Moorhouse*,[2] however, remains the leading Australian authority dealing with the liability of intermediaries for copyright infringement. It is also a striking example of copyright law dealing with the effects of a new technology – photocopying – and is a curtain-raiser for current debates about uses of the internet and the implications of online communications. Other *Leitmotiven* are the collectivisation of authors and copyright owners in the print environment and the adoption of elaborate statutory licences as a solution to the issues of control and remuneration.

Some background – Australia in the 1960s

Both the present authors began their university studies in the mid-to-late 1960s. For the most part, this was still the age of notepads with real paper, fountain pens and ball points, typewriters, carbon paper, and roneoed notes produced by typing onto wax masters that could be printed off in multiple copies. The photocopier machine was certainly there, but only just,[3] and was an exciting innovation to

---

1 R Gulliatt, 'His Dark Material', *Weekend Australian Magazine*, 1–2 December 2007, pp. 24–8.
2 *University of New South Wales v Moorhouse* (1975) 133 CLR 1.
3 The first Xerox photocopier was produced by the Haloid Company, later the Xerox Corporation, in 1950, with the first commercial photocopier, the Xerox 914, being produced from 1959: see further B Atkinson,

98   LANDMARKS IN AUSTRALIAN IP LAW

be found in the basements of university libraries and in departmental offices, in the form of large clunky machines that produced facsimiles copies on curious-smelling paper. Students, of course, are always swift to adopt new technologies, and the potential of the new machines was rapidly realised: lecture notes from the better note-takers (or attendees) could be readily reproduced, and no longer was it necessary to sit in libraries and make laborious handwritten notes of journal articles and books – key extracts could be easily copied and stored for later study and reflection.

Many of these uses, of course, were not infringements of anyone's copyright – it was either licensed or fell within the fair dealing defence for private study and research that had been included in s 40 of the recently enacted *Copyright Act 1968*. But little, if any, control was actually exercised over the use of these machines by the institutions concerned, raising the prospect that infringing uses were also occurring, and that the persons directly affected were authors and publishers, whose properties were being freely used without compensation. There is a story that the poet Judith Wright, at a literary conference, held up her tax returns over a number of years to show a steady reduction in her royalty income, which she directly attributed to the advent of the photocopier (rapidly making its presence felt in universities, schools and public libraries). Poems, like short stories, were peculiarly vulnerable to the ravages of facsimile copying, even though it is unlikely that any fair dealing defence was applicable where the whole of the work was taken. But while students, such as ourselves, were the immediate beneficiaries of this new technology, the institutions at which we were enrolled – and educational institutions at all levels – were becoming keenly aware of the possibilities offered for the copying and dissemination of teaching materials. Herein lay the real threat and challenge to copyright owners, as these kinds of new educational uses had never previously been in issue.[4]

This was a vibrant time in Australian society: it was the period of the Vietnam War, intense public debates over conscription, and the emergence of a new and robust, often intemperate, cultural awareness that was reflected in young writers such as Frank Moorhouse, Jack Hibberd, John Romeril, David Williamson and others. It was also a period of transition, quite lengthy as it turned out, from a long-reigning Liberal–Country Party coalition government to a more progressive and nationalistic reforming Whitlam Labor Party. A reflection of these changes is to be found in the fact that a collection of Frank Moorhouse's short stories, *The Americans, Baby*, was set as a prescribed text for one course at the University of New South Wales (Honours Political Science IV) and was recommended reading in another (Political Science I). That such a collection

---

The True History of Copyright: The Australian Experience 1905–2005, Sydney University Press, 2007, Sydney, p. 333.

4 Thus, Atkinson, op. cit., p. 334, notes that in 1969 the University of Sydney reported that in 1968 its machines had produced 873 780 copies while the University of New South Wales reported that students and staff made 325 000 copies in a 21-week period in 1969.

of stories, with its interconnected themes of sexual freedom and exploration, rural–city divide, anti-Americanism and political dissent, was now the object of university study was significant. Of more significance, though, was the fact that such a collection had been published by a mainstream publisher, Angus & Robertson, as part of a longstanding tradition of fostering and encouraging Australian writing, even when this pushed the boundaries of acceptable social and political mores.

But of even greater consequence, perhaps, was the fact that authors and publishers were now becoming more organised, with the formation of the Australian Copyright Council (ACC) in 1968 under the formidable leadership of Gus O'Donnell, a former PNG district official and a published author of various novels.[5] This new 'peak' body had come rapidly into conflict with another more venerable 'peak' body, the Australian Vice-Chancellors Committee (AVCC),[6] representing the rapidly burgeoning university sector which was the recipient of vast injections of central-government funding during the late Coalition period (beginning with Menzies) and culminating with the abolition of university fees by the Whitlam Government in 1973. The AVCC, too, had robust and determined leadership, including from Sir Bruce Williams of the University of Sydney (1972–74) and Sir David Derham of the University of Melbourne (1975–76). Both were reluctant to acknowledge that any infringements of copyright might be occurring on university premises. As Hutley JA discreetly expresses in the first instance decision in the *Moorhouse* case[7] between these two bodies, 'there had been disputes ever since the *Copyright Act 1968* with respect to the proper construction of that Act in relation to Universities.'

Setting up a test case

While O'Donnell was the chief public propagandist for copyright owners, the legal legwork was being done by two young lawyers, David Catterns and Peter Banki, who were employed by the ACC as legal officers. There is nothing quite like the initiation of legal proceedings to instigate a conversation between warring parties, and both Banki and Catterns spent a great deal of time researching the potential liabilities of universities for copyright infringement. The issues were far from simple: many of the uses occurring were undoubtedly covered by one of the special defences in the *Copyright Act 1968*, such as fair dealing for

---

5 See the biography of Gus O'Donnell on the website of the Australian Copyright Council, available at http://www.copyright.org.au/policy-research/essayprize/gusodonnell. O'Donnell is described by one commentator as 'a man of bomb-proof self-righteousness in the cause of authors': Atkinson, op. cit., p. 336. See also the history of the Copyright Agency Ltd by Peter Meredith: *Realising the Vision: A History of the Copyright Agency Limited*, 1974–2004, chap. 1, available at http://www.copyright.com.au/history_of_cal.htm.
6 Founded in 1920 with only six university members, the number of which had increased significantly by the early 1970s with the establishment of second, third and even fourth and fifth universities in the various states and the ACT. The body was renamed 'Universities Australia' in May 2007. See further http://www.universitiesaustralia.edu.au/content.asp?page = /about/index.htm.
7 *Moorhouse and Angus & Robertson (Publishers) Pty Ltd v University of New South Wales* (1974) 3 ALR 1, 4.

100   LANDMARKS IN AUSTRALIAN IP LAW

private study and research under s 40, or by the library copying provisions under ss 49 and 50. The status of much copying, however, was uncertain, particularly where universities themselves were preparing and distributing large quantities of photocopied materials. And the universities were reluctant to acknowledge that they might be infringing copyright in any way or allowing this to occur through their provision of photocopiers for student use.

Of these bodies, it appeared that UNSW had been the most abrupt and dismissive in its treatment of approaches from the ACC, in particular when it sought statistics on photocopying. Thus, a request from the ACC for permission to station an observer in the photocopying area had received the following reply from the Vice-Chancellor, Professor Rupert Myers: 'The University is of the view that the requirements of the law of copyright are being observed and declines to consent to your request'.[8] The indications were that the university was paying little, if any, attention to what was happening on its premises, and the university's internal memoranda and directives to staff were misinformed, even misleading, on the effect of key provisions of the Act and/or difficult to apply in specific circumstances. One particular instance was a notice that was attached to the library photocopying machines that referred only to s 49 of the *Copyright Act 1968*, which dealt only with what librarians could do and was quite irrelevant in the case of an individual using the machine. Supervision of the machines and their use also appeared to have been superficial at the best, with no instance of a breach of copyright being reported in the space of four years. The state of mind of the librarian on the issue of possible copyright infringements was effectively one of indifference to directives from higher up within the university on these matters, reflecting a determination 'that photocopying facilities without restriction would be available to users of the library irrespective of whatever safeguards his superiors might prescribe or the University's legal advisers might suggest.'[9] At levels higher up, the 'less the University knew about the real facts and the law, the easier it would be to maintain its propaganda.'[10] The frustration on the part of copyright owners was clear: it must have been a little like David being faced with the huge and immovable figure of Goliath. Attempts at polite dialogue had failed and legal proceedings appeared to be the only way forward.

While UNSW offered the most tempting target for a test case, it seems that this was in the nature of a shot across the bows in that the above facts could not really raise the wider issue of whether what the universities themselves were doing required permission from copyright owners. The target provided by UNSW

---

8 Quoted in ibid., p. 12 (Hutley JA).
9 ibid., pp. 13–14. In fact, Hutley JA did not accept the evidence of the librarian, Allan Horton, that he was unaware of the fact that the notices on the machines did not comply with the *Copyright Act* and that he had been part of a 'campaign to protect what he regarded as the interests of users of the library by concealing what has been going on.' It should be noted that Horton was an extremely distinguished member of the librarians' profession, with notable service to Australian libraries and archives, and a subsequent member of the Copyright Tribunal. For tributes concerning his role as librarian see the *Australian Library Journal* at http://www.alia.org/publishing/alj/54.2/full.text/allan.horton.html.
10 (1974) 3 ALR 1, 13–14.

was therefore an extremely limited one and care was needed to ensure that the parameters were set correctly. Thus:

- The author and copyright owner (Moorhouse) was not informed in advance, so as to remove the possible argument that the copying was licensed by him. There was also no advance knowledge on the part of the publisher, Angus & Robinson, which held the licence to publish the work. Both, however, consented to the bringing of the action after the copying had occurred.

- The person (Paul Brennan) who did the actual copying was an outsider: in particular, he was not a student (who might otherwise have had available the defence under s 40, particularly if enrolled in one of the courses for which the Moorhouse stories were prescribed). Nor could it be said that he was making the copies by virtue of the library copying provisions of the Act.

- Brennan made two copies of one of the stories (10 pages in all), so as to fall outside the fair dealing provisions in any event.

It is clear that all parties accepted that this was a test case and that 'this was done deliberately at the behest of the Australian Copyright Council to test the vigilance of the defendant and show that its supervision was deficient'. The claim of authorisation, however, was an imaginative one, given that prior authorities had been primarily concerned with performing rights and the role of owners of public entertainment venues. On the other hand, extension of these principles into the new hard copy environment provided by the advent of the photocopying machine was logical, and the proceeding had the effect of making the university sector (and educationalists generally) suddenly aware that they were no longer operating in a copyright-free environment. While they themselves might not be making the infringing copies in the present case, their slackness in supervision of machines under their control put them in the same position as the committee of the leagues club offering live performances of music.[11] The claim for authorisation of infringement of copyright by the UNSW, although a concept long embedded in the Act, provided a more promising tool by which to impose liability than, for example, a claim of liability based on principles of joint tortfeasorship, where it would have been necessary to establish some kind of common design between the university and the users of their photocopying machines. Furthermore, it was obvious that copyright owners could not hope to deal with individual students: the authorisation doctrine therefore offered a way to sheet responsibility home to the university, with a view to convincing it to enter into blanket licensing arrangements of the type offered by performing right societies such as the Australasian Performing Right Society (APRA) for the performance of musical works.

---

11 As, for example, in *Australasian Performing Right Association Ltd v Canterbury-Bankstown League Club Ltd* [1964–5] NSWR 138.

Public policy issues

Given its test case character, there were various interesting preliminary legal issues raised by the action, not the least the scope of any possible declaratory relief (see further below). One preliminary issue worthy of note, however, as it does not emerge in the subsequent High Court appeal, concerned the non-admission by the defendant of the subsistence of copyright, on the basis that the Moorhouse book was contrary to public policy and therefore not entitled to copyright protection. While Moorhouse's stories were considerably more explicit on matters of sexuality and sexual morality[12] than the early 20th-century novels of Elinor Glyn[13] or the 19th-century poems of Robert Southey,[14] such an argument 'came strangely from a University in which it is recommended reading for first year students and is available in the library without restriction'.[15] While it is unlikely that counsel for the UNSW[16] (as well as Hutley JA) were being swept along by the increasing sexual liberalism of the late 1960s and early 1970s, the burden was on the university to make good such a claim and it is refreshing to read that it was not seriously pursued. As Hutley JA said:

> The concept of public policy is obscure and counsel for the University did not assist the Court by argument. As the burden of proof on this contention is on it, I reject it. Whether public policy can take away copyright, as distinct from deriving the writer of the assistance of the Court to enforce it, requires consideration but it does not arise here.[17]

Moorhouse's authorial status (and entitlement to claim copyright protection) was therefore endorsed by the court, and posterity was denied the opportunity of extended argument and judicial consideration of the role of public policy in copyright law.[18]

The scope of possible relief

It was clear that the test case character of the proceeding raised real issues as to the kind of relief being sought. Compensation was hardly a realistic concern, and the plaintiff therefore sought both declaratory and injunctive relief against UNSW. Thus, declarations were sought in both specific and more general forms that the university had infringed their copyright (through authorising Brennan to make the infringing copies) and that by providing any coin-operated photostating machines in its library for use by users of the library, the university

---

12 Consider, in particular, the last story in the volume, 'The Letters to Twiggy'.
13 *Glyn v Weston Feature Film Co* [1916] 1 Ch 261.
14 *Southey v Sherwood* (1817) 2 Mer 435, 35 ER 1006.
15 (1974) 3 ALR 1, 4 (Hutley JA).
16 CJ Bannon QC and JM Spender (GG Masterman QC and RS Hulme appeared for the plaintiffs).
17 (1974) 3 ALR 1, 4.
18 Note however that the Full Court of the Federal Court has recently revisited these issues in the context of X-rated films: see *Venus Adult Shops Pty Ltd v Fraserside Holdings Ltd* [2006] FCAFC 188.

had authorised, within the meaning of s 36 of the Act, any infringement of the respondent's copyright which might occur as a result of the use by such a user of said machines.[19]

The odd aspect of Hutley JA's judgment is that while he was prepared to find that Brennan had infringed the plaintiff's copyright by making the photocopies, this particular infringement, in his view, had not been authorised by UNSW in that there was no proof he was induced to do what he had done by reason of any act or omission of the university, including the 'atmosphere of disregard for authors' rights which the University has encouraged'.[20] Logically, this was correct; Brennan was clearly a knowing infringer whose actions were prompted by those outside UNSW, that is, the ACC. But given the stricture of his findings against the university – their failure to supervise and inform users of the relevant copyright provisions – did this leave the university off the hook?

Hutley JA thought not. He viewed this as an instance of where the court's jurisdiction to make declarations might be usefully deployed, particularly where the plaintiffs had a real interest in the conditions under which UNSW permitted use of its photocopying machines in relation to works subject to copyright, and where the university itself had an interest for the benefit of its students to 'encourage the use of photocopying machines with a minimum of restriction'.[21] Oddly enough, the university was reluctant to avail itself of this opportunity to clarify its position and to identify what steps it might take in future to avoid such cases arising by framing an appropriate declaratory order – an attitude Hutley JA thought to be 'somewhat strange for a public body'. This meant that he was unable to formulate declaratory orders in a more general form that might henceforth assist both parties in understanding what they may or may not do in the future. Perhaps this circumstance simply reflected the large distance between the parties – reconciliation and cooperation were not in the air at this stage. Nonetheless, Hutley JA felt able to make a more limited declaration tied to the particular work of the plaintiff and the possibility that breaches of this copyright might have occurred during the relevant period of time:

> I therefore declare that between the date when the subject book was entered in the defendant's library and the hearing the University has authorized such breaches of copyright as have occurred by the photocopying of the whole or part of the library copy of *The Americans, Baby* by the use of the photocopying machines where such photocopying was not a fair dealing within the terms of s 40 of the *Copyright Act 1968* and where such breaches were in any way due to reliance upon any library guides issued by the defendant in the years 1970, 1971, 1972 and 1973 or the notices appearing upon the self-service photocopying machines in the said library or by the lack of supervision of the use of such machines or any combination thereof.[22]

---

19 See the description in (1975) 133 CLR 1, 9 (Gibbs CJ).
20 (1974) 3 ALR 1, 15 (Hutley JA).
21 ibid.
22 ibid., p. 17.

This turned out to be the issue over which Hutley JA was reversed by the High Court when the case went on appeal. While, as will be seen, the judge's explication of the principles governing authorisation were essentially upheld by the High Court (which then reached a different conclusion in their application to the facts of the case), one is left with the feeling that he was strongly impressed by the justice of the plaintiff's case and, in particular, by the evidence concerning the university's disregard of what was going on in its library. In short, he did not want to send the plaintiff away empty-handed. Thus, the plaintiff had 'substantially succeeded', but had lost on the issue as to whether the defendant authorised the specific breach of copyright by Brennan. Nonetheless, this had useful costs implications for the plaintiff to whom he awarded the whole costs, other than their costs of the amended and re-amended statements of claim. As to the latter, the defendant's costs of pleading to the amended and re-amended statements of claim were ordered to be paid by the plaintiff.

The mounting of an appeal

The decision of Hutley JA was clearly unsettling to UNSW as it began to appreciate its broader significance. While, at one level, its practical effect was narrow, and steps to avoid future infringements could be readily taken – for example, by placing prominent and correctly drawn copyright notices on the machines, adopting and publicising appropriate copyright policies, arranging for more vigilant supervision of the machines and so on – a warning bell had been sounded. Universities could no longer proceed on the unarticulated assumption that they were either in a copyright-free environment or that their broader educational and public purposes somehow removed them from potential liability. The mouse had roared, and the fact that its bite had proved miniscule did not remove the wider doubts that now arose: what else might universities be doing, no doubt for the broader public good, that might bring them within the scope of copyright owners' claims? Furthermore, the findings of Hutley JA with respect to senior and highly respected university officers, were both forthright and extremely damaging; he simply did not accept the evidence of Horton, the librarian, whom he found to have been pursuing a campaign to ensure that photocopying machines were available to users of the library 'irrespective of whatever safeguards his superiors might prescribe or the Universities' legal advisers might suggest', while Myers, the Vice-Chancellor and other senior officers, were, at best, wilfully blind as to what was actually occurring. Universities are respected institutions within society, and such findings no doubt caused some anguish and hurt to educators who believed in the higher public benefits of their vocation. On the other hand, authors and copyright owners, headed by the redoubtable O'Donnell, now had the satisfaction, after years of fruitless interchanges with vice-chancellors, of knowing that a court had taken their concerns seriously and these had not been rejected as trivial or unimportant.

An appeal was therefore inevitable, and was taken directly to the High Court. No cross-appeal was lodged within the time allowed by the rules[23] (this subsequently had serious costs consequences for the respondent), but leave was granted in the course of argument. This was on the ground that Hutley JA should have found that the breach found to have been committed by Brennan was authorised by the university, and on the further ground that the declaration should have been made in a more general form.

Having the matter heard by the High Court was not free of its own particular difficulties. Judges historically have felt free, perhaps even obligated, to play their part in the governance of public institutions such as universities. Of the members of the High Court at that time, Sir Garfield Barwick was Chancellor of Macquarie University,[24] Sir Douglas Menzies was Chancellor of Monash University,[25] and Sir Anthony Mason was Pro-Vice Chancellor of the Australian National University.[26] This issue was raised by counsel for Moorhouse and these judges did not sit on the appeal, leaving only three with no current university affiliations: Sir Edward McTiernan as Acting Chief Justice, Sir Harry Gibbs and Sir Kenneth Jacobs.

The High Court decision

The final result was something of a pyrrhic victory for the respondents: while they succeeded on the first ground of their cross-appeal, the declaration made by Hutley JA was held to be too wide and hypothetical in character. Accordingly, all that could now be the subject of declaratory relief was that the university had authorised the infringement by Brennan, even though the latter not been induced to do so by anything that the university had said, done or failed to do (matters which, to Hutley JA, were critical to his finding that no act of authorisation had occurred).

So far as the substantive issue of law is concerned, it can hardly be doubted that *UNSW v Moorhouse* remains the ultimate appellate decision dealing with the doctrine and scope of authorisation, a case that inevitably finds its place in every submission to court that is made today. Yet the decision does not involve any radical departure from principles established in the previous case law, namely that authorisation goes beyond any limitations that might be imposed by concepts of agency and actual or deemed authority; that it encompasses the giving of both direct and indirect or implicit permission, being summed up in the phrase 'sanction, approve, countenance'; that it requires some ability to control or prevent the infringing act; and that the presence of knowledge or recklessness on

---

23 The delay may have been due to lack of funding, and both counsel who ultimately appeared on behalf of the respondents (Masterman QC and Hulme) acted *pro bono*.
24 Barwick was the first Chancellor of that university, serving from 1967 to 1978: see http://www.lib.mq.edu.au/exhibitions/2006/#barwick.
25 Menzies was Chancellor of Monash from 1968 to 1974, dying shortly after the hearing, in any event.
26 The other member of the High Court, Sir Ninian Stephen, also had longstanding connections with the University of Melbourne.

106   LANDMARKS IN AUSTRALIAN IP LAW

the part of the alleged authoriser must be shown. All that was novel was that the concept of authorisation was now untethered from its historic link with the public performing right and the activities of promoters and venue operators, and was brought into play in the environment of educational institutions. The principles, however, were applicable across the board, as has been demonstrated by their more recent deployment in the online environment.

For both sides, moreover, the decision was of limited immediate legal value. For the universities, it did nothing to remove the stain of the factual findings against its officers, although the language of liability was somewhat more muted: 'I hold that the University did not take measures reasonably sufficient for the purpose of preventing infringements taking place.'[27]

The errors and omissions of its officers had therefore led UNSW to authorise Brennan's infringement of copyright and the university had the necessary mental element for this, even if it had no actual knowledge at the time of what Brennan was doing. On the other hand, the factual matrix of this finding was extremely narrow: all the university had to do was to sharpen its communication of copyright information to library users and to improve its internal procedures and supervision practices. No Pandora's box of potential liability in other areas of activities was opened up. In particular, the vexed question of the university's own photocopying practices was entirely untouched by the court's decision. As Jacobs J described it:

> This case was frequently described by counsel for the first-named respondent as a test case but it could only be so described in relation to the circumstances proved in evidence. If it was intended that in some way to be a test case then it is unfortunate that the occasion of testing was one where this University had inadvertently failed to qualify in any material way the invitation which it extended to make use of the photocopying machines to copy material in the University library.[28]

There was also an unexpected, and damaging, financial consequence in the final orders made by the court for the respondents/cross-appellants. The appellant (the University) won its appeal in relation to the declaration made by the Supreme Court of New South Wales, with the result that it had the costs of the appeal. While the respondent/cross-appellant won its cross-appeal, no order for costs was made on the basis that leave was only sought for this during the hearing itself and, in any event, the 'respondents' success is so limited that it should not carry costs'.[29] This left the respondents/cross-appellants with a significant costs bill. Some of this was recovered under the Suitor's Fund.

---

27 (1975) 133 CLR 1, 18 (Gibbs J).
28 ibid., p. 23 (Jacobs J). In the same way, a year later the Franki Committee said: '[I]t is difficult to see that this case provides an authority for any proposition other than that the placing of coin-operated self-service machines in a library without adequate notices at least drawing users' attention to relevant provisions of the *Copyright Act* constitutes an authorisation within section 36.' *Report of the Copyright Law Committee on Reprographic Reproduction* (Franki Committee), AGPS, Canberra, October 1976, p. 22.
29 (1975) 133 CLR 1, 18 (Gibbs J).

The aftermath of the case

If the practical legal effect of the High Court's decision in *Moorhouse* was limited to a narrow and specific set of facts, its symbolic and political value was undoubtedly far greater. For the first time, there was judicial acknowledgment of the legitimate claims of authors and copyright owners against the interests of educationalists, and a specific declaration that the particular university had hardly shown good faith or observed proper procedures in its relations with the ACC. Things, however, were moving on other fronts, and these were ultimately to prove more successful (at least from the perspective of authors and copyright owners).

Most closely linked to the *Moorhouse* decision was the incorporation of a not-for-profit company, the Copyright Agency Limited (CAL) in May 1974, the month that Hutley JA handed down the decision at first instance. This was intended to provide the collective organisation that would be required to collect the fees that might now be anticipated, and had a board membership that was identical to that of the ACC, with Gus O'Donnell as chair.[30] As events were to prove, CAL's time had not yet come and it was not to be until the mid-1980s that it was to begin to achieve the stream of revenue payments from universities and educational institutions that was seen by visionaries such as O'Donnell as the just outcome of the struggle for authors' rights. And, as CAL's history was to show, these results were only to be achieved after legislative change, proceedings before the Copyright Tribunal, the adoption of a more businesslike approach and, above all, a close collaboration with the publishers.[31] Movement towards voluntary licensing arrangements with the universities and other educational institutions (the preferred option of CAL and O'Donnell) was painfully slow and was to be superseded by statutory schemes (see below). While *Moorhouse* was a shot across the bows, universities were still somewhat grudging in facing up to their wider responsibility. Nonetheless, as Peter Banki said: 'After that they took a bit more notice of us, because they knew they were responsible.'[32]

On 20 June 1974, following Hutley JA's decision and as a result of the ACC's lobbying, of which *Moorhouse* was part, the then Attorney-General, Sen the Hon Lionel Murphy QC, appointed an expert committee under the chairmanship of Justice RJ Franki with the following terms of reference:

> To consider the question of the reprographic reproduction of works protected by copyright in Australia and to recommend any alteration to the Australian copyright law and any other measures the Committee may consider necessary to offer a proper balance of interest between owners of copyright and the users of copyright material in respect of

---

30 The members were Keith Kersey of the Musicians' Union, Peter Holderness of the Institute of Australian Photography, George Ferguson of the Australian Book Publishers Association and David Kinden of the Australian Institute of Architects. O'Donnell at this time was also chair of the Australian Society of Authors: Meredith, op. cit.
31 Differences with publishers led to a damaging and sad split with authors, and the ultimate exclusion of O'Donnell from the organisation he had founded: Meredith, op. cit., chap. 3 ('A House Divided').
32 ibid.

108   LANDMARKS IN AUSTRALIAN IP LAW

reprographic reproduction. The term 'reprographic reproduction' includes any system or technique by which facsimile reproductions are made in any size or form.

It is clear that pressure from copyright owners' interests, including CAL, had brought this about and this was, in any event, an Australian government that was far more overtly committed to the arts than any of its predecessors. The inquiry was able to range far more widely over the issue of photocopying and its implications for fair dealing, educational and library uses, but it also had a downside so far as copyright owners were concerned. Their overriding goal, at least in the purest O'Donnell form, was the full recognition of authors' claims through proper voluntary licensing schemes (such as the infant CAL was beginning to formulate). The terms of reference, however, directed the committee to consider the 'proper balance' between copyright owners and users, and this led inexorably towards proposals for imposed statutory solutions, an outcome that was vigorously resisted by the ACC.[33] As a collectivist solution, CAL was perhaps founded too late to be able to work out the same kind of strong voluntary licensing agreements that a body like the APRA had been able to do half a century before.

The committee reported in October 1976, more than a year after *Moorhouse*, but the only recommendation that touched directly on the issues in that case was the proposal that the Act be amended to make clear that the installation and use of self-service copying machines in libraries did not of itself impose any liability for copyright infringement upon the librarian or librarian's employer, provided that notices in a prescribed form were displayed drawing users' attention to the relevant provisions of the Act.[34] This was completely consistent with the decisions of both the Supreme and High Courts and now finds its place in s 39A of the *Copyright Act 1968*. The Franki Committee recommendations, of course, went much further than this, with proposals covering the fair dealing and library provisions and, most importantly, for the introduction of statutory licensing schemes in educational institutions where more than six copies of a work were made. Following various permutations, these recommendations finally came into the *Copyright Act* in 1980 as ss 53A and 53B, with complicated requirements for record-keeping on the part of educational users.[35] Following various further amendments since this time, the statutory licence schemes now reside in all their prolix glory in Pt VB and provide a detailed and complex framework for peak body negotiations between CAL, now a powerful and highly successful collecting

---

33 This reflects a similar conflict at the international level, where compulsory licences have long been resisted by authors' groups. Such 'solutions', often justified as being the only solution to 'market failure' problems, are only indirectly acknowledged or accommodated within the interstices of international instruments such as the Berne Convention for the Protection of Literary and Artistic Works: see generally S Ricketson and J Ginsburg, *International Copyright and Neighbouring Rights: The Berne Convention and Beyond*, Oxford University Press, Oxford, 2006, chap. 13.

34 Franki Committee report, op. cit., Appendix A, p. 139, recommendation (2).

35 One of the authors, as a young academic, has vivid memories of filling out the detailed forms required for this purpose in the early 1980s and the oddities of identifying authorship in the case of Acts of parliament and judicial decisions, for example, the Queen of Australia and all the members of parliament passing a particular Act, or Barwick, G, Mason, A, etc.

society, and the universities, schools and other user groups. These are collectivist and corporatist solutions that now seem very far removed from the shoestring operation that mounted the *Moorhouse* case over 30 years previously.

The relevance of *Moorhouse* was that it established the liability of the university itself. Modern technological uses of copyright material often require a relationship (e.g. licensing) between an organisation of copyright owners on one hand, and a person representing, or at least legally responsible for, multiple copyright users on the other.[36] Authorisation is still a central concept in establishing, or compelling, that relationship.

---

36 Refer here to the litigation over the *KaZaa* peer-to-peer software: *Universal Music Australia Pty Ltd v Sharman License Holdings Ltd* [2005] FCA 1242, and see further J Ginsburg and S Ricketson, 'Inducers and Authorisers: A Comparison of the US Supreme Court's Grokster Decision and the Australian Federal Court's Kazaa Ruling' (2006) 11 *Media & Arts Law Review* 1.

7

Foster v Mountford: cultural confidentiality in a changing Australia

Christoph Antons

Introduction

Foster v Mountford[1] is a case belonging to the period in which Australian courts were finding their identity in deciding intellectual property disputes. As the first decision in Australia taking into account Aboriginal customary rights to culturally defined notions of secrecy, it is a landmark case. It symbolises a shift from assimilation policies based on the notion of Australia as *terra nullius* at the time of 'discovery'[2] towards a growing understanding of Aboriginal customs and associated rights. As a case dealing with anthropological publications, it has to be seen against its contemporary background of anthropological paradigms and the emergence of the academic discipline of anthropology in Australia. The case also has significance beyond Australian borders. In an ongoing debate about violations of indigenous cultural secrecy and 'rights to cultural privacy', the case has been regarded as one of the few legal actions examining such violations.[3]

The facts of the case are straightforward and well known. Charles Pearcy Mountford was the author and Rigby the publisher of *Nomads of the Australian Desert*,[4] a book containing details and pictures of secret ceremonies of Central Australian Aborigines. The details had been revealed to Mountford some 35 years earlier during the course of his research in the area. Members of the Pitjantjara Council, an unincorporated body, on behalf of the communities concerned sought and obtained an *ex parte* injunction in the Supreme Court of the

---

1 *Foster and Others v Mountford and Rigby Ltd* (1976) 14 ALR 71.
2 S Macintyre, *A Concise History of Australia*, Cambridge University Press, Cambridge, 1999, pp. 34–5.
3 MF Brown, *Who Owns Native Culture?* Harvard University Press, Cambridge, Mass. and London, 2003, p. 33.
4 CP Mountford, *Nomads of the Australian Desert*, Rigby, Adelaide, 1976.

Northern Territory to prevent the publication of the book in that territory. The equitable doctrine of confidential information was applied in the case decision.

In this chapter, I will approach the topic from various angles. First, I would like to explain the social and political context of the case, both at the time when Charles Mountford undertook his research, and the confidence to keep the secrets revealed to him was allegedly imposed, and at the time when the decision in the case was made. The case has implications for anthropologists and other researchers working within Indigenous communities as a particular group of actors not usually targeted in confidential information cases. In the second part of the chapter, I will discuss the significance of the case and more importantly, the questions it leaves open. In the final part, I will look at various extended interpretations of the doctrine of confidential information, which have been suggested over the years, and their usefulness in this context. In particular, US anthropologists such as Michael F Brown in his famous book *Who Owns Native Culture?*[5] have discussed the problems associated with an extension of the US-style right to privacy to cover 'cultural privacy'.

The social and political background of the case: *Foster v Mountford* and the emergence of anthropology as an academic discipline

In his discussion of *Foster v Mountford* as one of the few cases worldwide that have dealt with violations of indigenous secrecy by outsiders, Michael Brown speaks of the 'distinguished anthropologist' Charles Mountford and his work with the Pitjantjara.[6] This requires further explanation. South Australian Charles Pearcy Mountford[7] worked at first as an electrical mechanic for the Adelaide Municipal Tramways Trust and then for the Postmaster-General's Department in Adelaide from 1913 to 1920. He became interested in Aboriginal culture when he was appointed as senior mechanic at the Darwin Post Office in 1920. He continued this interest after his return to Adelaide. In 1926 he published his first paper on Aboriginal rock carvings together with the entomologist Norman Tindale of the South Australian Museum.[8] In the same year, he became a foundation member of the Anthropological Society of South Australia. His career as a gifted fieldworker, photographer and ethnographer began in 1935 on an expedition to the West Australian Warburton Range, again with Tindale and with support from the Board for Anthropological Research of the University of Adelaide. Many expeditions and further work in South Australia, the Northern Territory, Western

---

5 Brown, op. cit.
6 ibid., p. 33.
7 For a biographical sketch of Mountford see P Jones, 'Mountford, Charles Pearcy (1890–1920)' in *Australian Dictionary of Biography* (online edn), available at http://www.adb.online.anu.edu.au/biogs/A150500b.htm.
8 For a biography of Tindale see P Jones, 'Tindale Biography', The South Australian Museum, available at http://www.samuseum.sa.gov.au/page/default.asp?site=2.

112   LANDMARKS IN AUSTRALIAN IP LAW

Australia and Queensland followed during three decades of fieldwork, which ended only in 1965 when Mountford reached the age of 75.

In spite of his growing reputation as an ethnographer and his prolific output of books and films about his expeditions, Mountford continued to work in government service until 1946 in the Postmaster-General's Department, and from then on until his retirement in 1955 as lecturer in the Commonwealth Department of Information. It was only after retirement that Mountford embarked on a formal education in anthropology, acquiring a diploma in anthropology from the University of Cambridge in 1959 and an MA from the University of Adelaide in 1964. Apart from many other honorary awards, two honorary doctorates followed; from the University of Melbourne in 1973 and from the University of Adelaide shortly before his death in 1976.

Mountford belongs to the first generation of gifted Australian ethnographers who began their work without much formal education in anthropology. Although two of the founding fathers of modern British social anthropology, Malinowski and Radcliffe-Brown, wrote influential classics on Australian Aborigines,[9] anthropology as an academic discipline in Australian universities only began in 1926 with the establishment of a Chair in Anthropology at the University of Sydney and the appointment of Alfred Radcliffe-Brown as its first holder. The Australian Government and colonial administrators initially were by no means convinced of the necessity and usefulness of university training in anthropology.[10] A number of factors, however, combined to affect a change in attitude. A few years after the proclamation of the Commonwealth of Australia, Britain had handed over the administration of Papua (British New Guinea) to Australia in 1906. The Commonwealth of Australia further governed the former German Colony New Guinea from 1914 as a League of Nations Mandated Territory from 1921, and it had acquired the Northern Territory from South Australia in 1911.[11] The sudden responsibility for many different groups of 'natives' within Australian territory led to a division at the second Pan Pacific Science Congress in Sydney in 1923, under which Australia became responsible for ethnographic research in Australia itself and (jointly with Britain and France) in Papua, New Guinea and Melanesia.[12] Funding for the Sydney Chair was secured from the Australian states and from the US American Rockefeller Foundation, whose funds where distributed via the Australian National Research Council (ANRC).[13]

The choice of the University of Sydney came as disappointment for the University of Adelaide and South Australian researchers. After a visit of a delegation of the Rockefeller Foundation to Adelaide in 1925, Adelaide-based researchers

---

9 B Malinowski, *The Family among the Australian Aborigines*, University of London Press, London, 1913; AR Radcliffe-Brown, *The Social Organization of Australian Tribes*, Oceania Monographs No. 1, Sydney, 1930–1, both cited in RM Berndt, 'Social Anthropology and Australian Aborigines' (1967) 37 *Oceania* 255.
10 G Gray, *A Cautious Silence: The Politics of Australian Anthropology*, Aboriginal Studies Press, Canberra, 2007, pp. 8ff; R McGregor, *Imagined Destinies: Aboriginal Australians and the Doomed Race Theory, 1880–1939*, Melbourne University Press, Melbourne, 1997.
11 Gray, op. cit., p. 31.
12 ibid., p. 8.
13 ibid., pp. 11–13.

with an interest in anthropology had come to believe that the city was a contender for the chair or at least as a separate centre for anthropological research, none the least because of its proximity to significant Aboriginal communities in Central Australia. After the chair had been awarded to Sydney, the committee set up to liaise with the Rockefeller Foundation delegation, continued as Board for Anthropological Research. The board continued to apply successfully for ANRC grants and for funds from foundations and other private sources such as the US American Carnegie Foundation. Unlike Sydney, however, there was a lack of trained anthropologists in Adelaide and research on Aboriginal communities was largely carried out by academics in the medical department of the University of Adelaide and by natural scientists like Tindale in the Museum of South Australia. This led to a concentration on physical anthropology.[14] The social anthropologists in Sydney had little interest in this kind of research, while the Adelaide Board largely controlled research that was being carried out in Central Australia.[15] This rivalry in anthropological research between Sydney and Adelaide continued until the early 1950s. With the Rockefeller Foundation throwing its weight firmly behind the social anthropologists, however, and with a further anthropology department opened at the Australian National University in Canberra in 1951, the Adelaide researchers found it increasingly difficult to find sources of funding for their expeditions.

Charles Mountford was at a particular disadvantage for not only was he not anthropologically trained, but he had no academic qualification at all. His career in anthropological research was, therefore, marked by a persistent struggle with the academic establishment of the discipline. In particular Professor AP Elkin, successor to Radcliffe-Brown and Raymond Firth on the Sydney chair since 1933, was influential not just within academic circles, but also as an ordained Anglican cleric with missionary bodies.[16] Elkin promoted the anthropologist and scientific expert as an intermediary between colonial official and Indigenous communities and usually insisted on academic training in anthropology for these experts.[17] He did not recommend amateur ethnographers such as Mountford and even referred to Donald Thomson, who acquired a diploma in anthropology after his training in scientific disciplines as 'a mixture of zoologist, anthropologist and journalist'.[18] Elkin dissuaded the Carnegie trust from funding the particular expedition, which Mountford undertook in 1940 and the results of which were later included in *Nomads of the Australian Desert*, on the ground that Mountford was an amateur ethnographer.[19] Similarly, he wrote to the American National Geographic Society, a financial backer of Mountford's 1947 expedition to Arnhem Land, stating that 'Mr Mountford, who is a good photographer, especially of still subjects, and who has done valuable work in the recording and copying of native

14 ibid., pp. 49–51.
15 ibid., pp. 58–9.
16 McGregor, op. cit., p. 194.
17 ibid., pp. 216–17.
18 Gray, op. cit., p. 124.
19 Jones, op. cit.

114 LANDMARKS IN AUSTRALIAN IP LAW

art, is not a trained anthropologist, much to his own regret.'[20] Elkin's student Catherine Berndt was even more unequivocal, describing Mountford in a letter as knowing 'just enough really to prevent him from realising his ignorance'. She wrote that 'there are so many details that can't be discovered by casual expeditions such as his, obliged always to use an interpreter and never becoming intimate with the people.'[21]

Mountford, according to his biographer, shrugged off Elkin's criticism with the following remark: 'In Australia, there is so much to do that there is ample scope for everyone ... So much information must be gathered before it is gone forever.'[22] The remark shows that Mountford, in accordance with the prevailing thinking among many ethnographers at the time, whether trained anthropologists or not, believed that he was recording a dying culture virtually at the last moment. This was a point particularly often stressed in funding applications and Mountford was no exception. In support of his funding application to the Board of Anthropology of the University of Adelaide for the 1940 expedition, he wrote to the Vice-Chancellor of the university as follows:

> The Aborigines are rapidly drifting into civilised areas, and in a short time all opportunity of ascertaining the significance of cave paintings and the associated myths in the desert will be lost for ever. The symbolism of the central Australian native is the most primitive in the world, and I feel that it is in this area that many of the puzzling questions as to the origins of art can be answered.[23]

The National Geographic Society grant and support from the American Smithsonian Institute came after visits to the US as lecturer of the Commonwealth Department of Information in 1945 and 1948, during which his presentations of films and photographs became a great success. A few anthropologists of this period, such as Olive Pink, objected to the showing of film footage of ceremonies including secret-sacred material in overseas institutions as a matter of principle.[24] Other researchers on the margins of Australian anthropology, such as the linguist TGH Strehlow, on occasion made disparaging remarks about Mountford's use of his footage,[25] but Strehlow himself used footage of his research to promote it among audiences in Europe in 1951.[26]

At a time when travel between the continents was still by steamship and the 'tyranny of distance' was still firmly in everyone's mind, researchers probably thought it unlikely that harm could be done by such film and photo presentations. Overseas university audiences, in particular, were seen as a different matter, and book and journal publications overseas revealing secret and/or sacred material were not regarded as impacting on Aboriginal communities back home. This

---

20 Gray, op. cit., p. 192.
21 Cited in ibid., p. 193.
22 M Lamshed, 'Monty': The Biography of CP Mountford, Rigby Ltd, Adelaide, 1972, p. 73.
23 ibid., p. 74.
24 B Hill, Broken Song: TGH Strehlow and Aboriginal Possession, Vintage Books, Milsons Point, NSW, 2003, p. 334.
25 ibid., p. 609.
26 ibid., pp. 484–5.

attitude was still firmly entrenched when *Foster v Mountford* was decided in 1976. During the late 1960s and early 1970s there were several publications that became controversial because of secret-sacred content, such as *Yiwara* by the American anthropologist Richard A Gould, published in 1969. Ronald Berndt carefully removed such content from early editions of *The World of the First Australians*[27] but left it in a book published in 1974 in Denmark.[28] After the *Foster v Mountford* decision, a further major controversy along similar lines involved the publication in 1978 in the German magazine *Stern* of colour photographs taken at secret-sacred Aranda ceremonies by TGH Strehlow. In spite of assurances from *Stern* that the material was not to be passed on to any Australian magazine, it was published only a few months later in Australia in the magazine *People*. As in *Foster v Mountford*, Aboriginal communities in the Alice Springs region joined by the Australian Institute of Aboriginal Studies considered applying for injunctions against *People*. In this case, however, further legal steps were considered unnecessary after *People* agreed not to distribute the magazine in Alice Springs.[29]

As Barry Hill explains, Strehlow had published secret-sacred material in the past and he did so in this case to raise funds for his research after his retirement from the University of Adelaide. However, 'the simple fact was that the ground of acceptability in these matters had been changing and was still hard to define with clarity.'[30] Seven years later, Ronald and Catherine Berndt wrote the following with regards to secret-sacred material in the foreword to the 1985 edition of *The World of the First Australians*:

> In tackling this problem, we have tried to keep in mind two issues: one, the need to provide at least some material of this kind to give breadth and understanding to the study of Aboriginal society and culture, since omission of it could be detrimental to any broader appreciation; and, two, the need to delete those features which could conceivably prove offensive to traditional Aborigines living in situations where their religion is a living reality. To achieve more rapprochement in this respect, between two seemingly incompatible aims, has proved extremely difficult ... However, to the best of our ability we have withheld secret-sacred knowledge of a detailed kind, although we have at the same time provided fragmentary glimpses into some of those aspects – but, in our opinion, in such a way as not to give the uninitiated access to them ... There seems to be a major difference here between not revealing non-accessible material, and discussing the overall significance of that material. Also, we do not include in this volume any photographs of secret-sacred ritual.[31]

It is against this background of changing attitudes to what is appropriate in carrying out research in Aboriginal communities and publishing the results of such research that *Foster v Mountford* was decided. Changing attitudes in the academic

---

27 RM Berndt and CH Berndt, *The World of the First Australians: Aboriginal Traditional Life: Past and Present*, Aboriginal Studies Press, Canberra, 1996.
28 Hill, op. cit., p. 743.
29 ibid., pp. 741–9.
30 ibid., p. 744.
31 Berndt and Berndt, op. cit. n. 27, 'Foreword to the 1985 Edition', pp. XVI–XVII.

116   LANDMARKS IN AUSTRALIAN IP LAW

community, however, are only part of a much wider change in Australian society that had become visible during the 1960s. The Aboriginal movements had fought for and obtained welfare benefits, equal pay for Aboriginal pastoral workers and the right to vote. After the national referendum of 1967, the Commonwealth took over the power to legislate for Aboriginal people from the more conservative state governments. Aboriginal writers, artists and academics began to present their versions of Aboriginal life in Australia and multiculturalism began to replace the previous policies of assimilation.[32]

The significance of *Foster v Mountford*, then and now

Today, *Foster v Mountford* is usually cited as a case that demonstrates the diversity of the subject-matter that has come to be protected by the equitable doctrine of confidential information.[33] It places Aboriginal cultural secrets next to the more familiar cases on commercial or trade secrets and private secrets of famous persons going back to the case of *Prince Albert v Strange*.[34] It treats the information as sufficiently developed to qualify for protection and not as mere 'trivial' private information.[35] The case is also quoted as an example of 'relative secrecy', where the information is known and distributed among 'insiders' but remains protected from 'outsiders'.[36] Beyond that, it is achieving wider significance as a case where an appropriate remedy was provided for breaches of 'cultural privacy'[37] via flexible, judge-made doctrines such as breach of confidence.[38] It has been included in what is regarded as Australia's 'groundbreaking body of case law located at the intersections of indigenous interests and intellectual property' where 'a growing pattern of creative lawmaking and dicta shows that judges are beginning to recognize the need for such reconfiguration.'[39] Nor should

---

32 Macintyre, op. cit., pp. 229–30.

33 R Meagher, D Heydon and M Leeming, *Meagher Gummow & Lehane's Equity: Doctrines & Remedies*, 4th edn, LexisNexis Butterworths, Chatswood, NSW, 2002, p. 1109; L Bently and B Sherman, *Intellectual Property Law*, 2nd edn, Oxford University Press, Oxford and New York, 2004, p. 1000; J McKeough, A Stewart and P Griffith, *Intellectual Property in Australia*, 3rd edn, LexisNexis Butterworths, 2004, Chatswood, NSW, pp. 74–5; S Ricketson, 'Confidential Information – A New Proprietary Interest? Part I' (1977–8) 11 *Melbourne University Law Review* 223.

34 (1849) 18 LJ Ch 120; M Richardson, 'Breach of Confidence' in P Parkinson (ed.), *The Principles of Equity*, 2nd edn, Lawbook Co., Sydney, 2003, p. 440.

35 M Richardson and J Stuckey-Clarke, 'Breach of Confidence' in Parkinson (ed.), *The Principles of Equity*, LBC Information Services, Sydney, 1996, pp. 438–9.

36 W Cornish and D Llewelyn, *Intellectual Property: Patents, Copyright, Trade Marks and Allied Rights*, 5th edn, Sweet & Maxwell, London, 2003, p. 308; Richardson, op. cit. n. 34, p. 446; M Richardson, 'Breach of Confidence, Surreptitiously or Accidentally Obtained Information and Privacy: Theory Versus Law' (1993–4) 19 *Melbourne University Law Review* 673.

37 Brown, op. cit.

38 R Sackville, 'Legal Protection of Indigenous Culture in Australia' (2003) 11 *Cardozo Journal of International & Competition Law* 711, 711; M Blakeney, 'The Protection of Traditional Knowledge under Intellectual Property Law' (2000) 22 *European Intellectual Property Review* 251, 255; S Frankel and M Richardson, 'Cultural Property and "the Public Domain": Case Studies from New Zealand and Australia' in C Antons (ed.), *Traditional Knowledge, Traditional Cultural Expressions and Intellectual Property Law in the Asia-Pacific Region*, Kluwer Law International, The Hague, forthcoming.

39 MM Carpenter, 'Intellectual Property Law and Indigenous Peoples: Adapting Copyright Law to the Needs of a Global Community' (2004) 7 *Yale Human Rights & Development Law Journal* 63.

FOSTER v MOUNTFORD   117

this be surprising since the judge who handed down the decision, Muirhead J of the Supreme Court of the Northern Territory, is well known in Australia as 'a leading advocate for reconciliation both in what he practised as well as preached'.[40]

A closer examination of *Foster v Mountford* reveals the usefulness as well as the limitations of the breach of confidence action in this context. As an *ex parte* injunction, its status as precedent is obviously limited.[41] Equally limited was the geographical scope of the measure. The injunction prevented the sale, display for sale or distribution of *Nomads of the Australian Desert* only in the Northern Territory. This included Alice Springs as the regional centre of greatest concern to the Pitjantjara Council. Even at the time of the decision it was obvious, however, that Australian state and jurisdictional boundaries did not coincide with the boundaries of the Pitjantjara lands. Muirhead J pointed out that the plaintiffs represented Aboriginal people identifiable by their use of the Pitjantjara language, but that more than one tribal group may be involved and that the lands of these communities were to be found in the south-west corner of the Northern Territory, a large area of the north-west of South Australia and a portion of central Western Australia adjacent to the eastern border of that state.[42] Mountford, in fact, made a distinction between tribal groups in his book and referred to the study of the 'art, myth, and totemic geography' not only of the Pitjantjara but also of the Jukandjara, whose tribal lands he located in the Musgrave Ranges and around the missions station of Ernabella from where Mountford started his expedition.[43] Muirhead J's careful distinction between tribal groups and people speaking Pitjantjara in this regard acknowledged the difficulties anthropologists associate with distinguishing between major and smaller tribal groups and between major languages and dialects, especially in central Australia, which means that they have regarded tribal territories and boundaries as 'relatively flexible'.[44]

In spite of these various overlaps of communities and territories, the Pitjantjara Council at the time apparently was satisfied with the prevention of the publication in the main regional centre frequented by Pitjantjara speaking people. A limited injunction of this nature was also in line with the prevailing thinking, outlined in the previous part of this chapter, that it was first of all important to prevent the return of the material into a geographical area where uninitiated people from

---

40 Evelyn Scott (chairperson of the Council for Aboriginal Reconciliation) quoted in 'Chairperson Pays Tribute to Justice Muirhead', CAR Media Release 217, 21 July 1999, available at http://www.austlii.edu.au/au/special/rsjproject/rsjlibrary/car/mr/car217.html.
41 Sackville, op. cit. n. 38.
42 *Foster and Others v Mountford and Rigby Ltd* (1976) 14 ALR 71, 72.
43 Mountford, op. cit., p. 40.
44 Berndt and Berndt, op. cit. n. 27, p. 33 and more generally pp. 28–40. Peter Sutton speaks of similar problems with the now popularly used term 'Aboriginal community', which may refer to 'a place, a population of residents (in some cases shifting about, in other cases very sedentary), a collection of subsets of ethnic, territorial and other groups, a focal concentration point in a regional system of overlapping egocentric social networks, a local cultural milieu, a mini-economy, a rallying badge of identity in competitive and combative contexts such as football and fighting, a political unit both formal and informal, and a unit of local governance'. P Sutton, *Native Title in Australia: An Ethnographic Perspective*, Cambridge University Press, Cambridge, 2003, p. 98.

118   LANDMARKS IN AUSTRALIAN IP LAW

'traditional' communities could come into contact with it. Mountford himself had included the following caveat in his book prior to his acknowledgements:

> Where Australian Aborigines are concerned, and in areas where traditional Aboriginal religion is still significant, this book should be used only after consultation with local male religious leaders.

> The restriction is important, it is imposed because of the concept of what is secret or may not be revealed to the uninitiated in Aboriginal religious belief and action, varies considerably throughout the Australian Continent and because the varying views of Aborigines in this respect must on all occasions be observed.[45]

In spite of the limited geographical scope of the injunction, however, the publisher Rigby finally decided to withdraw the book from circulation. For this chapter, a copy available in the library of the University of New England was consulted, which in addition to a note that the book had been withdrawn from circulation included an exchange of letters between the deputy librarian of the university and the publisher Rigby as well as the Aboriginal Arts Board of the Australia Council. Due to the note accompanying the publication, the library had restricted access to the book by placing it in a protected area of its collection. The deputy librarian inquired about the status of the publication after the library received request from users who wanted to consult the book. Rigby responded that about 2000 copies of *Nomads of the Australian Desert* had been sold by the time it was withdrawn. Several hundred more were destroyed in a warehouse fire and the remainder of the edition was purchased by the Aboriginal Arts Board.[46] The Aboriginal Arts Board in turn confirmed that placement in the protected area of the library and restriction of access was appropriate, but that researchers should be given the opportunity to refer to the book for special study purposes. The letter concluded that 'the Pitjantjatjara people do not wish the book to be freely available and seen by women and children. The steps you have taken are adequate to meet their requirements.'[47]

In view of the increasing distances travelled by 'traditional' people in the following years and the increasing interaction of their communities with outsiders such as tourists, teachers and various government personnel, such simple safeguards as Mountford's cautionary note were soon to become inadequate to protect the secrets of what may then still have been regarded as relatively secluded living groups. Geographical limitations as in the *Foster v Mountford* injunction appear even more inadequate in the current internet age, when attempts are being made to bring communications technology to remote areas to assist with educational needs and foster local development.[48]

---

45 Mountford, op. cit.
46 Letter from Rigby Ltd to Karl G Schmude, Deputy Librarian (Reader Services) of the University of New England, Armidale, 9 November 1979.
47 Letter from the Director of the Aboriginal Arts Board, Robert Edwards, to Schmude, 3 March 1980.
48 AS Latukefu, 'Remote Indigenous Communities in Australia: Questions of Access, Information and Self-determination' in K Landzelius (ed.), *Native on the Net: Indigenous and Diasporic Peoples in the Virtual Age*, Routledge, London and New York, 2006, pp. 43–60.

There were other limitations to this particular action for breach of confidence in *Foster v Mountford*, which the judge either circumvented or declined to discuss within the limited scope of an injunction and in view of the urgency of the matter. It has been correctly pointed out that there could be a question here as to whether the Pitjantjara Council actually had standing to sue.[49] In general terms, the party to whom the confidence is owed will be the appropriate plaintiff.[50] Muirhead J quoted this principle from the relevant case of *Fraser v Evans*,[51] but seemed to be satisfied that it was met in spite of the many years that had passed between Mountford's visit and the application for the injunction. Earlier in the decision, the judge mentioned that some members of the Pitjantjara Council still remembered Mountford's visit,[52] indicating that he may have regarded the Pitjantjara Council as at least partly identical to the Aboriginal elders who imposed the confidence to keep their tribal knowledge secret on Mountford some 35 years earlier. Alternatively, he may have regarded the obligation of confidence as being directly owed to the various Pitjantjara communities represented by the plaintiff council. Such an approach may create difficulties where, as mentioned above, community boundaries are difficult to establish. The judge further found that the plaintiffs were entitled to proceed as individuals who were threatened with damage, and that this was not a case for a relator action brought in the name of the Attorney-General to prevent public nuisance.[53]

A further matter, which Muirhead J raised briefly towards the end of the decision but declined to discuss further within the limited scope of this injunction, was the potential for the defendant Mountford to raise a public interest defence/exception, in particular by stressing his right to disseminate the results of his scientific and anthropological research.[54] The public interest defence is well accepted in English law[55] but has been used sparingly by Australian courts and largely confined to government information and so-called disclosures of iniquities.[56] Even statements implying a broader exception, such as that of Mason J in *Commonwealth v John Fairfax & Sons*, have been narrowly construed as necessary 'to protect the community from destruction, damage or harm'[57] or as a reflection of the implied constitutional freedom of political discussion.[58] This broadening of the scope is of relatively recent origin. Even if a broad defence of this nature had been available at the time of the decision, however, and the

---

49 McKeough et al, op. cit., p. 85.
50 Meagher et al, op. cit., p. 1125; McKeough et al, op. cit., p. 85, with reference to *Fraser v Evans* [1969] 1 All ER 8.
51 (1976) 14 ALR 71, 75.
52 ibid., p. 73.
53 ibid., p.75.
54 ibid., p. 76.
55 S Ricketson and M Richardson, *Intellectual Property: Cases, Materials and Commentary*, 3rd edn, LexisNexis Butterworths, Chatswood, NSW, 2005, p. 642; McKeough et al, op. cit., p. 104.
56 *Gartside v Outram* (1856) 26 LJ Ch 113, 114 (Wood VC). See in general GE Dal Pont and DRC Chalmers, *Equity and Trusts in Australia*, 3rd edn, Lawbook Co, Pyrmont, NSW, 2004, pp. 177–8. See also Richardson, op. cit. n. 463.
57 *Commonwealth v John Fairfax & Sons Ltd* (1980) 147 CLR 39, 57.
58 *Australian Broadcasting Corporation v Lenah Game Meats Pty Ltd* (2001) 208 CLR 199, 224 (Gleeson CJ), cited in Ricketson and Richardson, op. cit. n. 55, p. 643.

120   LANDMARKS IN AUSTRALIAN IP LAW

case would have moved beyond the stage of injunctive relief, it seems difficult to imagine that a judge would have upheld a public interest defence. Muirhead J examined the argument of a dying and vanishing culture raised typically by anthropologists and also by Mountford in this case, but he was not persuaded by it:

> Despite Mr Mountford's prognosis that their life and beliefs 'are so quickly vanishing', there is still an urgent desire in these people to preserve those things, their lands and their identity, and the existence of the council itself illustrates these objectives.[59]

Muirhead J also stressed the undermining of the social and religious stability of the Pitjantjara community and gave more weight to all of these arguments than to the research interests of Mountford. It seems difficult to imagine with the improved understanding of indigenous cultural secrecy today that a current court in a similar situation would elevate the interests of anthropological research above that of an Aboriginal community in its cultural secrets, especially considering the emergence of codes of conduct that regulate the balancing of such interests.

As Sackville J has pointed out, however, this does not necessarily mean that cultural information of this nature imparted on a confidential basis will necessarily be confined to the recipient.[60] In an interesting decision 10 years after *Foster v Mountford*, the Federal Court was asked to conduct a judicial review of a decision by the Aboriginal Land Commissioner of the Northern Territory, who had ordered the Aboriginal Sacred Sites Protection Authority to produce documents prepared by anthropologists and others in connection with a land claim to have secret sites in the area recorded.[61] In this rather unusual case, Aboriginal interests were represented on both sides, since the production of the documents helped to finalise a long-running land claim. The Federal Court (Bowen CJ, Woodward and Toohey JJ) was satisfied that the order required disclosure of the documents only to the Commissioner sitting in camera, his associate, counsel assisting, counsel for the Attorney-General of the Northern Territory, possibly a consultant anthropologist and the researcher who had gathered the material. This restricted use of the material and the interest of the Central Land Council in a swift decision of the land claim tipped the balance in favour of the order made by the Commissioner and dismissal of the application for review.

For the requirement that the information given to Mountford was imparted in confidence, an anthropologist expert witness and a staff member from the Aboriginal Legal Service were heard to confirm the affidavit of the chairman of the Pitjantjara Council. The anthropologist gave evidence that in his experience the information revealed could only have been supplied and exposed in confidence.[62] The judge took Mountford's own caveat at the beginning of the book

---

59 (1976) 14 ALR 71, 73.
60 Sackville, op. cit n. 38, p. 738, fn. 144.
61 *Aboriginal Sacred Sites Protection Authority v Maurice; Re: The Warumungu Land Claim* (1986) 10 FCR 104.
62 (1976) 14 ALR 71, 72.

FOSTER v MOUNTFORD   121

as confirmation that the author was well aware that the book contained secret-sacred material. It was this understanding rather than 'evidence by document or conversation or indeed by recognized legal relationship'[63] that persuaded the judge to grant the injunction based on breach of confidentiality. Neither *Nomads of the Australian Desert* nor the description of the 1940 expedition in Mountford's biography expressly refer to restrictions imposed on Mountford at the time the knowledge was revealed. However, *Nomads of the Australian Desert* contained detailed sections on 'sacred objects'. Further, both *Nomads of the Australian Desert* and the Mountford biography mention that during the expedition Mountford and his young companion Lauri Sheard were allotted totems and tribal relationships within the organisation of the Pitjantjara; they became totemically associated with the land.[64] This association, in the view of the Pitjantjara, would have brought him rights as well as responsibilities and obligations towards maintaining and observing their customs and laws. Thus, it would not have been inappropriate for the judge to regard confidentiality here as flowing simply from Mountford's particular relationship with the Pitjantjara community.

The *Foster v Mountford* case also indicates a more restricted role for the anthropologist as expert, and a shift from the central role of earlier years in representing Aboriginal life in a 'scientific' manner to that of an expert witness merely confirming court statements and affidavits of Aboriginal parties to the proceedings. It has been the practice, in land rights disputes as well as other proceedings, in recent years to combine Aboriginal evidence and the statements of expert witnesses.[65] Gary Edmond finds that 'most of the leading native title and heritage protection judgments devote considerably more space to the evidence of anthropologists, historians and archaeologists than the evidence of Aborigines'.[66] As an example, he contrasts about five pages of Aboriginal evidence in the case of *Ward v Western Australia* with over 20 pages on 'Historial evidence', 'Liguistic evidence', 'Anthropological evidence' and 'Genealogical evidence'.

The relationship between lawyers and anthropologists, however, is also not always unproblematic. While lawyers have expressed difficulties 'in coming to terms with the language and ideas of anthropologists',[67] anthropologists such as Ronald Berndt have warned colleagues not to fall 'into the trap of over-simplifying data for legal consumption'. Berndt described the problematic relationship in the following way:

> In a sense, and perhaps being deliberately a little unfair, one could say that the legal practitioners regard anthropologists, when they do not consider them to be obstructive, as being 'raw' material; or to put it more kindly, as a kind of resource. To follow

---

63 ibid., p. 73.
64 Mountford, op. cit., p. 86; Lamshed, op. cit., pp. 93–4.
65 C Antons, 'Folklore Protection in Australia: Who is Expert in Aboriginal Tradition?' in E Kurz-Milcke and G Gigerenzer, *Experts in Science and Society*, Kluwer Academic/Plenum Publishers, New York, 2004, p. 95.
66 G Edmond, 'Thick Decisions: Expertise, Advocacy and Reasonableness in the Federal Court of Australia' (2004) 74 *Oceania* 220.
67 Maurice J in the Warumungu land claim, cited in G Neate, *Aboriginal Land Rights Law in the Northern Territory (Vol. 1)*, Alternative Publishing Co-operative Ltd, Chippendale, NSW, 1989, p. 239.

122 LANDMARKS IN AUSTRALIAN IP LAW

Levi-Strauss, legal practitioners, in contrast, are 'cooked' – they have the final say, irrespective of anthropological opinion and irrespective of Aboriginal views.[68]

More recently, anthropologists have complained that their heterogenous approaches are difficult to represent within the confines of legal proceedings.[69] As a final point on the complicated relationship between law and anthropology, it is perhaps ironic that the earlier detailed ethnographic studies conducted by people like Mountford are now important again for a younger generation of anthropologists and Aboriginal claimants in the context of native title claims because they can be used to demonstrate the continuing traditional link to the land required by native title legislation.

Foster v Mountford and the wider debate on indigenous knowledge and cultural secrecy

Michael F Brown has pointed to the frequent use, mainly in the US and Canada, of an as yet undefined 'right of cultural privacy' within the indigenous movement and in policy documents dealing with indigenous issues.[70] If this right is regarded as a desirable extension of current privacy principles, its adoption in Australia faces considerable legal and factual obstacles. While privacy rights have been given statutory protection in most US states and some Canadian provinces,[71] the US protection of privacy tort first advocated in 1890 by Warren and Brandeis in the *Harvard Law Review*[72] has been overshadowed by freedom of speech considerations based on the First Amendment.[73] In *Australian Broadcasting Corporation v Lenah Game Meats*,[74] Gummow and Hayne JJ quoted David Anderson as follows:

> But privacy is not the only cherished American value. We also cherish information, and candour, and freedom of speech ... The law protects these expectations too – and when they collide with expectations of privacy, privacy almost always loses. Privacy law in the United States delivers far less than it promises, because it resolves virtually all these conflicts in favour of information, candour and free speech. The sweeping language of privacy law serves largely to mask the fact that the law provides almost no protection against privacy-invading disclosures.[75]

---

68 RM Berndt, 'Long View: Some Personal Comments on Land Rights' (1981) 16 *AIAS Newsletter* 5–20, cited in Neate, op. cit., p. 284.
69 Edmond, op. cit, p. 215.
70 Brown, op. cit, pp. 27–8.
71 E Barendt, 'Privacy and Freedom of Speech' in AT Kenyon and M Richardson (eds.), *New Dimensions in Privacy Law*, Cambridge University Press, Cambridge, 2006, p. 14.
72 SD Warren and LD Brandeis, 'The Right to Privacy' (1890–91) 4 *Harvard Law Review* 193.
73 Barendt, op. cit.; AT Kenyon and M Richardson, 'New Dimensions in Privacy: Communications Technologies, Media Practices and Law' in Kenyon and Richardson (eds.), op. cit. n. 71, pp. 1–2.
74 *Australian Broadcasting Corporation v Lenah Game Meats Pty Ltd* (2001) 208 CLR 199.
75 DA Anderson, 'The Failure of American Private Law' in BS Markesinis, *Protecting Privacy*, p. 140, cited in ibid., pp. 34–5. See also D Lindsay and S Ricketson, 'Copyright, Privacy and Digital Rights Management (DRM)' in Kenyon and Richardson (eds.), op. cit. n. 71, p. 138.

While the New Zealand Court of Appeal has been prepared to accept a public disclosure tort in *Hosking v Runting*,[76] British courts following the European Convention on Human Rights and the UK *Human Rights Act* were careful to couch a right to privacy in the familiar language of the breach of confidence doctrine, a development that Lindsay and Ricketson refer to as 'a creative, but potentially fraught, fusion of a "rights-based" conception of privacy, reflecting the influence of the European Convention on Human Rights, with the traditional incremental approach of the English common law.'[77] In Australia, the High Court in *Australian Broadcasting Corporation v Lenah Game Meats* did not take up the opportunity to shift decisively towards a privacy right,[78] although the possibility of such a right within the Australian context was extensively discussed and explicitly advocated in the minority opinion of Callinan J.[79] Even if a right to privacy was established, it would seem difficult to extend it to something as elusive as 'culture' and 'cultural communities'. In *Australian Broadcasting Corporation v Lenah Game Meats*, three of the judges held that a right to privacy could not be claimed by a corporation. Gummow and Hayne JJ with Gaudron J concurring quoted US decisions focusing on 'the humiliation and intimate personal distress suffered by an individual',[80] while Kirby J quoted the International Covenant on Civil and Political Rights, which appeared to relate only to the privacy of the human individual.[81] It seems difficult to transfer these individual rights to entire cultural communities. As Brown has pointed out:

> From the perspective of anthropology, cultural privacy flirts with self-contradiction. The salient features of culture are, by definition, shared and therefore public. Yet the collective nature of culture does not mean that its elements are uniformly distributed. Information is nearly everywhere held differentially along lines of age, gender, social class, kinship, and occupation. It may be acquired through interactions with other peoples. Through selective borrowing, cultures come closer together; through dialectical contrast, they mark themselves as different. We are left with interweaving and to some extent paradoxical visions of culture: as shared yet differentiated, as segmented yet intrinsically free-flowing, as something that exists unto itself yet which is also defined by opposition. At first glance, this intricate bundle of dichotomies is hard to reconcile with a concept as deceptively simple as privacy.[82]

On the other hand, there is arguably scope for a greater use of other doctrines of equity in cases involving indigenous cultural property.[83] Von Doussa J's decision

---

76 [2005] 1 NZLR 1. See Barendt, op. cit., p. 14; Lindsay and Ricketson, op. cit. n. 75, p. 138; M Richardson and L Hitchens, 'Celebrity Privacy and Benefits of Simple History' in Kenyon and Richardson (eds.), op. cit. n. 71, pp. 250–1.
77 Lindsay and Ricketson, op. cit. n. 75, p. 137.
78 Barendt, op. cit. n. 71, p. 13.
79 M Richardson, 'Whither Breach of Confidence: A Right of Privacy for Australia?' (2002) 26 *Melbourne University Law Review* 381.
80 (2001) 185 ALR 1, 37.
81 ibid., pp. 55–6.
82 Brown, op. cit., p. 28.
83 See also J Gibson, 'Justice of Precedent, Justness of Equity: Equitable Protection and Remedies for Indigenous Intellectual Property' [2001] 42 *Australian Indigenous Law Reporter* 1; and C Antons, 'Traditional Knowledge and Intellectual Property Rights in Australia and Southeast Asia' in C Heath and A Kamperman

124   LANDMARKS IN AUSTRALIAN IP LAW

in *Bulun Bulun v R & T Textiles*,[84] with its discussion of a fiduciary relationship between the individual artist and his clan in appropriately representing the symbols of his community, is a frequently cited example.[85] Both the Canadian and New Zealand courts[86] have occasionally found a fiduciary obligation to exist between their respective governments and indigenous peoples. Australian courts, however, have cautioned against imposing prescriptive duties via the doctrine of the fiduciary relationship, preferring instead to focus on the exaction of loyalty.[87] In the specific case of Mountford, who had been allotted a totem and a tribal relationship, it would be difficult to see why his responsibilities to his community should be judged differently than those of Bulun Bulun with regard to his Arnhem Land–based clan. In a more general sense, it could also be argued that many anthropologists at the time of Mountford's research were in a fiduciary relationship because of the vulnerability of the Aboriginal communities and the paternalistic role of the anthropologist in representing them. It would be much more difficult, however, to apply the same argument to current relationships between Aboriginal communities and researchers.

Some of the difficulties outlined above, especially with regards to standing to sue, could be avoided if the courts were to adopt a view of information as property[88] or regard breach of confidence as a *sui generis* action.[89] Thus far, however, Australian courts have not been prepared to adopt a proprietary analysis and are continuing to base confidentiality on the equitable principle of good faith.[90] Apart from availability of the equitable doctrine of breach of confidence, a case of research such as Mountford's would under current circumstances also most likely be covered by protocols, which have been developed for research activities in various Aboriginal communities.

At the international level, the Intergovernmental Committee on Intellectual Property and Genetic Resources, Traditional Knowledge and Folklore of the World Intellectual Property Organisation (WIPO) has drafted separate sets of 'revised objectives and principles' for the protection of traditional cultural expressions (TCEs) and traditional knowledge (TK) respectively. Among its various measures to prevent misappropriation of the material, the revised objectives and principles for the protection of TCEs foresees in particular in Art 3(c) that

---

Sanders (eds.), *New Frontiers of Intellectual Property Law: IP and Cultural Heritage, Geographical Indications, Enforcement and Overprotection*, Hart Publishing, Oxford and Portland, Oregon, 2005, pp. 44–5.

84 *Bulun Bulun v R & T Textiles Pty Ltd* [1998] 1082 FCA (3 September 1998).

85 Gibson, op. cit.; Antons, op. cit. n. 65; Antons, op. cit. n. 83.

86 *Te Runanga o Wharekauri Rehohu Inc v Attorney-General* [1993] 2 NZLR 301, 304; *R v Sparrow* (1990) 70 DLR (4th) 385, both cited in and critically examined by P Parkinson, 'Fiduciary Obligations' in Parkinson (ed.), op. cit. n. 34, pp. 375–6 and fn. 104.

87 *Breen v Williams* (1996) 186 CLR 71, 113, cited in Dal Pont and Chalmers, op. cit., pp. 84–5. Dal Pont and Chalmers quote Sir Anthony Mason in a speech delivered to the Canadian-Australian legal-judicial exchange in 1988, in which he observed that 'all Canada is divided into three parts: those who owe fiduciary duties, those to whom fiduciary duties are owed, and judges who keep creating new fiduciary duties!': cited in Dal Pont and Chalmers, p. 85, fn. 19.

88 McKeough et al, op. cit., pp. 80–3. See also Ricketson, op. cit. n. 33; and S Ricketson 'Confidential Information – A New Proprietary Interest? Part II' (1977–78) 11 *Melbourne University Law Review* 289.

89 Bently and Sherman, op. cit., pp. 994–5.

90 McKeough et al, op. cit. n. 33, pp. 78–9. See also Cornish and Llewelyn, op. cit., pp. 332–4.

there shall be adequate and effective legal and practical measures to ensure that communities have the means to prevent the unauthorized disclosure, subsequent use of and acquisition and exercise of IP rights over secret traditional cultural expressions/expressions of folklore.[91]

The commentary attached to Art 3(c) seeks to clarify that existing protection for confidential and undisclosed information covers TCE-related subject-matter, 'building also upon case law to this effect'. In a footnote to this commentary, *Foster v Mountford* is explicitly mentioned as example for relevant case law.[92]

Conclusion

In sum, *Foster v Mountford* is the first of a number of cases dealing with Aboriginal secret information. At the time of the decision in the mid-1970s, Australian courts had become sensitised to these issues and placed the welfare of Aboriginal communities over the research interests of anthropologists documenting what they believed were vanishing cultures. The decision appears eminently sensible, even more than 30 years later, and has inspired other courts to turn to equitable principles when dealing with Aboriginal cultural items. It is also included as a still relevant example in the commentary to the revised objectives and principles drafted by the WIPO Intergovernmental Committee on Intellectual Property and Genetic Resources, Traditional Knowledge and Folklore for the protection of traditional cultural expressions. While the court in *Foster v Mountford* declined to comment on a few issues, such as the standing of the plaintiffs to sue, in the context of an *ex parte* injunction the results were satisfying for the Aboriginal plaintiffs at the time. Today, however, and in view of the internet and other new media reaching remote Aboriginal communities, limited injunctive relief of this nature would no longer be sufficient. In view of the difficulties in precisely delineating cultures and communities, a right to 'cultural privacy' seems difficult to realise. Established doctrines of equity such as confidential information, fiduciary obligations and unconscionability combined with protocols and other forms of contracts may not always offer ideal answers to the problems surrounding Aboriginal cultural secrecy. If used in a pragmatic manner, however, as in the case of *Foster v Mountford*, these doctrines may lead to reasonably acceptable and practicable solutions.

91 WIPO/GRTKF/IC/12/4(c) of 6 December 2007, Art 3(c).
92 ibid., Annex, p. 22.

8

Cadbury Schweppes v Pub Squash: what is all the fizz about?

Mark Davison

Introduction

The soft drink market in Australia is big by Australian standards. By the early 1970s, the annual wholesale value of soft drink sales was about $300 million and growing.[1] In that expanding market, Solo made a dramatic impact. Solo has been one of the best-selling new sugar soft drinks in the Australian soft drink market since World War II.[2] It was one of very few new soft drinks that were able to make a dent in the control of the Australian soft drink market by Coca-Cola.

Its impact is primarily attributable to one of the most successful advertising campaigns in Australian commercial history. Advertising in 1974 and 1975 cost Cadbury Schweppes approximately $1 million.[3] In return, by the end of 1975, sales of Solo totalled 6 081 000 dozen (72.972 million individual cans and bottles).[4] Its success has continued for over 30 years. In a 1999 ACCC[5] consideration of a move by Coca-Cola in Australia to acquire the international soft drink trade marks of Cadbury Schweppes, such as Schweppes, Dr Pepper and Canada Dry,

---

1 *Cadbury Schweppes Pty Ltd v The Pub Squash Co Ltd* [1981] RPC 429 (*Pub Squash* case), 440.
2 One of the few other soft drinks to make an impression after the war was 'Fanta', a Coca-Cola company product made for the first time in Germany during World War II in response to the lack of access to the Coca-Cola syrup. A recent Australian television advertisement for Fanta thanked Hitler for Fanta. The advertisement did not run for long. Other soft drinks to make a big impression have been those with sugar substitutes, such as Diet Coke, Pepsi Max and Coke Zero.
3 *Cadbury Schweppes v Pub Squash* [1981] RPC 429, 444–6.
4 ibid., p. 446. Actual monetary sales figures are not available. In any event, high levels of inflation in Australia at that time would make it difficult to compare 1974 and 1975 sales figures.
5 The Australian Competition and Consumer Commission (ACCC) is responsible for the enforcement of Australia's restrictive trade practices regime, which is contained mainly within Pt IV of the *Trade Practices Act 1974* (Cth), and for the enforcement of the consumer protection provisions of the legislation, which are contained mainly within Pts IVA and V of the same legislation. Individuals also have personal rights of action in respect of various breaches of the restrictive trade practices and consumer protection provisions of the legislation.

126

the ACCC noted that after such an acquisition, only Solo, a brand restricted to the Australian market, and Sunkist would remain of Cadbury Schweppes brands with any brand strength.[6]

The legal interest in the marketing of Solo derives from two basic issues arising out of this case. The first is that the defendant adopted a very similar advertising campaign and some similarities in packaging which resulted in the passing off action brought by Cadbury Schweppes. Associated with this passing off action was a plea of unfair competition and an attempt to establish in law a new tort of this nature.

The second issue is that the appeal from the first instance decision went directly to the Privy Council and was one of the last appeals to the Privy Council from Australia. While there was no great technical legal controversy about the question as to whether the Privy Council had jurisdiction to hear the appeal, the case is a manifestation of the then emerging Australian judicial independence from the UK. The first steps towards limiting appeals to the Privy Council were made in 1968 in the *Privy Council (Limitation of Appeals) Act 1968* (Cth), which abolished appeals in relation to matters of federal law. The Whitlam Labor Government[7] later abolished appeals from the High Court to the Privy Council on any matter.[8] The states, such as New South Wales, retained the right of appeal to the Privy Council from their courts. The plaintiff, upon losing the decision at first instance, then had the option of pursuing the matter through the New South Wales Court of Appeal and then possibly to the High Court or directly to the Privy Council.[9]

The initial Solo campaign

Solo was first sold in Australia in 1973 by Cadbury Schweppes in a strategy designed to take market share from Coca-Cola. The new product was coupled with its marketing strategy to appeal to those seeking 'a man's drink' and a particular taste. The two approaches were closely linked.

Solo is a lemon-flavoured soft drink that is 'light on the fizz, so you can slam it down fast'. Consequently, it can be 'sculled'[10] just like beer[11] and indeed most

---

6 ACCC, 'ACCC Opposes Revised Coke/Schweppes Acquisition', press release, 8 June 1999.

7 The Whitlam Government was elected in December 1972 after 23 years of conservative government. During those 23 years, the Prime Minister from 1949 until 1966 was Sir Robert Menzies, who famously described himself as 'British to the bootstraps'.

8 *Privy Council (Appeals from the High Court) Act 1975* (Cth).

9 For a history of appeals to the Privy Council and why an appeal from a single judge of the New South Wales Supreme Court directly to the Privy Council was possible see M Gleeson, 'The Birth, Life and Death of Section 74', speech delivered at the Samuel Griffith Society, 14 June 2002, available at http://www.hcourt.gov.au/speeches. The effect was that the plaintiff could prevent the matter ever getting to the High Court, which could have happened if there had been an appeal to the New South Wales Court of Appeal, the decision reversed and the defendant had then appealed to the High Court.

10 The term, as used in this context, has a peculiarly Australian meaning. The *Macquarie Dictionary* (an authoritative Australian dictionary) defines it as follows: 'Scull – to drink, especially beer, as in a boatrace'. In sculling games, individuals or teams of drinkers race to finish their drinks. In team races, each drinker starts after the previous one has finished.

11 Per capita consumption of beer per annum in 1973–4 in Australia peaked at 136.5 litres but has since declined to about 95 litres per annum. See http://www.aihw.gov.au/publications.

128 LANDMARKS IN AUSTRALIAN IP LAW

television advertisements involved an actor doing just that after engaging in some vigorous, physical activity. The association of the drink with sculling was emphasised by the fact that in those advertisements, the actor invariably spilled some of the drink down his chin and onto his chest in his eagerness to consume it as quickly as possible. Those who recall beer-sculling competitions from their university days will be familiar with the concept of 'spillage' in which contestants may be disqualified for excessive spillage of the contents of their glass. Perhaps even more intriguing is that the spilling of the drink during consumption was not part of the original script for the advertisements. When filming the first advertisement, the actor was so nervous that he spilled some of the drink. The director liked the effect and required it in all future advertisements.

The association of Solo as a man's drink was heightened by two themes that ran through the advertising. The first was the association of Solo with 'those great lemon squashes the pubs used to make ... extra tang ... not too many bubbles'. By associating it with pubs, it became an acceptable substitute for both the alcoholic and non-alcoholic drinks traditionally served by pubs. In 1973, Australian pubs were very much the domain of the Australian male. For example, women were only permitted to drink in hotels in Canberra, the nation's capital, for the first time in the 1960s[12] and many hotels still had a very male culture which made women unwelcome. The pub drink theme was further enforced by the 'medallion type of label very similar to the labels on beer sold in Australia'.[13] In the first instance judgment, Powell J stated that the label was based on the medallion label for the well-known American beer Budweiser.[14]

In reality, while not stated in the case, the product, the labelling and part of the advertising theme were recycled versions of a soft drink previously sold in the US. The label was very similar to the label for the American soft drink called Rondo, which was very similar, if not identical, to Solo and advertised as 'Lightly carbonated, so you can slam it down fast!' and 'The Thirst Crusher'.[15]

Added to the radio advertisements and television voice-overs, with their references to 'just like the pubs used to make', were other advertising scenarios in which one rugged individual (solo) male engaged in adventures that involved activities such as kayaking down wild rapids. He would then pull into the riverbank and proceed to drink a can of Solo while engaging in the obligatory spillage. The reference to pubs was dropped in the advertising from September 1976 onwards[16], but the image of the Solo man engaging in exciting adventures remained. The end result was that a soft drink was turned into the drink of tough, solo men.

---

12 See http://www.abs.gov.au/AUSSTATS/abs@.nsf/0/B43FFBFD93BFC572CA2571E600180BCF.
13 *Cadbury Schweppes v Pub Squash* [1981] RPC 429, 486.
14 ibid., p. 441.
15 Rondo also had a somewhat similar advertising theme with advertisements of men engaged in martial arts combat. The winner then drank a Rondo and crushed the can, which is not particularly difficult when it is made of aluminium.
16 *Cadbury Schweppes v Pub Squash* [1981] RPC 429, 452.

The image before the product

One of the intriguing aspects of the marketing campaign is that the advertising campaign preceded the creation or at least the identification of the product being promoted. The concept of the masculine drink was the starting point for marketing, and the product, its labelling and its advertising were built around this concept. From an Australian perspective, it is one of the clearest and earliest examples of the sale of an image rather than a product. In that sense, it was a precursor of those developments in trade mark law which reflect the idea that the trademark (or the image it evokes) is what is primarily sold and the particular product is incidental to the sale.[17]

For many famous marks, this became the reality after the product was created. In the field of soft drinks, Coca-Cola is a classic example with its emphasis throughout the decades on so many different images that have little to do with the fact that Coca-Cola is a black, carbonated liquid with large amounts of sugar and the capacity to act as a very effective bleaching agent.[18] But Coca-Cola existed well before the sophisticated marketing strategies that were adopted for it.[19]

The Solo soft drink was created or, more accurately, adopted from the US to fit the pre-existing marketing image. In this sense, Solo was an embodiment of the more modern trend to sell the sizzle as much, if not more than, the sausage.

Pub Squash's television campaign

As was later decided in litigation, the Pub Squash company decided to adopt a similar marketing strategy in an attempt to take part of Solo's new market. It adopted the name Pub Squash for its lemon soft drink but later changed that name to Pub Soda Squash because of food and beverage regulations which prevented the use of 'squash' alone in the absence of a specified percentage of real lemon juice. The label on the can consisted primarily of the swing doors seen in a saloon from the Wild West and old-style hotels. Not surprisingly, the can was yellow, as was Solo's can, although there was actually a finding at first instance that it was not industry practice at that time to equate the colour of containers with the colour usually associated with the relevant fruit flavour.[20] Also, unsurprisingly, the cans and bottles containing Pub Squash were the same size as Solo's cans. Perhaps more to the point, the defendant adopted similar advertising themes and slogans. It also borrowed heavily from the concept of *The Six Million Dollar Man*,

---

17 See F Schechter, 'The Rational Basis of Trademark Protection' (1927) 40 *Harvard Law Review* 813 and N Klein, *No Logo*, Picador, New York, 2000 for more detailed treatment of this issue.
18 See http://www.superbrands-brand. com./volIII/brand coke.htm for details of some of the themes around advertising of Coca-Cola such as 'It's the real thing', 'Things go better with Coke' and 'Coke is it'.
19 See http://www.superbrands-brands. com/volIII/brand_coke.htm for a history of Coca-Cola, which was first made in 1886.
20 [1981] RPC 429, 460.

130 LANDMARKS IN AUSTRALIAN IP LAW

an American action television series playing at the time in which the action hero played by Lee Majors was part human, part bionics, due to being reconstructed after suffering near fatal injuries.[21]

Some of the Pub Soda Squash television advertisements were run only during the showing of *The Six Million Dollar Man* and involved

> the 'hero' . . . engaged in vigorous physical endeavour (unarmed combat with an 'evil villain') . . . the 'hero' 'rips' the top off the can, the 'spurt of mist' from the top of the can is featured, and the 'hero' crushes the can when he is finished drinking. At the end, the 'voice over announcer' says 'When your [sic] through with the hassles, rip into a Pub Lemon Soda Squash.[22]

Pub Squash also ran two other advertisements during its television campaign. One was the 'Furnace' advertisement in which a man was working near a blast furnace. The voice-over said: 'When the heat is on, and your throat is aching for the local, rip into a Pub Soda Squash; drown that thirst with the biting taste of lemon in Pub Soda Squash.'[23]

A third advertisement involved a 'young surfer-looking bloke', and the advertisement and the voice-over told the story of the young surfer hitching to the beach with his kneeboard and being picked up by a 'chick' who 'laid that can of "Pub Squash" on me'.[24] In the original script, the surfer was to spill the drink as he drank but, on legal advice, this was deleted from the actual commercial as shot and shown on television. The use of a kneeboarder rather than an actual surfer was an interesting choice. At the time, the shortboard surf scene was probably a bit too bohemian for the demographic being sought, of those perceiving themselves as rugged, male beer drinkers. The IPS (International Professional Surfing) events were not started until 1976,[25] and surfing was, at the time, associated with the young, wild and, possibly, drug-addled. The popularity of surfing today among many generations would not yield such an approach today.[26]

The first instance decision

The plaintiff based its case on two separate claims. The first was passing off and, at the trial itself, it amended its pleadings to claim a second cause of action in

---

21 The program was very popular, its theme was used by many and the expression entered the common language at the time. For example, while the program was playing, the Australian fast bowler Jeff Thomson was placed on a $600 000 contract by a Brisbane radio station, an extraordinary sum for a cricketer at that time, and he was promptly dubbed 'The Six Million Dollar Man'. The judgment in the case incorrectly refers to this program as *Million Dollar Man*.
22 [1981] RPC 429, 448.
23 ibid., p. 449. The advertisement theme is somewhat similar to an advertising campaign for Victoria Bitter's theme of 'a hard earned thirst needs a big cold beer'. In those advertisements, blue-collar workers were portrayed engaging in hot, manual work and slaking their thirst at the end of the working day with Victoria Bitter, a popular beer sold primarily in Victoria but also throughout Australia.
24 ibid., p. 455.
25 See http://www.surfermage.com./magazine/archivedissues/asphist.
26 For example, a recent television advertising campaign in Australia for Panadol involves a middle-aged man surfing a longboard cautiously on relatively gentle waves.

unlawful or unfair competition. With regard to the first of these claims, Powell J found on the evidence that passing off had not occurred, and as to the latter of these claims, he found that no such tort existed in Australian law.

Unfair competition and passing off (and a bit of law and literature)

The discussion about a tort of unfair competition was somewhat obscure in terms of defining the tort. The precise elements of such a tort were never clearly defined, probably because its existence was rejected and therefore such a detailed exposition of a non-existent tort was not required. However, the judgment seems to suggest that it would involve an intent to trade off the goodwill of the plaintiff and the achievement of that goal without necessarily going so far as to involve a misrepresentation of an association between the two products.

Consequently, the intention of the defendant was a critical concern of the judgment. In its submissions and evidence, the defendant vehemently denied attempting to 'trade off' the Solo image. It claimed that the idea for a Pub Squash had been devised prior to the launch of Solo and that it was already committed to launching Pub Squash at the time that the defendant became aware of Solo and its advertising campaign.

Powell J was equally emphatic in his rejection of most of the defendant's claims. It would be difficult to find a case in which a judge has more clearly expressed the view that he or she simply did not accept the evidence of a defendant's witnesses and yet the defendant managed to win its case. In the judgment, Powell J explained in some detail why each and every witness for the defendant should not be believed. In particular, he found that the defendant possessed a Solo can and showed it to the person responsible for the Pub Squash artwork, the name and formula for Pub Squash were adopted with Solo in mind, and the defendant deliberately sought 'to approximate the get-up of "Solo" without crossing the dividing line which would lead to a "passing off" of "Pub Squash" as "Solo"'.[27]

In summarising his conclusions Powell J came close to setting a world record for the longest sentence ever written in English – a 182-word sentence which also purported to be a paragraph:

> From what I have written above it will appear that it is my view that, as from a time being no later than the latter part of August 1974, the defendant, having by means of one or more of its officers become aware of the successful launch of 'Solo' in Victoria and of the sale of Solo in southern New South Wales, and, thus, appreciating that in all probability the Victorian launch would be followed by a large scale launch of Solo upon the New South Wales market, set out in a deliberate and calculated fashion to take advantage of the plaintiff's past efforts in developing Solo and of the plaintiff's past and anticipated future efforts in developing a market for a product such as Solo and that, in

---

27 [1981] RPC 429, 483.

132 LANDMARKS IN AUSTRALIAN IP LAW

particular the defendant, by its officers, sought to copy or to approximate the formula for Solo and chose a product name and package for the defendants' proposed product derived from and intended to gain the benefit of the plaintiff's past and anticipated advertising campaign, and the plaintiffs' package for their product.[28]

On his retirement from the bench, it was noted that one sentence in a judgment of Powell J, while not as long as the one above, contained 11 commas and one colon.[29] The sentence above contained a mere 10 commas. Lord Denning would not have been amused by either sentence.

Yet on a crucial allegation for passing off purposes, Powell J found for the defendant. He rejected the proposition that the defendant copied the plaintiff's form of advertising.[30] As the plaintiff had pleaded that the defendant had, 'with fraudulent intent, set out to compete unfairly with the plaintiffs by 'pirating' the formula for 'Solo', 'pirating' the colour of the containers in which 'Solo' was marketed, and 'pirating' the theme upon which the advertising for 'Solo' was based', this finding was critical.

> The suggested similarities with the 'Solo' advertisements, as for example, 'ripping off' the top of a can of Pub Squash', 'the spurt of mist' (both in 'The Million Dollar Man' and the reference to 'the local' (in 'Furnace') are, in my view, naturally suggested by, and would be hard to avoid, in a commercial for a canned soft drink named 'Pub Squash'; while the proposed incident in 'Kneeboard' was, in my view, not unnatural and was different, in its context, from the incident of the canoeist, in the 'Solo' advertisement, spilling 'Solo' down his chin.[31]

Having considered the two advertising campaigns and other factors such as similarities of the can, Powell J found that 'the facts ... do not reveal any relevant misrepresentation on the part of the defendant as to its goods, [and] the plaintiffs have not made out a case for relief based upon the extended concept of passing off'.[32]

However, the process in his judgment by which he reached that conclusion was the basis of the subsequent appeal. In particular, Powell J first examined the evidence and concluded that there was no misrepresentation supporting a passing off action. After this, he then proceeded to consider the defendant's intention to trade off the plaintiff's reputation only in the context of the allegation of unfair competition. On appeal, the complaint made by the plaintiff was that the judge had therefore failed to take into account the defendant's intention in determining whether it had actually achieved its intention. This issue is addressed in more detail below in the discussion of the Privy Council appeal.

---

28 [1981] RPC 429, 484.
29 See 'Address upon the Occasion of the Retirement of the Honourable Justice Philip Powell AM', 8 November 2002, available at http://www.lawlink.nsw.gov.au/lawlink/supreme_court.
30 [1981] RPC 429, 484.
31 ibid.
32 ibid.

Ancillary matters

There are some ancillary matters worthy of note. In particular, this case was not the only litigation between Cadbury Schweppes and Pub Squash. Pub Squash actually initiated passing off litigation against Cadbury Schweppes prior to this case. It complained of two matters. First, it complained of an advertisement that Cadbury Schweppes had published in the *Daily Mirror* in December 1975 which featured pictures of the cans of various lemon-flavoured soft drinks, including Pub Soda Squash. A Solo can was displayed in the foreground of the photograph and the double-page colour advertisement was headed 'Solo separates the men from the boys'. Pub Squash wrote to Cadbury Schweppes alleging that they were representing that Pub Soda Squash was a product of Cadbury Schweppes and, at the same time, that Solo was a superior product to Pub Soda Squash. They also objected to the use of the trade marks 'Pub Squash' and 'Pub Soda Squash' but only in that it constituted false advertising rather than trade mark infringement. The latter allegation may well have been worded to avoid a groundless claim of trade mark infringement which could have resulted in Cadbury Schweppes instituting proceedings.[33] Cadbury Schweppes later indicated that it would not engage in such advertising in the future and removed posters with the advertisement from various retail outlets.

The second allegation, of passing off, was made after Cadbury Schweppes sought registration of the business name 'Pub Squash Company' in South Australia and Tasmania. Business name registration is required in each state so that consumers and other traders can ascertain the legal entity behind any particular business name. However, registration of a business name confers no legal rights of a trade mark nature[34] and does no more than confer immunity from prosecution for failure to register a business name. Litigation was commenced in South Australia and interim injunctions granted which included undertakings by Cadbury Schweppes not to manufacture or distribute or to accept orders for aerated waters under the style of 'the Pub Squash Company'.[35] Why Cadbury Schweppes attempted to register that business name is unclear. It is possible that it was wrongly advised as to the value of a business name registration, a common error made by both lay people and lawyers who assume that registration of a business name confers rights instead of simply an immunity from prosecution for failing

---

[33] Under Australian trade mark law, a groundless threat of trade mark infringement proceedings is itself a cause of action. Accusing a large corporation such as Cadbury Schweppes of trade mark infringement is likely to lead to such proceedings being instituted. See *Trade Marks Act 1995* (Cth) s 129; and N Weston and M Davison 'Groundless Threats of Trade Mark Infringement: How to Avoid Getting Court' (2000) *Australian Intellectual Property Journal* 151.

[34] One possible exception to this proposition is that registration of a business name is one basis upon which an entity can claim registration of a '. com.au' domain name. See http://auda.org.au for details of the policies concerning the registration of Australian domain names.

[35] [1981] RPC 429, 453.

134 LANDMARKS IN AUSTRALIAN IP LAW

to register the business name.[36] The issue remains one of considerable confusion to this day and the subject of much debate and discussion on the relationship between business names and trade marks.[37]

The appeal to the Privy Council

The jurisdiction issue

One of the interesting aspects of the case was that the plaintiff chose to appeal directly to the Privy Council rather than the New South Wales Court of Appeal and, if necessary, from there to either the High Court or the Privy Council.[38] At the appeal, the respondents argued that the Privy Council had no jurisdiction in the matter as it involved a question of federal law. Appeals to the Privy Council on matters relating to federal law were abolished in 1968 and all appeals from the High Court to the Privy Council were abolished in 1975. These moves were a reflection of a political desire to demonstrate greater Australian independence from Great Britain.

Other moves included the Whitlam Labor Government's refusal to recommend imperial honours such as knighthoods which were awarded by the Queen on the recommendation of the federal government. Imperial honours were retained by several states as recommendations were made directly by the state governments to the Queen. The national anthem was changed from 'God Save the Queen' to 'Advance Australia Fair'.

In terms of legal independence, the effect of the abolition of Privy Council appeals was to free the High Court from the binding precedential force of Privy Council decisions and the quasi-binding force of House of Lords decisions. Despite this freedom, the High Court remained a conservative court under the Chief Justiceship of Sir Garfield Barwick who retired in 1981 and then Sir Harry Gibbs who succeeded him. The court was steeped in the approach to appellate work that its role was to 'find' the common law and espouse it rather than to create it.

Of course, these political niceties were not the primary concern of litigants. From a purely tactical perspective, the losing plaintiff had to elect between pursuing its case through to the High Court or via the Privy Council. It chose the Privy Council although the reasons for doing so are not readily apparent. The conservatism of the High Court may explain the decision to appeal to the Privy Council. As indicated in the Privy Council decision, there had been some suggestions in

---

36 See, for example, *Business Names Act 1962* (Vic) s 5, which requires the registration of a business name in the circumstances specified. The legislation confers no rights on the registrant.
37 See Advisory Council on Intellectual Property, *A Review of the Relationship between Trade Marks and Business Names, Company Names and Domain Names*, March 2006, available at http://www.acip.gov.au.
38 The *Supreme Court Act 1970* (NSW) referred to appeals to the Privy Council from the judgment of the court. As the court was defined as the Supreme Court of New South Wales, a party could appeal directly to the Privy Council.

various English decisions of either the existence or the desirability of creating a tort of unfair competition. Such a cause of action, in various legal forms, exists in most countries of the EU and English law was becoming increasingly influenced by the law of other European nations as a consequence of the UK's relatively recent entry into the EU.

In addition, the English courts had certainly indicated a preparedness to expand the operation of the tort of passing off, even if they were not willing to go to the next step of abandoning the need to prove some misrepresentation. Decisions such as the Spanish Champagne case and the Advocaat case demonstrated a willingness to push the boundaries of passing off and to take a broader view of what could constitute the relevant misrepresentation.[39]

In contrast, while Australian courts had embraced the expansion of passing off to factual situations beyond the traditional one of one trader passing off his or her goods as those of another trader,[40] a conservative High Court, although then technically freed from the constraints of being bound by the decisions of the highest English appellate courts, was highly unlikely to acknowledge the existence of such a tort of unfair competition without a much clearer signal from them that such a tort was known to the common law. To do otherwise would have been inconsistent with the approach of finding the common law as opposed to creating it. It would also have been inconsistent with the views of Dixon J in the *Victoria Park Racing* case, quoted later in this chapter.

The plaintiff's best prospect of a decision based on a tort of unfair competition was probably to argue the matter before the Privy Council and this may have been the inspiration for the decision to appeal directly to the Privy Council. On the other hand, this does not explain why the appellant abandoned the argument based on unfair competition when it appeared before the Privy Council. In the end, we are left without explanation of why the trip was made to London to argue the case when the delights of Canberra potentially beckoned.

From a jurisdictional perspective, the question for the Privy Council was whether the matters before it were matters of federal law or state law. If the former had applied, then the Privy Council would not have had jurisdiction. The original statement of claim raised an issue as to the validity of the defendant's trade mark as well as that of passing off. The laws relating to registered trade marks are and were clearly federal matters[41] and so it was argued that the appeal should not be heard by the Privy Council. However, at trial, while the claim in respect of the registered trade mark was never abandoned, both parties restricted their arguments and the submission of evidence to the passing off action. The first instance judgment made no reference to the trade mark claim other than to note that the plaintiff sought an order for the expungement of the defendant's

---

39 See *J Bollinger v Costa Brava Wine Co Ltd* [1960] RPC 16, *Erven Warnink BV v J Townend & Sons (Hull) Ltd* [1979] AC 731.
40 *Henderson v Radio Corporation Pty Ltd* [1960] SR (NSW) 576; 1A IPR 620.
41 The relevant legislation at the time was the *Trade Marks Act 1955* (Cth), passed pursuant to s 51(xviii) of the Australian Constitution which gave the Commonwealth jurisdiction in relation to trade marks.

136   LANDMARKS IN AUSTRALIAN IP LAW

trade mark 'Pub Squash' from the register. Consequently, the Privy Council was untroubled by the suggestion that the passing off action before it was a state matter and that it therefore had jurisdiction.

Perhaps more surprising is that the plaintiff did not plead a breach of s 52(1) of the *Trade Practices Act 1974* (Cth). The provision provides that 'a corporation shall not, in trade or commerce, engage in conduct that is misleading or deceptive or which is likely to mislead or deceive'. It has become the most litigated section of any Australian legislation because of its broad scope. Its close relationship to passing off is obvious and has been the subject of considerable commentary in numerous cases.[42] The non-pleading of s 52 is an interesting example of the slow speed at which the *Trade Practices Act* was initially taken up by practitioners, although by 1988 the case of *Pacific Dunlop v Hogan*,[43] which is discussed in Chapter 10, was brought in reliance on s 52. Today, it would be almost incomprehensible that such an action would not be brought in the Federal Court with the primary cause of action being s 52.

Revival of the Solo man

From time to time, Cadbury Schweppes has renewed its advertising campaign for Solo using the Solo man theme. For instance, in 1986, a number of television advertisements were run involving the Solo man in a raft in white water and on a windsailing device on a salt pan. In 1990, the Solo man was back in his kayak, this time entering the kayak on land at the top of a steep incline and sliding down the incline before entering the white water. Then, in 1995, the Solo man pulled his kayak into shore and unknowingly put his Solo can on the snout of a crocodile. The subsequent fight to regain the can from the crocodile that submerged with it was the central action of the advertisement. It concluded with the arm of the Solo man rising from the murky water triumphantly holding the intact can of Solo, somewhat reminiscent of the Lady of the Lake holding Excalibur.

It may be worth noting that Australia's own *Crocodile Hunter* episodes with Steve Irwin were first filmed in 1992 and 10 episodes were filmed in 1995. While the crocodile hunter's biggest reputation was probably in the US at the time, he had an emerging reputation in Australia. A 1995 episode of the quirky South Park engaged in a spoof of the crocodile hunter with a character who pursued wild animals with the statement 'I'm going to stick my thumb up his butt!'.

---

42 See M Davison, K Johnston and P Kennedy, *Shanahan's Australian Law of Trade Marks & Passing Off*, 3rd edn, Thomson, NSW, Pyrmont, 2003, chap. 22 for a discussion of the differences and similarities between s 52 and passing off. One possible distinction of relevance in the context of this decision is that s 52 may apply even if the misleading conduct is rectified prior to the point of sale. Powell J made the point that, in his opinion, any wrong selection of goods due to the similarities of the two cans would have been recognised before the completion of any purchase. See his judgment at p. 461. In theory, s 52 would apply to misleading or deceptive conduct prior to point of sale. See *Taco Co (Aust) Inc v Taco Bell Pty Ltd* (1982) 42 ALR 177 but also see the discussion of the issue in Davison et al, op. cit., para. 22.95.

43 *Hogan and Others v Pacific Dunlop Ltd* (1988) 12 IPR 225 and (on appeal) *Pacific Dunlop Ltd v Hogan and Others* (1989) 14 IPR 398.

Of course, it may have been coincidence that an advertisement involving a crocodile was filmed at about the same time, although no previous Solo advertisement had involved wild animals and this was the first in which the top was not ripped off a can and the contents consumed in the accustomed, awkward 'spillage' manner.

Recent advertising campaigns

The most recent Solo campaign is a combination of television advertisements, a website and tease advertising. In a very real sense, it departs considerably from the previous images used to promote Solo. The Solo man is no longer with us, it seems, but the emphasis on the male soft drink consumer remains.

Cadbury Schweppes registered the domain name 'mancans. com.au' and then proceeded to screen a number of television advertisements involving various scenarios in which the male actors were portrayed as being feminine in some respect. During the advertisements, they appeared to develop breasts, otherwise referred to as 'man cans'. There was no mention of the product being advertised but only references to the website.

The website itself also makes no reference to any product. Instead, the home page has comments such as these:

> Welcome … Maybe you had trouble understanding the difference between a V8 and flat 6. Perhaps you bought just a few too many hair products. Whatever the case, you acted in a distinctly unmanly way. And you grew yourself a nice little pair of Man Cans.

The website then goes on to explain the various causes of man cans and various means of avoiding their development or to rid oneself of them. For instance, it provides this advice to anyone who has man cans:

> **You've got 'em. Now what?**
>
> If you've really been acting like a big girl's blouse and sprouted a full-blown set of Man Cans, you're pretty well stuffed. But if you've just made a small mistake – like using your girlfriend's hair conditioner or accidentally watching more than a minute of *Sex and the City* – you can reduce the severity of you (sic) Man Cans with the following exercise:
>
> **The Mantra**
>
> Immediately remove yourself from the unmanly situation. Find a mirror, somewhere free of distraction and boldly and clearly repeat the following until the swelling reduces.
>
> > I am a man
> > I do manly things
> > I do not shriek, giggle or cry
> > I never watch romantic comedies. Ever.
> > I am an island . . .[44]

---

44 Copy on file with author.

The banner of the website refers to the 'Worldwide Organisation for Men Exhibiting Nanciness' which is an acronym for 'Women'. 'Nancy' is, of course, a reference to being effeminate or homosexual and the entire image is anything but that of the Solo man. Instead it has overtones of homophobia and traces of misogyny which have been the subject of some media discussion.[45]

The tease advertising in television advertisements referring to the website was subsequently backed up with television advertisements in which various men started to grow breasts. The men then engage in some manly adventure such as catching a shark by hand and dragging it out of the water into their home. Their breasts then disappeared and they drank a can of Solo without the trademark spillage occurring. However, the action is more a caricature of the Solo man than a real life representation as it is portrayed in such a way as to deny it being 'real'.

Feeding off each other and reaping where you have not sown

The case provides some interesting fodder for the long-running debate and discussion about the appropriateness of a general tort of unfair competition in Australia. At least one article published in UK journals decried the loss of an opportunity presented by the case to create such a tort.[46]

Yet both the facts and the subsequent history of the sales and advertising of Solo and Pub Squash demonstrate not only how unnecessary such a tort is but how difficult it would be to define and apply such a tort. If the heart of the tort would be the deliberate taking advantage of the goodwill generated by a particular advertising campaign, then one is struck by the number of potential claims that various advertising campaigns might have spawned.

For example, was Pub Squash to be enjoined because of its likeness to Victoria Bitter's 'hard earned thirst' advertising campaign? Should Pub Squash have been prevented from showing its advertisements with the hero action figure during the broadcasting of *The Six Million Dollar Man*? Should the crocodile ad for Solo which was broadcast at the time that Steve Irwin's reputation as the crocodile hunter was emerging in Australia and the US be considered an act of unfair competition? Should Solo have been prevented from using a medallion label modelled on well-known beer labels such as Budweiser in combination with an advertising campaign aimed at the macho beer-drinking male who has to occasionally content himself with a non-alcoholic beverage? Or should we embrace a more robust approach to competition in which deception and misleading are

---

45 See, for example, the *Herald Sun* blog of Andrea Burns, 14 August 2007, available at http://blogs.news.com.au/heraldsun/andreaburns.

46 G Dworkin, 'Passing off and Unfair Competition: An Opportunity Missed' (1981) 44 *Modern Law Review* 564, and see also J Lahore, 'The Pub Squash Case: Legal Theft or Free Competition' [1981] 2 *European Intellectual Property Review* 54.

prohibited but activities up to that line of misconduct are permitted? Why was it not enough for the defendant to sufficiently differentiate its product from that of the plaintiff?[47] Why would a free enterprise economy wish to embrace any other view of competition?

The case for preventing misrepresentation is a solid one. Economics suggests that misinformation must be prevented so that consumers may make their choice of goods but it imposes no greater requirement than that. As for commercial morality, it is hard to determine how morality and immorality are to be defined in this context. Powell J hinted that he considered the defendant's actions contravened commercial morality[48] but gave no indication as to the basis upon which such moral judgment was formed. The academic writing with its references to 'piracy' and 'theft'[49] are somewhat hyperbolical in nature. In particular, the point needs to be made that at the end of the day, Cadbury Schweppes was not deprived of the opportunity to continue to associate its product with rugged, manly activities and it has continued to profit from so doing in various forms for more than 30 years. If it had been able to demonstrate that the advertising image it portrayed was distinctive of its product, then it would have won its passing off case.[50] This latter point is also implicitly made in a brief note about the case published in the *Australian Law Journal* by one Susan Crennan, recently appointed to the High Court of Australia.[51]

The refusal to embrace a tort of unfair competition was one of the defining moments in the development of passing off in Australia. The possibility of the existence or creation of such a tort has been mooted in numerous cases in both Australia and England. While some judgments seem to have suggested the possibility of such a tort,[52] ultimately it has been rejected by the High Court of Australia on at least two separate occasions.[53] However, on those two occasions, the particular context was not one relating to a passing off type situation where the defendant was taking advantage of another's goodwill but without engaging in any misrepresentation. This case was the first of such a type in which an Australian court rejected the possibility of a tort of unfair competition in such circumstances.

The subsequent history of Solo suggests that the decision to do so was a wise one. Cadbury Schweppes has continued to thrive as has the Solo brand itself in the face of competition from Pub Squash. Despite losing the case, Cadbury Schweppes has been able to successfully use the 'man's drink' marketing approach

---

47 The test applied by the Privy Council. See [1981] RPC 429, 492.
48 ibid., p. 485.
49 'Theft is sanctified, it seems, provided there is no significant deception or confusion': Lahore, op. cit., p. 55.
50 The plaintiff did not have to meet a tougher test of 'universal and exclusive association' between the plaintiff's 'badge' and its goods or business. See the judgment at p. 457.
51 S Crennan, 'Trade Marks – Whether Similar Advertising Campaign Constitutes Passing Off' (1981) 55 *Australian Law Journal* 95.
52 *J Bollinger v Costa Brava Wine Co Ltd* [1960] Ch 262 and *Hogan v Koala Dundee Pty Ltd* (1988) 83 ALR 187.
53 *Moorgate Tobacco Co Ltd v Philip Morris Ltd* (1984) 156 CLR 414; 56 ALR 193 and *Victoria Park Racing and Recreation Grounds Company Ltd v Taylor* (1937) 58 CLR 479.

140   LANDMARKS IN AUSTRALIAN IP LAW

for more than 30 years. Despite the claims of 'piracy' made at the time, it still has what was allegedly pirated.

The words of Dixon J in *Victoria Park Racing and Recreation Grounds v Taylor*,[54] discussed in Chapter 4, remain of considerable force on the point:

> Courts of Equity have not in British jurisdictions thrown the protection of an injunction around all the intangible elements of value, that is, value in exchange, which may flow from the exercise by an individual of his powers or resources whether in the organisation of a business or undertaking or the use of ingenuity, knowledge, skill or labour. This is sufficiently evidenced by the history of the law of copyright and by the fact that the exclusive rights to invention, trade marks, design, trade name and reputation are dealt with in English law as special heads of protected interests and not under a wide generalisation.[55]

In that case and the *Pub Squash* case, the decision of the US Supreme Court in *International News Service v Associated Press*[56] was rejected as being an applicable authority and the dissenting views in that American decision were embraced by the courts.[57]

Conclusion

In summary, the *Pub Squash* case delivered a myriad of insights into the development of passing off and attitudes to unfair competition, the emerging use of trade marks and brand image without direct reference to their product and Australian society in the 1970s.

From a purely intellectual property law perspective, it was an intriguing example of the possibility of acquiring exclusive rights in relation to an abstract marketing image of a product. In the judgment of the judge at first instance, Cadbury Schweppes fell short of acquiring such rights but the courts acknowledged the possibility of it doing so. If the court action had been taken some time later, the defendant may have had some difficulty in achieving the same victory.

The case was also an interesting example of the emphasis on the marketing and brand image rather than the product itself. The marketing campaign was devised first and preceded the choice of the product. Cadbury Schweppes did not decide it had a great product and then try to create an image around it. It decided on the image that would sell and the product had to fit the image. Finally, the ancillary references to the passing off action instituted by Pub Squash against Cadbury Schweppes are but one example of the ongoing difficulties associated with the relationship between business names and trade marks.

---

54 *Victoria Park Racing and Recreation Grounds Company v Taylor* (1937) 58 CLR 479.
55 ibid., p. 509.
56 (1918) 248 US 215.
57 See A Kamperman Sanders, *Unfair Competition Law*, Clarendon Press, Oxford, 1997 for a discussion of unfair competition laws in Europe; and M Davison, *The Legal Protection of Databases*, Cambridge University Press, Cambridge, 2003, pp. 172–90 for a discussion of American unfair competition law and the decision in *International News Service v Associated Press* (1918) 248 US 215.

The other interesting legal aspect of the decision from a politico-legal perspective was the issue of the jurisdiction of the Privy Council. The late 1960s and the 1970s were a time of considerable political turmoil in Australia. One aspect of that turmoil was the attempt to develop and define a more distinctly independent Australian legal and political culture. The issues surrounding the ongoing role of the Privy Council were but one manifestation of that attempt.

From a more sociological/psychological perspective, the case is a fascinating time capsule. Brazen macho activity was embraced with the underlying suggestion of sculling of beer subliminally linked to the consumption of soft drink. On the other hand, real surfing was a bit too out there and advertisements needed to refer to kneeboard riders. Finally, a comparison of the original advertising theme with the more quirky 'man cans' advertising theme of today provides interesting fodder for thought about how masculinity is expressed in and appealed to by the mass media.

9

The *Firmagroup* case: trigger for designs law reform

Janice Luck

Introduction

The decision of the High Court in 1987 in *Firmagroup Australia v Byrne & Davidson Doors (Vic)*[1] (*Firmagroup* case) was concerned with the scope of protection granted to three-dimensional designs by Australia's then registered designs regime. Most would regard *Firmagroup* as Australia's leading designs case, notable for the profound effect it had in reforming the law, triggering the introduction of a new designs regime and influencing the establishment of a new second-tier patent regime.

On trial in the *Firmagroup* case was the effectiveness of protection granted to registered designs under Australian law. The registered design in question pertained to a combination handle and lock for shutter doors. These types of doors, the High Court explained, 'consist of flexible metal screens. They open by sliding upwards, the screen rolling onto a revolving spindle. They are in popular use as garage doors.'[2] In Australia, where sprawling low-density suburbs engender a reliance on private cars as a major means of transportation, garages and garage doors are of particular interest and importance. The following Australian private car ownership statistics are given in an article in Year Book Australia 2005:

---

[1] *Firmagroup Australia Pty Ltd v Byrne & Davidson Doors (Vic) Pty Ltd and Others* (1987) 9 IPR 353.
[2] ibid., p. 354

THE *FIRMAGROUP* CASE   143

Since the 1950s the number of private cars has risen dramatically, and continues to do so ... In 2003 there were 10.4 million registered cars and station wagons, compared with 769 000 in 1950 and 76 000 in 1920.[3]

The Series 1 Roll-A-Door roller doors marketed by the respondents in the *Firmagroup* case appeared to dominate the relevant prior art, with the trial judge stating that in 1978 the respondents enjoyed about 90 per cent of the Australian market for residential roller doors. The 'History' page of the current website of B&D Doors sets out the development of the Roll-A-Door roller door, describing it as an Australian invention and icon.[4] It thus seems fitting that the important question raised by the *Firmagroup* case was concerned with a design for a part of a garage door.

The application to register the design for the combination handle and lock was filed on 12 May 1976, and the writ in the *Firmagroup* case was issued on 15 March 1982. Remarkably however, the relevant law to determine the issues in the case was an Act passed by the Commonwealth parliament at the beginning of the century – the *Designs Act 1906* (1906 Act). As enacted, the 1906 Act was small: eight pages in length and containing 49 sections. In 1936, Dixon J of the High Court remarked that the Act

> shows a marked economy in the statement of its principles. It does not explain what it means by the very general expressions employed. The case law, as might be expected, cannot reduce to certainty the vagueness which the legislation exhibits, but the cases do contain statements which I think afford some guidance in the application of this rather peculiar Act.[5]

Although the 1906 Act was substantially amended in 1981[6], Dixon J's observation was quoted and endorsed by the High Court as recently as 2005.[7]

The parliamentary debates on the bill for what became the 1906 Act provide limited assistance as to the meaning of its provisions. In the second reading speech in the senate, Senator Keating said:

> The Bill may be said to be a legislative expression of the English law as it exists at present. The English statutory law is found in the *Patents Designs and Trade Marks Act* of 1883, subsequently amended by Statutes up to as far as 1888. That legislation, together with what has been the interpretation of it by the Judiciary in Great Britain, may be said to be the substance of this Bill.[8]

---

3 Australian Bureau of Statistics, *Use of Urban Public Transport in Australia*, Year Book Australia 2005 – 1301.0, available at http://www.abs.gov.au/ausstats/ABS@.nsf/Previousproducts/1301.0Feature%20Article292005.
4 See http://www.bnd.com.au.
5 *Macrae Knitting Mills Ltd v Lowes Ltd* (1936) 55 CLR 725, 729.
6 These amendments were not relevant to determining liability in the *Firmagroup* case.
7 *Polyaire Pty Ltd v K-Aire Pty Ltd* (2005) 64 IPR 223.
8 Commonwealth of Australia, *Parliamentary Debates*, Senate, 20 June 1906, p. 394. The historical development of Australia's designs law is considered by the Full Federal Court in *Hosokawa Micron International Inc v Fortune* (1990) 19 IPR 531 and by the High Court in *Polyaire v K-Aire* (2005) 64 IPR 223.

144 LANDMARKS IN AUSTRALIAN IP LAW

Most of the debate on the bill was directed to provisions which were thought to substantively depart from those of the *Patents, Designs, and Trade Marks Act 1883* (UK). Unfortunately, there was no further insight provided on the scope of protection granted by the infringement provisions in the bill.

The place that designs law should properly occupy in the overall protection of intellectual property has long been a difficult and vexed issue in Australia. Of particular concern, and one which existed at the time the 1906 Act was enacted, has been the appropriate scope of protection granted to designs in the light of protection granted by the patents regime. This concern – ensuring that designs protection does not encroach into areas the proper province of the patents regime by protecting function – lies at the heart of the issue in the *Firmagroup* case.[9]

The relevant designs law

The provisions of the 1906 Act relevant to the decision in the *Firmagroup* case were contained in ss 4 and 30(1)(a). In s 4, a design was defined as meaning 'an industrial design applicable, in any way or by any means, to the purpose of the ornamentation, or pattern, or shape, or configuration, of an article, or to any two or more of those purposes.' Section 30(1)(a) in substance provided that a person shall be deemed to infringe a registered design if he or she, without the licence or authority of the owner of the design, 'applies the design or any fraudulent or obvious imitation of it' to any article in respect of which the design was registered.[10] These definitions and infringement tests reflected the equivalent provisions in the *Patents, Designs, and Trade Marks Act 1883* (UK), and had not been changed since the enactment of the 1906 Act. In 1949, the tests of obvious and fraudulent imitation in the UK were replaced by a test of infringing by applying 'a design not substantially different from the registered design'.[11]

At the time the writ in the *Firmagroup* case was issued, s 30(1)(a) of the 1906 Act had received little judicial consideration and the authoritative interpretation

---

9 The case is not concerned with the more recent but equally difficult problem of the appropriate interrelationship between designs and copyright law that has emerged following the grant of a three-dimensional reproduction right to the owners of copyright in artistic works. The interrelationship between designs and copyright law has been the subject of much litigation and legislative activity in Australia. The area is particularly complex, but in broad terms two-dimensional designs based on drawings protected by copyright are now generally protected by that copyright but three-dimensional designs which have been commercially exploited are generally not protected by that copyright. There are, however, exceptions to these rules.
10 Section 30 also provided for indirect infringements and in fact originally referred to infringing the copyright in a registered design. However, subject to the nature of fraudulent imitation, the 1906 Act has always granted monopoly protection to registered designs.
11 *Registered Designs Act 1949* (UK) s 7(1).

of the provision remained that given by the High Court in the 1961 case of *Malleys v JW Tomlin*. The court stated:

> Turning to s 30 it is apparent that there is infringement in any one of three cases – ie where the design which has been applied is: (i) the registered design (ii) an obvious imitation of the registered design (ie not the same but a copy apparent to the eye notwithstanding slight differences) and (iii) a fraudulent imitation (ie a copy with differences which are both apparent and not so slight as to be insubstantial but which have been made merely to disguise the copying). Visual comparison will establish (i) or (ii) but a finding of fraudulent imitation must require something more because in such a case visual comparison is not of itself sufficient to establish imitation; otherwise it would be an obvious imitation.[12]

In order to establish infringement by applying the registered design or an obvious imitation, it was not necessary to prove that the alleged infringer had copied the registered design. On the other hand, in order to establish infringement by applying a fraudulent imitation, it was necessary to prove that the alleged infringer copied the registered design knowing or suspecting the design was registered or (possibly) the subject of a pending design application.[13] It was irrelevant that the alleged infringer may have honestly intended to make sufficient changes to avoid infringement, but it was necessary that the alleged infringing design be an imitation of the registered design; proving the necessary copying and knowledge or suspicion was not sufficient of itself.

Obviously critical to the determination of whether an alleged infringing design is an obvious or fraudulent imitation of the registered design is the degree to which the alleged infringing design visually differs from the registered design. It was well established, however, that the scope of protection granted to a registered design was influenced by the state of the prior art at the priority date. This principle was succinctly stated by Lockhart J in his judgment in the *Firmagroup* case, on appeal before the Full Federal Court:

> The scope of a registered design must be judged against the background of the prior art at the priority date. If the differences between the registered design and the prior art are only small then equally small differences between the registered design and the alleged infringing design will tend to lead to a finding of no infringement. On the other hand the greater the advance over the prior art in the registered design then, in general, the greater the scope of the protection afforded to the registered design: *Kevi A/S v Suspa-Verein UK Ltd*, supra; *Russell-Clarke: Designs* 5th ed pp 85–7; *Blanco White on Patents and Designs* 4th ed pp 326–7; *Ricketson: Law of Industrial Property* p 493 para 20.9.[14]

---

12 *Malleys Ltd v JW Tomlin Pty Ltd* [1961–2] 35 ALJR 352, 354.
13 The High Court in *Polyaire v K-Aire* (2005) 64 IPR 223, para. 18 stated that it was unnecessary in the case before it to decide whether it was also sufficient if the alleged infringer knew or suspected that an application to register the design was pending.
14 *Firmagroup Australia Pty Ltd v Byrne and Davidson Doors (Vic) Pty Ltd and Others* (1986) 6 IPR 377, 386.

146 LANDMARKS IN AUSTRALIAN IP LAW

The interpretation by the High Court in the *Malleys* case – that an obvious imitation is a copy apparent to the eye notwithstanding slight differences – indicated that this type of infringement was unlikely to protect the owner of a registered design against a person who was able to produce a design which copied the distinctive features of the registered design but with differences that were immediately apparent.[15] The High Court's interpretation of a fraudulent imitation, as a copy with differences that are both apparent and not so slight as to be insubstantial but which have been made merely to disguise the copying, provided little practical guidance on the degree of difference from the registered design that would still permit a finding of fraudulent imitation. Special leave to appeal to the High Court was granted in the *Firmagroup* case chiefly to consider the distinction between obvious and fraudulent imitations. The High Court, however, did not consider that the question arose in the case but went on to say: 'nothing that was submitted in argument before this court casts doubt upon the brief but accurate description of obvious and fraudulent imitations in the *Malleys* case.'[16] This comment needs some modification in light of the High Court's 2005 decision in *Polyaire v K-Aire*, where the court stated:

> However, a further examination of the whole of the reasons in *Malleys* shows that point (iii) would be accurate if the material in brackets were introduced, not by 'ie', but by 'eg'. While a copy with differences which are apparent and not so slight as to be insubstantial but which have been made merely to disguise the copying may answer the description in s 30 of a fraudulent imitation, this state of affairs does not exhaust the scope of that description.[17]

The *Firmagroup* case

While the High Court in the *Firmagroup* case may not have considered the distinction between obvious and fraudulent imitations, the decision nevertheless defined the scope of the rights granted under the 1906 Act by making a determination as to the circumstances where a design is not an imitation of the registered design but rather a different and thus non-infringing design.

As stated above, the registered design in the *Firmagroup* case was for a combination handle and lock for shutter doors. The statement of the nature of the registered design was as follows:

> The design resides in the application of the particular shape and configuration to a combination handle and lock for a shutter door as illustrated. The rear face of the handle and lock does not form part of the design. The design may be applied in any suitable manner and by any suitable means.[18]

The following are illustrations of the design:

---

15 See *Dunlop Rubber Co Ltd v Golf Ball Development Ltd* (1931) 48 RPC 268.
16 (1987) 9 IPR 353, 357.
17 (2005) 64 IPR 223, para. 28.
18 (1986) 6 IPR 377, 377.

THE *FIRMAGROUP* CASE 147

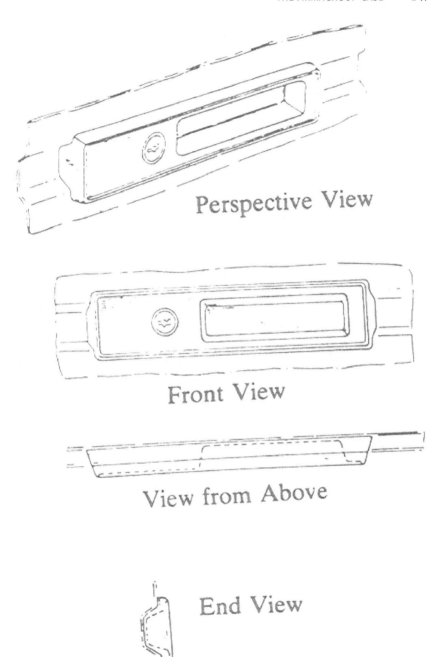

Figure 9.1 Door handle – registered design

In the *Firmagroup* case the owner of the registered design, Firmagroup Pty Ltd (the appellant), alleged that the manufacture and marketing by the respondents of the following combination handle and lock for shutter doors infringed its registered design:

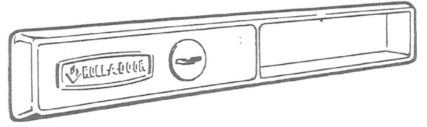

Figure 9.2 Door handle – alleged infringement

The trial judge, King J of the Supreme Court of Victoria, considered that the registered design 'was a substantial breakthrough in terms of novelty'.[19] As far as the prior art was concerned, King J noted that in 1978 the respondents' Series 1 roller door (the screen of which was different to the screen of the roller door the appellant went on to market) enjoyed about 90 per cent of the Australian market for residential roller doors. At this time, the respondents' lock was a rectangular flat metal plate with a lock in the centre, mounted on a screen with flat horizontal faces in front separated by backwardly extending semi-circular corrugations. The plate was placed on the flat surface with upper and lower flanges extending into the corrugations of the screen, thus providing a lower ledge users could grip to move the door up and down. The only other products forming part of the prior art were of the same general appearance. King J held that the registered design had thus incorporated into it a new concept of design in products of its kind; its new main features being a more elongated rectangular shape than was previously known and a recessed handle. As is clear from the above representation of the respondents' combination handle and lock, these new features were also present in the respondents' product.

King J held that the design of the respondents' combination handle and lock was not the same as the registered design, nor was it an obvious imitation of the registered design. In relation to the latter type of infringement, after stating that the appellant's design registration did not confer a monopoly over all articles with the features of an extended rectangular shape of the front face and a recess for use as a handle, King J said:

> [The appellant's] design incorporates such features in a particular form, and if another person uses the same features in a form substantially different in appearance, as the [respondents] have done in this case, there is no obvious imitation of the registered design.[20]

---

19 *Firmagroup Australia Pty Ltd v Bryne & Davidson Doors (Vic) Pty Ltd and Others* (1985) 4 IPR 631, 634.
20 ibid., p. 636.

THE *FIRMAGROUP* CASE   149

After reviewing the development of the respondents' combination handle and lock, King J considered that the necessary prerequisites to permit consideration of infringement by fraudulent imitation existed. He found that the respondents made use of the registered design knowing that it was a design registered under the 1906 Act. He thought that from the outset the respondents had considered the appellant a formidable competitor, with a product aesthetically superior to their own. In particular, the respondents thought the recessed handle was an excellent feature and wished to incorporate some form of it in their own face plate. However, the respondents also wanted to have a distinctively different face plate from that of the appellant, so as not to infringe the registered design, and believed they had achieved this. King J concluded that the respondents were right and held that there had been no fraudulent imitation:

> My conclusion is that although there are common features of construction in the compared designs, it must appear, to find fraudulent imitation, that the overall distinctive appearance of the registered design has been taken. In this case salient features of construction are taken, but the whole unit has been so redesigned to incorporate them that a different design has been produced. Thus the change in balance of the features and the lengthening of the article are not mere disguise but are themselves salient features of the defendants' design which are novel and unique in that design.[21]

In dismissing the appellant's appeal, the High Court approved this statement of King J, holding that it correctly summed up the position.

The appellant's appeal to the Full Federal Court was not successful,[22] nor was its appeal to the High Court. In delivering its very short judgment the High Court noted that a visual comparison of the registered design with the respondents' combination handle and lock revealed some points of similarity and some of distinction and went on to list these similarities and differences, placing particular emphasis on the latter. The court stressed that the 1906 Act was concerned with shape and configuration, not function. It accepted as correct the following passage from *Russell-Clarke on Copyright in Industrial Designs*:[23]

> What [the proprietor of a registered design] gets a monopoly for is one particular individual and specific appearance. If it is possible to get several different appearances, which all embody the general features which he claims, then those features are too general, and amount to a method or principle of construction. (See *Re Wolanski's Registered Design* (1953) 88 CLR 278 at 279–80; *Kestos Ltd v Kempat Ltd* (1935) 53 RPC 139 at 151.)[24]

The High Court went on to hold:

> The only design features that are susceptible to protection are those features which convey the idea of 'one particular individual and specific appearance', to repeat the

21 ibid., p. 640.
22 (1986) 6 IPR 377.
23 M Howe, *Russell-Clarke on Copyright in Industrial Designs*, 5th edn, Sweet & Maxwell, London, 1974, p. 27.
24 (1987) 9 IPR 353, 356.

phrase from *Russell-Clarke*. No design should be so construed as to give to its proprietor a monopoly in a method or principle of construction. The registration of the appellant's design thus gives no monopoly for the making of an article combining a plate in which a keyhole is set and a recessed handgrip; nor in our opinion does it give a monopoly for the making of an article combining a rectangular plate in which a keyhole is set and a recessed rectangular handgrip placed alongside horizontally. The idea of shape or configuration conveyed by those features is altogether too general to attract statutory protection.[25]

The court identified the particular conception of shape conveyed by the registered design as being of

a rather squat combination unit with the surface of the plate section extending into a broad surround of the recessed handgrip, a sloping recess in the handgrip, an absence of symmetry between the plate and handgrip sections of the unit and ends which are thick and irregularly shaped.[26]

These features, the High Court said, 'serve to distinguish the registered design from the respondents' article'.[27] The court concluded that what the respondents took from the registered design were not design features susceptible of protection and held:

As the points of similarity between the registered design and the respondents' article are general functional features, the article is not an imitation of the registered design within the meaning of section 30(1)(a).[28]

Analysis and impact of the *Firmagroup* case

The decision of the High Court in the *Firmagroup* case was greeted with dismay by many in Australia. The decision certainly did not protect the innovative elements of the registered design. An insistence that a design registration only grants protection to one particular individual and specific appearance is supported by long authority, and prima facie logical for a regime aimed at protecting how an article looks and not how it works. However, if the primary consideration in determining infringement is the principle that designs registration only grants protection to one particular individual and specific appearance, it is not surprising that the scope of protection granted is narrow. It seems preferable that the application of this principle be largely restricted to its original purpose of ensuring that the documentation filed with a design application clearly identifies one specific design.[29] In determining whether such a specific registered design has been infringed, primary consideration should be given to the infringement provisions. The concept of fraudulent imitation present in the 1906 Act clearly envisaged giving protection beyond the particular individual and specific appearance and

25 ibid.
26 ibid.
27 ibid.
28 ibid., p. 357.
29 See for example *Moody v Tree* (1892) 9 RPC 333 and *Re Bayer's Design* (1907) 24 RPC 65.

THE *FIRMAGROUP* CASE   151

provided an avenue for granting broader protection to the owner of a registered design. This appears to have been the view of the Designs Law Review Committee (DLRC), a committee appointed in October 1970 by the then Commonwealth Attorney-General to review the 1906 Act. The DLRC referred to the change in the UK law, which replaced the tests of obvious and fraudulent imitations with the test of a design not substantially different from the registered design, and expressed the view that the replaced tests appeared to provide wider protection. The DLRC went on to comment in relation to s 30 of the 1906 Act:

> The words 'obvious imitation' are, in our opinion, to be treated as broadly equivalent to the expression 'not substantially different' appearing in . . . the United Kingdom Act, but the words 'fraudulent imitation' have no equivalent in the United Kingdom Act.[30]

The High Court in the *Firmagroup* case did not take the opportunity to interpret the concept of fraudulent imitation expansively. Rather, the court confirmed that the rights granted by a registered design should be construed narrowly. It is to be remembered that the registered design in the *Firmagroup* case 'was a substantial breakthrough in terms of novelty' and its registered owner was therefore entitled to the broadest of protection.

As indicated above, the 1906 Act was substantially amended in 1981. The amendments were effected by the *Designs Amendment Act 1981* (1981 Amendment Act). These amendments, however, would not have affected the decision in the *Firmagroup* case. The 1981 Amendment Act substituted a new definition of design as follows:

> *design* means features of shape, configuration, pattern or ornamentation applicable to an article, being features that, in the finished article, can be judged by the eye, but does not include a method or principle of construction.

In the *Firmagroup* case, the High Court made it clear that the express exclusion in the new definition of methods or principles of construction made no difference to the law; the exclusion merely gave statutory expression to what was previously implied in the true conception of a design.[31] The 1981 Amendment Act did not also exclude from the definition of design 'features of shape or figuration which are dictated solely by the function which the article to be made in that shape or configuration has to perform', words that subsequent amendments had included in the UK definition of design. Rather, the 1981 Amendment Act introduced the following s 18 into the 1906 Act:

> An application for registration of a design shall not be refused, and a registered design is not invalid, by reason only that the design consists of, or includes, features of shape or configuration that serve, or serve only, a functional purpose.

This provision changed the law to some uncertain extent. Under the previous law it was no bar to the registrability of a design that it may serve a functional

---

30 Designs Law Review Committee, Parliament of Australia, *Report on the Law Relating to Designs, First Term of Reference*, 1973, para. 128.
31 (1987) 9 IPR 353, 356.

purpose, but a design which was dictated solely by the function of the article was not registrable. That is, when the features of shape and configuration of a design were attributable only to the function which the article, in that shape, was to perform, the design was not registrable even if the same function could be performed by an article of a different shape. The scope of this exclusion was not clear, but it appeared that if a designer had a choice as to shape or configuration, the resultant design was unlikely to be one whose features were dictated solely by function.[32] But these functional registrability issues were not relevant to the decision in the *Firmagroup* case. There was rightly no suggestion in that case that the registered design fell foul of such limitations and that it should not have been registered because of the functional nature of its features of shape and configuration. The *Firmagroup* case was concerned with determining the scope of protection to be given to the registered design's functional features of shape and configuration.

Inevitably the High Court's decision in the *Firmagroup* case raised the important question of whether the 1906 Act was achieving its objective of encouraging design innovation and, if not, whether amendments to the Act or new measures were necessary to ensure adequate protection of designs. Several review bodies were given the task of considering these questions.[33] Of major significance to such deliberations was whether the distinction between appearance and function so critical to the decision in the *Firmagroup* case was a tenable or appropriate distinction to make in relation to modern design. As the Bureau of Industry Economics stated in 1995:

> Once an activity whose chief concern was the application of decoration to utility articles, design has evolved to become an integral part of the innovation process. Rather than appearance being separate from function, these two aspects have fused for many products ... The uncertainty as to the economic role of designs law contrasts with the increasing economic importance of design activity. Design nowadays occupies a critical role in the production of goods. Design enhances functionality.[34]

The Australian Law Reform Commission's review

Introduction

The most comprehensive review of the 1906 Act was that undertaken by the Australian Law Reform Commission (ALRC). In August 1992 the then

---

32 The law prior to the introduction of s 18 by the 1981 Amendment Act is discussed at length in *Hosokawa Micron International Inc v Fortune* (1990) 19 IPR 531.
33 These were the Committee Inquiring into Intellectual Property Protection for Industrial Designs which completed its report, *Inquiry into Intellectual Property Protection for Industrial Designs*, in 1991; the Australian Law Reform Commission which completed its report, *Designs* (Report No. 74), in 1995; the Bureau of Industry Economics which completed its report, *The Economics of Intellectual Property Rights for Designs* (Occasional Paper 27), in 1995; and the Advisory Council on Industrial Property which completed its report, *Review of the Petty Patent System*, in 1995.
34 Bureau of Industry Economics, *The Economics of Intellectual Property Rights for Designs*, Occasional Paper 27, 1995, pp. 37–8.

Commonwealth Attorney-General referred the 1906 Act to the ALRC for inquiry and report. Paragraph 6.3 of the ALRC's final report stated:

> The terms of reference given to the Commission impel reform of the infringement provisions. They refer specifically to the need to 'remove the difficulties that have arisen in the operation of the *Designs Act 1906*.' A major impetus for this review is the strong concern, clearly expressed during the Commission's consultations, about the narrow scope of protection given to designs by the courts' interpretation of the Act. These concerns escalated as a result of the decision in *Firmagroup*.[35]

Most of the ALRC's recommendations for reform were accepted by the Commonwealth government and resulted in the repeal of the 1906 Act and the enactment of the *Designs Act 2003* (2003 Act), which came into force on 17 June 2004.

Recommendations relating to registered designs

Not surprisingly, the ALRC's surveys and consultations and the submissions received revealed that the protection granted by the 1906 Act was not highly regarded. Particular dissatisfaction was expressed at the inability to protect the innovative functional features of designs. Others pointed out that there is a broad range of factors involved in modern design and many, such as durability, ease of operation, feel and environmental considerations, are either not protected or not sufficiently protected. The ALRC's terms of reference, however, related to a review of the 1906 Act and, like many judges and legislators before them, the ALRC was concerned that any significant extension of designs protection could interfere with patent, copyright and trade mark law and the policies underlining them. Thus the ALRC divided its recommendations into two categories: those which could be achieved within the current framework of intellectual property protection and those that required a broader review. Consistent with this approach, the ALRC recommended that the registered designs regime continue to protect only the visual features of designs but that incidental protection of function continue to be permitted. Thus in the 2003 Act a design, in relation to a product, 'means the overall appearance of the product resulting from one or more visual features of the product'.[36] 'Visual feature' is defined to include 'the shape, configuration, pattern and ornamentation of the product'[37] and it is provided that 'a visual feature may, but need not, serve a functional purpose'.[38] It follows from these recommendations that reform of the infringement provisions were critical to ensuring broader protection for registered designs.

The relevant infringement provisions of the 2003 Act, largely based on the ALRC's recommendations, are contained in s 71(1)(a) which provides:

> A person infringes a registered design if, during the term of registration of the design, and without the licence or authority of the registered owners of the design, the person:

---

35 ALRC, *Designs*, Report No. 74, 1995.
36 Section 5, definition of 'design'.
37 Section 7(1).
38 Section 7(2).

154 LANDMARKS IN AUSTRALIAN IP LAW

(a) makes or offers to make a product, in relation to which the design is registered, which embodies a design that is identical to, or substantially similar in overall impression to, the registered design;[39]

The rights granted to the owner of a registered design are thus no longer shackled by the concept of an imitation. Instead, the owner's rights extend to preventing the use of a design substantially similar in overall impression to the registered design, regardless of whether the registered design has been copied or not. The ALRC preferred the word 'substantially' to 'significantly' because it believed the word 'substantially' implied a qualitative test which would assist the court in evaluating the importance of the similarities and differences between competing designs. The ALRC believed that the phrase 'overall impression' would encourage courts to focus on the whole appearance of competing designs instead of counting the differences between them.[40]

Section 19 of the 2003 Act sets out various factors to be considered in assessing whether a design is substantially similar in overall impression to another design.[41] Section 19 provides:

(1) If a person is required by this Act to decide whether a design is substantially similar in overall impression to another design, the person making the decision is to give more weight to similarities between the designs than to differences between them.

(2) The person must also:
 (a) have regard to the state of development of the prior art base for the design; and
 (b) if the design application in which the design was disclosed included a statement (a *statement of newness and distinctiveness*) identifying particular visual features of the design as new and distinctive:
  (i) have particular regard to those features; and
  (ii) if those features relate to only part of the design – have particular regard to that part of the design, but in the context of the design as a whole; and
 (c) if only part of the design is substantially similar to another design, have regard to the amount, quality and importance of that part in the context of the design as a whole; and
 (d) have regard to the freedom of the creator of the design to innovate.

(3) If the design application in which the design was disclosed did not include a statement of newness and distinctiveness in respect of particular visual features of the design, the person must have regard to the appearance of the design as a whole.

(4) In applying subsections (1), (2) and (3), the person must apply the standard of a person who is familiar with the product to which the design relates, or products similar to the product to which the design relates (the *standard of the informed user*).

(5) In this section, a reference to a person includes a reference to a court.

---

39 The further provisions of s 71(1) provide for indirect design infringements.
40 ALRC, op. cit., para. 6.7.
41 The test of substantially similar in overall impression is also the test to determine whether a design is registrable – see ss 15 and 16 of the 2003 Act.

THE *FIRMAGROUP* CASE 155

To ensure that the new infringement provisions grant the owner of a registered design broader rights than s 30 of the 1906 Act granted, as held by the *Firmagroup* case, it is important that the factors set out in s 19 achieve the ALRC's intention that the test of substantially similar in overall impression results in a qualitative assessment. Several of the subsections of s 19 appear to achieve this. First, s 19(4) provides that in applying the factors the court must apply the standard of the informed user, that is, the standard of a person who is familiar with the product to which the design relates or similar products. The informed user is apparently the person or group for whom the registered design is intended. According to the ALRC:

> The informed user will usually be the consumer or person using the designed article, depending on the nature of the design, but will not be a design expert. For example, the informed user of car replacement parts may be the mechanic who repairs the vehicle, but for domestic items it may be the consumer.[42]

This is in contrast to the position under the 1906 Act where it was the judge's eye, assisted where necessary by expert evidence, which assessed the visual similarities and differences between the registered design and the alleged infringing design. Assessing these similarities and differences from the perspective of an informed user should assist in ensuring that the importance and significance of the similarities and differences in relation to the particular product in question are taken into account.

Likewise the factors set out in s 19(2) and (3) should produce a qualitative assessment. Section 19(2)(c), by providing that if only part of the design is substantially similar to another design, the court must have regard to the amount, quality and importance of that part in the context of the design as a whole, clearly includes a qualitative assessment. Having regard to the state of the development of the prior art base for the design and to the freedom of the creator of the design to innovate, factors respectively mandated by s 19(2)(a) and (d) require consideration of the quality of the advance made by the registered design. This makes a finding of substantial similarity in overall impression more likely when the registered design is a significant advance over the prior art or where, given the nature of the product involved, the scope for innovation is limited. As indicated above, case law considering the 1906 Act had enunciated rules to the same effect. The mandatory nature of s 19, however, should ensure that the rules are consciously applied by the court in all cases.

Section 19(2)(b) also requires the court to have particular regard to any visual features identified in the design application as new and distinctive. If those features relate to only part of the design, the court must have particular regard to that part of the design but in the context of the design as a whole. Greater weight should thus be given to the identified new and distinctive features in the assessment of overall impression. It follows that the use where appropriate

---

42 ALRC, above n. 35, para. 6.13.

of statements identifying particular visual features of the design as new and distinctive should make a finding of substantial similarity in overall impression more likely if those features have been copied by the alleged infringer. The 1981 Amendment Act introduced statements of monopoly that design applicants could lodge with their applications which probably had the potential to operate in a similar way to the statements referred to in s 19(2)(b), a potential that for various reasons was not generally used.[43]

Perhaps the most significant factor set out in s 19 is that contained in sub-s (1) which provides that in determining whether the alleged infringing design is substantially similar in overall impression to the registered design, the court is to give more weight to similarities between the designs than to differences between them. This provision appears to have been recommended by the ALRC to ensure that undue emphasis is not placed on minor differences between competing designs instead of considering the overall similarities. But sub-s (1) goes further than this because it applies to all similarities regardless of their significance or importance. Thus this provision in the context of infringement clearly favours the owner of the registered design, arguably to an inappropriate extent.

It remains to be seen whether the new infringement provisions of the 2003 Act will be successful in granting more expansive protection to registered designs. The test under these provisions, however, remains one of comparing the competing designs as a whole in relation to the product in question; relevant to the comparison is not only what has been reproduced from the registered design, but also what the alleged infringer has produced. If infringement in the *Firmagroup* case had been determined by the 2003 Act provisions, it may well be that the respondents' design would have been held to infringe the appellant's registered design, at least if a statement identifying the recessed handle as the new and distinctive feature had been included in the application.

Protection of function

Not unexpectedly, the ALRC's inquiry revealed that many considered the *Firmagroup* case had resulted in a gap in the protection of function.

> There was a widespread view that the designs law did not adequately protect the functional features of articles and that many of these articles, whilst innovative in their particular markets, would not satisfy the standard of inventiveness necessary for patents.[44]

The ALRC was of the view that this gap is a gap in patent protection, not designs protection. The petty patent system was then being reviewed by the Advisory Council on Industrial Property (ACIP), and accordingly the ALRC recommended:

---

43 See the 1906 Act, ss 4 (definition of 'statement of monopoly') and 20(4).
44 ALRC, op. cit., para. 2.44.

ACIP should take the new designs legislation recommended in this report into account in its review of the petty patent system. ACIP should address any gap in the protection of function in its recommendations for reform of the petty patent system.[45]

This recommendation was accepted by the government.

Broader reform issues

The appellant in the *Firmagroup* case was not able to bring an action attempting to restrain the copying of its registered design on the basis that the copying was unfair. Australia does not recognise a general tort of unfair copying or unfair competition, as discussed in other chapters, although infringement by fraudulent imitation had the potential to operate in appropriate circumstances as a remedy against the unfair copying of registered designs. The action of passing off, and related actions for contraventions of the provisions in the *Trade Practices Act 1974* proscribing misleading and deceptive conduct, are of limited assistance to creators or owners of new designs. Effectively, such actions will not be successful unless the new design has been used to such an extent that the owner has acquired a reputation in the design amongst a sufficient number of his or her customers. However, even if the owner of the design can establish such a reputation, adequate labelling that clearly sets out the true trade source of the articles embodying the copied design may well be effective in preventing passing off or anyone being misled or deceived.

In relation to such broader issues, the ALRC recommended:

> The Attorney-General should commission a review of the advantages and disadvantages of introducing a broad anti-copying right into Australia's intellectual property law. The review should consider unfair copying and unfair competition laws. It should be conducted jointly by bodies with expertise in economic policy and legal policy.[46]

The government responded to this recommendation by stating that it would decide on this recommendation after it had had an opportunity to assess the operation of the new designs legislation. As yet, no such review has been commissioned.

The ACIP's petty patent review

The ACIP, in its report following its review of the petty patent system, stated that from its consultation sessions and reports received it was clear that there was broad agreement with the ALRC's findings that a gap exists in the industrial property regime: a gap relating to functional innovations that are neither inventive enough under the then standard or petty patent system to warrant protection, nor protectable under the designs system. The ACIP stated:

45 ibid., para. 3.5.
46 ibid., para 3.71.

The *Firmagroup Case* illustrates this claim [that a gap in protection exists] ... The defendant was found to have imitated the functional ideas of the plaintiff's design, but not the plaintiff's design. There were sufficient differences between the appearance of the two designs to warrant finding that the design itself had not been copied. If the functional ideas embodied in the plaintiff's design could not be patented, a second tier protection aimed at protecting low level innovations, but for a shorter time than full patent protection, would seem suited to filling the vacuum.[47]

Although the ACIP found the economic significance of any gap in protection difficult to assess, it recommended that Australia should adopt a second tier patent protection system by modifying the petty patent system, with the new system to be known as the innovation patent system. The ACIP concluded:

From the consultation process we determined that the key objectives of a second tier patent system should be to provide a protection system for minor or incremental innovations which:
- fills the 'gap' between designs and standard patents;
- is quick to obtain;
- is cheap to obtain and enforce;
- is simple;
- helps small/medium businesses enterprises;
- has certainty; and
- lasts for a sufficient time to encourage investment in the developing and marketing of the innovation.[48]

The petty patent system was designed to provide many of these features but the inventive step required for the grant of a petty patent was the same as that for a standard patent. This was to be remedied for the innovation patent, the ACIP recommending that the inventive level for innovation patents should be lower than that for standard patents. More particularly, the ACIP recommended that the test for an innovation patent should be a modified form of the expanded novelty test set out in *Griffin v Isaacs*,[49] and that if an innovation varies from a previously publicly available article, product or process only in ways that make no substantial contribution to the effect of the product or working of the article or process, then it cannot be considered novel and should not be patentable. The Commonwealth government accepted the above recommendations of the ACIP and most of its other recommendations.

The *Patents Amendment (Innovation Patents) Act 2000* amended the *Patents Act 1990* by repealing the petty patent system and implementing the recommended innovation patent system. An innovation patent was granted a term of eight years and the procedure for obtaining an innovation patent was intended to be quick and inexpensive. In order for an invention to be patentable for the purposes of the innovation patent, the invention need only involve an

---

47 ibid., para. 4.3.
48 ibid., para 4.6.
49 (1938) 12 ALJ 169.

innovative step rather than an inventive step. An invention is to be taken to involve an innovative step unless the invention only varies from publicly available information in ways that make no substantial contribution to the working of the invention.[50] It remains to be seen whether the innovation patent will be successful in granting more expansive protection to functional features of designs. The appellant's combination handle and lock, the subject of its registered design in the *Firmagroup* case, appears to have produced a handle and lock unit that was more efficient than similar products in the prior art and thus arguably made the necessary substantial contribution to qualify for the grant of an innovation patent.

There has been a review of the innovation patent by IP Australia. In its final report IP Australia concluded:

> At this stage it appears that the objectives of the innovation patent are generally being met, and public awareness of the system appears to be reasonable ... Although it is difficult to objectively measure whether low-level innovation has been stimulated by the innovation patent, the higher use of the system than was the case for the petty patent suggests that it has to some degree. The innovation patent is predominantly being used by Australian individuals and SMEs for less-knowledge intensive innovations. The innovation patent system is also generally speedier and has lower fees than the standard patent system, although the cost difference is marginal when an agent is employed.[51]

IP Australia further commented:

> Most of those who made submissions believed that the innovative step was clearly a lower threshold than inventive step, and was a main reason for the reasonable level of use of the system. The latest opposition decisions by IP Australia support this view, however the level and effectiveness of innovative step can ultimately only be determined by the courts. Also, recent worldwide concerns over a possible proliferation of 'trivial' patents creating barriers to innovation mean that the appropriateness of the innovation patent should be regularly assessed.[52]

Conclusion

It can be seen that the High Court's decision in the *Firmagroup* case belongs in a book concerned with significant Australian intellectual property decisions, even though its 'story' is essentially a legal one. The reaction to the narrow scope of protection granted to registered designs under the 1906 Act by the High Court has generated much reform activity. Such reform has hopefully resulted in the provision of adequate protection for innovative, three-dimensional functional designs in Australia.

---

50 See in particular the *Patents Act 1990* (Cth) ss 7(4) and 18(1A).
51 IP Australia, *Review of the Innovation Patent, Final Report,* July 2006, p. 4.
52 ibid., p. 6.

10

Larger than life in the Australian cinema: *Pacific Dunlop v Hogan*

Megan Richardson*

Introduction and scene setting

In 1919 cinema-going outstripped going to church in Australia.[1] Cinema was also more popular than theatre, opera and horse racing, football, cricket and going to the pub.[2] In the 19th century, when cinema began, an aim may have been to document society. But by the early 20th century fictional features were a dominant form. With fictional features came film stars and with film stars came promotional value that could be turned to account. Most obviously, if films made stars, stars in turn sold films. The 'star' magically combined elements of their own personas with the personalities of the characters they played, and cinemagoers were drawn to the personalities that appeared and reappeared onscreen in countless new forms. Film-makers who appreciated this could see the possibility of selling by association. But why stop at film? Entrepreneurs soon saw that sales of other products could be just as successful under the banner of a star's 'pulling power', conveying an emotional appeal that mere descriptions of quality could not.

The Hollywood star system was unmatched by any other in the world. This system saw Mary Pickford's salary rise from $175 a week in 1911 to $10 000 a

---

* I am grateful to Andrew Kenyon for helpful comments, to Michael Kraaz, Fiona Rotstein, Joel Shortman and Thomas Vranken for background information, and to Jennifer Digby for valuable research assistance. Thanks also to the Duty Judge and Deputy District Registrar at the Federal Court in Sydney for providing access to the case file (and associated practical advice) for *Paul Hogan; Rimfire Films Limited and Burns Philp Trustee Company Limited v Pacific Dunlop Limited* No. G584 of 1987.
1 C Hamann, 'Heralds of Free Enterprise: Australian Cinemas and Their Architecture from the 1900s to the 1940s' in J Sabine (ed.), *A Century of Australian Cinema*, Heinmann Australia, Melbourne, 1995, p. 84.
2 D Collins, 'Shopfronts and Picture Showmen: Film Exhibition to the 1920s' in Sabine, op. cit., p. 40 (1921 data).

week in 1916, combined with 50 per cent of profits derived from all products.[3] Similarly, Charlie Chaplin's income by 1916 included a $10 000 weekly salary as well as a $150 000 signing bonus,[4] as well as a share of the revenue derived from the photocards, books, toys, sheet music and fan cards that were sold under his and Paramount's labels.[5] Chaplin certainly appreciated the importance of the publicity which came from his films, advertising projects and relationship with the press. As he said:

> publicity is one of the essential things in the career of a man, whatever his profession, whose popularity depends in no small way upon keeping himself before the public.[6]

England also had its share of screen idols and, in a minor way, film-makers Cyril Hepworth and Alfred Hitchcock followed the Hollywood star system.[7] In particular, Hepworth capitalised on the fame of his star 'Stewart Rome', the most popular screen presence in Britain in 1915 apart from Charlie Chaplin according to a public poll, by advertising films under his stage name. Even so, his failure to appreciate Ryott's worth – there were no product endorsements, publicity given to 'Stewart Rome' was limited to roles in Hepworth films, and Ryott was precluded from exploiting the name on his own account under a contractual provision in which he was paid a mere £10 a week for his services (held to be an unlawful restraint of trade)[8] – may help to explain the postwar demise of the Hepworth company while the success of the Hollywood brand grew.

Surprisingly, in Australia, although there were theatre and opera stars and sporting legends galore, there were no fully fledged film stars or mega-hits until the 1980s when Mel Gibson shot to international fame in *Mad Max 2*[9] and Paul Hogan followed in *Crocodile Dundee*.[10] In part this may have been due to the centrally controlled manner in which films were usually funded in Australia, these films being notable exceptions. But earlier the low-budget *Mad Max 1*[11] had also not sought funding by the Australian Film Commission and

---

3 C, 'Incorporating the Star: The Intersection of Business and Aesthetic Strategies in Early American Film' (1990) 64 *Business History Review* 383, 383–4.
4 C Maland, *Chaplin and American Culture: The Evolution of a Star Image*, Princeton University Press, Princeton, NJ, 1989, p. 25.
5 See JA Aberdeen, 'Charlie Chaplin: Biography – Independent Profile', Hollywood Renegades Archive, available at http://www.cobbles.com/simpp_archive/charlie-chaplin_biography.htm.
6 Maland, op. cit., p. 27, citing an interview in *New Orleans Daily States*, 23 July 1916.
7 See generally J Hawkridge, 'British Cinema from Hepworth to Hitchcock' in G Nowell-Smith (ed.), *The Oxford History of World Cinema*, Oxford University Press, 1996, p. 130; and Francois Truffault with the collaboration of Helen Scott, *Hitchcock*, rev edn, Paladin Grafton Books, London, 1986, chap. 2.
8 *Hepworth Manufacturing Company Ltd v Ryott* [1920] 1 Ch 1. As David Vaver says, the case shows 'the importance of publicity as an element of the market value of labour': 'Authors' Moral Rights' (1987) 25 *Osgoode Hall Law Journal* 749, 764.
9 George Miller (director), Bryon Kennedy (producer), Terry Hayes, George Miller and Brian Hannant (screenplay), Kennedy-Miller Entertainment, Sydney, 1981. For further details and some clips of the film see Australian Screen, http://australianscreen.com.au/.
10 Peter Faiman (director), John Cornell (producer), Paul Hogan, Ken Shadie and John Cornell (screenplay), Rimfire Films, Northern Territory and New York, 1986. For further details and some clips of the film see Australian Screen, http://australianscreen.com.au/.
11 George Miller (director), Bryon Kennedy (producer), James McCausland and George Miller (screenplay), Kennedy-Miller Entertainment, Melbourne, 1979. For further details and some clips of the film see Australian Screen, http://australianscreen.com.au/.

162   LANDMARKS IN AUSTRALIAN IP LAW

this was a sensible decision.[12] The AFC's chairman, Phillip Adams, called the film a 'dangerous pornography of death' in *The Bulletin*, comparable to *Mein Kampf*.[13] Nevertheless, it achieved a certain cult status. Similarly, *Mad Max 2* and *Crocodile Dundee* did not seek AFC funding – and again it probably would not have been granted. *Mad Max 2* was as violent as *Mad Max 1* and *Crocodile Dundee* was characterised by Adams in *The Australian* as falling into a worn-out genre of 'overstated antipodean reactions to northern hemispherical sophistication'.[14] The films were instead financed by investors, supported by Div 10BA of the *Income Tax Assessment Act 1936* (Cth), which in the 1980s allowed generous deductions for investment in Australian films and gave a preferential tax rate on any profits.[15] And, as if to anticipate a massive popular response no matter what the critics might say, the advertising and other promotional material for the films emphasised rather than played down their more populist features.[16]

Various convincing accounts of the films' enormous popular success in Australia and internationally have been given – the anti-establishment themes, the typically Australian remote settings (in *Crocodile Dundee* juxtaposed with scenes from highly urbanised New York), the simple plot recounting the innocent hero's journey from oblivion to success, overcoming obstacles placed in his way in the typical pattern of a favourite folk tale,[17] the celebrations of mateship and humour long associated with the Australian psyche. Even the violence in *Mad Max 2* has a darkly humorous aspect.[18] And the insensitive treatment of sensitive cultural issues in *Crocodile Dundee* can more easily be accepted as amusing when supported by the willing participation of respectable representatives of those cultures – most notably Linda Kozlowski as the feminist New Yorker 'Sue', who compares Mick Dundee to Tarzan, and David Gulpilil as the Aboriginal 'Nev', who wears a watch in the desert and displays simple photographic expertise. The importance of the film stars, however, should not be underestimated. *Crocodile Dundee* traded off the celebrity of Paul Hogan, or 'Hoges', who was a popular Australian television personality in the 1970s and 80s (and

---

12 D Stratton, *The Last New Wave: The Australian Film Revival*, Angus & Robertson, Sydney and Melbourne, 1980, p. 241.
13 'The Dangerous Pornography of Death', *Bulletin*, 1 May 1979.
14 'Sorry Hoges, But This Time You've Blown It', *Australian*, 26 April 1986.
15 See D Stratton, *The Avocado Plantation: Boom and Bust in the Australian Film Industry*, Pan Macmillan, Sydney, 1990, chap. 1 and further p. 81 (*Mad Max 2*) and p. 335 (*Crocodile Dundee*).
16 See, for instance, the poster for the Paramount distribution of *Crocodile Dundee* by Australian graphic artist Brian Clinton, shown on his website at http://brianclintonauthentics.com/portfolio_film_posters.html. Clinton here uses a hyper-realist style to present Dundee as suffused with inner-heroism, quietly admired by the woman (Sue) in the background. The careful juxtaposition of crocodile, bush knife and (New York's) Statue of Liberty gives the distinct impression that somehow, despite his remote far-North Australian background, Dundee survives and conquers in highly urbanised New York.
17 Although as Meaghan Morris comments, his style was more 'mock-heroic' than fully heroic: 'Tooth and Claw: Tales of Survival and *Crocodile Dundee*' in A Ross (ed.), *Universal Abandon? The Politics of Postmodernism*, University of Minnesota Press, 1988, p. 112.
18 As David Stratton – who along with most of the other Australian critics (barring Phillip Adams perhaps), seems to like this film better than *Crocodile Dundee* – points out: op. cit. n. 15, p. 84.

Australian of the Year in 1985), and was internationally renowned for his Foster's beer and Australian Tourism Commission advertisements.[19] Similarly, *Mad Max 2* had the benefit of Mel Gibson's cult status, derived from the first *Mad Max*. And throughout and certainly in their most cinematic moments in which the stars feature with their distinctively Australian look and accent – the final country road death scene in *Mad Max 2*, the 'knife scene' in *Crocodile Dundee* (which, although set in New York, only serves to highlight the [Australian] fish-out-of-[New York] water theme) – the stars are absolutely central to the films' impact.

As David Stratton says, those associated with *Mad Max 2* 'could have gone almost anywhere'.[20] The same is true of those associated with *Crocodile Dundee*. Neither Gibson nor Hogan chose widespread merchandising. Both went to Hollywood but they mostly stuck to film. Similarly, before *Crocodile Dundee*, which he co-wrote, Hogan was primarily a television star and his advertising decisions were carefully made by himself and John Cornell, his friend, business partner, and producer of *Crocodile Dundee*.[21] Foster's beer and Australian tourism were vehicles for the 'Hoges' character, which was drawn upon in the film. Hogan obviously could not claim to be a real crocodile hunter, but in other ways his character matched his familiar persona and possibly his underlying personality as well. Mick Dundee frequented pubs, drank beer and was a tour guide of sorts. He also had the dry humour present in the 'shrimp on the barbie' advertisements for the Australian Tourism Commission. And in the same way as Hogan looked and sounded like 'a very ordinary Australian' male,[22] with Dundee there is a sense of 'the everyman', a socially representative type modelled on a 'self-deprecating masculinity',[23] only represented on a larger and slightly hilarious scale. In short, *Crocodile Dundee* may have broadly been aimed at entertaining the audience and making a great deal of money but its important subsidiary aim and effect was to serve as 'part of a larger discursive web – a component part of the ongoing biographical legend of Hogan'.[24]

However, such image-defining and refining features were not carried through in the unauthorised 'spoof' advertisement for Grosby Leatherz Shoes, which featured in the case of *Hogan v Pacific Dunlop* and on appeal *Pacific Dunlop Ltd v Hogan*.[25]

---

19 See generally T O'Regan, '"Fair Dinkum Fillums": The *Crocodile Dundee* Phenomenon' in S Dermody and E Jacka (eds.), *The Imaginary Industry: Australian Film in the Late '80s*, Australian Film, Television & Radio School, Sydney, 1988, p. 156.
20 Stratton, op. cit. n. 15, p. 84.
21 See O'Regan, op. cit., p. 161.
22 Andrew Denton, interview with Paul Hogan on *Enough Rope*, ABC Television, 19 May 2003, available online at http://www.abc.net.au/tv/enoughrope/transcripts/s858507.htm.
23 O'Regan, op. cit., pp. 164–5.
24 ibid., p. 163.
25 *Hogan and Others v Pacific Dunlop Ltd* (1988) 12 IPR 225 and (on appeal) *Pacific Dunlop Ltd v Hogan and Others* (1989) 14 IPR 398.

Facts and judgments

The Grosby advertisement aired on television in Australia from May 1987 and was followed up with a poster campaign. It is not surprising that it led to the institution of legal proceedings for passing off and breach of ss 52 and 53(c) and (d) of the *Trade Practices Act 1974* (Cth). No one who knew the film and watched the advertisement could fail to notice the referencing to the famous 'knife scene' from *Crocodile Dundee*. Both involved a couple meeting a mugger at night (and although the scene from the film is set in a well-lit public area while in the advertisement the setting is a dingy street, as the trial judge noted, there were plenty of dingy streets in other scenes in *Crocodile Dundee*).[26] The couple in the advertisement were a blond-headed woman (like Sue in the film), and a man who looked like Mick Dundee and was dressed in 'a hat with a band displaying "animal teeth" and a vest worn over an open-necked shirt with the sleeves rolled up above arm bands' (as was Dundee in the film).[27] Before the mugger revealed himself in the advertisement, the female character said 'He looked just like you, Mick' (another obvious reference).[28] In both the advertisement and the film the mugger pulled a knife but what followed was somewhat different. In the film, it led to the following exchange:[29]

> SUE: Mick! Give him your wallet.
> MICK (relaxed): What for?
> SUE: He's got a knife.
> MICK (laughing): That's not a knife (producing his hunting knife). That's a knife (followed by some jacket-slashing, the mugger then running off with his accomplices).
> MICK: Just kids having fun.

In the advertisement, the situation degenerated into the following:[30]

> FEMALE CHARACTER: Mick, give him your wallet. He's wearing leather shoes.
> MALE CHARACTER: You call those leather shoes. Now these are leather shoes – Grosby leather, soft, comfortable, action-packed leather (followed by some kicking, the mugger flying into the air and out of the frame of the film).
> MALE CHARACTER: Made right here in Australia and only 40 bucks.

The words 'He looked just like you Mick' were meant, it was said, 'to give the impression that the couple had just left the theatre showing the film *Crocodile Dundee* and the character in the commercial was imitating his hero whom he had just seen in the movie'.[31] If so, the message did not reach the audience, in part no doubt because *Crocodile Dundee* was emphatically *not* the kind of film for which audiences dressed like, talked like or otherwise imitated the characters. Rather,

---

26 See (1988) 12 IPR 225, 230 (Gummow J).
27 ibid.
28 ibid., p. 231.
29 ibid., p. 230.
30 ibid., p. 231.
31 ibid., p. 232.

the more obvious message was simply that the advertisement was a 'send-up' of the knife scene from the film. It was claimed to be a parody but had nothing of the 'social and literary criticism' that the law has traditionally associated with parody,[32] although in a broader sense it may be considered to fall within a generic creative practice in which 'material is borrowed, imitated or appropriated, often but not always for the purpose of commentary or humour, such that there is a playful, ironic or reflective relationship between the object of parody and the new text or practice'.[33] It may still be argued that any properly informed audience should appreciate the disjunction between the desire of Hogan and others to maintain image control and the respondent's disruptive activities. Nevertheless, the difficulty for the casual observer, with limited knowledge of the advertising strategies behind the film and Hogan's professional career, was assessing whether Hogan or others associated with the film would have consented to the send-up, or would have been asked to do so.

Gummow J

On the applicants' part, much was made of character merchandising practices as supporting common assumptions about consent. The trial judge, Gummow J, upheld the claims of passing off and breach of s 52 of the *Trade Practices Act*.[34] The judge also referred to 'the strong body of evidence as to the extent of character merchandising, sponsorship and testimonial advertising in Australia', adding that 'those practices are part of the relevant surrounding circumstances' in the case[35] – as is the circumstance that 'television is an engaging medium because it has movement, sound, and light', evoking 'pleasant memories' of the film.[36] More difficult to assess was the evidence of confusion from the handful of lay witnesses who appeared at the trial. As detailed later below, a number of these showed anxiety and even doubt as to whether consent would have been obtained or even sought. Nevertheless, there was held to be sufficient support for the finding of passing off and misleading or deceptive conduct for the purposes of s 52 of the *Trade Practices Act*, without needing to frame protection in terms

---

32 ibid., p. 224. Compare M Rose, *Parody: Ancient, Modern and Post-Modern*, Cambridge University Press, Cambridge, 1993, chap. 1 (parody is dependant upon the object for criticism).
33 J Griffith and A Kenyon, 'Taking Forward the Gowers Review of Intellectual Property – Proposed Changes to Copyright Exceptions', submission to UK Government, 8 April 2008, London and Melbourne. Griffith and Kenyon offer an understanding of parody as blending into a family of '[c]aricature, parody and pastiche', unlike Rose who distinguishes parody from other modes of borrowings, imitations and appropriations including travesties which draw on the original for purely comic purposes: see Rose, op. cit., chap. 2. The Grosby advertisements might be described as a travesty of the *Crocodile Dundee* knife scene. Compare Burchett J in *Pacific Dunlop v Hogan* (1989) 14 IPR 398, 430 (it is 'more accurately described as a parasitic copy – parasitic because its vitality is drawn entirely from the audience's memory of the original').
34 But not the claim brought under s 53 of the *Trade Practices Act*, which was rejected on the basis that the language of the provision, specifying 'sponsorship, approval or affiliation', required 'authoritative or formal commendation': (1988) 12 IPR 225, 254, citing Franki J in *Weitmann v Katies Ltd* (1997) 29 FLR 336, 344.
35 (1988) 12 IPR 225, 246–7.
36 ibid., 246–7.

166 LANDMARKS IN AUSTRALIAN IP LAW

of a looser and more tenuous doctrine of 'misappropriation of reputation'.[37] As Gummow J observed:

> it is not to the point to emphasise (as the respondent's counsel perhaps sought to do) that viewers would not necessarily be likely to sit and ponder these matters, and worry whether any particular consideration had actually been paid by the respondent and so forth. The viewers would have other things immediately to take their attention after the advertisement finished. But, like Miss Timbs (who saw only the bus poster), many would have presumed there was such a commercial connection. For others, such a thought might, as Mr Wilson [sic, Watson?] put it, have flashed across their mind.[38]

Full Court

The decision of Gummow J was upheld on appeal but a division emerged on the issue of whether the evidence supported the findings. Beaumont J took the traditional position of an appellate judge, stating that where an issue involves matters of impression 'particular respect and weight should be given to the decision of the trial judge unless some error in his judgment has been demonstrated'.[39] Sheppard J, however, pointed out that conflicting and in some instances changing evidence of witnesses was not strongly supportive of the applicants,[40] adding that there was a risk that those witnesses who thought there was consent might have done so because they erroneously presumed that 'in some general way permission was needed', based on 'vague thoughts by members of the community concerning the legal rights film-makers might have in ideas or characters'.[41] Moreover, to rely on judicial impressions in this case was risky because '[e]ach of the judges who has had to consider this matter has had the benefit, or has been under the disadvantage – it depends on how one looks at the matter – of seeing the knife scene from the film and the advertisement one after the other'.[42] Clearly, Sheppard J, a judge of great trial experience who has publicly declared that 'facts are always critical and come before the law or at least its detail',[43] was troubled by the scope in this case for vague and shifting perceptions in the minds of those later called on to account for their impressions, sitting uncomfortably with the precision normally expected of evidence in court.

It may be helpful at this stage to consider precisely what was said by the witnesses in their affidavits and evidence in court, paraphrased in the trial judgment as follows:[44]

---

37 As had been found by Pincus J in *Hogan v Koala Dundee Pty Ltd* (1988) 12 IPR 508, but it seems clear that Gummow J who mentioned this judgment only in passing (on the relevance of fraud to damages) was not enamoured of such reasoning, especially if liability could be premised on a narrower basis.
38 (1988) 12 IPR 225, 247.
39 (1989) 14 IPR 398, 427.
40 ibid., p. 417.
41 ibid., p. 407.
42 ibid., p. 414.
43 The Hon Ian Sheppard, address given at graduation ceremony, Faculty of Law, University of Sydney, 15 May 2006, available at http://www.gsu.uts.edu.au/graduation/speakers/pdf/2006/address2006sheppard.pdf.
44 To provide an authentic flavour, the summary below follows what was said in the trial judgment as closely as possible to the language (including the manner in which witnesses were identified). That a full and detailed

PACIFIC DUNLOP v HOGAN   167

Witnesses	Evidence
Miss Ashby	Recognised the poster as a look-alike of Hogan as Crocodile Dundee. In her affidavit said she thought the people advertising the shoes probably would have asked permission from him or the makers of the film. In cross-examination conceded she had no means of knowing if they had.
Mr Watson	Recognised the television commercial and poster as an attempt to use the humour in the knife scene from *Crocodile Dundee*. In his affidavit said that he had assumed when he saw the television advertisement for the first time that the makers of the advertisement had obtained permission in some way, or that they were linked with the people who held rights in the film. Held position in cross-examination.
Miss Timbs	Recognised the poster as a take-off of the knife scene from Crocodile Dundee. In her affidavit said that she had presumed there would have been some permission given by the makers of the film or Paul Hogan to use the Mick Dundee character. In cross-examination agreed that this had only occurred to her at the time of her affidavit.
Mr Greenheld	Recognised the lead character in the television advertisement as 'a take-off of Mick Dundee'. In his affidavit said he would have thought as a matter of normal or sound business practice the producers would have gained permission. In cross-examination agreed that when he first saw the advertisements thoughts such as these did not cross his mind, explaining that 'it would be a bit cynical if you started to think of the possible repercussions'.
Miss Kiffin	Recognised the television commercial as a send-up. It never occurred to her that there was a business arrangement.
Mrs Eddy	It did not cross her mind that the man in the billboard advertisement was Paul Hogan or that consent was obtained.
Mr Jedlin	Thought the television advertisement was a 'terrible' send-up, made in fun, and it never occurred to him that the makers of the film or Hogan must have authorised and nor did he think this was likely in circumstances.

As Sheppard J said, '[i]t crossed the mind of only two of the seven members of the public who were called [presumably Miss Ashby and Mr Watson] that Mr Hogan must, in some way, have approved of the advertisements'.[45] Yet this technically correct statement is difficult to reconcile with the findings of passing off and misleading or deceptive conduct on the part of the trial judge and Beaumont J on appeal. On close analysis, there is an element of ambiguity in the evidence, which may suggest a wider range of possible responses on the question of witness confusion than either a conscious assumption – entailing crossing the mind – that permission would have been obtained, or the absence of such an assumption. Notably, two witnesses (Miss Timbs and Mr Greenheld) said under cross-examination that they had given no conscious thought to the question of permission when they saw the advertisement or poster, yet at the time of their affidavits said they had assumed permission would have been given. Were they simply correcting themselves as to the true state of their minds at the relevant time? Or is it plausible to think they had initially made a subconscious assumption as to approval of some kind and later were acknowledging their lack of conscious thought? The fact that one of these witnesses (Miss Timbs) was explicitly referred to by Gummow J in supporting the finding of passing

---

analysis was given is confirmed by a review of material held on the case file for *Paul Hogan; Rimfire Films Limited and Burns Philp Trustee Company Limited v Pacific Dunlop Limited* No. G584 of 1987.
45 (1989) 14 IPR 398, 427.

168 LANDMARKS IN AUSTRALIAN IP LAW

off as well as misleading or deceptive conduct[46] slightly reinforces the second interpretation.[47]

Finally we come to Burchett J, who made up the majority (with Beaumont J) in the Full Federal Court. Here we see the judgment which comes closest to acknowledging the subtle and inarticulate nature of impressions which may be formed in a case such as this. Indeed, this judgment makes little reference to what the witnesses actually said and is almost Freudian in its implication that the conscious and unconscious self should be carefully distinguished. Yet it is not a judgment that uses the language of psychology and science, or even marketing, as in some more recent cases.[48] Rather, Burchett J – who, like Gummow J, referred to television as a unique medium for carrying vague advertising messages – drew on literary references and associations to posit the following:

> No logic tells the consumer that boots are better because Crocodile Dundee wears them for a few seconds on the screen ... but the boots *are* better in his eyes, worn by his idol. The enhancement of the boots is not different in kind from the effect produced when an alpine pass makes a grander impact on the tourist whose mind's eye captures a vision of Hannibal urging elephants and men to scale it.

> To ask whether the consumer reasons that Mr Hogan authorised the advertisement is therefore to ask a question which is a mere side issue, and far from the full impact of the advertisement. The consumer is moved by a desire to wear something belonging in some sense to Crocodile Dundee (who is perceived as a persona, almost an avatar, of Mr Hogan). The arousal of that feeling by Mr Hogan himself could not be regarded as misleading, for then the value he promises the product will have is not in its leather, but in its association with himself. When, however, an advertisement he did not authorise makes the same suggestion, it is misleading; for the product sold by that advertisement really lacks the one feature the advertisement attributes to it.[49]

We might wonder about the references here to Dundee wearing the boots, the consumer seeing him as an 'idol', and the situation as 'not different in kind' to Hannibal scaling an impasse. The idea of Dundee as a classic hero, in the nature of a famous Carthaginian military commander, or even the classic screen idol of earlier 20th century, sits uneasily with his image of self-deprecating masculinity.[50] And there appears to be a slight gap in the reasoning that the misrepresentation lies in the absence of a real, or genuine, association with the character with whom the audience feels an emotional connection. Surely the audience must be

---

46 See the observations of Gummow J in (1988) 12 IPR 225 quoted at n. 38 above.

47 And Gummow J seemed to see this as an issue of confusion which might 'feed' into the ultimate legal question of deception or likely deception, for purposes of establishing passing off and misleading or deceptive conduct under s 52 of the *Trade Practices Act*: see the brief discussion, ibid., p. 245.

48 Probably wisely, given the lack of expert evidence. Subconscious, or subliminal, confusion is a notoriously contentious concept in modern psychological theory (especially cognitive psychology which insists that mental processes should be measured rather than reflected upon introspectively), as well as being exceptionally difficult to prove to any legal standard. See R Tushnet, 'Gone in Sixty Milliseconds: Trademark Law and Cognitive Science' (2008) 86 *Tex L Rev* 507, 542 (disputability of subliminal confusion in cognitive psychology, which purports to function as a science) and 564 ('so far the evidence in favor of the cognitive model is not persuasive enough to justify realigning doctrine around it').

49 (1989) 14 IPR 398, 429.

50 Compare O'Regan who asks, '[i]s Hogan a classic hero?' (answering no): op. cit., p. 164.

encouraged to assume falsely a real, or genuine, association, even if only sub-consciously (as hypothesised above), for there to be a *mis*representation?[51] That this may have been intended only becomes clearer later when the judge refers to the pervasive feature of such cases as the 'inveigl[ing of] the emotions into false responses'.[52] All that said, we can still appreciate a fine attempt to give a rendered account of the emotional attraction of a well-loved character and the audience's need to be able to believe in the character as a person in order for the emotional connection between character and audience to work.[53] Moreover, there is some satisfaction to be found in an account that reflects on the character of Crocodile Dundee and the audience's response to him as if this *matters*[54] – treating such things as not merely frivolous aspects of the case but as profoundly important to its resolution.

It is important also that the account is more about the audience's experience than about Dundee, or rather Hogan, as an injured party. This belies any sugges-tion that the case can be taken as an exemplar of Australian courts developing a US-style publicity right, *sub nom* passing off. It simply does not fit with the absence of any reference to coercion of the person whose identity is being bor-rowed without authority. Rather, the damage, if damage is to be found, lies in the inveigled emotions of the audience lulled into an unwilling suspension of disbelief. In this respect, also, we may be seeing the pervasive influence of the consumer-focused *Trade Practices Act*, which by the late 1980s had become a tandem action with passing off. Thus *Crocodile Dundee* represents a nice con-trast to the older case of *Henderson v Radio Corporation*,[55] where damage was premised on the position that wrongfully appropriating a person's professional or business reputation is like stealing the person's goods or money,[56] and *Pub Squash* (featured in Chapter 8 of this book), where passing off was seen as more naturally aligned to 'unfair competition' than misleading or deceptive conduct which was not even claimed.

Of course, there are still those who might argue that, from an audience/consumer perspective, challenging and disrupting an audience's assumptions may sometimes be beneficial rather than harmful and may even

---

51 Gummow J put it rather more precisely: the misrepresentation conveys 'a representation of a commercial connection ... which connection does not exist': (1988) 12 IPR 225, 248.

52 *Pacific Dunlop v Hogan* (1989) 14 IPR 398, 430.

53 Literary critic James Wood expresses this well in *How Fiction Works* (Jonathan Cape, 2008) when he says: 'Perhaps because I am not sure what a character is, I find especially moving those postmodern novels, like *Pnin*, or *The Prime of Miss Jean Brodie*, or *The Year of the Death of Ricardo Reiss*, or Roberto Bolaño's *The Strange Detectives*, in which we are confronted with characters who are at once real and unreal. In all these novels, the author asks us to reflect on the fictionality of the heroes and heroines who give the novels their titles. And in a fine paradox, it is precisely such reflection that stirs in the reader a desire to make these fictional characters "real", to say, in effect, to the authors: "I know that they are only fictional – you keep on telling me this. But I only *know* them by treating them as real"': p. 84.

54 As Wood says, the audience must become aware that the vital character's actions are 'profoundly impor-tant': that is how readers 'retain in their minds a sense of the character': ibid., p. 98.

55 [1960] SR(NSW) 576; 1A IPR 620.

56 ibid., p. 285 (Evatt CJ and Myers J), a judgment misconstrued by Pincus J in *Hogan v Koala Dundee* (1988) 12 IPR 508 as giving a claim of 'wrongful appropriation of a reputation or, more widely, wrongful association of goods with an image properly belonging to the applicant': p. 520.

be liberating for the audience.[57] And it might be posited that a particular place for working out such ideas can be found in the remedy awarded in *Crocodile Dundee*, which permitted the advertisements to continue subject to a disclaimer of endorsement by Hogan or the makers of the film to the advertisement and its contents.[58] But there is little support for this reasoning in the language of the judgments. A more plausible explanation of the limited remedy awarded in the case was an acknowledgment of the – at most – limited evidence of sub-conscious confusion. In other words, this was simply seen as a marginal case of likely deception which was best dispelled by a marginal remedy. So it was rather easily assumed that a suitably worded disclaimer would be sufficient to release the audience from any misconceptions that might disrupt their sense of what the film and its central character signified for them. Still, such a simple treatment of remedy was a not unfitting response to the simple free market philosophy and, it has to be said, success of the film as well.

Concluding comments

Academic commentators have often been critical of the *Crocodile Dundee* decision. Many also appear not to like the film. In legal terms, however, the case was, and remains, pivotal in insisting that in Australia the basis of a passing off or misleading conduct claim is a 'particular type of misrepresentation', as Gummow J said.[59] With *Crocodile Dundee*, what constitutes a misrepresentation may have become a more fluid and contestable concept than before. Nevertheless, in imagining how an audience might respond to the subtleties of advertising messages, the discourse is firmly focused on audience effects. This is particularly evident in the references made by the judges to the emotional appeal of personalities and their avatar-like characters, and to the vivid impact of moving visual forms, exemplified by television and, it should be added, by film.

---

57 See, for instance, A T Kenyon and E Milne, 'Images of Celebrity: Publicity, Privacy, Law' (2005) 10 *Media & Arts Law Review* 311, 314, and authorities cited there.
58 See *Hogan v Pacific Dunlop* (1988) 12 IPR 225, 255. The order was confirmed on appeal.
59 ibid., p. 248.

11

O Fortuna! On the vagaries of litigation and the story of musical debasement in Australia

Elizabeth Adeney*

O Fortuna	*O Fortune*
velut luna	*just like the moon*
stau variabilis . . .	*you are changeable . . .*[1]

O Fortuna, Carmina Burana

Introduction

Like the moon, the fortunes of men wax and wane. Such was the wisdom of the medieval poet who composed the lyric that forms the conceptual and structural framework of Carl Orff's choral piece, the *Carmina Burana*. It is a wisdom that international litigators do well to remember as, encouraged by previous success, they venture ever further from the legal systems that have favoured them.

The incorporeal character and international regulation of intellectual property mean that much of its litigation has global dimensions. The current case is no exception. As traced in this chapter, it begins in Germany, continues in the Netherlands, and ends in Australia. It concerns one of the most widely used pieces

---

* My thanks to Kate Haddock of Banki, Haddock and Fiora (solicitors for the applicants) for her helpful comments on the litigation of this case.

1 In full, the poem reads: 'O Fortune, just like the moon you are changeable, always waxing or waning. Hateful life first grinds us down and then soothes the mind's alertness with play; it melts both penury and power like ice. O monstrous and meaningless fate, you turning wheel! [Because of you] bad luck and empty wellbeing are always liable to change. Obscured and veiled, you oppress me too. Now, as part of your game, I submit my bare back to your wickedness. The fate of wellbeing and of virtue is now against me. [This man] is impaired and weakened, always in anguish. Here, at this hour, without delay, pluck the quivering strings. Since the strong man is prostrated by fate, everyone weep with me!' My thanks to Professor Mary Dove of Sussex University for this translation.

172   LANDMARKS IN AUSTRALIAN IP LAW

of music of the 20th century,[2] Carl Orff's *O Fortuna* chorus from the *Carmina Burana* cantata, and its somewhat controversial composer. In its Australian phase the case concerns the concept of 'debasement' of a musical work, a concept once contained in the statutory licensing provision of the Australian *Copyright Act*.[3] It concerns the legal struggle of Orff's representatives to maintain the integrity of the *O Fortuna* chorus in the face of postmodern creative practices, and to ensure its presentation to the public in the form originally envisaged by the composer. It is therefore closely linked with the history and practice of authorial moral rights as they are understood in the continental European countries. This linkage then begs the question of the relevance of the Australian decision to the development of moral rights in this country.

The Australian limb of the litigation is most fully documented in the first instance and appeal decisions of the Federal Court of Australia in the case of *Schott Musik International v Colossal Records of Australia*.[4] This Australian limb represents the convergence of several prior histories, and it is with these that we shall start.

The composer

Carl Orff and the *Carmina Burana*

Carl Orff[5] wrote the music for the *Carmina Burana* between 1934 and 1937, at a relatively advanced stage in his career. He had been born in Munich in 1895 into a family both military and musical. From an early age he had shown a passion for composition and performance, his first published works dating back to his teens.[6] He had studied at the Munich Academy of Music but had been rather disappointed by this formal training.[7] Much of his pleasure as a child, and hence inspiration, was derived from his Bavarian homeland,[8] from ancient languages and writings[9] and from folk theatre.[10] From 1924 Orff became involved in music and dance education through his work at the *Güntherschule*, where he developed and realised his concept of the unity of speech, music and movement.[11] This

---

2 See, among other sites, http://www.answers.com/topic/orff-s-carmina-burana-in-popular-culture for a list of the many uses to which the *O Fortuna* chorus has been put, including its use in the 1981 film *Excalibur*; in the films *The Doors, Glory* and *Natural Born Killers*; in television commercials for *Carlton Draught* beer and *Old Spice* aftershave; and in the advertising of *The Twilight Zone Tower of Terror* attraction at Walt Disney World Resort.
3 *Copyright Act 1968* s 55(2), repealed by Act 159 of 2000, s 3, Sch 1, item 1A.
4 *Schott Musik International GmbH & Co v Colossal Records of Australia Pty Ltd* (1997) 36 IPR 267; (1997) 38 IPR 1.
5 For information about the composer's life and works see, generally, W Thomas, *Carl Orff*, trans. V Maschat, Schott, London, Mainz, New York, Tokyo, 1985; H Wolfram Schmidt, *Carl Orff, sein Leben und sein Werk in Wort, Bild und Noten*, Wienand Verlag, Cologne, 1971; A Liess, *Carl Orff*, trans. A and H Parkin, Calder and Boyars, London, 1966; C Orff, 'Erinnerung' in *Carl Orff und sein Werk: Dokumentation*, Vol. 1: *Frühzeit*, Hans Schneider, Tutzing, 1975.
6 Orff, 'Erinnerung', op. cit. n. 5, p. 42.
7 ibid., pp. 44–5.
8 ibid., pp. 35–7.
9 ibid., pp. 35–8; Thomas, op. cit., p. 3.
10 Orff, op. cit. n. 5, p. 25.
11 Thomas, op. cit., pp. 7–8.

THE *SCHOTT* CASE   173

interest in music education was to remain with him throughout the rest of his long life, and his work in the area was to bring him international fame. In addition to his educational work, Orff was a relatively prolific composer.

Orff produced works in various genres: *Lieder,* choral works,[12] opera[13] and also orchestral music and concertos. Prior to 1930, he set many contemporary texts to music, a number of them by Franz Werfel and Bertold Brecht.[14] However in the 1930s, during the early National Socialist period, Orff was in search of new, less politically contentious sources.[15] It was at this time that he came across an edition of 12th- and 13th-century lyric poetry.[16] The poetry, by a variety of authors known and unknown, had been preserved in manuscript form in the abbey of Benediktbeuern in Bavaria; hence the name of the collection – the *Codex Buranus.* This collection of songs (*carmina*) in Latin and vernacular languages was to inspire what is now the most famous of Orff's works – the *Carmina Burana* (songs of Beuern), a staged cantata. It was first performed in 1937 when Orff was 42.[17] At the time, Orff saw this composition as a personal breakthrough. This, he claimed histrionically and no doubt with an eye to contemporary politics, must be considered the starting point of his compositional work. All his previous works, which his publisher Schott had 'unfortunately' printed, could now be pulped.[18]

Of the hundreds of lyrics available to him from the *Codex Buranus,* Orff chose 24,[19] setting them to his own music.[20] The songs he chose are sometimes rueful, sometimes celebratory, occasionally lyrical and delicate, at times grotesque. Orff's *Carmina Burana* consists of several thematic groupings of songs, representing various aspects of human vitality. The framework is provided by the theme of 'Fortune, Empress of the World', in which the *O Fortuna* chorus appears. In this chorus the poet rails at the subjection of humankind to the cruelties of fortune, laments his own suffering and invites his audience to share his musical lamentation. The printed score of the work featured an image of the Wheel of Fortune,

---

12 *Fremde sind wir; Der Gute Mensch; Veni Creator Spiritus; Vom Frühjahr; Öltank und vom Fliegen; Carmina Burana; Catulli Carmina; De Temporum Fine Comoedia; Trionfo di Afrodite; Comoedia de Christi Resurrectione;* and *Ludus de Nato Infante Mirificus.*

13 *Antigonae, Astutuli; Die Bernauerin; Die Kluge; Der Mond; Oedipus der Tyrann;* and *Prometheus.*

14 M Kater, 'Carl Orff im Dritten Reich' (1995) 43 *Vierteljahresheft für Zeitgeschichte* 1, 5.

15 Werfel was Jewish and Brecht communist, and Orff's cantatas based on their works were removed from the market by Orff's publisher, Schott: KH Kowalke, 'Dancing with the Devil: Publishing Modern Music in the Third Reich' (2001) 8 *Modernism/Modernity* 1, 15. Michel Hofmann, Orff's collaborator, describes the composer's sometimes 'desperate' search for suitable older material: F Dangel-Hofmann (ed.), *Carl Orff – Michel Hofmann: Briefe zur Entstehung der Carmina Burana,* Hans Schneider, Tutzing, 1990, pp. 19, 196.

16 JA Schmeller (ed.), *Carmina Burana: Lateinische und Deutsche Lieder und Gedichte einer Handschrift des XIII. Jahrhunderts aus Benedictbeuern auf der K Bibliothek zu München,* Stuttgart, 1847.

17 Indeed it was first performed in Frankfurt at the 68th and last annual Festival of Composers of the General German Music Society, prior to the society's disbanding under the National Socialist government. The premiere (supposed to have taken place in Berlin) had been delayed due to Orff's poor reputation in National Socialist circles. See Kater, op. cit., p. 9.

18 Letter from Orff to Schott in June 1937, quoted in Dangel-Hofmann, op. cit., p. 7.

19 Orff consulted his friend Dr Michel Hofmann, an archivist and philologist in Bamberg, in his choice of lyrics and in the writing of the cantata. This collaboration was subsequently to lead to litigation as the Hofmann heirs claimed that their ancestor was a joint author of the cantata. Orff was held, however, to have been the sole author, with Hofmann having played only an advisory role: Decision of the Munich Regional Court of 2 July 2002, case No. 7 O12953/01. Hofmann was, however, the author of German translations of the *Carmina Burana* lyrics.

20 The originality of Orff's music has been challenged on the basis that the manuscript contains some notation. It was not sufficiently comprehensible, however, to have been used by Orff. This was established during the Dutch action, described below. See n. 59 below and associated text.

174   LANDMARKS IN AUSTRALIAN IP LAW

first raising up a king to the pinnacle of success and power, then throwing him
onto his back beneath the wheel as it turned.[21] The illustration, taken from
the *Codex*, was an image that Orff had constantly in mind in composing the
music.

> The music of the chorus, according to Orff's collaborator Hofmann, expresses the
> eternal and unbending dominance of fate and also the defiance of the human spirit as
> it confronts its destiny.[22]
>
> In the music is reflected the unbending fixedness (*Statik*) of fate's timeless domi-
> nance, but also the unbroken courage (*Daseinsmut*) of those who are not silent in the
> face of fate, but who exorcise, banish and conquer her. The closing refrain correspond-
> ingly embodies the same aggressive attitude to life.[23]

The musicologist Helm described Orff's general musical approach as follows:

> He does not propose to 'revitalize' old works, but to turn to the advantage of the
> contemporary stage the vitality that is inherent in those works. To this end Orff has
> evolved a musical style that is extraordinarily direct, elemental and primitive. It is a
> kind of return to musical innocence that stands at the opposite pole from Romanticism,
> post-Romanticism, neo-Romanticism, and Impressionism. Nor is it in any sense neo-
> Classical. Orff's style, in all its variations, is based on the principle of simplification, on
> the reduction (or return) of music to its elements . . . [R]hythm is the primary factor
> of his style, the factor that gives much of his music its characteristic drive and vitality.
> He reduces rhythm to its simplest terms . . . The resemblance between Orff's melodic
> substance and that of plainsong is striking . . . The point of departure in Orff's music is
> always the text. In a sense, indeed, the music is an illustration or decoration of the text
> and has little or no *raison d'être* apart from the words to which it is fashioned. In the
> synthesis of sung and spoken word, dance, and scenic art that is Orff's ideal, the word
> plays the most important role.[24]

Orff wrote the *Carmina Burana* music in a Germany increasingly controlled by
the musical conservatives who supported the National Socialist government. He
did not particularly appeal to these conservatives.[25] He did not much appeal to
the avant garde either.[26] Orff was not modernist after the manner of Hindemith
or Schoenberg, nor was he traditionalist. He was accused of lack of respect for
the old masters[27] and of decadence.[28] The extreme Germanists looked askance
at his use of Latin texts in a number of his works.[29] Indeed Orff feared that

---

21 Reproduced in Dangel-Hofmann, op. cit., p. 239.

22 This defiance is considerably less evident in the Latin text (translated at n. 1 above) than in Hofmann's
extraordinary and bombastic German translation of its closing lines: 'Tune the strings without delay, to their
best and fullest tones; Though the storm wind should fell oaks, mightier still swells our song'.

23 Dangel-Hofmann, op. cit., pp. 143–4. The wording of this description is so typically National Socialist,
with its emphasis on defiance and aggression, that one suspects it was formulated in a way most calculated
to please the ruling group. Hofmann's very pointed justification for the use of Latin lyrics is in the same vein,
emphasising the superiority of German medieval Latin over classical Latin.

24 E Helm, 'Carl Orff' (1955) 41 *The Musical Quarterly* 285.

25 Kater, op. cit., pp. 6 (mentioning Orff's associations with 'persons with an orientation towards the left')
and 7 (mentioning his associations with the Jewish Karl Salomon, Erich Katz and Matyas Seiber).

26 Stravinsky labelled Orff's music 'neo-Neanderthal': I Stravinsky and R Craft, *Memories and Commentaries*,
University of California Press, Berkeley, 1959, p. 123, cited in KH Kowalke 'Burying the Past: Carl Orff and
his Brecht Connection' (2000) 84 *The Musical Quarterly* 58, 78.

27 Kater, op. cit., p. 8.

28 ibid., p. 7.

29 See the review of the premiere by Friedrich Herzog in the *Rheinische Landeszeitung* of 11 June 1937,
lamenting that the German language had not been used. Reprinted in Dangel-Hofmann, op. cit., p. 222.

the *Carmina Burana* would be considered '*undeutsch*', not German enough to be printed and performed.[30] A number of the planned early performances of the *Carmina Burana*, including the planned premiere, were cancelled due to fear of offending the National Socialist conservatives.[31] The work was called 'Bavarian nigger music' ('*bayerische Niggermusik*') by Drewes, head of the music department in the Ministry of Propaganda;[32] the pianist Elly Ney labelled the work a *Kulturschande*, a disgrace to the culture.[33]

There is little evidence in Orff's music that he took much heed of these judgments. Certainly he did not further change his subject-matter, his style or the languages of his lyrics to conform to conservative taste. He claimed after the war that his use of Latin had been a subversive expression of universalism.[34] He continued throughout the war to create works that could be taken as critical of government.[35] In this he was no doubt fortified by popular opinion, which was largely in favour of his work, and especially of the *Carmina Burana*. Despite the disapprobation of some, the cantata achieved great success in wartime Germany. Orff himself said that approval of it among the critics ran at 90 per cent.[36] The work was even produced at La Scala, conducted by the young Herbert von Karajan.[37] Its popularity has continued to this day,[38] though in ways that might have dismayed Orff.

Orff lived for more than 40 years after the composition of the *Carmina Burana*, continuing his work in musical education and composition, drawing, as before, on both German and foreign material for inspiration. He died in 1982. Always conscious of his legacy, he provided in his will for a Carl Orff foundation, intended to carry on his work and to maintain his 'artistic, educational and spiritual heritage'.[39] This foundation is still active in Germany today, operating in part through the Carl Orff Centre in Munich.

The publisher

Orff's publisher from 1927 was B Schotts Soehne in Mainz.[40] Formed in the 18th century, Schott was one of the foremost German music publishers. It had

---

30 Kater, op. cit., p. 10. See also Kowalke, op. cit. n. 26, p. 70, who states that Orff's 'daughter Godela remembers him sweating profusely at the premiere, fearing that *Carmina Burana* would be rejected by the cultural authorities as "*undeutsch*"'. Such fears appear to have built up during the writing of the cantata, Orff having initially seemed to think the material quite suitable for 1930s tastes.
31 Kater, op. cit., pp. 9, 10 and 11, referring to rejections in Dresden, Berlin and Munich.
32 ibid., p. 11.
33 ibid., p. 13.
34 ibid., p. 9.
35 ibid., p. 13, quotes lines from *Die Kluge* which premiered in 1943: 'Fidelity is dead. Justice lives in penury. Piety goes begging. Tyranny carries the sceptre'. Even the positing of the ever-fickle Fortuna as Empress of the World might have seemed subversive to a ruling group that had just declared the Thousand Year Reich.
36 ibid., p. 20.
37 Kowalke, op. cit. n. 26, p. 78; see also n. 15 above.
38 Kowalke, op. cit. n. 15, p. 3, stating in 2001 that earnings from the *Carmina Burana* exceeded a million dollars annually.
39 See the Carl Orff institutions website, http://www.orff.de/Institutions.1578.0.html?&L=1.
40 Liess, op. cit., p. 19.

176 LANDMARKS IN AUSTRALIAN IP LAW

published, most notably, Beethoven's *Ninth Symphony* and Wagner's *Ring*.[41] Schott was always concerned to safeguard its investment and Orff's reputation, and to maximise his chances of success.

Schott weathered the 12 years of National Socialism well. It gave every appearance of embracing the new movement while continuing to publish banned works.[42] It was Schott that, in 1935, warned Orff that there were concerns about his use of Latin lyrics for what was to become the *Carmina Burana*.[43] It was Schott that suggested the expansion of what was originally quite a brief cantata into something more substantial. On a more political note, Schott did not appear entirely supportive of Orff accepting a commission to compose an alternative score to *A Midsummer Night's Dream*, replacing the music of the Jewish Mendelssohn.[44] Schott also discouraged Orff from composing music for the Hitler Youth.[45]

Schott was not only Orff's adviser and publisher; Schott had, and still has, the task of defending the authorial rights as they exist from time to time and from place to place. Schott has a history of taking its defence of its composers very seriously, too seriously for the tastes of some.[46]

Background to the legal action: moral rights in Europe

Throughout Orff's career, German law offered the composer two kinds of inalienable right over his music.[47] On the one hand were the economic rights that

---

41 Kowalke, op. cit. n. 15, p. 6. The Schott publishing house was founded in 1770 by Bernhard Schott in Mainz. In 1780 he obtained an exclusive printing privilege and the title of 'Court music engraver'. The house published the piano scores and first editions of Mozart's *Don Giovanni* and *Die Entführung aus dem Serail*. It also published late works of Beethoven, including the *Ninth Symphony*, the *Missa Solemnis* and the last two string quartets. In 1859 Franz Schott, the grandson of Bernhard, brought Richard Wagner onto the list of Schott composers and the house published *Die Meistersinger von Nürnberg*, the complete *Ring des Nibelungen* and *Parsifal*. In 1874 the Schott family appointed Dr Ludwig Strecker as their successor. His sons, Dr Ludwig Strecker and Willi Strecker (with whom Orff dealt), continued to run the business until succeeded by Heinz Schneider-Schott. Information available at http://www.schott-music.com/world/history/index.html.
42 See Kowalke, op. cit. n. 15, pp. 15–16. In particular he writes: '[D]isplays of loyalty to the cause apparently afforded Schott considerable latitude in the conduct of its daily operations . . . Even after the ban on performances of Hindemith in 1936, Schott continued to publish his works . . . It was a 'sport', Strecker [one of the Schott partners] later told the composer, 'for me to bring out all these things despite the Nazi ban, and fortunately we weren't caught'.
43 Kater, op. cit., pp. 9–10. Orff did not, however, abandon his use of Latin. He used the language again a few years later when he wrote the *Catulli Carmina* (1942).
44 The head of the company, Willy Strecker, commented on Orff having got himself into a wasps' nest with this venture; however Orff did not desist: Kater, op. cit., pp. 18–19.
45 Kater, op. cit., p. 16. For the history of Orff's unsuccessful attempts to interest the Hitler Youth in his work, see Kater, pp. 16–18.
46 See the complaints of Kowalke, published in his epilogue to 'Burying the Past: Carl Orff and His Brecht Connection', op. cit. n. 26, pp. 75–6. Schott is quoted as having stated in a letter to Kowalke that 'The Orff heirs and Orff Foundation have given Schott (and Schott has accepted to take) an explicit mandate to safeguard Orff's interests in cases [where criticisms of Orff's wartime activities are made that in Schott's view are unfounded]'.
47 First in the LUG (the literary and musical authors' rights Act of 1901) and then in the new *Urheberrechtsgesetz* of 1965, where the moral rights were much more fully elaborated. The rights were and are inalienable in the sense that, unlike copyright in the common law countries, they cannot be sold outright.

protected the author against unauthorised exploitation of the music, and on the other were the moral rights (*Urheberpersönlichkeitsrecht*) that allowed the author to control uses made of the work and to maintain the bond between author and work. The two sets of rights were intertwined in German 'copyright' law as components of the *Urheberrecht*, the general authorial right. Both could be used to protect the author against uses of the work that were inimical to the artistic vision.[48] Of most interest to us here are the moral rights.

Where a new arrangement of a musical work takes place, the right that must be taken account of is what law-makers in the English-speaking countries often call the 'right of integrity'. The various ways in which this right is worded in different jurisdictions are significant. Under the Berne Convention and in many pieces of domestic legislation, mention is made of the 'distortion', 'mutilation' or other 'modification' of the work.[49] A prima facie case is established if this treatment produces prejudice to the honour or reputation of the author.[50] National jurisprudence, however, and particularly that of Germany and France, has employed other ways of describing the relevant detriment to the author. Some writers have spoken of the misrepresentation of the author to the public,[51] and of the work ceasing to convey what the author intended.[52] It has been held that the author has 'the absolute right to object to any alteration, modification, correction or addition, no matter how small, which is susceptible to distort his thought'[53] and that the author has

> the moral right of control and of supervision, a right that he retains over the productions of his mind and which permits him to oppose any enterprise that results in the compromising of his work's integrity and the betrayal of his thought.[54]

It has been stated that the most important general principle underlying the right is that the author should have his work communicated to the present and future world substantially *as he has created it*.[55] The current German legislation refers to distortions and other impairments of the work that are apt to endanger the author's intellectual and personal interests,[56] a broad formulation capable of embracing the earlier formulations of the courts and commentators.

---

48 The economic rights allowed the authorial representatives to license only those uses of the music that were not inimical to authorial interests, and they allowed litigation against all those, licensees or non-licensees, who had used the work in ways contrary to these economic rights.

49 See 'Comparative Table of National Moral Rights' in E Adeney, *The Moral Rights of Authors and Performers*, Oxford University Press, Oxford, 2006 for national laws and the types of terminology they use. See also Berne Convention for the Protection of Literary and Artistic Works, opened for signature 14 July 1967, 1161 UNTS 3, Art 6bis (entered into force 10 October 1974).

50 See Adeney, op. cit. n. 49.

51 J Mittelstaedt, 'Droit Moral im Deutschen Urheberrecht' [1913] GRUR 84, 88–9. For further detail see Adeney, op. cit. n. 49, para. 2.39.

52 *Cappiello c Métais, Dupuy, Leprince et la Société du Chocolat Poulain*, Paris, 20 March 1928, Gaz Pal 1928.1.786. For further detail see Adeney, op. cit. n. 49, paras. 2.35–36.

53 *Dlle Chasles c Dlle Soutzo*, Trib civ Seine, 17 February 1926 (Gaz Pal 1926.1.597).

54 *Maeterlinck c Février et autres*, Trib civ Seine, 25 March 1909 (Gaz Pal 1909.1.451).

55 Mittelstaedt, op. cit, p. 86 (emphasis added). Mittelstaedt added the rider that an alteration which was consistent with the spirit and quality of the work would not infringe. In other words, the alteration would not constitute a misrepresentation of the author in the relevant sense (p. 89).

56 *Urheberrechtsgesetz* § 14.

178 LANDMARKS IN AUSTRALIAN IP LAW

Schott's *O Fortuna* litigation in Europe

During the 1990s, approximately 10 years after Orff's death, Schott became aware of uses of the *O Fortuna* chorus that seemed to infringe the moral right of integrity. Two such uses had occurred in the Netherlands, another in Germany. Schott took action in the respective local courts.

At first fortune smiled on Schott and its co-plaintiffs. Judgments were passed in favour of the authorial interests first in Amsterdam (January 1992) and then Munich (July 1994). In the Netherlands the success was spectacular, leading to the withdrawal of highly successful musical arrangements. While the German action concerned a breach of the integrity right rather different from that which was later to occur in Australia,[57] the Dutch action had much in common with its Australian counterpart. It is therefore worth considering the Dutch action in more detail.

The Dutch litigation

The Dutch action arose out of the fact that a company, Indisc, had marketed in the Netherlands compact discs containing a house version of the *O Fortuna* chorus produced through sound sampling by the group Apotheosis.[58] Orff was named on the CDs as the composer. This version reached third place on the Dutch top 40 chart. A second company, Red Bullet, had marketed compact discs in the Netherlands containing a disco version of *O Fortuna*. Again Orff was named as composer. In this disco version some parts of the chorus, for example the opening, had been removed and certain additions made, most notably in the form of a disco rhythm and the sound of a horse neighing. This version stood at number one on the national top 40 chart. Schott joined with STEMRA, the Dutch collecting society responsible for granting musical recording licences, to take legal action against Indisc. Associated with this action[59] was a technically separate action by Red Bullet against STEMRA and Schott.[60]

In 1992 STEMRA, in a circular to the recording industry, had specifically prohibited the production and distribution of adaptations of the *O Fortuna* chorus where the permission of the rights holders in the original work (i.e., the Orff representatives) had not been gained. Despite receipt of this circular, Indisc ordered continued sale of the offending compact disc and was sued.

Red Bullet, for its part, mounted a number of challenges to what it saw as the interference with its rights represented by the circular. It argued that Orff

---

57 The German action concerned a boxer who had used the *O Fortuna* chorus to accompany his entry into the ring. The music was also used in television advertising for his fights. Schott instituted proceedings in the Munich *Landgericht* or state court which granted an injunction against the continued use of the work in this way. For commentary on the case, see C Russ, 'Das Lied eines Boxers' (1995) ZUM 32.

58 In fact at least six techno versions of the chorus have been created by the bands Apotheosis, FCB (released as 'Excalibur'), Highland, Nick Skitz-Excalibur 2001, Spiritual Project, and Headhunterz. See http://www.answers.com/topic/orff-s-carmina-burana-in-popular-culture.

59 KG 92/425 V reported at [1992] 6 *Informatierecht* 112.

60 KG 92/426 V reported at [1992] 6 *Informatierecht* 112.

THE *SCHOTT* CASE 179

could not be considered the author of the music, given the medieval origins of the *O Fortuna* song. This challenge was rejected on the basis that Orff had had no access to the original medieval music and therefore had to compose his own.[61] Red Bullet also challenged the capacity of Schott to take action for infringement of the Orff rights, invoking issues of the rights' transfer and inheritance. The court rejected this argument too.[62] Since the allegation that the Red Bullet version changed the work was undoubtedly true, and since STEMRA had no authority to authorise altered reproductions of a musical composition, it was ultimately held that Schott was entitled to claim infringement of the moral rights. The STEMRA dictate contained in the circular was therefore well founded.

Taking into account the type and extent of the alterations, the court ordered the disco version to be withdrawn from circulation. It refused Red Bullet's request that it engage in a 'balancing of interests'. This would have involved a balancing of the damage to the Orff interests against the significant financial detriment that would be suffered by Red Bullet in withdrawing the CDs, with a view to finding in favour of the most disadvantaged party. The two sets of interests were not sufficiently unequal to justify this.[63]

In the case of Indisc, which did not receive such detailed analysis, the court came to a similar conclusion. It was fortified by the fact that the alterations to the *O Fortuna* chorus evident in the Apotheosis house version were even greater and more obvious than those on the Red Bullet CD. Counsel for Indisc had raised the argument that the sound sampling which had occurred did not constitute alteration of the work *as a whole*. This argument was rejected. The *O Fortuna* track was considered to be not just a snippet but a total, albeit altered, reproduction of the chorus. Also to no avail were the arguments that the sampling had been taken from a legitimate recording of the chorus and that the Apotheosis version was legitimate as a parody or, alternatively, as an aural quotation from the original. As the moral rights of Orff were at play, the conclusion had to be drawn that any permission granted by STEMRA for the recording of the CD did not extend to the alterations. This track too had to be withdrawn.[64]

In the case of both recordings, the power of the authorial moral rights and their separateness from the economic rights allowed Schott's allegations to prevail, to the considerable financial detriment of the distributors. In neither case was the Dutch right of integrity, contained in Art 25 of the Dutch statute, discussed in any detail. It seemed to go without saying that arrangements of the kind marketed by the two parties would infringe it. The crucial point was that both arrangements involved significant *unauthorised alterations* to the work, and no relevant defences were available.

---

61 ibid., p. 113. See also n. 20 above.
62 Red Bullet argued unsuccessfully that neither Schott nor the widow Orff was empowered to exercise the rights in the Netherlands: [1992] 6 *Informatierecht* 112, 113–14.
63 ibid., p. 114.
64 ibid.

180 LANDMARKS IN AUSTRALIAN IP LAW

Schott considers an Australian foray

No doubt encouraged by these outcomes, Schott considered a much more risky venture – action in Australia, a common law country. Schott evidently wanted to rely on moral rights principles in a country that at the time did not formally recognise the existence of moral rights in its law. The publisher's legal representatives were hoping to breathe life into nascent moral rights thinking in this country, aware that the Australian government had long considered itself to be in compliance, one way or another, with the moral rights provisions of the Berne Convention.[65] It was thought that an Australian statutory licensing provision, blocking the licence when the arrangement 'debased' the work, might be interpreted by a court as protecting authorial moral rights.

Statutory and compulsory licences: a curtailment of power

Copyright owners (and authors if the two are the same) derive a significant part of their power from the exclusive economic rights over their work. Not only do these rights allow the copyright owner to profit from the commercial use of the work, but they can also be used for the incidental purpose of controlling the way the music is exploited. In this they are effective in two ways. They allow the owner to license only those uses of the music that are not inimical to the interests of the rights holder, and they allow litigation against all those, licensees or non-licensees, who have made unauthorised use of the work. Thus, they allow contractual control over the uses to which the music is put, and an incidental control over misuses of the work if those misuses coincide with infringement of the economic rights. To lose the power to control exploitation contracts is therefore to lose a significant degree of control over the work itself.

Such loss of power has been produced through the institution in domestic law of statutory or compulsory licensing provisions.[66] Under such a provision, once a first recording company has produced an arrangement of the music, other recording companies are entitled to do likewise. Either the composer is obliged to

---

[65] Such a conviction seemed to explain Australia's failure, in the years after 1935, to enact any express protection of moral rights. The conviction had, however, faded since the 1960s. In 1990 the Attorney-General, Michael Duffy, stated: 'At the time Australia . . . joined the Berne Convention, it was clearly considered that existing legislative and judicial remedies were adequate to comply with that part of the Convention on moral rights. Yet today, different perceptions, different expectations, are leading governments including this government to re-examine the way in which it might give effect to convention provisions on moral rights.' Attorney-General Michael Duffy, 'Treaty Obligations: Cost of Consent', speech delivered at the Conference on the Role of Consent and the Development of International and Public Law, organised by the Centre for International and Public Law, Australian National University, Canberra, 15 August 1990, published at (1990) 61 *Department of Foreign Affairs and Trade: The Monthly Record* 526.

[66] These terms tend to be used interchangeably in the common law jurisdictions. It would be logical to distinguish between them, however, on the basis that a statutory licence is given by legislation whereas a compulsory licence is given, under statutory compulsion, by the rights holder.

THE *SCHOTT* CASE 181

grant a licence for this secondary use, as was the case in Germany until recently,[67] or the statute of the country concerned will itself grant the licence, as is the case in Australia.[68] The effect of this is a promotion of competition and the increased access of the public to the musical work. Royalties must, of course, be paid by the user, but the power to pick and choose the recipients of a licence and to determine the conditions of the use are largely lost to the rights holder. This loss has long been a cause of concern to authors.[69]

Controlling the loss of power: limits on compulsory licensing and the link to moral rights

The diminution of power represented by the compulsory or statutory licence has, typically, been subject to its own control mechanism. There are certain things that a recording company, in the enjoyment of its statutory freedom, has not been entitled to do to a work. These mechanisms vary from one country to another, but they are normally designed to protect the non-economic interests of the composer. In some countries the limits on compulsory or statutory licences have been linked to 'moral rights' in the legislation itself. In others the link to non-economic authorial protection may be found in preliminary legislative documents.

The US copyright regime, for example, contains a limited statutory licence provision in s 115 of Title 17. The US House report dealing with the provision states:

> [The clause] is intended to recognize the practical need for a limited privilege to make arrangements of music being used under a compulsory license, *but without allowing the music to be perverted, distorted, or travestied.*[70]

The UK copyright legislation for many years also contained a statutory licence.[71] When it was under discussion in the House of Lords in the 1950s it was stated for the government that the proposed control on it 'is put in specifically to prevent the vulgarisation or the "jazzing up" of a distinguished piece of work which, naturally, might annoy and aggravate the composer'.[72]

In Germany the controls on the compulsory licence – embodied in §§ 62 and 63 of the Authors' Rights Act – actually drew on and reinforced the moral rights elsewhere recognised by the Act.[73] For Schott's purposes, the most significant

---

67 *Urheberrechtsgesetz* § 61, now repealed.
68 *Copyright Act 1968* (Cth) s 55(1).
69 It was an important factor leading to the 1928 introduction of moral rights into the Berne Convention: see *Actes de la conférence réunie à Rome du 7 mai au 2 juin 1928* (Rome Actes), Bureau de l'Union Internationale pour la Protection des Œuvres Littéraires et Artistiques, Berne, 1929, pp. 175–7, 236.
70 HR Rep No. 94-1476, 94th Congress (1976), reprinted in 1976 USCCAN 5659 (emphasis added).
71 *Copyright Act 1911* (UK) 1 & 2 Geo V, c 46, s 19.
72 *Hansard*, HL (series 5) Vol. 194, col. 1031 (1 December 1955) (Lord Mancroft, Joint Parliamentary Under-Secretary of State for the Home Department).
73 Most notably in §§ 12, 13 and 14 of the Act, but also in further sections such as § 39.

182 LANDMARKS IN AUSTRALIAN IP LAW

control was provided by § 62 of the Act. This reiterated a limited prohibition on any *alterations* to the work that might take place when the compulsory licence was used.[74] The section referred to and relied on § 39, a provision recognised as helping to complete and clarify Germany's main protection of the work's integrity.[75] Section 39 provides that a person in whom an exploitation right is vested may not alter the work, its title or the authorial designation without authorisation. Thus, those who were defending the Orff legacy were accustomed to a system in which a direct relationship existed between the then compulsory licensing provisions and a moral rights–based prohibition on significant alterations to the work.

It was a control mechanism of this type that the Orff-Schott representatives were to rely on in the Australian action. The legislative history of the statutory licensing provisions in Australia encouraged their view that an argument based on moral rights principles might have some prospect of success in this country.

The *Schott* action in Australia

A case of converging stories

The Australian action was mounted by Schott Musik International, Boosey & Hawkes (Australia) and the Australasian Mechanical Copyright Owners Society (AMCOS). Schott was applying in its capacity as the owner of the economic rights in the music, and was acting with the support of Orff's widow, Liselotte. Despite acting in its capacity as copyright owner, Schott was motivated not by economic concerns but rather by concern at the treatment that Orff's work had undergone.[76] Boosey & Hawkes made the application in its capacity as the exclusive licensee of the copyright in Australia. The collecting society AMCOS[77] also applied in its capacity as the exclusive licensee of certain aspects of the copyright. It was responsible for administering the Australian statutory licence and also had licensing agreements in place with the Australian Record Industry Association and the Australian Music Publishers Association.

The respondents in the action were Colossal Records of Australia and its directors, who had made or authorised the making of certain compact discs.[78] These CDs embodied a sound recording 'Excalibur, '95 Remix of O Fortuna' performed by the Italian music group FCB. It was this remix, consisting of four tracks, to which the applicants took exception, claiming an injunction, delivery of the offending CDs and damages.

---

74 The section states: 'To the extent that the provisions of this Part allow the use of a work, alterations to the work may not be undertaken. Section 39 applies correspondingly.'
75 Contained in § 14 of the German Authors' Rights Act. See E Ulmer, *Urheber und Verlagsrecht*, 3rd edn, Springer, Berlin, Heidelberg, New York, 1980, p. 217.
76 I am indebted to the legal representatives for the applicants for confirming this.
77 The Australasian Mechanical Copyright Owners Society.
78 Authorisation of an infringing action constitutes a primary infringement under the *Copyright Act 1968* (Cth) s 36.

THE *SCHOTT* CASE   183

The remixed tracks could be classified as 'adaptations' of the musical work under Australian law[79] and hence within the exclusive rights of the musical copyright owner. They consisted of techno dance music arrangements of the *O Fortuna* chorus. More specifically, the first of the four tracks, taken from a legitimate recording of *O Fortuna*, had transformed the original music by means of

> electronic sounds, transposition, electronic distortion giving a harshness to the choral voices, pumping rhythms, various voices interspersed, including at one stage a voice saying 'do the honky stomp, do the honky stomp, do the honky, do the honky, do the honky, do the honky stomp', piano riffs and a variety of electronic effects.[80]

One witness listed the following alterations to the original musical work: change of key; change of time values; interruptions between consecutive bars; separation of consecutive passages; linkage of separated passages; distortion of sound; glissandi applied to chords; extraction, manipulation and repetition of fragments; reversal of chord progressions; overlay of various percussion sounds; overlay of synthesised chords; contraction of passages; sampled chords switched on and off to provide techno rhythms; overlay of voices enunciating common phrases; and manipulation of choral chords to sound as though the choir was singing common words.[81] Another stated:

> The FCB remix contains music created by electronic instruments, with sampling of an original recording of the work fading in and out. The recording is alienated by scratching and other manipulations. It is my observation that instead of the complex alternating rhythm which contributes essentially to the effect of the original work, the rhythm of the arrangement is a monotonous synthesis [sic?] techno beat . . . [the] hymnic invocation has been forcibly adapted to the tonal language of the techno music movement.[82]

Generally speaking, the making of an adaptation without authorisation of the copyright owner was permissible under s 55 of the *Copyright Act*, the statutory licensing provision. The adaptation could be impugned, however, if it 'debased' the original *O Fortuna* music.[83] The concept of 'debasement' was the peculiarly Australian control on its statutory licence. Because it appeared to safeguard the non-economic interests of the composer, it was also regarded in Australia as providing protection analogous to moral rights protection.[84] Its existence was one of the reasons why a more complete set of moral rights provisions was for decades not deemed necessary in this country.

---

79 *Copyright Act 1968* (Cth) ss 10(1), 31.
80 *Schott Musik International GmbH & Co v Colossal Records of Australia* (1997) 38 IPR 1, 6.
81 *Schott Musik International GmbH & Co v Colossal Records of Australia* (1997) 36 IPR 267, 275–6.
82 ibid., p. 277.
83 Section 55(2) read: 'The last preceding subsection does not apply in relation to a record of an adaptation of a musical work if the adaptation debases the work'.
84 See Parliament of Australia, Bills Digest No. 99, 1999–2000, Copyright Amendment (Moral Rights) Bill 1999: 'It may also be argued that sections 35(5) and 55(2) partly protect the right of integrity.' See also M Weir, 'The Story of Moral Rights or the Moral of the Story?' (1992) 3 *Australian Intellectual Property Journal* 232, 243.

184 LANDMARKS IN AUSTRALIAN IP LAW

It is not altogether surprising that the Orff publishers, particularly those who had known the composer and who understood the meaning of the *O Fortuna* music, should have considered the treatment described above as debasing. But did the 'debasement' control really protect the composer's interests?

This word 'debase' had never been interpreted by an Australian court and neither the plain meaning of the word itself nor its context in the statute cast much light on how it should be handled. It was therefore both permissible and necessary for the courts to look at the parliamentary comments surrounding the provision's introduction in order to gauge its effect.[85]

'Debasement' in parliamentary debate

The debasement limitation had been introduced into the statutory licensing provision in 1968. The parliamentary debates preceding its introduction indicate that it reflected a strong sympathy for the position of the composer rather than the copyright owner as such. As one member of parliament said: 'What we have to understand and to think about is that it is the originators who are the people who deserve basic protection in any legislation like this.'[86]

The most significant comment on the intentions behind the control was made by the Attorney-General, Nigel Bowen, quoting the words of Alexander Buchanan, the Member for McMillan:

[O]nce the composer had allowed his work to be put into record form by one manufacturer *a second manufacturer might come along and 'muck up his work'* . . . An attempt has been made to cover that possibility in sub-clause (2) of clause 55. If the production is a debased form of the work it is not covered by the freedom from copyright.[87]

It is rather typical of Australian discourse (even parliamentary discourse) that the defining words of the legislators should have been the slang phrase 'muck up his work'. This statement focuses attention on the adaptation itself and on the composer–work relationship. The emotional overtones of the phrase suggest that the new clause was indeed intended to protect some personal interest that bound the composer to the work. However, only the copyright owner could take advantage of the limitation, so the provision represented a hybrid form of protection, halfway between copyright and moral rights. It is in the light of these facts that the judgments in the *Schott* case were made.

The arguments on behalf of Schott

The applicants, in keeping with European moral rights tradition, based their case primarily on the unauthorised *difference* between the techno version of *O Fortuna* and Orff's original score. Counsel for the applicants, David Catterns,

---

85 *Acts Interpretation Act 1901* (Cth) s 15AB.
86 Vol. H of R 59, p. 1937 (Duthie).
87 ibid., p. 1961 (emphasis added).

THE *SCHOTT* CASE 185

presented the debasement test as similar in meaning and scope to various tests for infringement of the integrity right. He argued that to 'debase' means 'to alter the quality or integrity of the work "Carmina Burana" or to adulterate it'.[88] He argued that the work had been altered so much that it no longer represented the artistic vision of Orff. One of the applicants' expert witnesses considered that a debasing adaptation would be one that would destroy aspects of the work's 'integrity':

> that is, its wholeness or one-ness – I don't mean wholesomeness; I mean its one-ness. One that destroys the form of the piece. One that injures the composer's emotional intentions. One which veers far enough away from the original to change its nature, its structure and message.[89]

Other opinions put forward for the applicants were that the techno version 'mutilated' and 'distorted' the work,[90] that it showed no 'respect' for the work,[91] that the remix was 'derogatory' to the work and 'damaging to the reputation' of Orff's music,[92] and that the 'dignity' of the music was lowered.[93]

These are all well-established arguments, some of which have been used for more than a century to establish infringements of the authorial right of integrity in Europe. The reference to 'mutilation and distortion' seemed to be taken either directly from Art 6bis of the Berne Convention[94] or from the UK moral rights provisions.[95] So did the reference to the authorial 'reputation'. The reference to a 'derogatory' treatment of the work was likewise borrowed from the UK right of integrity.[96] The reference to 'dignity' might have been derived from Berne Convention debates.[97] Use of the word 'respect' seemed to allude to the French right of integrity, the author's 'right of respect for his work'.[98] The notion of injury to the composer's emotional intentions seemed to derive from older European judgments.[99]

Despite these arguments, three of the judges who heard the case did not accept that moral rights were at issue at all. They considered that they were engaged in an entirely independent process of ascertaining both the ordinary meaning

---

88 (1997) 36 IPR 267, 273.
89 ibid., pp. 276–7.
90 ibid., p. 277.
91 ibid.
92 ibid.
93 ibid.
94 Article 6bis(1) currently reads: 'Independently of the author's economic rights, and even after the transfer of the said rights, the author shall have the right . . . to object to any distortion, mutilation or other modification of, or other derogatory action in relation to, the said work, which would be prejudicial to his honor or reputation.'
95 A treatment of a work must be derogatory to infringe the integrity right under UK law. A treatment will be derogatory if 'it amounts to a distortion or mutilation of the work or is otherwise prejudicial to the honour or reputation of the author or director': *Copyright, Designs and Patents Act 1988* (Cth) s 80(2)(b).
96 ibid., s 80(1).
97 Piola Caselli at the Rome Revision Conference of the Berne Convention noted that moral rights were about the protection of the author 'with respect to his reputation, his honour and his dignity': *Actes de la conférence réunie à Rome du 7 mai au 2 juin 1928*, Bureau de l'Union Internationale pour la Protection des Œuvres Littéraires et Artistiques, Berne, 1929, pp. 291–2.
98 *Intellectual Property Code* Art L 121–1.
99 See ns. 52–4 above.

186   LANDMARKS IN AUSTRALIAN IP LAW

of the word 'debasement' and what the Australian legislators had meant when they wrote the concept of debasement into the Act. None of the judges thought that the legislature had been trying to introduce moral rights into Australian jurisprudence.

Tamberlin J's reasoning at first instance

At first instance Tamberlin J found that no debasement had taken place. His reasoning was, in short:

- that there had been no reduction in the value of the copyright as a result of the Excalibur remix;[100]
- that there was no widespread perception of reduction in quality, rank or dignity of the work as a result of Excalibur;[101]
- that how 'widespread' a perception was should be assessed considering 'the overall impression which [the adaptation] is likely to make on a community with a wide range of tastes and attitudes in relation to adaptations and musical forms';[102]
- that Excalibur preserved substantial and essential elements of the original intact, and communicated a powerful exuberance and rhythmic character quite consistent with the character of Orff's *O Fortuna* chorus.[103]

Tamberlin J was not impressed by the defendant's argument that the musical value of the chorus had already been impaired by its so-called kitsch character and its expression of 1930s ideals, and could therefore be 'debased' no further.[104] Nor was he impressed by the fact that the chorus had already been much used in advertising, even with the permission of the Orff representatives, and had thereby lost some of its association with high art.[105] Musical debasement, he thought, would have to be brought about by something that altered the perception of the music itself rather than by the mental distractions conjured up by its performance.

The appeal

Tamberlin J's judgment against Schott and the other applicants was unanimously affirmed on appeal by Hill, Wilcox and Lindgren JJ, but each of the three members

---

100 (1997) 36 IPR 267, 281. Reduction in the copyright value could be interpreted as evidence of the work having fallen into disrepute, hence as having been debased.
101 ibid.
102 ibid., p. 274.
103 ibid., p. 281.
104 ibid., p. 278.
105 Evidence had been adduced that the chorus had been used in advertisements for Nescafé, a Michael Jackson concert, an Arnold Schwarzenegger film and an advertisement for Sea World. It had been used in films such as *The Doors*, *The Omen* and *Excalibur* and in advertisements for other films. It had been licensed for use in advertisements for Old Spice products and also for modern versions of the chorus: ibid., p. 280. The policy of the Orff representatives appears to have been to object, not to the context in which the work was used, but only to actual distortions of the music.

of the appeal bench had his own reasons for the affirmation. What was clear from the aggregated decisions, however, was that 'debasement' was considered a very strong term indeed and much would be needed to prove its existence. This perception ran counter to the implication of parliamentary discussion that all that was needed was a 'mucking up' of the work, a term that suggests no more than that the work is disarranged and spoilt.

Hill J noted that the fact of making a new arrangement of a work, altering its style and approach for example, cannot in itself entail 'debasement' since the whole statutory scheme allowing adaptations is predicated on change.[106] On the other hand, 'debasement' is still possible even though no adaptation can ever touch the value or quality of the 'original'.[107] For a work to be debased the adaptation must have 'some characteristic which affects the way the original work is regarded'.[108] How a work is regarded might, in turn, be illustrated by the effects of the adaptation on the copyright owner's commercial interests.[109] Hill J concluded that the proper test to adopt is 'whether it is a consequence of the adaptation . . . that a reasonable person will be led to think less of the original work'.[110] For example, an adaptation that brought to the original associations objectionable to a reasonable person might be considered debasing, as might a parody of the work, or an arrangement that associated the work with a terrorist or racist body.[111]

Wilcox J took a different approach. He thought that 'debasement' must come about through the extreme musical inferiority of the adaptation and should not be measured solely by public perceptions.[112] He introduced the terms 'degradation' and 'integrity' to the test – 'the adaptation must be so lacking in integrity or quality that it can properly be said to have degraded the original work'.[113] An adaptation that had its own integrity and that did not constitute a 'mere travesty' of the original[114] was unlikely, in his view, to degrade the original.

Lindgren J took yet another path. He considered that the legislative intention was to exclude from the statutory licence adaptations of a work 'very generally of a kind protected against by the "droit moral"'.[115] Picking up the language of moral rights, he thought that the debasement question could be formulated as 'whether the arrangement is an impermissible distortion, mutilation or other modification of the musical work'.[116] The issue needed to be considered, however, not through the eyes of the composer or musicologist, but in the light of contemporary life,

---

106 (1997) 38 IPR 1, 10.
107 ibid., p. 11.
108 ibid.
109 ibid.
110 ibid., p. 12.
111 ibid.
112 ibid., p. 3.
113 ibid., p. 4.
114 ibid., p. 5.
115 ibid., p. 15.
116 ibid., p. 17.

188   LANDMARKS IN AUSTRALIAN IP LAW

musical technology, societal phenomena and new musical genres.[117] Neither a poor performance[118] nor anything external to the music such as lyrics or visual images could create such an impermissible modification.[119] Lindgren J ventured the opinion that an arrangement is less likely to be a debasement where it makes the original musical work available to the tastes of a different era or subculture, and 'thereby acquires its own integrity'.[120]

Based on their respective reasoning, the three judges decided that the rhythmic distortions, the interpolations and the other alterations of the *O Fortuna* chorus did not constitute a debasement and that the statutory licence had therefore been properly exercised. Costs were awarded against Schott and its fellow applicants. The wheel of fortune had turned.

The place of *Schott* in Australian law

This decision was the only one ever to consider the 'debasement' control on the Australian statutory licence. The control was subsequently repealed,[121] leaving the current licence with no internal control mechanism. At the same time extensive moral rights provisions came into force in Australia.[122] The implication is that statutory licensing is henceforth to be controlled by Australia's now quite fully articulated moral rights concepts.

While it should not be supposed that the *Schott* decision caused the legislators to adopt moral rights for Australia, it did demonstrate a few reasons why the replacement of the debasement control was desirable:

1. The lack of a clear line of reasoning among the judgments demonstrated the difficulty of applying a concept as indeterminate as 'debasement' to the treatment of copyright material. Neither international nor domestic sources could provide much insight into its meaning. The moral right of integrity, by contrast, has received much attention by courts, commentators and international bodies. It is altogether a better documented right.

2. It was evident in the judgments that the functional incoherence of the 'debasement' mechanism was a problem. Its primary beneficiary was the composer, yet the composer could not invoke it; it could only be invoked by the copyright owner and was expressed to safeguard the 'work'. Except where the composer remained, or controlled, the copyright owner, the composer's interests were largely unprotected under the Australian statute.

---

117 ibid.
118 ibid., p. 15.
119 ibid., p. 16.
120 ibid., p. 17.
121 Act 159 of 2000 (*Copyright Amendment (Moral Rights) Act 2000*) s 3, Sch 1 item 1A.
122 ibid., s 3, Sch 1 item 1.

THE *SCHOTT* CASE 189

3. For the above reason, it was evident that the debasement control was unlikely ever to protect foreign composers in the way required by the 1928 Act of the Berne Convention, to which Australia had become a party in 1935. Though for a time it had been thought that the debasement control offered one way in which this country might comply with Art 6bis of the Convention, it was now clear that this was a vain hope. Australia did not offer foreign composers a protection equivalent to that offered in, for example, the Netherlands.

The future

It is not therefore surprising that the legislators abandoned this form of control in favour of controls that were more clearly directed at Berne Convention compliance. These controls, though they raise their own issues of indeterminacy, are directed expressly at authorial protection. They are far more detailed than the debasement provision and greater legislative assistance is given in their interpretation. They also connect to over a century of judicial and scholarly comment, which helps to elucidate their meaning.

Whether the new moral rights provisions will lead to different outcomes for composers, however, still remains questionable. The unanimity of the outcome in the *Schott* case demonstrated a reluctance of Australian courts to make negative value judgments about derivative creativity. We may find that the same is the case under the new moral rights provisions.

There are, however, several reasons to think that future courts may be less resistant to a finding in favour of authorial interests than the *Schott* courts were. For one thing more than 10 years have passed since the *Schott* decisions. Australia has in that period – through the introduction of moral rights – committed itself legislatively to the repositioning of authorial interests in the general scheme of 'copyright' protection. A new generation of judges may therefore be persuaded, as the judges in the *Schott* case were not, that the distortion of a work in ways that impair the work's function as a vehicle for authorial communication is a serious act that should not be tolerated during the statutory protection period. The interests of the derivative creator (and those commercially exploiting that creativity) may not always trump the authorial interests. Reference in the current integrity provision to the author's 'honour or reputation', particularly the 'honour' component, would seem broad enough to accommodate the finding that certain alterations, which the author would have found offensive or demeaning, are capable of infringing.[123]

A further consideration needs to be borne in mind. The Australian moral rights provisions are worded in such a way as to bring our copyright system

---

123 On the question of 'honour', see E Adeney 'The Moral Right of Integrity: The Past and Future of Honour' (2005) *Intellectual Property Quarterly* 111.

190   LANDMARKS IN AUSTRALIAN IP LAW

into compliance with the current Berne Convention text. The key words used to delineate the Australian integrity right ('prejudicial to . . . honour or reputation') are the very words used in Art 6bis of the Convention. Therefore, the intentions of the negotiating parties at Berne Convention conferences may be taken into account in interpreting the words in the case of ambiguity.[124] For this reason the meaning given to moral rights in other countries, particularly the predominantly European countries that negotiated Art 6bis, cannot be ignored. The type of values that underpinned the Dutch decisions in this stream of litigation may over time come to influence Australian thinking.

---

124 *Koowarta v Bjelke-Petersen* (1982) 153 CLR 168, 265 (Brennan J); *'Applicant A' v Minister for Immigration and Ethnic Affairs* [1997] HCA 4 (Unreported, Brennan CJ, Dawson, McHugh, Gummow and Kirby JJ, 24 February 1997), available at http://www.austlii.edu.au/au/cases/cth/HCA/1997/4.html.

12

The protection of *At the Waterhole* by John Bulun Bulun: Aboriginal art and the recognition of private and communal rights

Colin Golvan

Introduction

John Bulun Bulun is an Aboriginal artist who lives in the area of Maningrida, an Aboriginal township about 600 km east of Darwin in central Arnhem Land. When I first met him in 1988, he lived in an outstation known as Garmedi with a population of about 20 people. Bulun Bulun was one of a group of three highly successful bark painters living at the outstation, with the other artists being Jack Wunuwun and his son Michael. These artists painted on bark using traditional ochres, applying the ochres mixed with water using both traditional and western brushes. They would also use glue to give a sheen to the surface of the bark on which they were painting. Their work was often very elaborate, combining complex tribal imagery with detailed cross-hatching.

Bulun Bulun has been among the best known bark painters in Australia over a period of many years, and his work is widely admired by western art critics and curators of the major Aboriginal art collections. His work is represented in most major public collections of bark painting. At the time, Jack held the distinction of having received more than any other bark painter for a single work – $10 000 paid by the Australian National Gallery for the painting known as *Banumbirr, the Morning Star* in 1987. One of Bulun Bulun's paintings had been sold in 1988 for $5000. Today his leading works would sell for many multiples of this price. The market for Aboriginal art has blossomed since 1998; in 2007, Sothebys recorded a record price for the sale of an Aboriginal artwork (an oil painting) of $2.4 million.

In 1987, a T-shirt manufacturer reproduced one of Bulun Bulun's paintings, known as *At the Waterhole*, on T-shirts without his permission. Subsequently, a revised version of the T-shirt was created, which drew on another of Bulun

192   LANDMARKS IN AUSTRALIAN IP LAW

Bulun's paintings, known as *Sacred Waterholes Surrounded by Totemic Animals of the Artist's Clan'* (painted in 1981) as well as *At the Waterhole*. Again, no permission was sought. The work of other artists was also reproduced. There were a number of significant markings on the T-shirts which included the title 'At the Waterhole', the label 'The Aboriginals', and a swing ticket with the following script:

> AT THE WATERHOLE – a design originated from Central Arnhem Land. The art depicts magpie geese and waterlilies around a central waterhole with tortoises also shown. It's characterized by excellent draughtsmanship, curved flowing lines and close intertwining forms. The motifs create an overall curvilinear pattern on a plain black background. The aboriginals painted these designs on large pieces of bark often treated with a layer of brown or red ochre. The design is built up using red, yellow, black and white ochres, applied with a hair or chewed twig 'brush'. Modern day artists are beginning to take advantage of modern materials like masonite board, acrylic paints and conventional artists' brushes. However, the subject-matter and traditional styles are still retained.[1]

An early version of the T-shirt bore the notation Flash Screenprinters (c).

In 1989, Bulun Bulun and the other artists concerned took the unprecedented step of bringing an action for infringement of copyright and breaches of the *Trade Practices Act 1974* (Cth) in the Federal Court in Darwin, arising from these unauthorised reproductions. The manufacturers and two Darwin tourist shops which sold the T-shirts gave undertakings to the court agreeing to cease manufacturing and selling the T-shirts, and to deliver up all remaining stocks. The outcome was described by the coordinator of the Association of Northern and Central Australian Aboriginal Artists, Martin Hardie, as a 'landmark' for Aboriginal artists as it showed that the interests of Aboriginal artists could be protected through reliance on the *Copyright Act 1968* (Cth) and associated protection under the *Trade Practices Act*. Mr Hardie said that the case would be recalled as the occasion on which the rights of Aboriginal bark painters in their works have been formally recognised by means of undertakings given to a court.

The case was the first occasion on which Aboriginal artists had successfully litigated to protect their imagery from unauthorised reproduction, and provided a foundation for later authority in which the Federal Court confirmed the copyright foundations for the protection of Aboriginal artistry from illegal copying.[2] It was also the first occasion on which Aboriginal artists asserted a private right of ownership of artworks under copyright in a court proceeding, a step which was met with a degree of criticism concerning the claim of private, rather than communal, rights in traditional works of tribal imagery. In fact the case was subsequently settled (there being no judgment published by the court) with a substantial payment being made to the artists in question and the offending T-shirts being withdrawn and delivered up to the artists.

---

1 Copy on file with author.
2 See, in particular, *Milpurrurru v Indofurn Pty Ltd* (1994) 30 IPR 209.

Figure 12.1 Johnny Bulun Bulun, *Magpie Geese and Waterlilies at the Waterhole*
© Johnny Bulun Bulun, licensed by VISCOPY, Sydney, 2008

The case

The evidence prepared in the proceeding was of interest as it was the first attempt to document the copyright foundations of a claim of the kind under consideration. This section sets out key passages of the evidence, outlining the factual and opinion underpinnings for this landmark claim.

194   LANDMARKS IN AUSTRALIAN IP LAW

One of the chief deponents for Bulun Bulun was Margaret West, the curator of Aboriginal Art and Material Culture at the Northern Territory Museum of Arts and Sciences. The museum had one of the largest collections of bark paintings in Australia, including the work known as *At the Waterhole,* painted by Bulun Bulun in 1978. West deposed that

> bark painting was one of a number of mediums used for ceremonial purposes amongst Aboriginal communities in central and northern Australia, as is body painting and rock painting. Bark painting tends to take its origins from body painting, and has been actively pursued in recent years arising from a growing interest in acquiring Aboriginal art among art collectors in Australia and around the world.[3]

West deposed:

> The technique involved in producing a bark painting involves the following steps. First, bark is stripped from stringybark eucalyptus trees during the wet season. The bark is dried and compressed, and the inner surface is then smoothed. A range of colours are used – mostly red, brown, yellow, black and white. The colours are obtained from grinding coloured rocks, which are obtained in the artist's area or exchanged between tribes. Some artists mix their colours with glue for a shiny effect, and some artists use orchid juice for the same purpose. The painters do not mix colours, and deliberately strive to reproduce the natural colours in their works. A variety of brushes are used, including a thin strip of bark which is chewed and used for broad lines and a brush made of human hair used for fine lines, as well as thin sticks softened at one end. Artists are also using western style brushes.

West also deposed:

> While many bark paintings represent traditional designs, it nevertheless remains that particular artists have their own distinctive ways of expressing the traditional designs. Tribal groupings will have the right to depict particular designs by virtue of Aboriginal custom. Members of a tribal group will be entitled to depict particular designs in their artwork, with some inheriting the right to depict a complete version of a design by virtue of their proficiency and skill as artists. The artists will have the right to deal with the works as they consider appropriate, including the right to sell the works.

West said that most artworks have religious significance to the artists and their communities, and added that the artists would not deal in their works in such a way as to undermine the dignity and significance of their work. She continued:

> There is no separate class of artists as such in Aboriginal society. Rather, all adults are expected to participate in the process of remembering and recording the dreaming rituals of their tribe. Nevertheless, some painters have come to establish special reputations by virtue of their proficiency and popularity in the Western art market. Despite this commercial influence, the creation of a painting is regarded as an act in itself which conjures the spirit power of a tribe. The paintings are also used to educate members of a tribe in the tribe's rituals and dreaming, and may be studied by younger tribe members, under the supervision of an artist, in order that the rituals of the tribe are properly imparted. This is done sometimes before an artwork is released for sale. In traditional

---

3 Copies of affidavits on file with author.

Aboriginal society, the designs of a tribe are amongst the most important possessions of the members of the tribe. When an artwork is sold, it is never considered that the title to the design has passed. This always remains with the artist who is permitted by his tribe to depict the design in question. It is an unspoken understanding, on the part of the artists, that the purchasers will properly look after the artworks.

West said that she was aware of one particular artist, who was deceased, and who stopped painting for an extended period of time because of the anguish he felt at seeing one of his artworks reproduced on a tea towel, which is regarded as an act of theft in both a material and spiritual sense. In an affidavit, Bulun Bulun deposed that he was the author of the two works in question and that they were original works. He deposed that he had

> never approved of the reproduction of any of my artworks on T-shirts, and never approved the mass reproduction of any of my artworks, other than the reproduction of photos of my works in art books. None of the respondents have ever spoken to me, or attempted to speak to me, about the matter. Had they sought my permission, I would not have given it.

Bulun Bulun said that he had been impeded from carrying out his activities and duties as an artist because of the unauthorised reproduction of his artworks:

> This reproduction has caused me great embarrassment and shame, and I strongly feel that I have been the victim of the theft of an important birthright. I have not painted since I learned about the reproduction of my artworks, and attribute my inactivity as an artist directly to my annoyance and frustration with the actions of the respondents in this matter. My interest in painting has been rekindled by the efforts being made on my behalf to resolve this problem, and I am just starting to paint again, although I am doing so in anticipation that this problem will be resolved in the near future. If it is not resolved satisfactorily, I have considered never painting again.

Bulun Bulun deposed that

> my work is very closely associated with an affinity for the land. This affinity is at the essence of my religious beliefs. The unauthorized reproduction of artworks is a very sensitive issue in all Aboriginal communities. The impetus for the creation of works remains their importance in ceremony, and the creation of artworks is an important step in the preservation of important traditional customs. It is an activity which occupies the normal part of the day-to-day activities of the members of my tribe and represents an important part of the cultural continuity of the tribe. It is also the main source of income for my people, both in my tribe and for the people of many other tribes, and I am very concerned about the financial well-being of my family should I decide that I cannot go on painting.

Bulun Bulun was trained as a painter by his father, who was himself a painter.

> My father lived at a mission settlement at Milingimbi where he sold works to the mission. He painted the dreaming stories of our tribe, the Gunilbingu, including waterhole scenes. He painted such scenes in his own way. I do not have any of his works, and have never tried to copy any of them. His teaching was of importance in imparting to me the traditional techniques of bark painting, and the dreaming traditions and images of our tribe. I am training my own son in the same manner.

Bulun Bulun said that he had particular responsibilities as a ceremonial manager to ensure that ceremonies and traditions were observed correctly, and that his painting was a significant part of this duty:

> Many of my paintings feature 'waterhole' settings, and these are an important part of my dreaming, and all the animals in these paintings are part of that dreaming. Many of the paintings include the long-necked turtle, called barnda, the magpie goose, or gumang, the file snake, or bipuan, and water lily, or yarrman. The bands of cross-hatching or rarrk represent a marrawurrurr yiritdja site.
>
> The story being told in my waterhole works concerns the passage to Garmedi from my traditional land, and illustrates different ways of interpreting the same aspects of the story. The story is generally concerned with the travel of the long-necked turtle to Garmedi, and, by tradition I am allowed to paint the part of the story concerning the travel of the turtle to Garmedi. According to tradition, the long-necked turtle continued its journey, and other artists paint the onward journey. The many different versions of the waterhole story, as illustrated in the photos of my work exhibited to the Affidavit of Margaret West, are indicative of the range of possibilities in telling the traditional story. I also paint other stories in my work, such as the story of the Morning Star ceremony, and another series concerning the story of two sisters who released maternal milk into a waterhole.

Originality

One of the principal issues in the case was that of whether the works were original for the purposes of copyright protection (as required under s 32(2) of the *Copyright Act*. Originality in copyright has been likened to an act of authorship, in the sense that a work claimed to be 'original' may not be a copy of another work. In *Walter v Lane*,[4] a decision of the House of Lords, Lord James of Hereford stated:

> Whilst the Act supplies no definition of the word 'author', and whilst it may be difficult for any judicial authority to give a positive definition of that word, certain considerations controlling the meaning of it seem to be established. A mere copyist of written matter is not an 'author', within the Act, but a translator from one language to another would be so ... an 'author' may come into existence without producing any original matter of his own. Many instances of the claim to authorship without the production of original matter have been given at the bar. The compilation of a street directory, the reports of proceedings in courts of law, and the tables of the times of running of certain railway trains have been held to bring the producers within the word 'author'; and yet in one sense no original matter can be found in such publications. Still there was something apart from originality on the one hand and mere mechanical transcribing on the other which entitled those who gave these works to the world to be regarded as their authors.[5]

Thus, it was held that newspaper reports prepared from speeches were capable of protection as original works.

---

4 [1900] AC 539.
5 ibid., p. 554.

Other similar cases involve copyright protection being granted to the chrono-logical list of football fixtures,[6] a catalogue of books available at a book shop,[7] and directories of traders, businesses and professional services.[8] Peterson J in *University of London Press v University Tutorial Press*[9] stated:

> Copyright Acts are not concerned with the originality of ideas, but with the expression of thought and, in the case of 'literary work', with the expression of thought in print or writing. The originality which is required relates to the expression of the thought. But the Act does not require that the expression must be in an original or novel form, but that the work must not be copied from another work – that it should originate from the author.[10]

In *Computer Edge v Apple Computer*,[11] Gibbs CJ adopted this dicta and stated: 'The expression "original" in that section [s 32] does not mean that the work must be the expression of original or inventive thought.'[12] Gibbs CJ went on to state: 'Originality is a matter of degree, depending on the amount of skill, judgment or labour that has been involved in making the work.'[13]

As regards the adaptation of works which are common property, *Hatton v Keane*[14] involved an adaptation of one of Shakespeare's plays, with alterations in the text, original music, scenic effects, and other accessories. It was held that the production as a whole was a proper subject of copyright protection, although the play itself was, in its original form, common property. In *Robertson v Lewis*,[15] it was held that copyright in a traditional air had been acquired by virtue of writing it down, to the extent that anyone who was proved to have made a copy directly or indirectly from the version so written infringed that copyright.

The key originality issue in the Bulun Bulun matter was whether a contemporary depiction of ancient tribal imagery was entitled to be claimed as 'original' for the purposes of copyright protection. The evidence in the proceeding put the issue beyond doubt, but at the time there was a divergence of opinion on the issue, in particular as expressed in the report of an enquiry into the issue. A working party set up in 1975 by the Commonwealth government to investigate the protection of Aboriginal folklore noted in its 1981 report that there was concern as to the ability of Aboriginal artists to satisfy the threshold requirement of originality in order to claim copyright protection. The view was expressed that the artists draw upon tradition and pre-existing works, and that although the level of independent contribution required to establish originality is not great, it could be argued that the derived nature of many works of Aboriginal artists could deprive those works of copyright protection. This statement of opinion was

---

6 *Football League Ltd v Littlewoods Pools Ltd* [1959] 1 Ch 637.
7 *Hotten v Arthur* (1863) 11 WR 934.
8 *Lamb v Evans* [1892] 3 Ch 462.
9 *University of London Press Ltd v University Tutorial Press Ltd* [1916] 2 Ch 602.
10 ibid., pp. 608–9.
11 *Computer Edge Pty Ltd v Apple Computer Inc* (1986) 6 IPR 1.
12 ibid., p. 6.
13 ibid., pp. 6–7.
14 (1859) 7 CB 268.
15 [1976] RPC 169.

198 LANDMARKS IN AUSTRALIAN IP LAW

a matter of much controversy which was ultimately debunked in cases involving the protection of Aboriginal copyright.

On the originality issue, Margaret West deposed that while the settings in the two works may have been painted on numerous occasions by Bulun Bulun himself and his forebears, it remained

> that the works are clearly products of considerable skill, and reflect facets of the Applicant's distinctive style. I note, for example, the fineness and detail of the cross-hatching, which is one of the most important features in any Aboriginal bark painting. I also note the particular depiction of the figures and composition, which are unique to the Applicant. For example, I am not aware of any other artist who depicts magpie geese, long-necked turtle and water snake at waterholes in the fashion of the Applicant. I would describe the works as very decorative, very busy and very nicely composed. I note that they share a number of important features in common, such as the bark, or cross-hatching, the placement of the figures relative to the waterholes, the depiction of large footprints, the depiction of the waterholes, the striping on the magpie geese figures, the depiction of the geese figures in a red ochre, the depiction of the snake figures and the use of leaves. These are all distinctive features of the Applicant's work. I would rate the Applicant as amongst the best exponents in his artform just as one might rate a particular Western artist as a leading exponent in his particular artform of, say, sculpture or water-colour painting. The Applicant's standing as an artist is recognised by those in the market for Aboriginal artworks, with his works fetching substantial sums at galleries in Sydney and Melbourne.

Peter Cooke was an art adviser in Maningrida for many years. He deposed:

> Bark paintings of the size and complexity which the Applicant usually produces are invariably very time-consuming works to produce. The bark may take up to a month to prepare in the first place. The painting time will then involve approximately a week's full-time work, although the production process will be slowed down by ceremonial commitments and time spent hunting. The very fine cross-hatching in the Applicant's work requires an immense amount of precision. People who produce this kind of work often complain of back ache from sitting over a painting, as well as eyestrain. The quality of the cross-hatching work is often the feature which appeals most readily to art buyers. Few artists are able to produce cross-hatching of the fineness and precision of the Applicant.

Charles Godjuwa worked as an art adviser at Maningrida. In his affidavit he deposed:

> There are about 20 artists actively selling works in the region, and each one produces their own individually styled work. These works are not copies of other works, but are all distinctive in their own ways, which is why I am able to command reasonable prices for the artworks.

Godjuwa said that individual items sold at the Maningrida Art and Craft Centre ranged in price from tens of dollars to $10 000. He deposed that he had

> known the Applicant for nearly 11 years. He is a very important artist, and he commands tremendous respect from his peers. He plays a significant role in the management of the ceremonies of his tribe.

Godjuwa said that Bulun Bulun's painting style was

distinctive in particular ways. He adopts a particularly distinctive approach to the depiction of magpie geese. I know of no other artist who paints these birds as the Applicant does. As it happens, magpie geese are a prized food in the Applicant's area, and the emphasis on the bird by the Applicant is of significance to the area. Included amongst other prominent figures in his work are depictions of the long-necked turtle, flying fox and water snake. I know of no other artist who paints these figures in the manner of the Applicant. I note the particular prominence these figures assume in his work, and, of course, the Applicant's distinctive cross-hatching style.

Because of the Applicant's detailed personal knowledge of the country of his tribe, through his hunting and ceremonial experience, he has an intimate understanding of the manner of these creatures, all of which are common to the Applicant's tribal land, as well as of the significance of them as totems in his tribe's dreaming practices. This understanding guides the Applicant in his attention to detail, for which his works are much sought after. He is amongst a small group of artists in the Maningrida area entitled by tribal custom to depict designs in very precise detail, with this entitlement following from the skill he has demonstrated in understanding the dreaming customs of his tribe and by virtue of his particular gifts as an artist.

These views were confirmed by affidavits in the proceeding from a Sydney gallery operator, Kerry Steinberg, and the curator of Aboriginal Art at the Australian National Gallery, Wally Caruana. Kerry Steinberg deposed that she rated Bulun Bulun as one of the top bark painters in the Maningrida area: 'His work sells for between $600 and $5000. There are few living Aboriginal bark painters who can command fees of over $5000 for their work.' She said that Bulun Bulun had a very special painting style:

In particular, I note the detail of his work and the strong story content. His work is also not readily available. In a review of the 1987 exhibition at the Hogarth Gallery in Sydney, the critic of the 'Sydney Morning Herald', Bronwyn Watson, wrote in that newspaper on 18 September 1987 that the Applicant was 'one of the most eminent exponents of bark painting'. Ms Watson said the exhibition showed the development of his work from his early style (depicting animal and plant forms) to a more complex style of his dreamtime paintings.

Steinberg said:

The Applicant is particularly well known for his depiction of 'waterhole' settings. These settings are of special importance to him because they are key parts of the dreaming of his yiritdja moiety. His depiction of the 'waterhole' setting is quite distinctive, particularly as regards the detail and style of the internal cross-hatching.

Caruana deposed that the Australian National Gallery collection of Aboriginal works contained eight works by Bulun Bulun, including three bark paintings, three colour screen prints and two lithographs: 'I regard the Applicant as one of the most important artists in Australia. He is a particularly able bark painter, with an established exhibition record and artistic reputation.' In addition to the Northern Territory and Australian National Galleries, Bulun Bulun's work was also exhibited at the Department of Defence building in Canberra, where a large

200   LANDMARKS IN AUSTRALIAN IP LAW

mural was on display illustrating all of his tribe's main totems. His work had also
been displayed at the Sydney Opera House and was included in the National
Ethnographic Collection. In July 1986 Bulun Bulun's work was exhibited at
Osaka as part of an exhibition of Australian Aboriginal art, and he travelled to
Japan as a guest of the museum in question. His work had also been exhibited
in New York, again as part of an exhibition of Australian Aboriginal art. He had
two exhibitions at the Hogarth Gallery in Sydney in 1981 and 1987. While Bulun
Bulun painted in a genre which dated back over a long period, it was nevertheless
clear that he was an artist of highly respected skill. In the absence of any evidence
of copying, this evidence concerning his skill was an issue of particular note in
the satisfaction of the test for originality.

Direct infringement and copying

The rights of a copyright owner are set out in s 32 of the *Copyright Act*. Under
s 14(1)(a), a reference to an act comprised in the copyright in a work is to be
read as a reference to the doing of an act in relation to a substantial part of
the work. 'Substantiality' has been interpreted as referring to the quality rather
than quantity of a reproduction.[16] In *Hawkes & Son (London) v Paramount Film
Service*,[17] it was held that the musical work 'Colonel Bogey' was infringed by the
use of 28 bars, or half a minute, out of total playing time of the song of about four
minutes. The court regarded this part as 'substantial' as it contained the principal
air of the 'Colonel Bogey' march.

In *Bauman v Fussell*,[18] the court was concerned with the alleged infringement
of a photograph by a later painting. The test for substantiality was stated as follows: 'Has this picture reproduced the original in its essential features, looking at
it as a whole?' In this case the photographer was required to rely on the 'positioning' of the features in the photograph as being the essence of the work capable
of copyright protection. The court did not regard this positioning as having sufficient originality for the purposes of subsistence of copyright, although Somervell
LJ indicated that it was possible to envisage a case where a photographer had
'made an original arrangement of the objects animate and inanimate which he
photographs in order to create a harmonious design'. In the view of Somervell
LJ, such arrangement would constitute a substantial part of the work capable of
protection in its own right.

In *Brooks v Religious Tract Society*,[19] the plaintiff was the owner of copyright
in a painting which represented a collie dog seated on his haunches on a stone
floor looking down at the upturned face of a child. There was a cat in the background. The defendant reproduced the painting, but replaced the child with a

---

16 *Hawkes & Son (London) Ltd v Paramount Film Service Ltd* [1934] 1 Ch 593; *LB (Plastics) Ltd v Swish
Products Ltd* [1979] FSR 145.
17 [1934] 1 Ch 593.
18 [1978] RPC 485.
19 (1897) 45 WR 476.

tortoise and two cats. An injunction was granted in the case prohibiting what was regarded as a substantial reproduction. In *Lerose v Hawick Jersey International*,[20] the plaintiff owned the copyright in a painted called *Nature's Mirror*, which portrayed the draped figure of a 'psyche' with wings, kneeling on a rock and looking into a pool of water. There was a background to the picture. The picture was reproduced without the wings and the background was significantly reduced. The reproduction was held to be an infringement.

In *Hanfstaengl v Empire Palace*,[21] relief was refused by the Court of Appeal where the defendant's sketches gave only a 'rough idea' of the plaintiff's work. The degree of resemblance was taken to be the test, with the value and essential qualities of the original work having to be reproduced. The approach was confirmed by the House of Lords,[22] although it should be noted that court was interpreting the *Fine Arts Copyright Act 1862*, which arguably extended to the protection of ideas, and not just form of expression.

In the *Hanfstaengl* case, it was noted that intention is irrelevant in relation to establishing infringement. A defendant will be guilty of infringement, even though he acted quite innocently and without knowledge of the plaintiff's rights. In the Bulun Bulun case, the question of substantiality was relevant to the particular T-shirt which used an image which copied aspects of two artworks of Bulun Bulun. Margaret West identified the following elements of copying from the two artworks in question of Bulun Bulun with respect to the revised T-shirt design:

(a) The waterholes have been copied in the manner of the multi-coloured cross-hatching in black, white and red, and using the same cross-hatching style.
(b) The colouring of the cross-hatching of the Applicant's magpie geese.
(c) The striping on the necks of the magpie geese.
(d) The striping on the snakes.
(e) The use of black for some of the magpie geese and the colouring of the cross-hatching inside these black magpie geese.
(f) The bird footprints.
(g) The placement of the magpie geese in relation to the waterholes.
(h) The depiction of geese eggs.
(i) The use of white dots and the presentation of leaves and the colouring of the leaves.
(j) The use of yellow and red colouring for the magpie geese.
(k) The depiction of the legs of the magpie geese.
(l) The placement of the long snake figure on the left of the design, and the particular manner of the placing of the heads of the various animal figures in or close to the waterhole.
(m) The style of snakes, but for the alteration of the tail of the smaller snakes.
(n) The border cross-hatching, including the black, white and red colours of the cross-hatching and the angle of the lines of the cross-hatching adopted by the Applicant, but reversed in the other direction.

---

20 *Lerose Ltd v Hawick Jersey International Ltd* [1973] FSR 15.
21 [1894] 3 Ch 109.
22 [1895] AC 20.

West said that the only aspects of the T-shirt design which she could not recognise as copied were the lizard and crayfish figures and the diamond shapes inside the turtle:

> The diamond cross-hatching inside the turtle is definitely not a feature of the Applicant's work. Used as it is amongst an array of features that would be known, by those who follow Aboriginal bark painting, as features common to the work of the Applicant, there may be some confusion as to whether the Applicant himself has attempted to imitate another form of cross-hatching which is not characteristic of his work, but which belongs to another artist. I note that both of the relevant works of the Applicant are shown at page of the book *Arts of the Dreaming – Australia's Living Heritage* by Jennifer Isaacs and page 22 of the book *Australian Aboriginal Art* by Wally Caruana. If one turns to page 203 of the firstmentioned book and page 27 of the secondmentioned book, there are examples of diamond cross-hatching, with the secondmentioned reproduction showing diamond cross-hatching inside a turtle figure. I would suggest that the maker of the design on the artwork may well have turned a couple of pages of the books to pick up a design feature which was not an obvious design feature of the Applicant. Similarly, the crayfish figure is used in the design at page 27 of the secondmentioned work.

West deposed that

> the T-shirt design could not have been made without detailed reference to the form of artistic expression of the artistic works of the Applicant to which I have been referring. In my opinion, there is virtually nothing original about the T-shirt designs. I also note the indebtedness of the T-shirts' designers to the Applicant through their adoption of the 'At The Waterhole' title. The Applicant enjoys a particular reputation for his 'waterhole'-based work.

Trade practices issues

There were two aspects to the substantive claims based on breaches of the *Trade Practices Act 1974* – the first turning on Bulun Bulun's reputation in the paintings themselves and the second as to matters of association or sponsorship arising from the markings on the T-shirts.

As to the first matter, a reputation may exist in an artist's name or his work where the artist has a public reputation and where the work itself is the subject of some reputation (associated with the artist), and the artist is thus presumed to have approved or endorsed the reproduction of his artwork on T-shirts. This approach was endorsed in two decisions, at the time, involving the protection of the character 'Crocodile Dundee' and aspects of the films based on the character, in *Hogan v Koala Dundee*[23] and *Hogan v Pacific Dunlop*[24] (as discussed in another chapter in this collection).

---

23 *Hogan and Another v Koala Dundee Pty Ltd* (1988) 12 IPR 508.
24 *Hogan and Others v Pacific Dunlop Ltd* (1988) 12 IPR 225 and (on appeal) *Pacific Dunlop Ltd v Hogan and Others* (1989) 14 IPR 398.

In the Bulun Bulun matter, a number of deponents had sworn that they could identify Bulun Bulun's work, and furthermore believed that Bulun Bulun and other artists may be profiting from the sale of the shirts such as to indicate a common endeavour. The use of 'The Aboriginals' name and the text on the tag was also suggestive of commendation. There was additional evidence of false and misleading conduct from purchasers of the T-shirts. Lynn Hall, a Melbourne medical practitioner, deposed that in June 1988 she attended the World Expo in Brisbane with her family:

> I visited a souvenir shop at the Expo and purchased a T-shirt marked with the name 'The Aboriginals' on the label of the T-shirt and on a tag attached to the T-shirt and bearing the words 'At The Waterhole' on the T-shirt.

She deposed:

> I bought the T-shirt because I liked the design, but furthermore I believed that I was supporting the artist who created the design on the T-shirt. I considered, at the time I purchased the T-shirt, that it was a good idea that Aborigines were promoting their artworks at the Expo through the sale of such T-shirts. I was influenced in holding these beliefs by the use of The Aboriginals name in association with the T-shirt, and the text on the tag, which made the T-shirt seem authentic, and at the very least approved by the artist, if not manufactured by the artist or people associated with the artist. While I discarded the tag shortly after the purchase of the T-shirt, I recall it contained some text about the origins of the design shown on the T-shirt.

Issues arising – collective protection

While the outcome of the proceedings (by a comprehensive settlement) and the analysis of the matters before the court effectively confirmed that copyright protection was available to protect Aboriginal artists in the situation of Bulun Bulun, with any general rejection of the availability of copyright protection for Aboriginal designs accordingly being dismissed, the case also indicated some concerns about copyright protection. Most importantly, the notion of individual ownership was not consistent with tribal customs which emphasise communal ownership, even though the tests for ownership under the *Copyright Act* are still satisfied. The notion of communal ownership of copyright is not consistent with the *Copyright Act*, nor the Berne Convention under which the *Copyright Act* was adopted.

At the time, the concept of tribal ownership of confidential ideas was recognised in *Foster v Mountford*,[25] in which the Federal Court accepted that representatives of the tribal leadership of a particular tribe could bring an action in breach of confidence to restrain the use by an archaeologist of the tribe's secrets, imparted to him in confidence. The issue came to be considered in a copyright setting in the case of *Bulun Bulun v R & T Textiles*.[26] This proceeding involved

---

25 (1977) 14 ALR 71.
26 *Bulun Bulun and Another v R & T Textiles Pty Ltd* (1998) 41 IPR 513.

204   LANDMARKS IN AUSTRALIAN IP LAW

claims by Bulun Bulun and his clan group, in respect of copyright infringement – a subsequent infringement, but again involving the artwork *At the Waterhole*. There was no defence to the claims of copyright infringement brought in that proceeding by Bulun Bulun.

Nevertheless, the action proceeded on behalf of the clan owners of rights in the artwork in question (through their representative) on the basis of the proposition that they were equitable owners of copyright in the artwork, or otherwise entitled to seek the protection of the court as beneficial owners of the artwork (created by Bulun Bulun as a fiduciary). They asserted such right on the basis that they, in effect, controlled the copyright in the artwork, and that they were the beneficiaries of the creation of the artwork by the artist acting as trustee on their behalf. Accordingly, they claimed to be entitled to a form of collective right with respect to the copyright in the work over and above any issue as to authorship.[27]

The case provided an opportunity for the court to give consideration to the nature of relationships between clan groups and artists with respect to the creation of traditional artworks. In so doing, the court had an opportunity to give attention to the shortcoming of copyright protection addressing only private rights of ownership in artworks in a manner inconsistent with notions of communal ownership, which corresponded with perceptions of ownership held by artists and their communities. In other words, it was sought to bridge an obvious gap in the treatment of the problem of infringement as between Western and communal law.

The evidence expanded on the tribal issues involved in Bulun Bulun undertaking the making of the artwork. Bulun Bulun described the artwork as depicting a place which he described as his 'soul', being the location where the creator ancestor of the Ganalbingu, Barnda (or long-necked turtle) emerged from inside the earth.[28] According to Ganalbingu custom, it was Barnda that shaped the natural features of Ganalbingu land, including the waterhole depicted in the artwork, known as Djulibinyamurr.[29] Barnda also is believed to have created the Ganalbingu people and given them their ceremonies and customs. The importance of the site was such that desecration of the site was believed to result in punishment to the Ganalbingu – such desecration may include inappropriate depiction of images of the site.[30] Bulun Bulun gave evidence to the effect that he was responsible for the proper conduct of ceremony concerning Djulibinyamurr.[31] He deposed:

> I am permitted by my law to create this artwork, but it is also my duty and responsibility to create such works, as part of my traditional Aboriginal land ownership obligation. A painting such as this is not separate from my rights in my land.[32]

27 ibid., p. 513.
28 ibid., p. 518
29 ibid.
30 ibid.
31 ibid.
32 ibid., pp. 518–19.

He said that the artwork had encoded messages of a secret and sacred nature which only an initiate can understand. He said that 'unauthorized reproduction of "At the Waterhole" threatens the whole system and ways that underpin the stability and continuance' of his society.

> It interferes with the relationship between people, their creator ancestors and the land given to the people by their creator ancestor. It interferes with our custom and ritual, and threatens our rights as traditional Aboriginal owners of the land and impedes in the carrying out of the obligations that go with this ownership and which require us to tell and remember the story of Barnda, as it has been passed down and respected over countless generations.[33]

While von Doussa J held that there was no need for any order as such in favour of the clan owners of the claimed rights, he considered that the clan group was nevertheless entitled to maintain claims to protect the copyright in the artwork. In doing so, the court gave detailed attention to the customary law pertaining to the relationship between the artist and clan group of the kind noted above. Some of the evidence was taken from clan leaders in Ramingining in Arnhem Land, rather than in court in Darwin, and the court also carried out an inspection of the Djulibinyamurr site at the request of the tribal owners of the site.

Of particular interest is that the respondent in the proceeding did not take any role in the case brought by the clan group, but rather the claims made by the clan group were challenged by the federal Minister for Aboriginal and Torres Strait Island Affairs and the Attorney-General for the Northern Territory, both of whom sought to intervene in the proceeding.[34] Much of this intervention was concerned with the separate issue of claims of native title and rights attaching to native title in land, but in the case of the Federal Minister extended to the issue of the remedies available to the clan group.

Von Doussa J accepted the view expressed on behalf of the applicant that there was no basis under common law to establish communal title in the copyright in the artwork, and that the issue of ownership was governed at law by the *Copyright Act*.[35] The judge noted that the High Court had clearly established that rights and interest of Aboriginal people were governed by the laws of the Commonwealth, the states and the common law,[36] and that no separate or additional law was available by reference to the customary law and practices of the Ganalbingu clan.

Nevertheless, applying the principle of fiduciary duties, von Doussa J considered that a fiduciary relationship existed between the artist and the clan group and that the artist had a fiduciary duty towards his community accordingly.[37] The fiduciary relationship was said to arise from the nature of the ownership of artistic works among the Ganalbingu people.[38] The judge noted that the categories of fiduciary relationships are not closed, and that a fiduciary relationship

---

33 ibid., p. 519.
34 ibid., p. 522.
35 ibid., p. 525. Note, in this regard, s 8.
36 ibid. (per *Coe v Commonwealth* (1993) 118 ALR 193, 200).
37 ibid., p. 530.
38 ibid., p. 529.

206   LANDMARKS IN AUSTRALIAN IP LAW

will be imputed to arise if a relationship of mutual trust and confidence can be said to exist. Referring to the fiduciary obligation of the Crown to Indigenous people, Brennan CJ in *Wik Peoples v Queensland*[39] stated:

> It is necessary to identify some action or function the doing or performance of which attracts the supposed fiduciary duty to be observed: *Breen v Williams* (1996) 186 CLR 71 at 82. The doing of the action or the performance of the function must be capable of affecting the interests of the beneficiary and the fiduciary must have so acted that it is reasonable for the beneficiary to believe and expect that the fiduciary will act in the interests of the beneficiary (or, in the case of a partnership or joint venture, in the common interest of the beneficiary and fiduciary) to the exclusion of the interest of any other person or the separate interest of the beneficiary.[40]

Von Doussa J considered that the relationship between Bulun Bulun, as artist and owner of copyright, and his clan group was 'unique', in particular in that he used 'with permission' the tribal knowledge of the clan, which was permitted 'in accordance with the law and customs of the Ganalbingu people'.[41] Such permission was 'predicated on the trust and confidence which those granting permission have in the artist'.[42] Part of the relationship of trust was considered by the judge to involve a responsibility on the part of the artist to take appropriate steps to prevent misuse of the artwork: –'The artist is required to act in relation to the artwork in the interests of the Ganalbingu people to preserve the integrity of their culture, and ritual knowledge'.[43] The judge stated that it was not inconsistent with this obligation for the artist to pursue his own interests, such as by selling the artwork, 'but the artist is not permitted to shed the overriding obligation to act to preserve the integrity of the Ganalbingu culture where action for that purpose is required'.[44]

The judge concluded that Bulun Bulun was in a fiduciary relationship with his clan group, stating that this did not mean that Ganalbingu law and custom formed part of the law of Australia, but rather that such law and custom was 'part of the factual matrix' which indicated the fiduciary relationship. Thus, the judge held:

> I have no hesitation in holding that the interests of the Ganalbingu people in the protection of that ritual knowledge from exploitation which is contrary to their law and custom is deserving of the protection of the Australian legal system.[45]

The judge found that

> equity imposes on him [Bulun Bulun] obligations as a fiduciary not to exploit the artistic work in a way that is contrary to the laws and customs of the Ganalbingu people, and,

---

39 (1996) 187 CLR 1.
40 ibid., p. 95.
41 (1998) 41 IPR 513, 529.
42 ibid.
43 ibid.
44 ibid., p. 530.
45 ibid., pp. 530–1.

in the event of infringement by a third party, to take reasonable and appropriate action to restrain and remedy infringement of the copyright in the artistic work.[46]

The judge did not find that the fiduciary relationship extended to vest in the clan an equitable interest in the ownership of the copyright in the artistic work, but rather a 'right in personam to bring action against the fiduciary to enforce the obligation'.[47] In the circumstances, the judge found that there was nothing further to be done as the relevant copyright rights had been enforced. He found though that, had the position been otherwise, equitable remedies would have been available to the clan group, including the imposition of a constructive trust on the legal owner of the copyright in favour of the beneficiaries where it was necessary to do so 'to achieve a just remedy and to prevent the fiduciary from retaining an unconscionable benefit'.[48]

If Bulun Bulun had failed to enforce his rights, the judge considered that equity might allow the beneficiaries to bring an action in their own names against the infringer and the copyright owner, enabling the enforcement of copyright rights through mandatory orders against the copyright owner. If Bulun Bulun denied the existence of the fiduciary relationship and refused to enforce his copyright rights, the court might impose a remedial constructive trust on him 'to strengthen the standing of the beneficiaries to bring proceeding to enforce the copyright'.[49] This would also be appropriate where the copyright owner could not be identified or found and the beneficiaries were unable to join the legal owner. A practical application of these principles would involve a clan group being entitled to take steps to protect an artwork of a deceased artist where the trustee of the artist's estate failed or refused to take action appropriately required by the clan. This might apply where the Public Trustee, assuming that an artist has died intestate, refuses or fails to bring an action to protect the copyright in the artist's work.

Conclusion

Von Doussa J's judgment is an important one in linking obligations under Aboriginal law into the Australian legal concept of fiduciary obligations, and giving recognition to the 'standing' of the clan in certain circumstances – as required by equity. It also illustrates the flexibility of courts in adapting copyright and associated legal principles to the requirements of the protection of age-old cultural practices, reinforcing that the instinct to advocate more or new law is not necessarily appropriate in this context.

The judgment also recognises the relationship between artists and clan groups, recording the court's understanding of the importance of the cultural and spiritual role of artists such as Bulun Bulun, and reinforcing the special place of such

---

46 ibid., p. 531.
47 ibid.
48 ibid.
49 ibid.

art in the broader context – being work created in an environment of a close spiritual relationship with the community whose stories and culture it was depicting. The identification of this relationship assists in understanding the special role of the Aboriginal arts in the visual arts culture of Australia, and shows the flexibility of copyright and equity in protecting Aboriginal artworks from unauthorised reproduction.

13

The grapes of wrath: the Coonawarra dispute, geographical indications and international trade

Matthew Rimmer*

It is clear that inherited landscape myths and memories share two common characteristics: their surprising endurance through the centuries and their power to shape institutions that we still live with.
Simon Schama, *Landscape and Memory*[1]

Introduction

The famous wine region of Coonawarra in South Australia has been promoted as 'Australia's other Red Centre', emphasising its terra rossa soil and its cabernet sauvignon.[2] In his atlas of the wine regions of Australia, John Beeston comments upon the rich and contested history of the region: 'Coonawarra is certainly the most famous cabernet sauvignon region in Australia, and some would argue, the most renowned wine region in Australia per se'.[3] A reporter, Penelope Debelle, captures a sense of the legal conflict over the parameters of the boundaries of Coonawarra: 'Behind the name Coonawarra, an inglorious contest is being waged that pits the romance of South Australia's terra rossa cool-climate wine region against the cold commercial reality of the label.'[4]

---

* The author would like to acknowledge the work in this field of Kathy Bowrey, Michael Handler, William van Caenegem and Antony Taubman, and the advice of the editors, Andrew Kenyon, Megan Richardson and Sam Ricketson. He would also like to acknowledge the contribution of the cartographer, Jennifer Sheehan, of the Research School of Pacific and Asian Studies at the Australian National University, who produced the maps in Figures 13.1 and 13.2.
1 S Schama, *Landscape and Memory*, HarperCollins, London, 1995, p. 15.
2 'Coonawarra: Australia's Other Red Centre', available at http://www.coonawarra.org/wines.asp.
3 J Beeston, *The Wine Regions of Australia*, 2nd edn, Allen & Unwin, Sydney, 2002, p. 263.
4 P Debelle, 'Vignerons See Red Over Coonawarra Boundary', *Age*, 24 February 2001, p. 11.

209

210 LANDMARKS IN AUSTRALIAN IP LAW

The dispute over the boundaries of the Coonawarra has its origins in the European Community—Australia Wine Agreement 1994.[5] As a result of this bilateral trade agreement with the EU, Australia amended the *Australian Wine and Brandy Corporation Act 1980* (Cth) and introduced comprehensive protection of geographical indications in respect of wines and spirits in 1994. In 1995 the Joint Committee of the Coonawarra Grape Growers Association Inc and the Coonawarra Vignerons Association Inc lodged an application to the Geographical Indications Committee for it to determine a region called 'Coonawarra'. In 2000 the committee made a final determination as to the boundaries of the Coonawarra region. Dissatisfied with the narrow scope of the determination, 46 applicants sought a review of the decision by the Administrative Appeals Tribunal (AAT). In *Coonawarra Penola Wine Industry Association and Geographical Indications Committee*,[6] the AAT emphasised the importance of the historical construction of the boundaries of Coonawarra, stressing the industry and market acceptance and recognition of the Coonawarra region. Five parties appealed against the decision of the AAT to the Full Court of the Federal Court. In *Beringer Blass Wine Estates v Geographical Indications Committee*,[7] the court was sympathetic to the efforts of the tribunal, noting that the task was not an easy one. Ruling that the AAT had made a number of errors of law, the court further enlarged the boundaries of the Coonawarra region to include the five properties.

The *Coonawarra* case has been productive in inspiring a range of academic discourse about the development and evolution of geographical indications in Australia. Legal historians, such as Brad Sherman, have considered the roots of appellations of origin in the regulation of agriculture.[8] Comparative scholars, such as William van Caenegem, have examined how geographical indications have been developed in the EU and translated to other jurisdictions.[9] Furthermore, intellectual property and international trade scholars have been interested in the interplay between bilateral, regional and international trade agreements, dealing with appellations of origin and geographical indications.[10] There has

---

5 Agreement between Australia and the European Community on Trade in Wine, and Protocol, 26–31 January 1994, [1994] ATS 6 (entered into force 1 March 1994) (hereinafter European Community—Australia Wine Agreement 1994).
6 *Coonawarra Penola Wine Industry Association Inc & Others and Geographical Indications Committee* [2001] AATA 844 (5 October 2001).
7 *Beringer Blass Wine Estates Ltd v Geographical Indications Committee* [2002] FCAFC 295 (20 September 2002).
8 L Bently and B Sherman, *Intellectual Property Law*, 2nd edn, Oxford University Press, Oxford, 2004, pp. 962–89; L Bently and B Sherman, 'The Impact of European Geographical Indications on National Rights in Member States' (2006) 96 *Trademark Reporter* 850.
9 W van Caenegem, 'Registered Geographical Indications: Between Intellectual Property and Rural Policy, Part I' (2003) 6 *Journal of World Intellectual Property* 699; W van Caenegem, 'Registered Geographical Indications: Between Intellectual Property and Rural Policy, Part II' (2003) 6 *Journal of World Intellectual Property* 861; and W van Caenegem, 'Registered GI's: Intellectual Property, Agricultural Policy and International Trade' (2004) 26 *European Intellectual Property Review* 170.
10 PJ Heald, 'Trademarks and Geographical Indications: Exploring the Contours of the TRIPS Agreement' (1996) 29 *Vanderbilt Journal of Transnational Law* 635–60; M Handler, 'The EU's Geographical Indications Agenda and its Potential Impact on Australia' (2004) 15 *Australian Intellectual Property Journal* 173; M Handler, 'The WTO Geographical Indications Dispute' (2006) 59 *Modern Law Review* 70; B Tamberlin and L Bastin, 'Australia and the World Trade Organization: Decision Enforcement' (2007) 81 *Australian Law Journal* 802; and R Chesmond, 'Protection or Privatisation of Culture? The Cultural Dimension of the International

been some legal and academic discussion about the interplay between trade marks and geographical indications.[11] Critical legal scholarship has also taken a keen interest in the development of geographical indications. Law and science theoreticians – notably, Gary Edmond – have considered the use of expert evidence in cases such as the *Coonawarra* litigation.[12] Cultural studies experts – notably Kathy Bowrey – have explored the representation of geographical indications in the popular media.[13] Critical legal scholars, such as Malcolm Voyce,[14] have contemplated whether geographical indications reflect a larger enterprise of empire.

The *Coonawarra* case emphasises the dynamic interplay between property rights and intellectual property rights. The law and geography movement is interested in the tropes of land and property, boundaries and maps, culture and nature, identity and knowledge.[15] Geographers have sought to analyse such concerns in legal disputes over geographical indications such as Coonawarra.[16] The *Coonawarra* case also involves larger considerations of law and cartography. As Alexander Reilly has observed of the phenomenon of map-making in the context of native title disputes:

> The legal process of transforming relationships to land into a cartographic form brings into focus the distinction between space and place, and what it is about these concepts that ought to be reflected in property rights.[17]

Intellectual Property Debate on Geographical Indications of Origin' (2007) 29 *European Intellectual Property Review* 379.

11 D Ryan, 'Geographical Indications and Trade Marks' (1998) 9 *Australian Intellectual Property Journal* 127; B Amani, 'A Penchant for Persian Rugs over Palatable Products: The Use of Geographical Appellations as Trade Marks. Part 1' (2000) 14 *Intellectual Property Journal* 185; B Amani, 'A Penchant for Persian Rugs over Palatable Products: The Use of Geographical Appellations as Trade Marks. Part 2' (2000) 14 *Intellectual Property Journal* 313; W Taylor, 'Trade Marks and the Overlap with Geographical Indications' (2000) 5 *Flinders Journal of Law Reform* 53; S Stern, 'The Overlap between Geographical Indications and Trade Marks in Australia' (2001) 2 *Melbourne Journal of International Law* 224; and S Stern, 'The Conflict between Geographical Indications and Trade Marks or Australia Once Again Heads Off Down the Garden Path' (2005) 61 *Intellectual Property Forum* 28.

12 G Edmond, 'Disorder with Law – Determining the Geographical Indication for the Coonawarra Wine Region' (2006) 27 *Adelaide Law Review* 59.

13 K Bowrey, 'Geographical Indications: The Controversy over the Coonawarra Boundary Decision', Australian Centre for Intellectual Property in Agriculture Seminar Series, Australian National University College of Law, December 2001.

14 M Voyce, 'Geographical Indications, the EU and Australia: A Case Study on "Government at a Distance" through Intellectual Property Rights' (2007) 7 *Macquarie Law Journal* 155.

15 See N Bromley, *Law, Space, and the Geographies of Power*, The Guilford Press, New York and London, 1994; N Bromley, D Delaney and R Ford (eds.), *The Legal Geographies Reader*, Blackwell Publishers, Oxford, 2001; J Holder and C Harrison, *Law and Geography: Current Legal Issues*, Oxford University Press, Oxford, 2003; and W Taylor (ed.), *The Geography of Law: Landscape, Identity and Regulation*, Hart Publishing, Oxford and Portland (Oregon): 2006.

16 W Moran, 'Rural Space as Intellectual Property' (1993) 12 *Political Geography* 263; D Harvey, *Spaces of Capital: Towards a Critical Geography*, Edinburgh University, Edinburgh, 2001, pp. 394–411; M Foale and D Smith, 'The Coonawarra: A Viticultural Frontier?: Or Just a Case of Sour Grapes?' (2004) 55 *Globe* 43; and G Banks and S Sharpe, 'Wine, Regions and the Geographic Imperative: The Coonawarra Example' (2006) 62 *New Zealand Geographer* 173.

17 A Reilly, 'Cartography, Property and the Aesthetics of Place: Mapping Native Title in Australia' in A Kenyon and P Rush (eds.), *An Aesthetic of Law and Culture: Texts, Images and Screens*, Elsevier, Amsterdam, 2004, pp. 221–40, 223. See also M Sparke, 'A Map that Roared and an Original Atlas: Canada, Cartography, and the Narration of Nation' (1998) 88 *Annals of the Association of American Geographers* 463.

212   LANDMARKS IN AUSTRALIAN IP LAW

Parallels have also been drawn between geographical indications and traditional knowledge. Jeffrey Grosset, a wine-maker from the Clare Valley, has suggested that instead of the French word *terroir*, Australians should use the indigenous word, 'pangkarra', to encapsulate all of the human and environmental influences on a vineyard.[18] Conversely, the indigenous lawyer Terri Janke has wondered whether geographical indications offer a useful schema by which to protect the combination of property and intellectual property interests in traditional knowledge.[19]

This chapter tells the story behind the *Coonawarra* litigation, addressing the parties to the dispute, the legal and historical context of the case, its immediate impact, and its lingering significance. It considers the *Coonawarra* case as quite literally a landmark in Australian jurisprudence in respect of intellectual property. This chapter engages in the methodology of 'legal storytelling'.[20] In the field of new historicism, the use of anecdotes – *petite histoire* – has been seen as a useful way of challenging grand historical narratives. Joel Fineman has observed that the anecdote is 'the literary form or genre that uniquely refers to the real'.[21] This chapter has three parts. The first part outlines the European Community–Australia Wine Agreement 1994 and the operation of the *Australian Wine and Brandy Corporation Act 1980* (Cth). The second part considers the various stages of the dispute over the Coonawarra region – moving from the decision of the Geographical Indications Committee to the ruling of the AAT and the conclusive decision of the Full Federal Court. The third part examines the implications of the *Coonawarra* case for other wine regions of Australia, most notably the King Valley in Victoria, but also the Hunter Valley in New South Wales and the Margaret River in Western Australia. The conclusion considers the ramifications of the European Community–Australia Wine Agreement 2007, which has been initialled by both sides.

Landscape and memory: the European Community–Australia Wine Agreement 1994

In the EU the cultivation, production and labelling of wine are governed by the wine laws of individual members. Such regulations are informed by the concept of *terroir*, which claims that the quality of agricultural products is determined by

---

18 J Grosset, 'Australia's Quality Focus Gives Closure to Terroir', Inaugural Lecture to Wine Press Club of New South Wales, available at http://content.worldwidewine.com/clients/winepressclub/0311_Inaugural_Lecture_NSW_WPC.pdf.

19 T Janke, *Minding Culture: Case Studies on Intellectual Property and Traditional Cultural Expressions*, World Intellectual Property Organization, Geneva, 2003, p. 36, available at http://www.wipo.int/tk/en/studies/cultural/minding-culture/studies/finalstudy.pdf. See also D Zografos, 'Can Geographical Indications be a Viable Alternative for the Protection of Traditional Cultural Expressions' in F Macmillan and K Bowrey (eds.), *New Directions in Copyright Law: Volume 3*, Edward Elgar, Cheltenham (UK) and Northampton (US), 2006) pp. 37–55. Interestingly, Coonawarra takes its name from the Aboriginal word for honeysuckle.

20 J Ginsburg and R Cooper Dreyfuss, *Intellectual Property Stories*, Foundation Press, New York, 2006.

21 J Fineman, 'The History of the Anecdote' in H Aram Veeser (ed.), *The New Historicism*, Routledge, New York and London, pp. 49–76.

the character of the place from which they come.[22] There remains great debate as to whether such laws are best classified as a species of intellectual property, or a feature of agricultural policy.[23]

In France there are several layers of legal protection afforded to 'appellations of origin' – geographical designations that signify the origin of agricultural products and the qualities and characteristics primarily related to the environment, both natural and human.[24] Each controlled appellation of origin is recognised by a decree which delimits the specific area to which the appellation pertains but also specifies the grape varieties and methods of planting, harvesting and production to be used. The purpose of such laws is to provide consumers with a guarantee that only approved practices are employed in the production of the wine and that standardised information regarding the nature and origin of the wine is as shown on the label. The system of 'appellations of origin' is administered by the Institut National des Appellations de Origine – a public body under the aegis of the French Ministry of Agriculture.

The Institut National des Appellations de Origine and French wine producers have taken concerted legal action, coupled with intense lobbying for the protection of geographical indications at a national and international level, to protect their established markets by playing for favourable rules in the court.[25] Australian courts, however, were somewhat wary of providing protection for French appellations of origin, such as Champagne.[26] This unsuccessful litigation in Australia led to a push by the EU for the development of a bilateral trade agreement governing geographical indications.

European Community–Australia Wine Agreement 1994

On 6 December 1992 it was announced that the Australian government and European Commission officials had negotiated the text of a bilateral wine agreement aimed at improving bilateral wine trade.[27] The European Community–Australia Wine Agreement 1994 entered into force in 1994.[28]

---

22 D Gade, 'Tradition, Territory, and Terroir in French Viniculture: Cassis, France, and Appellation Contrôlée (2004) 94 *Annals of the Association of American Geographers* 848.
23 S Stern, 'Are GIs IP?' (2007) 29 *European Intellectual Property Review* 39.
24 For a more extensive discussion of French law with respect to geographical indications, see W Moran, 'Rural Space as Intellectual Property' (1993) 12 *Political Geography* 263; E Barham, 'Translating Terroir: The Global Challenge of French AOC Labelling' (2003) 19 *Journal of Rural Studies* 127; and Gade, op. cit. n. 22, p. 848.
25 In *J Bollinger* v *Costa Brava Wine Co Ltd* [1960] Ch 262: the wine manufacturer, Bollinger, and 11 other producers from the Champagne district in France obtained an injunction restraining the sale of 'Spanish Champagne', on the grounds that the public would be deceived into thinking that it was wine produced in the Champagne district by the true *methode champenoise*.
26 In the case of *Comite Interprofessionel du Vin de Champagne* v *NL Burton Pty Ltd* (1981) 38 ALR 664, the French wine producers failed in their attempt to replicate in Australia their success in the Spanish Champagne case. It was held that since the term 'champagne' had come to connote any wine produced by something approximating the *methode champenoise*, whether in the Champagne district or not, Australian consumers would not be deceived by its use in connection with wines made outside that district.
27 D Ryan, 'The Protection of Geographical Indications in Australia under the EC/Australia Wine Agreement' (1994) 16 *European Intellectual Property Review* 521.
28 European Community–Australia Wine Agreement 1994.

214   LANDMARKS IN AUSTRALIAN IP LAW

In their second reading speeches, the Hon Simon Crean and Senator Bob McMullan commented that there had been a long tradition of Australian winemakers relying upon European geographical names to denote certain styles of wine-making.[29] The ministers observed of the content of the European Community–Australia Wine Agreement 1994:

> The Agreement provides for the mutual recognition of each Party's winemaking practices and standards; it affords mutual protection to each Party's geographical indications, that is, the names of our wine regions such as Coonawarra and Hunter Valley.[30]

The ministers observed that the legislation would help define the boundaries of Australian geographical indications, presciently mentioning Coonawarra:

> Where does Coonawarra end and Riverland start? This question is just as relevant for Australian wine consumers. By defining the boundaries of our geographical indications, this bill will give greater certainty to enforcement of the Label Integrity Program provisions of the Act, which require winemakers to keep records to substantiate label claims of the vintage, variety or geographical indication of wine. The bill will give consumers the guarantee that when wine is labelled 'Coonawarra', the grapes from which the wine was made came from within the defined boundaries of the Coonawarra region.[31]

The Australian government declined to adopt the restrictive 'appellations of origin' system used in the EU. It was of the view that the Australian wine industry had been able to flourish because of its ability to produce wine of good quality and with distinctive characteristics, without the outdated controls or restrictions of the *ancien regime* of the EU. The Australian government instead agreed to provide protection for 'geographical indications'.

Although supporting the agreement, Senator Meg Lees of the Democrats expressed reservations about the legislation authorising the Australian Wine and Brandy Corporation to define the names and boundaries of Australia's winemaking regions:

> Winemakers have expressed to me that they support the definition of boundaries as it protects the high prices that they often paid for their land. However, to again use the Coonawarra as an example, there is already one challenge to the boundary that has been drawn around this region. Clearly the drawing of boundaries is a very difficult task and there will be winners and losers.[32]

Nonetheless, Lees was of the view that Australian wine-makers would adapt to the new system: 'My discussions with winemakers in the Coonawarra region of South Australia suggest the process of phasing out European names is already well under way.'[33] She concluded: 'With proper marketing, it will not take Australian

---

29 Commonwealth of Australia, *Parliamentary Debates*, House of Representative, 29 September 1993, p. 1342 (Simon Crean); and Commonwealth of Australia, *Parliamentary Debates*, Senate, 28 October 1993, p. 2826 (Bob McMullan).
30 ibid.
31 ibid.
32 Commonwealth of Australia, *Parliamentary Debates*, Senate, 7 December 1993, p. 4055 (Meg Lees).
33 ibid.

THE *COONAWARRA* DISPUTE   215

consumers of wine and port long to learn that their favourite beverage is now sold under a new name.'[34]

There are two competing discourses at work in the parliamentary debate over the European Community–Australia Wine Agreement 1994. The dominant government narrative is that the phasing out of European appellations of origin and the development of Australian geographical indications is an opportunity to be welcomed and exploited by local agricultural producers. A dissenting discourse is that the international trade rules are a form of protectionism for European wine producers, which will undermine and sap the efforts of New World wine producers to increase their market share.

Australian Wine and Brandy Corporation Act 1980 (Cth)

The *Australian Wine and Brandy Corporation Act 1980* (Cth) is the primary piece of legislation in Australia regulating geographical indications.[35] The objectives of the legislation include the purposes to 'determine the boundaries of the various regions and localities in Australia in which wine is produced', 'give identifying names to those regions and localities' and 'determine the varieties of grapes that may be used in the manufacture of wine in Australia.'[36] The legislation also seeks to 'enable Australia to fulfil its obligations under prescribed wine-trading agreements', especially noting 'an agreement relating to trade in wine that is in force between the EEC and Australia.'[37]

Section 4 of the Act defines a 'geographical indication' in relation to wine as meaning 'a word or expression used in the description and presentation of the wine to indicate the country, region or locality in which the wine originated'; or

> a word or expression used in the description and presentation of the wine to suggest that a particular quality, reputation or characteristic of the wine is attributable to the wine having originated in the country, region or locality indicated by the word or expression.

The Act provides for penalties in respect of false and misleading description and presentation of wine.[38] Section 40C provides that a person must not, in

---

34 ibid.
35 For a discussion of the regime see S Stern and C Fund, 'The Australian System of Registration and Protection of Geographical Indications for Wines' (2000) 5 *Flinders Journal of Law Reform* 39; and R Smith, 'Australia's GIs (Geographical Indications): Is the Approach Rational? Smart Thinking on Viticulture' (2007) 22 *Australian and New Zealand Wine Industry Journal* 13.
36 *Australian Wine and Brandy Corporation Act 1980* (Cth) s 3(1).
37 ibid.
38 This regime was tested in the Federal Court case of *Comite Interprofessionel du Vin de Champagne v NL Burton Pty Ltd* (1996) 35 IPR 170. In this matter, French wine makers brought proceedings against the Tasmanian proprietors of 'La Provence Vineyards' who marketed wine under a label including prominently the words 'La Provence'. First, Heerey J found that the heading in para. 2.6 of the Schedule, 'Provence and Corsica regions', constituted a registration of 'Provence' as a geographical indication in respect of the region of Provence. Second, he declined to hold that 'La Provence' was a word or expression that so resembles the registered geographical indication 'Cotes de Provence' as to be likely to be mistaken for it. Third, the judge held that the defendants had not committed an offence under the provisions of s 40 C of the *Australian Wine*

216 LANDMARKS IN AUSTRALIAN IP LAW

trade or commerce, intentionally sell or export wine with a false description and presentation. Under s 40D(2), the description and presentation of wine is false if, relevantly, it includes a registered geographical indication and the wine did not originate in a country, region or locality in relation to which the geographical indication is registered. Under s 40E, a person must not, in trade or commerce, intentionally sell or export wine with a misleading description and presentation. Under s 40 F, the description and presentation of wine is misleading if it includes a registered geographical indication and the indication is used in such a way as to be likely to mislead as to the country, region or locality in which the wine originated. The Register of Protected Names maintained under s 40ZC reflects the European Community–Australia Wine Agreement 1994, and in particular provides for the phasing out in three stages of the use of certain European geographical indications.

There has also been a great deal of legal and academic discussion about the interplay between trade marks and geographical indications under this new regime.[39]

Australian Wine and Brandy Corporation Regulations 1981 (Cth)

Section 40N of the *Australian Wine and Brandy Corporation Act* provides for the establishment of the Geographical Indications Committee (GIC). Under s 40P, the function of the GIC is to make determinations of geographical indications for wine in relation to regions and localities in Australia, and it has power to do all things necessary and convenient in connection with this function. Section 40T(1) provides that the committee should identify the boundary of geographical indications and determine the names to be used to indicate those areas.

The *Australian Wine and Brandy Corporation Regulations 1981* provides criteria to be applied by the GIC in the determination of geographical indications.

Regulation 24 provides definitions of the terms 'zone', 'region' and 'subregion'. A 'zone' is defined as an area of land that 'may comprise one or more regions'. A 'region' is defined as a 'single tract of land that is discrete and homogeneous in its grape growing attributes to a degree that . . . is measurable and is less

---

and Brandy Corporation Act 1980 (Cth) in that they had not knowingly sold wine bearing a false description and presentation. However, his Honour pointed out that the defendants could not in future be said to be ignorant of the registration of the word 'Provence' as a geographical indication.

39 In the case of *Southcorp Wines Pty Ltd* [2000] ATMO 34 (14 April 2000), the Australian Trade Mark Office considered an application by Southcorp Wines Pty Ltd for registration of the trade mark 'Queen Adelaide Regency'. The Deputy Registrar, Helen Hardie, ruled that unless the trade mark is applied only to wine originating in the region defined by the registered geographical indication 'Adelaide', its use would contravene s 40C of the *Australian Wine and Brandy Corporation Act 1980* (Cth). Accordingly, she held that its use under those circumstances would be contrary to law and a ground for rejection would arise under s 42(b) of the *Trade Marks Act 1995* (Cth). By contrast, in *Ross & Veronica Lawrence* [2005] ATMO 69 (21 November 2005), the Australian Trade Mark Office accepted an application for registration of the trade mark 'Feet First' for use in respect of wine. The Hearings Officer, Ian Thompson, noted that the word 'First' was a name which existed on the Register of Protected Names under the *Australian Wine and Brandy Corporation Act 1980* as being a sub-region within the Einzellagen wine-growing area within Germany. He found that 'there is sufficient doubt as to the negative application of the legislation in this instance to render unsafe any conclusion that the use of the applied for trade mark *would* be contrary to law.'

substantial than in a subregion'. A 'subregion' is 'part of a region' and comprises 'a single tract of land that is discrete and homogeneous in its grape growing attributes to a degree that is substantial.' Furthermore, 'a region' or a 'subregion' 'usually produces at least 500 tonnes of wine grapes in a year' and 'comprises at least 5 wine grape vineyards of at least 5 hectares each that do not have any common ownership, whether or not it also comprises 1 or more vineyards of less than 5 hectares.'

Regulation 25 provides an extensive list of criteria to be taken into account by the GIC in the determination of geographical indications. The committee should have regard to 'whether the area falls within the definition of a subregion, a region, a zone or any other area.' The committee needs to examine 'the history of the founding and development of the area, ascertained from local government records, newspaper archives, books, maps or other relevant material.' The GIC considers 'the existence in relation to the area of natural features, including rivers, contour lines and other topographical features' and is also asked to examine 'the existence in relation to the area of constructed features, including roads, railways, towns and buildings'. The GIC is required to consider 'the boundary of the area suggested in the application to the Committee under section 40R', 'ordinance survey map grid references in relation to the area' and the 'local government boundary maps in relation to the area.' The GIC must also examine

> the existence in relation to the area of a word or expression to indicate that area, including: any history relating to the word or expression; whether, and to what extent, the word or expression is known to wine retailers beyond the boundaries of the area; whether, and to what extent, the word or expression has been traditionally used in the area or elsewhere; and the appropriateness of the word or expression.

Regulation 25(i) offers a final criterion concerning 'the degree of discreteness and homogeneity of the proposal indication' as determined by nine attributes. The attributes include the geological formation of the area; the degree to which the climate of the area is uniform; the date of harvesting for grapes in the area; whether part or all of the area is within a natural drainage area; the availability of water from an irrigation scheme; the elevation of the area; any plans for the development of the area by governmental authorities; any relevant traditional divisions within the area; and the history of grape and wine production in the area. In determining a geographical indication under s 40Q (1) of the Act, the GIC is not prohibited from having regard to other relevant matters.

Such regulations are designed to capture the elusive, impressionistic concept of *terroir* – the overall environment within which a grape variety grows. The convoluted, open-ended regulations, however, lend themselves to legal disputation and conflict. The application of nine criteria, nine further sub-criteria and any other extrinsic considerations allow for a wide spectrum of opinion. It is little wonder that the open-ended regime for geographical indications has

218   LANDMARKS IN AUSTRALIAN IP LAW

been accused of generating uncertainty and indeterminacy in rural and agriculture communities. As Glenn Banks and Scott Sharpe have observed: 'The *Coonawarra* case illustrates the difficulties that can arise in regional definition when the legislation and regulations can be read as ambiguous or apparently inconsistent.'[40]

The *Coonawarra* decision: *Beringer Blass Wine Estates v Geographical Indications Committee*

The litigation over the boundaries of Coonawarra was an epic affair, involving a large number of disputants, a 'hot tub' of expert witnesses, and a cascading series of appeals. The dispute featured institutional tensions between the GIC, the AAT, and the Full Court of the Federal Court of Australia, which took diverging approaches to the determination of geographical indications. The *Coonawarra* dispute was an instance of what a member of the Australian judiciary has evocatively described as 'mega-litigation'. Sackville J has used the phrase to describe large-scale legal disputes:

> By that expression, I mean civil litigation, usually involving multiple and separately represented parties, that consumes many months of court time and generates vast quantities of documentation in paper or electronic form.[41]

The judge adds: 'An invariable characteristic of mega-litigation is that it imposes a very large burden, not only on the parties, but on the court system and, through that system, the community.'[42] Such remarks are apropos of the *Coonawarra* litigation.

The AAT

On 12 December 1995 the Joint Committee of the Coonawarra Grape Growers Association Inc and the Coonawarra Vignerons Association Inc lodged an application to the GIC for it to determine a region called 'Coonawarra'.

The GIC made an interim determination of the Coonawarra region on 30 April 1997. After receiving further submissions, the committee proposed a variation to the interim determination on 3 February 1999. A final determination was made on 10 May 2000 (see Figure 13.1). The approach of the administrative body was to circumscribe the boundaries of Coonawarra by predominantly referring to scientific and historical criteria. The region of Coonawarra was contained alongside the adjoining areas of Penola and Wrattonbully.

---

40 Banks and Sharpe, op. cit. n. 16, p. 182.
41 *Seven Network Ltd v News Ltd* [2007] FCA 1062, para. 2 (Sackville J).
42 ibid.

THE *COONAWARRA* DISPUTE   219

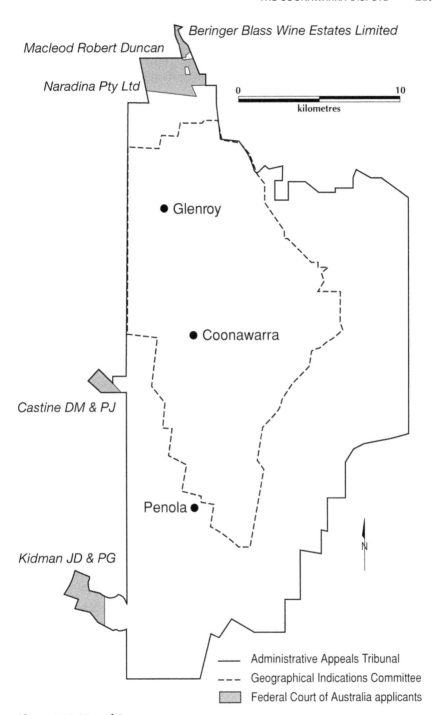

Figure 13.1 Map of Coonawarra

220   LANDMARKS IN AUSTRALIAN IP LAW

In *Coonawarra Penola Wine Industry Association and Geographical Indications Committee*,[43] the AAT considered applications by 46 parties who were dissatisfied with the ruling of the GIC. The tribunal relied upon historical evidence to develop an enlarged boundary for the geographical indication of 'Coonawarra'.

The AAT received a large volume of evidence from the parties and expert witnesses about the areas of 'Coonawarra', 'Penola' and 'Wrattonbully'. O'Connor J noted that the tribunal convened a 'hot tub' of expert witnesses within the fields of geography and geomorphology, soil science, hydrology, viticulture and mapping. The judge noted: 'Although descriptions varied, there was, not surprisingly, much common ground about the basic geology, topography, natural features and climate of Coonawarra and adjacent regions'.[44] However, there was significant scientific disagreement about soil and viticultural prospects of some localities and the implications of this for boundary determination.

In the end O'Connor J observed that such scientific evidence was ultimately inconclusive: 'None of the experts, despite voluminous scientific data from which to base their opinion, concluded that their particular area of expertise could provide the key to defining the Coonawarra region'.[45] She found that the boundaries of Coonawarra could not be determined by the presence of terra rossa soil alone:

> All experts rejected soil as a discriminator for this region unless one reduced the regional boundary to the outskirts of the cigar of terra rossa soil which no party agreed was feasible.[46]

The AAT concluded 'that an extension of the cigar to an area south of the township of Penola could be substantiated, and create homogeneity for those vineyards south of the town of Penola'.[47] O'Connor J also held 'based on the opinion of the expert geographers that a number of boundaries were "feasible" in scientific terms and that this process will depend on the weight given to other, non-scientific criteria'.[48]

As a result of the limitations of such scientific evidence, the AAT focused upon the history of the Coonawarra region:

> In our view history has a critical role in identifying the boundary of this region. As stated previously its importance is recognised in a number of the criteria which must be applied to establish the boundary, but also because, as we have stated above, the scientific criteria are difficult to use as the discriminators of a region to be called Coonawarra.[49]

The tribunal observed that the expert historians' 'historical conclusions are directed towards an expansive historical view of the area to which the name Coonawarra should be applied'.[50] O'Connor J noted, however, that '[n]one of

---

43 [2001] AATA 844 (5 October 2001).
44 ibid., para. 47.
45 ibid., para. 81.
46 ibid.
47 ibid., para. 82.
48 ibid., para. 83.
49 ibid., para. 85.
50 ibid.

THE *COONAWARRA* DISPUTE   221

these historical experts have ... suggested a particular boundary for the Coonawarra region, pointing to the possible effect of the other criteria on the process.'[51] The tribunal considered the historical significance of a 1984 Resolution of the Viticultural Council of South Eastern South Australia that Coonawarra's boundaries should be as 'within the Hundreds of Penola and Comaum'.[52] She noted: 'We consider that the 1984 Resolution was intended to extend the viticultural area accepted as Coonawarra beyond the area of the cigar.'[53] O'Connor J observed: 'It is particularly significant that no party to the proceeding before the Tribunal argues that the Tribunal should revert to the cigar boundary as the boundary of the Coonawarra wine region.'[54]

Summing up, the tribunal conceded that it was a difficult exercise to definitively determine the boundaries of the Coonawarra region:

> All parties acknowledge that the Hundred lines while having a great deal of historical integrity have less geographical or scientific integrity. They were not it seems, chosen to emphasise homogeneity or discreteness or with consideration of the natural features of the area but for reasons of utility ...
>
> The aim of the Australian government and, it appears, the wine industry, was to create regions by consensus between affected parties and the failure of that process in this case is to be regretted but it is, considering all the evidence and opinion, not surprising.
>
> We have concluded that there is no absolutely 'correct' boundary for this region. Which boundary, therefore, is preferable is, as all the parties concede, a matter of weight and judgement.[55]

O'Connor J noted:

> All parties have submitted that the development of this wine region had been a dynamic process and that 'lines in the sand', based under whatever criteria which is a necessary outcome in drawing a contested boundary may throw up disappointing solutions in particular cases, especially for those on the border of the region.[56]

The judge observed:

> The adoption of the two Hundreds as the wine region border was also, in our view, recognition by the local wine industry that the boundaries of the cigar shaped strip of terra rossa soil at the heart of the region was no longer an adequate marker for the boundary of the Coonawarra in 1984.[57]

O'Connor J concluded: 'Whether one characterises it as a 'marketing tool' or even challenges the homogeneity of the cigar itself, it is historically and scientifically the signature of the Coonawarra Wine Region'.[58] She ruled that 'land outside the two Hundreds and not proximate to the topography of the cigar' could

---

51 ibid., para. 90.
52 ibid., para. 92.
53 ibid., para. 116.
54 ibid.
55 ibid., paras. 127 and 129–30.
56 ibid, para. 137.
57 ibid.
58 ibid.

222 LANDMARKS IN AUSTRALIAN IP LAW

not, without countervailing reasons, 'justify inclusion in a Coonawarra Wine Region.'[59]

The Coonawarra Vignerons Association and the Coonawarra Grapegrowers Association issued a press release concerning the decision of the AAT. In it they said: 'There must be certainty about what Coonawarra means geographically in order to meet the requirements imposed by importing countries, and agreed to by Australia'.[60] The organisations hoped that the decision would settle the division and conflict in the region: 'While grapegrowers and winemakers have looked forward to resolution of this issue, it has been a long and difficult process for a tightly-knit community'.[61] Nonetheless, a number of wine-makers remained discontent with the ruling of the tribunal, and appealed to the Federal Court.

The Full Court of the Federal Court

In *Beringer Blass Wine Estates v Geographical Indications Committee*,[62] the Beringer Blass vineyards, known as 'Robertson's Well', and several other wineries appealed against the ruling of the AAT that their locations were excluded from boundaries of the geographical indication of 'Coonawarra'. Von Doussa, O'Loughlin and Mansfield JJ heard the matter.[63] The Full Court of the Federal Court enlarged the margins of the 'Coonawarra' boundary to include the applicants (see Figure 13.1 above).

The vineyards maintained that the AAT had committed four errors of law. First, the Beringer Blass vineyards submitted that the tribunal had required Robertson's Well to satisfy a higher threshold test under the *Australian Wine and Brandy Corporation Act* and the Regulations for the inclusion in the Coonawarra region boundary than it did for those parties whose properties fell within the Hundreds of Comaum and Penola. In particular it was argued that the AAT had erred in construing the Regulations so as to require the 'history' criteria in regulation 25 to amount to an overwhelming countervailing reason for including a property within the Coonawarra region. Second, it was submitted that the finding that there was no record of the use of Robertson's Well label or descriptor as Coonawarra was wrong in fact and constituted an error of law because it was unsupported by probative material. Third, it was submitted that the finding that Robertson's Well had no objective connection with the Coonawarra region was also wrong in fact and constituted an error of law. Fourth, it was argued that

---

59 ibid.
60 T Atkin, 'Drawing a Line under Coonawarra', *Harpers*, 18 October 2001.
61 ibid.
62 [2002] FCAFC 295 (20 September 2002).
63 In his time as a judge of the Federal Court, von Doussa J has earned a reputation as a pioneer and an innovator in matters of intellectual property – particularly for his decisions in respect of communal ownership of Indigenous art in *Milpurrurru v Indofurn Pty Ltd* (1994) 30 IPR 209 and *Bulun Bulun v R&T Textiles Pty Ltd* (1998) 41 IPR 513; von Doussa J also heard the proto-moral rights dispute between Charles Bannon and the Daubists, which was ultimately settled: M Rimmer, 'Daubism: Copyright Law and Artistic Works' (2002) 9 *Murdoch University Electronic Journal of Law*, available at http://papers.ssrn.com/sol3/papers.cfm?abstract_id=600864.

the AAT had erred in law in failing to take into account relevant considerations, including the proximity of Robertson's Well to the topography of the cigar and the homogeneity of the Coonawarra region.

The Federal Court was sympathetic to the complex task of the tribunal. Nonetheless, the judges ruled that the tribunal had misconstrued regulations 24 and 25:

> The task which confronted the AAT was not an easy one. As it noted, climate, water, drainage and soil conditions did not provide discernible boundaries. The cigar had long since ceased to delineate the grape producing area from which wine recognised as Coonawarra originated. The AAT found, at par 137 of the reasons, that proximity to the cigar was an important indication of the boundaries, and no party in these appeals has criticised that finding. But the notion of proximity was not alone enough to identify boundaries, or even approximate boundaries, with any precision.[64]

The judges observed:

> To simply adopt the boundaries of the Hundreds as the western boundary of the region when vineyards not much further to the west are much nearer to the cigar than many vineyards to the east that are included, produces a result that is not internally consistent and, without more, is both arbitrary and not based on the central identifier of a region prescribed in reg 24.[65]

The Federal Court held:

> The case for inclusion of the Robertson's Well vineyard and the lands of Naradina Pty Ltd and RD MacLeod within the boundaries is even stronger as the adverse soil profile which develops as one moves to the west of the cigar is not present in these lands.[66]

The Federal Court found that the AAT had placed too great an emphasis upon the history of the founding and development of the area:

> When the Regulations are so understood, the 1984 Viticultural Council resolution, which assumes major importance in the reasoning of the AAT, could be relevant only insofar as it provides probative material identifying boundaries of a single tract of land that is discrete and homogeneous in its grape growing attributes ... It seems clear that the boundary proposed by the resolution was not a boundary based on any research or expert evidence. At the most, the resolution provides some evidence that some viticulturists knowledgeable in and about the area considered that the region which produced grapes from which wine recognised as 'Coonawarra' was made, extended beyond – and well beyond – the cigar.[67]

The judges observed:

> The finding of the [AAT] in par 128 demonstrates the way in which its misconstruction of reg 24 and reg 25 has diverted its attention from the central issue, which is to identify a single tract of land that is discrete and homogeneous in its grape growing attributes to the requisite degree.[68]

---

64 *Beringer Blass Wine Estates v Geographical Indications Committee* [2002] FCAFC 295 (20 September 2002), para. 72.
65 ibid.
66 ibid.
67 ibid., para. 68.
68 ibid., para. 69.

224 LANDMARKS IN AUSTRALIAN IP LAW

The Federal Court held:

> The difficulties in identifying boundaries to an area that may reasonably be regarded as the Coonawarra region within the meaning of reg 24 provides reason for a decision-maker to have regard to historical information, but only insofar as that information is properly to be taken into account in light of the definitional requirements of reg 24, and the purpose of the criteria in reg 25. Accordingly the application by Beringer Blass must succeed.[69]

Second, the Federal Court considered whether there was a record of use of the name 'Robertson's Well' in association with the label or descriptor 'Coonawarra'. Beringer Blass relied on evidence that its holding company Mildara had, since 1993, marketed 'Robertson's Well' wines, the front label of which included the words 'Robertson's Well' and 'Coonawarra', and the back label of which read: 'John "Poor Man" Robertson was one of the most illustrious pioneers of the Coonawarra region and at one time ran 60 000 sheep on his property.'[70] In opposition, the Southcorp Group contended that the AAT did not fall into factual error because the wine marketed as 'Robertson's Well' with a Coonawarra descriptor on its labelling, originated from grapes grown not on Robertson's Well, but in another vineyard in Coonawarra. The judges concluded: 'We would agree with the submission made by Beringer Blass that the AAT erred in those findings of fact, and that the findings were unreasonable or arbitrary having regard to the evidence'.[71]

Third, the Federal Court dismissed the appeal that the AAT erred in finding that the Robertson's Well property had no objective connection with the Coonawarra region, holding: 'We do not think that evidence of the kind relied upon by Beringer Blass, namely evidence about their postal address and about the recognition by trade customers that Robertson's Well is at Coonawarra, assists the Beringer Blass case'.[72] The judges emphasised: 'Evidence of that kind is not evidence which bears on the question whether an area is a single tract of land that is discrete and homogeneous in its grape growing attributes.'[73]

Fourth, the Federal Court agreed that the tribunal erred in law in failing to take into account three relevant considerations:

> The Robertson's Well property is much closer to the topography of the cigar than many properties to the east of the cigar which are included in the geographical indication. Not only was there no evidence before the AAT that the land between the northern boundary of the geographical indicator determined by the AAT and the Robertson's Well property was not homogeneous or otherwise unsuitable so as to exclude the property, there are express findings as to similarity of climatic and soil conditions to those pertaining to the cigar.[74]

---

69 ibid., para. 73.
70 ibid., para. 77.
71 ibid., para. 81.
72 ibid., para. 82.
73 ibid.
74 ibid., para. 83.

The judges ruled: 'The failure to take into account these relevant matters is a product of the erroneous construction which the AAT placed upon regs 24 and 25.'[75]

The Federal Court also upheld an appeal by DM and PJ Castine, noting: 'The evidence therefore establishes a trade recognition of the characteristic of the wine as essentially attributable to its origin within the Coonawarra region.'[76] Similarly, the Federal Court held that the finding in relation to JD and PG Kidman reflected a 'failure to take into account relevant evidence and, for this reason, reflects an error of law'.[77] Finally, the Federal Court held that 'a boundary that included the Robertson's Well would inevitably include the properties of RD MacLeod and Naradina.'[78] However, the judges rejected the argument by the applicants, other than Beringer Blass, that the AAT had committed an error of law by failing to give written reasons for its decision.

The King Valley: *Baxendale's Vineyard v The Geographical Indications Committee*

The *Coonawarra* litigation produced a chiaroscuro effect with a range of responses, shedding light and dark on the decision of the Federal Court. There have been divergent opinions as to the significance and influence of the decision.

The Limestone Coast

Some commentators have suggested that the *Coonawarra* litigation has been a restorative tonic, which has helped to restore order and harmony in the viticultural community. Rell Hannah of Beringer Blass Wine Estates celebrated the decision of the Federal Court:

> We'd felt all along that the narrow 'cigar' definition of Coonawarra was much too narrow, that it didn't take account of many different grape growers and wineries who contributed to the region over the year. That was the basis that we initially entered into this so we are pleased that it's been finally recognised that Coonawarra is broader than that.[79]

Such a perspective suggests the legal ruling has brought certainty and stability to the industry of wine-making in the *Coonawarra* decision and has helped provide guidance to other regions in Australia engaged in similar boundary-making exercises. Alexander Reilly has noted in the context of native title law: 'Maps facilitate certainty through the reduction of the social and political landscape'.[80]

---

75 ibid.
76 ibid., para. 86.
77 ibid., para. 96.
78 ibid., para. 101.
79 ABC News, 'Wine Makers Celebrate Coonawarra Expansion', *ABC Rural News*, 23 September 2002, available at http://www.abc.net.au/rural/sa/stories/s683320.htm.
80 Reilly, op. cit. n. 17, p. 236.

226 LANDMARKS IN AUSTRALIAN IP LAW

Alluding to John Steinbeck's 'great American novel', the *Daily Telegraph* melodramatically declared that the Coonawarra ruling would 'bring grapes of wrath' and result in 'broken friendships and bitter feuds'.[81] In his critical legal commentary, Gary Edmond argues that the protracted litigation in the *Coonawarra* case highlights the indeterminate and capricious nature of the legislation and administrative regulations governing geographical indications:

> In this instance, the domestic ramifications of an international trade agreement between Australia and Europe generated frustration, animosity and eventually litigation. Attempts to repair the situation through ordinary legal mechanisms seem to have merely superimposed considerable expense and delay on the existing difficulties. Significantly, the move to law amplified uncertainty and contributed, though not always directly, to unprincipled and unsatisfactory outcomes.[82]

Edmond maintains that 'the inconsistent application of law produced a series of regional boundaries with little relevance to the statutory framework' and thus 'directly contributed to the legal alienation of many participants and attentive members of the public'.[83] His suggestion is that the case law produced rampant legal disorder, adding to the complexity and mystification of geographical indications.

Cartographer Max Foale and geographer Derek Smith questioned the rationales of the decision of the Full Court:

> An arbitrary boundary, based upon the inclusion of a group of vineyards claiming some historical/commercial rights at a particular arbitrary date and within a wider homogeneous environment has little logic, unless other factors are incorporated.[84]

The authors contended: 'The best approach is surely to draw the boundary on principles of regional geography to its maximum reasonable and definable extent'.[85] Geographers Glenn Banks and Scott Sharpe suggested:

> A more explicit attempt to either solely focus on biophysical elements (pursuing the chimera of purity) or to clearly acknowledge historical, economic and political factors, should reduce the confusion that occurred with Coonawarra.[86]

The wine writer Huon Hooke argued that the significance of the Coonawarra decision had been overrated by its supporters and detractors alike.[87] He maintained that the reputation of the producer was of greater import than the reputation of the larger region of wine-making:

---

81 'Ruling to Bring Grapes of Wrath: Coonawarra Line Ruling Due Today', *Daily Telegraph*, 5 October 2001, p. 5.
82 Edmond, op. cit. n. 12, pp. 59–60.
83 ibid., p. 60.
84 Foale and Smith, op. cit. n. 16, p. 63.
85 ibid., p. 64.
86 Banks and Sharpe, op. cit. n. 16, p. 182.
87 H Hooke, 'Drawing the Line in Coonawarra', *Sydney Morning Herald*, 16–22 October 2001, p. 16. See also C Shanahan, 'Defining Regions Leads to Border Skirmishes', *Canberra Times*, 21 October 2001, p. 37; and C Shanahan, 'Boundaries Await in the Coonawarra Case', *Canberra Times*, 21 October 2001, p. 41.

THE *COONAWARRA* DISPUTE   227

I'm sure to be branded a heretic, but I don't believe the Coonawarra boundary is very important. People in South Australia have been trying to invest the name with value it doesn't and shouldn't have. There is no region in the world which produces only great wine. There is bad Bordeaux, Burgundy, Rioja, Chianti and Napa. There is bad Coonawarra, and no amount of juggling lines or arguing about soil types will change that.[88]

Such a sceptical position suggests that there is greater value attached to the reputation of individual trade marks than the reputation of geographical indications for particular regions. Hooke did fear, though, that the creation of boundaries would limit the quantity of wine that could be produced and raise prices through creating conditions of scarcity: 'My pessimistic side suspects we will see the genuine Coonawarra wines gradually ratchet their prices up, to cash in on the new boundary'.[89]

As a result of the broad, inclusive boundaries determined for Coonawarra by the Federal Court, the GIC rejected a proposal to establish a wine region called 'Penola'. The executive officer Jock Osborne observed:

It's a bit silly to have a Penola wine region when the township of Penola is actually in the Coonawarra wine region. But there's a group in Penola that were keen for the determination to proceed and they'll be disappointed with this decision.[90]

The committee says those producers can make a fresh application for a new name or label their wine as coming from the 'Limestone Coast' region.

The King Valley

There has been much debate about whether the decision in the *Coonawarra* case is helpful in determining the boundaries and limits of other Australian wine-producing regions.

In *King Valley Vignerons v Geographical Indications Committee*, Downe J of the AAT considered whether the King Valley in Victoria should be defined as a single region for the purposes of geographical indications or whether there should be two regions – the King Valley and the Whitlands High Plateaux (see Figure 13.2).[91] The judge acknowledged that the determination of boundaries was an artificial exercise: 'Nature generally does not draw bright line boundaries'.[92] Applying the criteria and sub-criteria of the *Australian Wine and Brandy Corporation Regulations 1981*, Downe J held that King Valley was one homogeneous and discrete area, which included the valley, the plateau and the ridges:

---

88 ibid.
89 ibid.
90 ABC News, 'Penola Wine Region Plan "Too Confusing"', ABC News, 22 August 2007.
91 *King Valley Vignerons Inc and Ors v Geographical Indications Committee and Anor* [2006] AATA 885 (18 October 2006).
92 ibid., para. 50.

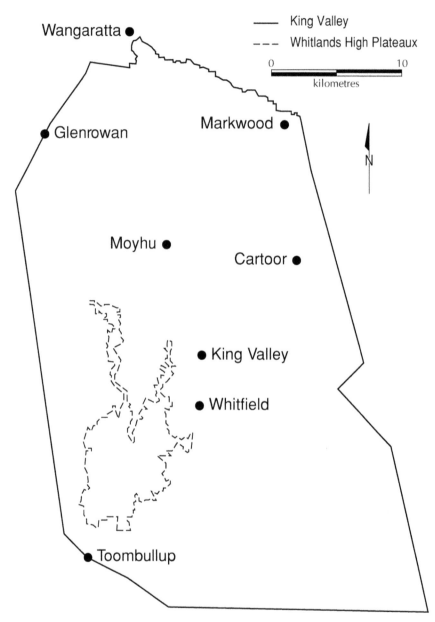

Figure 13.2: Map of King Valley

THE *COONAWARRA* DISPUTE   229

There are undoubtedly differences in grape growing characteristics within the area but there are high levels of homogeneity within separate parts such as the plains, the valley proper, the ridges and the Plateau.[93]

The judge held that 'there seems to me to be sufficient discreteness in grape growing attributes to qualify the areas under consideration as a region or regions.'[94]

In the case of *Baxendale's Vineyard v The Geographical Indications Committee*, the Federal Court considered the determination of geographical indications under the *Australian Wine and Brandy Corporation Act*.[95] It examined whether the Whitlands High Plateaux region should be part of or separate from the King Valley region in Victoria. Rejecting the appeal on this issue, Dowsett J questioned the heavy reliance upon the *Coonawarra* decision by the Whitlands vignerons:

> In my view many of the criticisms which the applicants make of the Tribunal's reasons are the result of their undue reliance upon the decision in the *Coonawarra* case. Many of the 'propositions' which they seek to draw from that case may be really observations relevant to its facts, having regard to the way in which it was conducted. This approach led the applicants to advance certain arguments by reference to that decision and without reference to the [*Australian Wine and Brandy Corporation Act 1980* (Cth)], the regulations or the EC agreement.[96]

The Full Court rejected the appeal by Baxendale's Vineyard, finding that the decision of the tribunal was consistent with the ruling in *Beringer Blass Wine Estates v Geographical Indications Committee*.[97] The judges doubted whether the factual matrix in the case was similar to the *Coonawarra* litigation.

Other sub-regions

Since the registration of the Margaret River as a wine region, John Gladstones has proposed a 'Conceptual Plan for Viticultural Subregions of Margaret River'.[98] He proposed six sub-regions: Yallingup, Carbunup, Wilyabrup, Treeton, Wallcliffe and Karridale. Although it is logically based upon climatic and geographical grounds, this proposal could be stymied on legal grounds. As John Beeston observes: 'The [GIC] seems to have no power to "revisit" wine regions and sub-regions once such are finally registered'.[99] Moreover, there would be difficulties in terms of marketing the sub-regions of the Margaret River.

There has also been some conflict in other parts of Western Australia. The GIC has been moving toward a final determination for two wine regions called Manjimup and Pemberton. Jerrard notes: 'It is shaping as the most protracted and bitter dispute in naming a wine region in Australia, surpassing the eight years

---

93 ibid., para. 118.
94 ibid., para. 121.
95 *Baxendale's Vineyard Pty Ltd v The Geographical Indications Committee* [2007] FCAFC 122.
96 ibid., para. 99.
97 [2002] FCAFC 295 (20 September 2002).
98 Beeston, op. cit. n. 3, p. 391.
99 ibid., p. 394.

230 LANDMARKS IN AUSTRALIAN IP LAW

taken to determine the Coonawarra region in South Australia, which ended in the Federal Court.'[100] The Manjimup Wine Region Association has threatened to take legal action to stop the proposal, arguing that the boundary is incorrect and will lead to Pemberton dominating. The Pemberton Wine Region Association has said that it will defend the decision, arguing that the marketability of its members' products is at stake.

In New South Wales there was much debate about the wine sub-regions of the lower Hunter Valley – Pokolbin, Belford, Rothbury and Mount View. The Hunter Valley Vineyard Association's president, Trevor Drayton, said sorting out the sub-regional issue had been tough:

> It was very important to us that we don't have a Coonawarra situation. The last thing we wanted was people fighting with each other.[101]

Drayton hoped the GIC would hand down its boundaries ruling based on the submission from his association. The boundaries of the proposed sub-regions broadly follow those of historic parishes from which they take their names. Drayton hoped that there would be no legal challenges to the division of the sub-regions.

One wonders whether the borders set for Coonawarra and other famous wine regions in Australia, such as the Margaret River and the Hunter Valley, will remain fixed and immutable. In France there has been great pressure to enlarge the boundaries of famous appellations of origin. In response to a potential shortage of grapes and demands from local mayors, the Institut National des Appellations d'Origine has embarked upon a major revision of the legal boundaries of Champagne.[102] In 2003 the institute worked on defining fresh criteria for entry and sent five scientists out to survey soil, climate and the historical location of vines. In 2007 the scientific team recommended 40 villages or communes for consideration.[103] In addition, two communes may lose their grape-grower status.[104] In March 2008 the national committee of the Institut National des Appellations d'Origine was due to vote upon the recommendations made by the scientific committee. There has already been great controversy over the inclusion and exclusion of communes from the list developed by the scientific committee. A group representing the landowners of Aisne has filed a complaint with the European Court of Human Rights in 2006, complaining that 25 communes from the area have been excluded from the list.[105]

---

100 S Jerrard, 'Growers in Gripe over Wine Names', *West Australian*, 6 June 2005, p. 7.
101 D Lewis, 'You Whine, but We Heard on the Vine You're Not Pokolbin', *Sydney Morning Herald*, 7 February 2004, p. 11.
102 S Nassauer, 'Demand for Champagne, Gives Péas a Chance: Small French City Gets Another Shot at Joining Lucrative Appellation', *Wall Street Journal*, 15 December 2007, B1.
103 ibid.
104 ibid.
105 ibid.

Conclusion: The European Community–Australia Wine Agreement 2007

The story of the *Coonawarra* litigation tells a compelling socio-economic tale. It provides a glimpse of the growth and transformation of the Australian wine industry, and the development of distinctive local and regional identities in the face of competition from well-established European traditions. There are a number of themes to this tale. The Coonawarra boundary dispute highlights tensions between local regionalism, national identity, and international trade rules. In the story, there are conflicts between several legal institutions: the GIC, the AAT, and the Federal Court. The *Coonawarra* litigation highlighted instabilities and uncertainties in the definition of geographical indications in the Australian regime. The determination of boundaries depends upon the complex interaction of scientific evidence, natural phenomena, history, economic pressures, and political decisions. The ruling raises issues about the interaction between individual trade marks and regional identities constructed by geographical indications. The dispute also emphasises the interplay between property rights and intellectual property rights – the inter-mingling of place and culture.

There has been both conflict and compromise between the Australian government and the European Community over geographical indications and international trade. In 2003 Australia and the US complained to the World Trade Organization (WTO) about European Community regulations concerning the protection of trade marks and the registration and protection of geographical indications.[106] In 2005, the WTO Panel found that the equivalence and reciprocity conditions in respect of geographical indications protection under the European Community regulation violated the national treatment obligation under Art 3 of the TRIPS Agreement 1994 by according less favorable treatment to foreign nationals than to European Community nationals. However, the WTO Panel determined that the regulation was justified under Art 17 of the TRIPS Agreement, which permits members to provide limited exceptions to the rights conferred by trade marks, provided that such exceptions take account of the legitimate interests of the owner of the trade mark and of third parties.

Surprisingly, given such conflict at a multilateral level, Australia and the European Community initialled a new bilateral agreement on geographical indications in 2007. Mariann Fischer Boel, Commissioner for Agriculture and Rural Development, observed: 'This accord safeguards EU interests by establishing principles for the protection of GIs and traditional expressions and protecting our wine labelling regime'.[107] The agreement expands upon the 1994 accord.

---

106 World Trade Organization Panel Decision on the European Union's Protection of Trademarks and Geographical Indications for Agricultural Products and Foodstuffs 2005 WT/DS290/R; Handler, 'The WTO Geographical Indications Dispute', op. cit. n. 10, pp.70–80; and B Tamberlin and L Bastin, 'Australia and the World Trade Organization: Decision Enforcement' (2007) 81 *Australian Law Journal* 802.
107 European Commission, 'European Commission and Australia Initial New Wine Agreement', IP/07/771, 6 June 2007.

232 LANDMARKS IN AUSTRALIAN IP LAW

The agreement provides for a full protection of EU geographical indications, including for wines for export. It will provide for the phasing out by Australia of the use of a number of important names such as Champagne and Port within one year from the entry into force of the agreement. It safeguards the EU wine-labelling regime by listing optional particulars which may be used by Australian wines, regulating the indication of vine varieties on wine labels, and eliminating the use within one year after the entry into force of the agreement of some of these vine varieties (such as Hermitage and Lambrusco). There has been much debate as to whether this new agreement will have a positive or negative impact upon the Australian wine industry. Matthew Harvey of Monash University has observed:

> The good news is that the Australian wine industry has responded creatively to the restrictions already imposed by using imaginative forms of naming and labelling and by establishing reputations for distinctive wine regions.[108]

Furthermore, the boundary determination for the Coonawarra region may have a larger significance, given developments in international trade. In a number of multilateral forums, there remain larger international tensions about providing protection of geographical indications in respect of quality regional products. The EU has provided protection of appellations in respect of food, such as hams, cheeses and olives.[109] The Community has been lobbying in a number of international forums to expand the definition of geographical indications to cover foodstuffs. Mark Davison of Monash University commented that the EU has moved to seek protection from the WTO for geographical indications such as 'edam, parmesan, Parma ham and gorgonzola in much greater detail than at present'.[110] There has been much debate among Australian agricultural producers as to whether such a development would be a threat to local markets or represent a marketing opportunity. The decision in the *Coonawarra* case may be helpful in determining the boundaries and limits of Australian food-producing regions.

---

108 L White, 'Clampdown Looms on Regional Names', *Foodweek*, 9 June 2006.
109 *Consorzio del Proscuitto di Parma v Asda* ('Parma Ham' case) 20 May 2003, Case C-108/01; *Ravil v Bellon* ('Grand Padano cheese' case) 2003 Case C-469/00; *Federal Republic of Germany and Kingdom of Denmark v Commission of the European Communities* ('Feta Cheese' case) 10 May 2005, Case C-465/02 and Case C-466/02; *Geographical Indications (Olive Oil 'Kalamata')*, Ministerial Decision, 20/08/1993, No. 379567 (Greece); *Commission of the European Communities v Federal Republic of Germany* ('Parmesan cheese' case) 26 February 2008, Case C-132/05.
110 White, op. cit. n. 108.

14

Waiting for the 'Billy'®[1] to boil: the *Waltzing Matilda* case

Leanne Wiseman and Matthew Hall

Once a jolly swagman camped by a billabong,
Under the shade of a coolibah tree,
And he sang as he looked at the old billy boiling
'Who'll come a-Waltzing Matilda, with me?'

Waltzing Matilda, Waltzing Matilda
'You'll come a-Waltzing Matilda, with me'
And he sang as he watched and waited 'til his billy boiled,
'You'll come a-Waltzing Matilda, with me'.

Down came a jumbuck to drink at the billabong,
Up got the swagman and grabbed him with glee,
And he sang as he stowed that jumbuck in his tucker bag,
'You'll come a-Waltzing Matilda, with me'.

Waltzing Matilda, Waltzing Matilda
'You'll come a-Waltzing Matilda, with me'
And he sang as he stowed that jumbuck in his tucker bag,
'You'll come a-Waltzing Matilda, with me'.

Down came the squatter, mounted on his thoroughbred,
Up came the troopers, one, two, three,
'Where's that jolly jumbuck you've got in your tucker bag?'
'You'll come a-Waltzing Matilda, with me'.

Waltzing Matilda, Waltzing Matilda
'You'll come a-Waltzing Matilda, with me'
'Who's that jolly jumbuck you've got in your tucker bag?'
'You'll come a-Waltzing Matilda, with me'.

---

1 Trade mark registration no. 596575.

Up got the swagman and jumped into the billabong,
'You'll never catch me alive,' said he,
And his ghost may be heard as you passed by that billabong,
'Who'll come a-Waltzing Matilda, with me?'

Waltzing Matilda, Waltzing Matilda
Who'll come a-Waltzing Matilda, with me
And his ghost may be heard as you passed by that billabong,
'Who'll come a-Waltzing Matilda, with me?'

AB (Banjo) Paterson (1895)

Introduction

In 2002, the Full Court of the Federal Court handed down its judgment in the case of *Lomas v Winton Shire Council and the Waltzing Matilda Centre*.[2] In so doing, the Full Court ended the long-running dispute over the rights of Lomas and others to obtain exclusive rights in the trade mark WALTZING MATILDA.[3] The action arose from the appeal by the Winton Shire Council and the Waltzing Matilda Centre (which was owned by the council) from the decision of the Registrar of Trade Marks who held that Lomas was the first user and therefore the proprietor of the trade mark.[4] On appeal to the Federal Court, Justice Spender overturned the decision of the Registrar and allowed, at least in part, the opposition brought by the council and the centre.[5] The Full Court of the Federal Court reversed that decision and held that the evidence relied on by the council and the centre did not amount to use of the mark WALTZING MATILDA as a trade mark in respect of the relevant foodstuffs or restaurant services.[6]

In many ways, *Lomas v Winton Shire Council* is an unremarkable decision: it is a fairly straightforward application of settled principles of trade mark law, dealing with proprietorship[7] and prior conflicting marks under the *Trade Marks Act 1995* (Cth). Having said that, the case and the ongoing fate of 'Waltzing Matilda' provide an insight into the extent to which words that have significant cultural and social meaning can operate as a sign or badge of origin to indicate the origin of particular goods or services. The case is also important in so far as it gives rise to the question: even if the words 'Waltzing Matilda' are capable of distinguishing a particular trader's goods or services, are they so laden with social, cultural, political and historical meaning that they should not be able to be used exclusively by a particular trader as a trade mark? That is, even if 'Waltzing Matilda' is able to function as a trade mark, are those words so important that no

---

2 *Lomas v Winton Shire Council and the Waltzing Matilda Centre Ltd* (2003) AIPC 35,165.
3 There was a number of applications in respect of various goods and services: in the case of Lomas, foodstuffs and restaurant services.
4 *Winton Shire Council and Another v Lomas* (2001) 51 IPR 174.
5 *Winton Shire Council and Another v Lomas* (2002) 56 IPR 72.
6 (2003) AIPC 35,165.
7 *Trade Marks Act 1995* (Cth) s 58.

THE *WALTZING MATILDA* CASE   235

individual should be given exclusive rights to use the words as a trade mark? This is an issue that is broader than 'Waltzing Matilda'. It is a question that affects any symbol or sign that is part of Australia's national identity or is seen as a cultural icon.

'Waltzing Matilda' was written by Banjo Paterson in 1895. In essence it is a ballad about an itinerant worker (a swagman) who is camped at a billabong (or waterhole). While he is waiting for his billy to boil to make his tea, a sheep comes down to the billabong for a drink of water. As often happened at the time, the swagman kills the sheep. When the sheep's owner arrives with three police officers to arrest the swaggie, the swagman drowns himself in the billabong. There has been considerable debate about 'Waltzing Matilda', particularly about when and how it was written.[8] As one commentator has noted, '[t]here are now more 'official' versions of "Waltzing Matilda" than there are unofficial versions of the plot that killed Kennedy'.[9] There are three main versions of "Waltzing Matilda", each with their own history, melody and lyrics. These are the Macpherson/Paterson rendition which is based on the 1895 song;[10] the popular version of the song which first appeared in print in an arrangement by Marie Cowan (c 1903)[11] (this has different tune and words to the Macpherson/Paterson version); and a third oral version, sometimes referred to as the Queensland version, which has Paterson's lyrics but to a different tune.[12]

While aspects of the song's legacy are disputed, there are some facts which are generally accepted. Most commentators agree that the words to 'Waltzing Matilda' were written by Banjo Paterson in 1895 when he visited Dagworth Station, a property about 100 km north-west of Winton (in western Queensland).[13] On one version of events, when Paterson was at Dagworth Station, Christina Macpherson played him a tune that she had recently heard at a race meeting in Victoria. The melody played by Macpherson is thought to be an imperfect recollection of the Scottish folk tune 'Thou Bonnie Wood of Craigielea' or 'The Bold Fusilier'. After hearing the tune, Paterson decided to write lyrics to accompany the music. It has been suggested that the lyrics that Paterson wrote were based

---

8 For the background, see S May, *The Story of 'Waltzing Matilda'*, 2nd edn, WR Smith & Peterson, Brisbane, 1955); C Semmler, *The Banjo of the Bush: The Work, Life and Times and AB Paterson* (Lansdowne Press, Melbourne, 1966); R Maggoffin, *Fair Dinkum Matilda: The Story of a Song its People & Times*, Mimosa Press, Charters Towers, 1973; R Maggoffin, *The Provenance of Waltzing Matilda: A Definitive Exposition of the Song's Origins, Meanings and Evolution from a Pivotal Episode in Australia's History*, Matilda Expos Publishers, Kynuna, 2000; R Maggoffin, *Waltzing Matilda: The Story behind the Legend*, ABC Books, Sydney, 1987; C Roderick, *Banjo Paterson: Poet by Accident*, Allen & Unwin, St Leonards, 1993; M Richardson, *Once a Jolly Swagman: The Ballad of Waltzing Matilda*, Melbourne University Press, Melbourne, 2006; and T Radic, 'The Matilda Knot' (1995) *Victorian Journal of Music Education* 3.
9 J Marx, 'The Meaning of Waltzing Matilda', *Sydney Morning Herald*, 23 July 2007, available at http://blogs.smh.com.au/thedailytruth/archives/2007/07/the_meaning_of_waltzing_matild.html. See also Radic, op. cit., pp. 5–6.
10 See Figure 14.2 below. Maggofin states that the Macpherson manuscripts were not found until the 1970s. Maggofin, *The Provenance of Waltzing Matilda*, op. cit. n. 8.
11 See Figure 14.1 below.
12 'Waltzing Matilda', The National Library of Australia, available at http://www.nla.gov.au/epubs/waltzingmatilda/2-Versions.html.
13 'However other part of the opponents' evidence suggest that the town of Kyuna which is considerably closer to Dagworth than is Winton has also promoted itself as connected with the song': *Winton Shire Council v Lomas* (2000) 51 IPR 174, 176.

Figure 14.1 Cover of Marie Cowan's 1903 arrangement of 'Waltzing Matilda' nla.mus-an7412026-s1-v, National Library of Australia

on a shearers' strike that had taken place at Dagworth Station in 1894. After the striking shearers had set fire to a woolshed and fired guns in the air, three policemen chased a man named Samuel Hoffmeister. However, rather than letting himself be captured by the police, Hoffmeister committed suicide by shooting himself at a waterhole on the station.

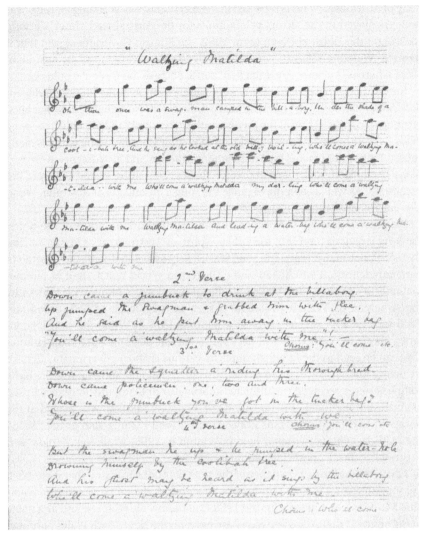

Figure 14.2 Christina Macpherson's transcription of 'Waltzing Matilda', c 1895, NLA MS 9065, National Library of Australia

While the provenance of the song may be unclear, its subsequent popularity cannot be disputed. In addition to its widespread popular appeal, the song also has also had some influential supporters. For example, Sir Winston Churchill is reported to have played the song to General de Gaulle, describing it as 'one of the finest songs in the world'.[14] For good or bad, 'Waltzing Matilda' is often seen as being quintessentially Australian. As one commentator noted, 'Waltzing Matilda has become known throughout the world, or at least a large portion of it, as the

14 May, op. cit., p. 12.

238 LANDMARKS IN AUSTRALIAN IP LAW

Song of Australia'.[15] This is reflected in the fact that when 'Waltzing Matilda' was wrongly played in the victory celebrations for the Australian sprinter Marjorie Jackson at the Helsinki Olympics in 1952, the Finnish Government said that it thought 'Waltzing Matilda' would be recognised by everyone as an Australian song, whereas 'Advance Australia Fair' and 'God Save the Queen' would not.[16]

Interestingly, particularly for a song widely seen as reflecting the independent Australian spirit, the international popularity of 'Waltzing Matilda' has been attributed to the decision of the English author Thomas Wood to publish the song in his *Cobbers* book.[17] Wood's version of 'Waltzing Matilda', along with his many subsequent arrangements for combinations of voices and instruments, were regularly used by schools, piano and voice classes, glee clubs, choral societies and orchestras. As well as helping to make the song a hit outside of Australia, Wood also earned substantial royalties.[18]

Despite, or possibly because of, the anti-authoritarian nature of the lyrics, the song is said to represent the 'official spirit' of Australia, or at least a version thereof.[19] For many years, the song was closely associated with the Australian national identity. It was linked to the Diggers in World War I, used in ceremonial military parades, and played at official functions.[20] Along with Ned Kelly, the swagman of 'Waltzing Matilda' is seen as 'an outcast of both urban and rural society' who is celebrated 'as a national icon'.[21] While the song's popularity may have waned, it still occupies a special place in Australian culture. This can be seen in the failed attempts by various (Labor) governments to have 'Waltzing Matilda' recognised as the Australian national anthem. Although the song has never received the ultimate imprimatur of being officially recognised as Australia's national anthem (although 'Waltzing Matilda' was played at the Montreal Olympic Games), as Prime Minister Paul Keating said at the 'Waltzing Matilda' centenary dinner held in Winton in 1995, 'Waltzing Matilda' was Australia's official 'unofficial' national song.[22]

Given the enduring popularity of the song, it is not surprising that it has been appropriated for a variety of purposes including as the name of sporting teams (the Matildas), as a mascot for the 1988 Commonwealth Games, and as a name of the highway that spans between Barringun on the New South Wales border to Normanton in the Gulf of Carpentaria. The name and associated imagery have

---

15 ibid., p. 24.
16 Radic, op. cit., p. 9.
17 *Cobbers: A Personal Record of a Journey from Essex in England, to Australia, Tasmania and Some of the Reefs in the Coral Sea, Made in the Years 1930, 1931, and 1932*, Oxford University Press, London, 1934.
18 *The Mirror* in Sydney reported in February 1971: 'The widow of the musician [Wood] who made 'Waltzing Matilda' a hit left a personal estate valued at $799 835'. See 'Waltzing Matilda Widow's $799 000', *Mirror* (Sydney), 10 February 1971.
19 B West, 'Crime, Suicide and the Anti-hero: "Waltzing Matilda" in Australia' (2001) 35 *Journal of Popular Culture* 127.
20 See May, op. cit., p. 12: 'So national a symbol has it become that it is used in the Navy, Army and Air Force at their ceremonial parades all over the world and not the least, by any means, was when the Coronation Contingent of Australian troops mounted guard at Buckingham Palace during the week prior to the Coronation of her Majesty the Queen Elizabeth II.'
21 West, op. cit., p. 137.
22 Radic, op. cit.

also been used to promote a variety of goods and services including service stations, internet service providers, film production companies, boat cruises, wine estates and luxury motorhomes. Many of these names have been registered as trade marks. The enduring power of the Matilda brand has also been used as a way of luring tourists to western Queensland. Indeed this was one of the motives for the establishment of the Waltzing Matilda Centre at Winton in 1998.[23] In 1995, to celebrate the centenary of the first performance of the song, the Queensland Government with the Winton Shire Council staged a centenary celebration in Winton.[24] As a result of the success of that celebration, the council subsequently established the Waltzing Matilda Centre in Winton as a permanent celebration of the song and the history that surrounds it and the region. The centre, which was the idea of 'Queensland Events' and funded by the Queensland Government, aims to promote and celebrate the centenary of the first public performance of the song.[25] Described as the 'only centre in the world dedicated to a song',[26] it is said to show the song's continuing relevance and centrality in Australian culture.[27] It is also testament to the ongoing commercial appeal of the song, a theme to which we will return to below.

The *Waltzing Matilda* litigation

In the mid-1990s, Tasmanian woman Brenda Lomas decided to set up a nation-wide franchised chain of restaurants. One of the main characteristics of the restaurants was that they were to have an Australian theme. To highlight the Australian theme, Lomas decided that the restaurants should operate under the name WALTZING MATILDA. Lomas sought to register the mark WALTZING MATILDA in classes 29, 30, 31, 35 and 42 for a variety of foodstuffs, franchising and restaurant services. The application was filed on 20 November 1997.

Winton Shire Council and the Waltzing Matilda Centre opposed Lomas' application on the grounds that the trade mark would be likely to deceive or cause confusion (s 43), the applicant was not the owner of the trade mark (s 58) and the trade mark was similar to a trade mark that had already acquired a reputation in Australia (s 60). The trade marks officer, Terry Williams, found that the song 'Waltzing Matilda' belonged to and indicated Australia as a whole. He also found that the song was part of the heritage of all Australians. This did not prevent him, however, from finding that the words could function as a trade mark. It also did not prevent him from finding that the opposition failed on all grounds.

Before the Trade Marks Office, the council and the centre argued that given the reputation of Winton and the centre as representatives and custodians of the

---

23 For a history of the centre see *Winton Shire Council v Lomas* (2002) 56 IPR 72, 76.
24 The first public performance of 'Waltzing Matilda' was at a banquet for the Premier of Queensland held at the North Gregory Hotel in Winton in April 1895.
25 *Winton Shire Council v Lomas* (2000) 51 IPR 174, 176.
26 Waltzing Matilda Centre, http://www.matildacentre.com.au/InteractiveTour.html.
27 West, op. cit.

240   LANDMARKS IN AUSTRALIAN IP LAW

history of the song, the use of the trade mark by Lomas would be likely to deceive or cause confusion and thus fall foul of s 43.[28] It was argued that at the filing date, the public would have expected that 'Waltzing Matilda' was affiliated with Winton in some way or another. It was also argued that the connotation between Winton and 'Waltzing Matilda' was inherent in the mark because of the strong and widely known historical links between the town and the song. The delegate of the Registrar did not agree. It was accepted that a significant number of people were familiar with the history of the song and that the council and the centre had built on this in promoting the bush or Australiana aspects of their activities in relation to accommodation, food and drink; nonetheless, the Registrar held that the song had outgrown both its origins and any possible exclusive links with either opponent. As a song, it belonged to and indicated Australia as a whole.[29] While the song may have belonged to Australia, this did not mean that the title of the words WALTZING MATILDA could not function as a trade mark. That is, there was no reason why WALTZING MATILDA could not distinguish a trader's goods or services that had no connection with either the song or the Winton area. It was held that there was nothing that suggested that when Lomas used the words WALTZING MATILDA as a trade mark for the specified goods or services this inherently denoted any sort of affiliation between Lomas' goods or services and the town of Winton, the council or the centre. Therefore, the opposition under s 43 failed.[30]

The council and the centre also opposed the application under s 58, which provides that a trade mark may be opposed on the basis that the applicant is not the owner of the mark in question. This was based on the fact that at the filing date of the application, the council had already held the centenary celebrations for the song and also begun construction of the centre. In promoting the yet-to-be-opened centre, the council had a clear intention that the centre would operate as a tourist attraction dedicated to the song. Winton Shire Council also had a very definite intention to put on a unique cultural event. The council had sought extensive sponsorship for the event and the centre from a wide range of companies and government agencies. Despite this, it was held that the connections between the opponents and those funding or sponsoring bodies, and between the opponents and the public who saw the promotion of the to-be-opened centre, were not relationships involving the use of a trade mark for either goods or relevant services. Instead, the words WALTZING MATILDA were used as the name of the upcoming centre, not as an indication of an offer to trade in, or to designate the origin of, goods or relevant services either then on offer or to be offered. On this basis it was held that if there was trade mark use by the centre prior to the priority date, that the use was limited to use as a cultural centre,

---

28 This provides that an application for the registration of a trade mark in respect of particular goods or services must be rejected if, because of some connotation that the trade mark or a sign contained in the trade mark has, the use of the trade mark in relation to those goods or services would be likely to deceive or cause confusion.

29 (2001) 51 IPR 174, 179.

30 ibid.

THE *WALTZING MATILDA* CASE   241

which was 'a far cry from any commerce under a trade mark used in relation to food or to any of the services specified in the current application'.[31]

The council and the centre also relied on s 60 of the *Trade Marks Act* to oppose Lomas' application. This provides that a trade mark may be opposed on the basis that another trade mark had acquired a reputation in the mark before the priority date, such that if the first mark was registered it would be likely to deceive or cause confusion. Because of the finding that WALTZING MATILDA belongs to and is part of the heritage of all Australians, however, it was unlikely that anyone would think that there was an affiliation between either the applicant or her goods and services and the opponents. This was the case even if the applicant opened a restaurant in Winton (whether franchised or not) or if stores in Winton sold Lomas' goods. Any speculation that arose about Lomas' marks causing confusion would primarily be due to the proximity or other circumstances of trade, not to the trade marks at issue.[32]

The council and the centre appealed the decision to the Federal Court.[33] Again, the council and the centre relied on s 43 to argue that the proposed use of WALTZING MATILDA was likely to deceive or cause confusion. As before the office, this argument was rejected by the court. Spender J held that the respondent's proposed use of the mark WALTZING MATILDA on or in respect of any of the goods or services only brought to mind the 'Waltzing Matilda' song. At most, the use of the mark was only likely to convey to the reasonable member of the public the Australian nature of those goods and services. On this basis Spender J held that there was no connotation of a connection with the centre at Winton, the town of Winton or the council. As such, he held that there was no deception or confusion.[34]

While Spender J rejected the arguments made in relation to s 43, he did accept the council's opposition in relation to ownership of the mark in respect of prepared foodstuffs in classes 29 and 30 and in respect of all services claimed in class 42 (restaurant services). Although the council and the centre had not coined the term 'Waltzing Matilda', it was held that they had better rights to ownership of the trade mark in respect of those goods and services than Lomas. The council and the centre established that they had used the mark 'Waltzing Matilda' in relation to the tourist centre in Winton from March 1998 and in respect of the centenary celebrations in 1995. In this context, the question was not whether there had been use of the mark 'Waltzing Matilda' by the applicants. Rather the question was whether there had been any use prior to the priority date in respect of any of the goods or services the subject of the opposed application. In response to this question, the council and the centre were able to provide evidence of

---

31 ibid., p. 179.
32 ibid., p. 180.
33 (2002) 56 IPR 72. The hearing is a complete re-hearing of the matter, with each party entitled to rely on new evidence and is not, strictly speaking, an appeal. See s 197 of the *Trade Marks Act 1995*. On appeal, the Winton Shire Council and the Waltzing Matilda Centre relied on each of the grounds before the office, and also that fact that it was an identical trade mark (s 44).
34 (2002) 56 IPR 72, 78.

their intent to use 'Waltzing Matilda' prior to the priority date of the trade mark application.

In October 1997 – which was prior to both the opening of the centre and the priority date of Lomas' application – the council had produced and circulated a brochure calling attention to 'The Waltzing Matilda Centre'. Relevantly, the brochure referred to an aspect of the proposed activities at the centre: 'Savour old fashioned, home baked bush fare at the Country Kitchen'. The council also placed an advertisement in the RACQ travel and accommodation guide, which was headed 'THE WALTZING MATILDA CENTRE' and showed a rural scene. The advertisement included the caption: 'Visit the Waltzing Matilda General Store for unique souvenirs and the Waltzing Matilda Country Kitchen for a traditional homestead meal'. Spender J held that this was evidence of use, 19 days prior to the priority date, that was sufficient to establish that Lomas was not the first user of the trade mark (and therefore not the owner) in connection with prepared foodstuffs and restaurant services.

Lomas sought leave to appeal Spender J's decision to the Full Court of the Federal Court.[35] On appeal, the council and the centre only pursued the arguments in relation to proprietorship. The other grounds, including arguments about deception and confusion under s 43, were not pursued.[36] As a result, the main issue argued on appeal was in relation to the ownership of the mark. More specifically, the issue that was addressed on appeal related to the question of what constitutes a use of a trade mark prior to registration.

Given that it is settled law that it is not necessary that there be an actual dealing in goods bearing a trade mark before there can be said to be use of that mark as a trade mark, the issue in the case was whether the brochure and the advertisement constituted use of the trade mark. The Full Court rejected Spender J's analysis and conclusions. In deciding that there had not been any use prior to registration, the court highlighted the fact that in talking about the Country Kitchen the brochure did not mention 'Waltzing Matilda'. The court also noted that when the Country Kitchen commenced operations in April 1998 it was called the 'Coolibah Country Kitchen'. On this basis the court held that the reference to 'Waltzing Matilda' in connection with the Country Kitchen in the advertisement was no more than a reference to the proposed facility within the centre. The court also held that the lack of consistency in the way the council used 'Country Kitchen' gave rise to an inference that the council had taken some time to decide the name which the restaurant would trade under.[37] The fact that in the advertisement Winton had separated the proposed facilities such as the 'country kitchen' and the 'souvenir shop' and then subsequently named the country kitchen the 'Coolibah Country Kitchen' suggested that the 'Waltzing Matilda' name applied to the centre rather than to every component within it.[38]

---

35 (2003) AIPC 35,165.
36 ibid., p. 35,167, para. 5.
37 ibid., p. 35,173, para. 42.
38 ibid., p. 35,173, para. 43.

Protection of icons

On one level *Lomas v Winton Shire Council* is a straightforward application of trade mark principles. Except for the question of whether permission should be granted to appeal a decision of a single judge on appeal from a registrar's decision on opposition proceedings,[39] there is little that is doctrinally interesting about the decision. When we look at the decision more generally, however, it offers a number of insights both into the legal and political processes that regulate the use of signs, words and images, as well as how intellectual property law deals with objects of cultural heritage more generally.

In Australia, a range of different names, images, symbols and logos are deemed to be so important, whether for cultural, social or political reasons, that they are not able to be appropriated for private use.[40] In some cases public outcry against the use of a name has ensured that the symbols are not appropriated for private ends.[41] A number of more formal mechanisms have also been used to ensure that culturally significant signs are not appropriated for private use. In addition to general causes of action such as passing off or those provided by the *Trade Practices Act*, specific provisions have also been used to protect specific signifiers. One of the ways this has been done is by limiting the types of marks that are able to be registered. This includes the arms, flag or seal of the Commonwealth or of a state or territory; and the arms or emblem of a city or town in Australia or of a public authority or public institution in Australia. A number of specific words are also unable to be registered including Austrade, CES, Olympic Champion, Repatriation, Returned Airman, Returned Sailor, Returned Soldier[42] and ANZAC.[43]

In some cases, non-trade mark mechanisms have also been used to protect specific items of cultural heritage. Perhaps the most well-known example is the special protection given to Donald Bradman, primarily as a result of the intervention of the then Prime Minister John Howard. The controversy over the

---

39 See *Special Effects Ltd v L'Oreal SA* [2007] EWCA Civ 1 (CA), para. 57.
40 There is specific protection in New Zealand for culturally significant words and symbols. See O Morgan, *Protecting Indigenous Signs and Trade Marks under the New Zealand Trade Marks Act 2002*, University of Melbourne Legal Studies Research Paper No. 80, 2004.
41 An example includes the 2002 decision of Athletics Australia to call the national athletics team 'The Diggers'. The ensuing public outcry led Athletics Australia to issue an apology and drop the name. Similar problems arose with the playing of the 'The Last Post' on the last Ansett flight and the naming of ANZAC Bridge in Sydney. Advisory Council on Intellectual Property, *The Protection of National Icons*, 2002, p. 3.
42 *Trade Marks Act 1995*, s 39(2) provides that certain signs may not be registered; reg 4.15 prescribes the relevant signs. The signs are specified in Sch 2 of the *Trade Mark Regulations 1995*, Sch 2(f). See Advisory Council on Intellectual Property, ibid., p. 19.
43 ANZAC is protected by the *Protection of the Word 'ANZAC' Regulations* which prevent the Registrar of Trade Marks and the Registrar of Designs from registering trade marks and designs, respectively, which include the word ANZAC. The word ANZAC is also prohibited from being the name or part of a name of a registered corporation unless permission is granted by the Minister for Veterans' Affairs under s 147 of the *Corporations Act 2001* and regs 2B.6.01, 2B6.02, 5B.3.01, 5B.3.02 and Sch 6 of the *Corporations Regulations 2001*. The word ANZAC is also protected under the *Customs (Prohibited Imports) Regulations 1956*. Item 13 of Sch 1 of those regulations prohibits absolutely the importation of 'Goods the description of which includes the word ANZAC or bearing the word ANZAC or a word so nearly resembling the word ANZAC as to be likely to deceive.' Advisory Council on Intellectual Property, op. cit., p. 18.

244   LANDMARKS IN AUSTRALIAN IP LAW

use of the Bradman name arose in 2001 after a road in Adelaide was renamed Sir Donald Bradman Drive in recognition of Bradman's cricketing achievements. Unsurprisingly, businesses on the renamed road started to use the Bradman name in relation to their businesses. While the use of the Bradman name to promote private commercial ends created a degree of public controversy, it was the renaming of a sex shop 'Erotica on Bradman' that caused the greatest concern. To prevent this from continuing, the *Corporations Regulations 2001* were amended to ensure that no company name is able to be registered if, in the context in which it is proposed to be used, it suggests a connection with Sir Donald Bradman that does not exist.[44]

Over time, many different types of words, names, logos and symbols have been deemed to be too important to allow them to be reserved to the exclusive use of a single trader by trade mark registration. This has not been the case, however, with 'Waltzing Matilda'. The fact that 'Waltzing Matilda' has not been signalled out for special treatment means that it

> remains, a ready tool for anyone who cares to exploit it, whether it's the tourist indus-
> try reaching for dollars in desperate country towns, or earnest nationalists intent on
> installing the swaggie as a hero of the working class, or the winner of the recent Spirit
> of Matilda poetry competition who has Matilda walking not a few tortuous miles, or
> God help us all, those who now want to harness it to the Sydney Olympics and the
> Federal Centenary celebrations.[45]

That is certainly the position in Australia, having regard to the reasoning of the trade marks office and the court, in the *Lomas* case. What those decisions also suggest, however, is that use of the name on or in connection with goods or services that are not Australian would be misleading. As Spender J recognised, the words WALTZING MATILDA are likely to convey to the reasonable member of the public the Australian nature of goods and services. This raises a question of whether an application by a trader who is not Australian, or in respect of goods or services that are not Australian, whether in Australia or overseas, would be able to be successfully opposed. It also raises the issue of if so, who has standing to be able to bring the opposition proceedings and argue that the words belong to and indicated Australia as a whole and are part of the heritage of all Australians.

The fate of 'Waltzing Matilda', particularly when compared to the approach that has been taken to other iconic names and figures such as Bradman and ANZAC, can be attributed to the song's anti-authoritarian sentiment. There is also a sense in which the fate of the song has been affected by its strong class

---

44 Sir Donald Bradman granted all rights to his name, likeness and image to the Bradman Foundation, a not-for-profit charitable trust. 'In this case what was required was the limitation of the commercial use of the name *Bradman* to use by those associated with Sir Donald Bradman, e.g., the Bradman Foundation wished to continue to exploit the name to raise money for its activities ... Inclusion in the *Corporations Regulations* gives much broader protection but would not, e.g., prevent further trade mark registrations or its use as a business or trading name. Similar issues have arisen in relation to commercial use of the name May Gibbs.' Advisory Council on Intellectual Property, ibid., p. 2.

45 Radic, op. cit., p. 9: 'only a marriage to the great Australia God of sport saved it from getting stuck with the leftist intellectuals of the folk music revivals of the 1950s.'

association. In this context it is important to note that Paterson wrote 'Waltzing Matilda' in a period where there was high level of class conflict between pastoralists, who were attempting to secure their hold on grazing land, and the growing underclass of farm labourers and itinerant workers, who were struggling to survive. This was a time where for 'a swagman or rural labourer at the time, killing one of the squatter's numerous sheep for food was thought of as a natural and a legitimate activity'.[46] The approach that has been taken towards 'Waltzing Matilda' is captured in Peter Carey's comment that Australians' attitudes to Ned Kelly tend to divide along class lines:

> I would think that the people who call him simply a horse thief and a murderer are in an absolute minority ... By and large, they're the genteel types who care what the British think about them – the same people who won't have Waltzing Matilda as their national song.[47]

The fact that 'Waltzing Matilda' has not been given any special protection has not been overlooked. For example, in its 2002 report *The Protection of National Icons* the Advisory Council on Intellectual Property said that 'Waltzing Matilda' meets even the most stringent example of possible for classification as a national icon.[48] The council recommended that in recognition of its special status as an Australian cultural term, 'Waltzing Matilda' should be declared a non-exclusive trade mark under the *Trade Marks Act 1995*. This provision was meant to be similar to s 18 of the *Trade Marks Act* that prohibits the *registration* or *use* of a trade mark while preserving any rights in trade marks that were registered or used in good faith before the date of commencement of the regulations.[49]

There are a number of reasons that might be given to justify why trade mark law should be amended to ensure that 'Waltzing Matilda' is not able to be appropriated for commercial ends. The concerns that have been raised about the negative impact of allowing registration of national icons such as 'Waltzing Matilda' is part of a wider concern that 'the law [is moving] more and more of our culture's basic semiotic and symbolic resources out of the public domain and into private hands'.[50] The main concern here is that culturally important words, names and songs may be the property of a few who have secured exclusive rights, rather than available to all to whom those words, names and songs have meaning and are important.

Another argument that is made against allowing trade mark protection for icons such as 'Waltzing Matilda' is that it undermines the values that these icons

---

46 West, op. cit., p. 131.
47 N O'Reilly, 'The Influence of Peter Carey's True History of the Kelly Gang: Repositioning the Ned Kelly Narrative in Australian Popular Culture' (2007) *Journal of Popular Culture* 488, 494.
48 Advisory Council on Intellectual Property, op. cit., p. 8.
49 ibid.
50 M Madow, 'Private Ownership of Public Image: Popular Culture and Publicity Rights' (1993) 81 *California Law Review* 127, 142. See also D Lange, 'Recognizing the Public Domain' (1981) 44 *Law & Contemporary Problems* 147; R Cooper Dreyfuss, 'We Are Symbols and Inhabit Symbols, So Should We Be Paying Rent? Deconstructing the Lanham Act and Rights of Publicity' (1995–6) 20 *Columbia VLA J L* 123.

246   LANDMARKS IN AUSTRALIAN IP LAW

embody. Here the fear is that inappropriate use of the icon may dilute, diminish, or bring the word, name, tune or image, along with the reputation of anyone related to it, into disrepute. In some cases the disrespectful treatment of national icons, because of their close association with national history, traditions and values, has provoked reactions of outrage and distress. In the same way in which allowing a sex shop to be called 'Erotica on Bradman' discredits the Bradman legacy, so too allowing a restaurant or fast food outlet to name itself after a national icon undermines and trivialises the legacy of the song.[51]

While a number of arguments can be made in favour of ensuring that trade mark law should be changed so that cases such as *Lomas v Winton Shire Council* do not arise again, there are a number of counter-arguments that need to be taken into account. In this context it may be helpful to heed the salutary advice that has been given about the protection of icons.

> Paramedics are reporting a marked increase in the amount of people collapsing from icon overload, and several major population centers are now in danger of becoming engulfed by what a leaked government report describes as a 'national icon epidemic' ... The icon glut is due chiefly to the definition of the term now being so loose that it will sleep with absolutely anybody.[52]

One issue that was raised but not clarified by the decision, which is relevant to both the applicant and the opponents in the case, is whether the term 'Waltzing Matilda' could operate as an indicator of origin or of particular qualities of a product or service. The claim made by the council and the centre to 'Waltzing Matilda' was based on a kind of geographical indication: Winton was close to the place where the song was written and where it was first publicly performed. As the Trade Mark Registrar said, however, most Australians would not recognise that Winton had any better claim to 'Waltzing Matilda' than other places in Australia. This was because 'the association of Waltzing Matilda with the town of Winton is not known by the public at large. Reports of the Winton Waltzing Matilda centenary celebrations in the press would have been quickly forgotten'.[53] Questions could also be asked about whether Lomas was able to overcome the fact that the song, both its words and tune, is instantly recognisable as Australian. Its themes appeal to a romantic notion of the Australian outback; it is arguably part of the Australian identity, a marker of our social and cultural attitudes, part of our nation's cultural heritage, and a clear cultural signature. With this cultural baggage, does this mean that it is impossible for 'Waltzing Matilda' to denote a particular trader's goods or services? That is, is 'Waltzing Matilda' so closely connected to the Australian identity that it is not able to operate as an indicator of a particular trader or origin or an indicator of quality? In a sense, the question

---

51 It also has been suggested that the use of the word 'Diggers' in relation to a sports team was not accepted by the Australian community because the use of the word, in association with sport, served to 'dilute or trivialise the horrendous sacrifice and loss suffered by Australian and New Zealand Defence Force personnel in the First and Second World Wars.' Advisory Council on Intellectual Property, op. cit., pp. 2–3.
52 J Schembri, 'The Age of Icon Overload', *Age*, 5 August 2005, available at http://www.theage.com.au/news/opinion/the-age-of-icon-overload/2005/08/04/1123125852965.html.
53 *Waltzing Matilda Centre Ltd v Jolly Swagmen Pty Ltd* (2002) 58 IPR 499.

THE *WALTZING MATILDA* CASE   247

is, is it possible for a sign to become geographically generic? While the trade marks officer found that the song 'Waltzing Matilda' belongs to and indicates Australia as a whole, this did not prevent him from finding that the words could function as a trade mark. While he held that it was possible for 'Waltzing Matilda' to operate as a trade mark, the issue was not addressed on appeal. It is, however, an issue that goes to the heart of the question as to whether iconic signs are able to be protected as trade marks.

Many of the arguments made against allowing trade mark protection for cultural icons such as 'Waltzing Matilda' are based on the romantic belief that the song was not only written at a time when you could leave your back door unlocked, but also that it was written when the malign influence of commerce had not yet had a chance to influence our cultural practices. As with many of the arguments made about the negative impact of commercial practices on our cultural heritage, the argument that we need to protect 'Waltzing Matilda' from commercial ends presupposes that until recently the song has been untouched by financial considerations. One of the interesting things about 'Waltzing Matilda' is the fact that it has long been connected with commercial interests.

The fact that Paterson sold copyright in 'Waltzing Matilda' to Angus & Robertson for £5 shortly after it was published ensured that the story was treated as an object of trade and commerce.[54] More importantly, commercial ends have also played a role in shaping the modern version of the song. Following his appointment as an Indian representative to the Melbourne International Exhibition of 1880–81, the Scottish merchant James Inglis set up a company to import Indian tea into Australia. The tea was sold as 'The Billy Tea' (which was subsequently registered as a trade mark) and marketed using an image of a swagman boiling his billy. In 1902, Inglis asked the librarian of the Sydney Book Club if he knew of a verse which the company could use to market The Billy Tea. The librarian replied: 'There's some stuff of Banjo Paterson's in Mr Robertson's office that nobody seems to bother about'. These included 'Waltzing Matilda' which Inglis felt was well suited to advertise The Billy Tea.[55] In 1903 Inglis & Co paid Angus & Robertson five guineas for copyright in 'Waltzing Matilda'. In order to enhance the advertising appeal of the song, Marie Cowan, wife of the manager of Inglis & Co, was asked to alter the lyrics of 'Waltzing Matilda' so that they better promoted The Billy Tea.[56] As well as changing the lyrics and music of the song written by Paterson in 1895, to help with brand identification 'billy' was capitalised and placed in inverted commas to become 'Billy'.[57] Cowan's revised lyrics, which form the basis of the popular contemporary version of the song, are as follows:

---

54 C Roderick, *Banjo Patterson: Poet by Accident*, Allen & Unwin, St Leonards, 1993, p. 87.
55 Maggoffin, *Fair Dinkum Matilda*, op. cit. n. 8, p. 119.
56 Roderick, op. cit., p. 87; Richardson, op. cit. n. 8, p. 85.
57 The 1903 sheet music clearly shows 'Billy', not only with a capital B, but also in inverted commas to signify its product status. J Safran, 'Waltzing Matilda, Courtesy of a Tea-leaf Near You', *Age*, 20 December 2002, available at http://www.johnsafran.com/pdf/waltzingmatilda.pdf.

248 LANDMARKS IN AUSTRALIAN IP LAW

> Once a jolly swagman camped by a billabong
> Under the shade of a coolibah tree
> and he sang as he watched and waited till his 'Billy' boiled
> Who'll come a waltzing Matilda with me?

This is in contrast to the original lyrics which read:

> Once a jolly swagman camped by a billabong
> Under the shade of a coolibah tree
> and he sang as he looked at the old billy boiling
> Who'll come a waltzing Matilda with me?

The revised words and music, replete with one of the earliest examples of product placement in Australia,[58] were printed by Allan and Co, the music printer and publisher, and distributed with packages of The Billy Tea.[59]

Another argument that may be made against treating 'Waltzing Matilda' as a special case draws upon arguments made in other contexts about the creative role that traders play in popular culture. For example it has been suggested that '[t]raders who seek to negotiate the line between expressive meaning and trade marks should not be penalised for the contribution to popular culture'.[60] Whatever merits these arguments have in other contexts, they have little to say about the fate of 'Waltzing Matilda'. The reason for this is that the *Waltzing Matilda* case is not an instance where the trader's proposed use of the name as a trade mark would add to popular culture; so much as the trader is parasitic on popular culture, they are merely appropriating the sign and associated imagery for their own commercial ends.

Another point highlighted by the fate of 'Waltzing Matilda', which is not so much a counter-argument to the push to deny trade mark protection for 'Waltzing Matilda' so much as a call for additional considerations, is that while trade mark protection does have the potential to undermine the iconic sign, on reflection, it seems that we should be as worried about the use that is made of copyright and the role that it might play in restricting the way that we interact with our national icons as with trade marks. The reason for this is that copyright owners have the potential to censor use of the song. For example, an author of a book written about 'Waltzing Matilda' in 1955 complained that the copyright owners in the lyrics refused to allow him to reprint the words of 'Waltzing Matilda'.[61]

---

58 ibid.

59 Richardson, op. cit. n. 8, p. 134.

60 Richardson notes 'the expressive power of the law, its capacity as a kind of prestige dialect to foster desirable social attitudes and behaviour, could work better in promoting a healthy relationship between trade marks and language.' M Richardson, 'Trade Marks and Language' (2004) *Sydney Law Review* 193, 220.

61 May, op. cit. See also J Greenway, 'Folklore in Australia' (1957) 70 *The Journal of American Folklore* 202, 203. The SA Film Commission made a nine-minute animated film using 'Waltzing Matilda' – paying royalties to a NY company if it were played in the US as rights were assigned over. Radic, op. cit. n. 8, 9.

THE *WALTZING MATILDA* CASE 249

Similar problems have also arisen in relation to 'Advance Australia Fair'[62] and 'Happy Birthday'.[63]

Conclusion

The central question at the heart of *Lomas v Winton Shire Council* is the extent to which a cultural sign can function as a trade mark. That is, to what extent can 'Waltzing Matilda' be the subject of exclusive rights granted to a registered owner? It is this issue which the Winton Council and Waltzing Matilda Centre sought to resolve through the trade mark oppositions and various court proceedings. Underpinning the opposition was a desire to protect the words so that they would remain available for all Australians, to prevent them from being reserved for use for a select few. Ultimately those efforts met with no success, as the words are clearly distinctive and capable of distinguishing goods or services. It was clear that there was no legislative basis on which it could be said that the words could not operate as a trade mark. The centre also lobbied the federal government to obtain protection similar to that afforded to other cultural icons, such as ANZAC[64] and DON BRADMAN.[65] Again, those efforts met with no success.

While, as we said before, there is little doctrinally interesting about the case, nonetheless it is still interesting in what it tells us about Australian law and the machinations involved in the effort to protect culturally significant signs. In this context, trade mark law pulls in a number of different directions. The ability of the public to use and adapt cultural items needs to be juxtaposed with the need to ensure that the sign and the stories that have developed alongside it are respected, preserved and not tarnished by inappropriate use.

One of the things highlighted by the treatment of 'Waltzing Matilda' is that legal protection is not only about ensuring that a sign is not undermined and discredited. It is also about receiving official imprimatur; the establishment's sign of approval. This can be seen in the comments made in relation to the decision to protect Bradman's name. For example, it was said that adding Bradman's name to the hallowed list assures his status as an icon in the development of a unique Australian identity along with the Queen and the 'Aussie Digger'.[66]

---

62 For discussion of some of the copyright-related problems in relation to 'Advance Australia Fair' and 'Australia Land of Ours', see M Minell, *A Nation's Imagination: Australia's Copyright Records, 1854–1968*, National Archives of Australia, Canberra, 2003, pp. 132–3. Minell refers to a Hansard report from 30 April 1942 in which a 'member of the House of Representatives expressed concern that APRA was collecting royalties for broadcasting *Advance Australia Fair*. The Prime Minister, Mr Curtin, responded that the claim for copyright had been reviewed and reported on by a parliamentary committee but that the report had not been presented to the Parliament, which was occupied with the war. However, a memo dated 29 November 1942 indicates that Hon Arthur Calwell (then Minister for Information) had arranged that *Advance Australia Fair* and, in some cases, the British and American national anthems would be played in picture theatres.
63 On the copyright in 'Happy Birthday', see K McLeod, *Owning Culture: Authorship, Ownership and Intellectual Property Law*, Lang Publishers, New York, 2001, p. 50.
64 See n. 43 above.
65 See n. 44 above.
66 H Black, 'Corporations Law Goes into Bat for Bradman' (2000) 4 *Telemedia* 97.

In a similar vein it was also said that the amendments to the *Corporations Law* in 2000 'confirms Bradman's unique status among his diehard Australian fans and elevates the protection of his name to a statutory level.'[67] Given the anti-authoritarian sentiment of 'Waltzing Matilda', in many ways it is perhaps fitting that it has not been given any special protection. Is it better that 'Waltzing Matilda' gains the legal imprimatur, like Bradman and ANZAC, or is it better to be left to the vagaries of the public domain where it is free to be used by anyone? What would Paterson have found worse: the fact that the song was being used to sell food to tourists in a remote Queensland town,[68] or the fact that for a small fee you can get a Slim Dusty rendition of 'Waltzing Matilda' as a ringtone for your mobile phone?[69] As in the case itself, the key question here is who is entitled to own and control the sign. Should it be Paterson as author of the original song? If so, what stake does Marie Cowan have in the revised lyrics? What of Winton as the place where the song was first performed? Should the name 'Waltzing Matilda' be controlled by those who spend the time and effort adapting the sign to promote their specific trading ends? Or should it be the Australian public?

---

67 ibid.

68 According to one report, Paterson was not overscrupulous about what and where he published. Greenway, op. cit.

69 Or that Paterson's creation has been merged with Qantas, which was founded in Winton, to create the Qantilda Museum?

15

The *Panel* case

Melissa De Zwart[*]

Introduction

The story of 'the *Panel* case' sheds more light on the nature of the Australian broadcasting industry and some of its larger-than-life personalities, than it does upon the scope of Australian copyright law that was ostensibly the concern of the case. The concept of what constitutes a 'substantial part' of a television broadcast remains unclear and the application of the test of fair dealing was demonstrated as producing highly subjective and unpredictable results, subject to personal issues of taste and interpretation. Overall, the *Panel* case was a frustrating and expensive journey and the outcomes of the litigation were unsatisfactory and unhelpful to those involved and the television industry at large.

The case was first heard by Conti J in the Federal Court in November 2000. Conti J was to issue two judgments, one relating to the re-broadcast of the relevant images[1] and one relating to making a cinematograph film of the broadcast.[2] The matter was then appealed to the Full Federal Court, which issued judgment in 2002.[3] The High Court handed down its opinion on the appeal from the Full Federal Court in March 2004, leaving a number of matters to be decided by the Full Federal Court.[4] The Full Federal Court's second decision was produced in

---

[*] The author would like to thank Channel Ten for permission to interview participants regarding this case; Richard Cobden SC, Robert Todd and Karen Gettens for their personal insights into the running of the case; and Michael Hirsh for his ongoing patience with my obsession with this case. Any errors are, of course, those of the author. It is noted that Channel Nine was also contacted and invited to participate in this project but, due to the extensive change in personnel at that network, declined this invitation.

[1] *TCN Channel Nine Pty Ltd v Network Ten Pty Ltd* (2001) 50 IPR 335.

[2] *TCN Channel Nine Pty Ltd v Network Ten Pty Ltd* [2001] FCA 841.

[3] *TCN Channel Nine Pty Ltd v Network Ten Pty Ltd* (2002) 55 IPR 112.

[4] *Network Ten Pty Ltd v TCN Channel Nine Pty Ltd* (2004) 59 IPR 1.

252   LANDMARKS IN AUSTRALIAN IP LAW

May 2005[5] with the final hearing of the matter, being the unsuccessful application for special leave to appeal again to the High Court, in October 2005.[6] This long and draining litigation produced greater uncertainty for practitioners and television producers alike, and ultimately, benefited neither of the networks nor the public. The case gives us some interesting insights into the nature of the Australian broadcasting industry, however, and surprisingly, given the nature of the program the subject of the dispute, the importance of sport to Australian television broadcasting. This chapter will focus on the background to and context of the litigation, as well as the legacy of the decision.[7]

The media mogul, the cricket hero and the bride

Our story begins, according to industry insiders, with Kerry Packer watching the television one Wednesday evening when *The Panel* was broadcast on Channel Ten.[8] Kerry Packer was a larger-than-life character. He had inherited a large media empire in 1974 upon the death of his father, Sir Frank Packer, which included Australian Consolidated Press and the Channel Nine stations in Melbourne and Sydney. Although initially preoccupied by the print side of his empire, Packer developed a special vision for his television network. Modelled upon the Hollywood star system, Packer developed a stable of Australian stars and built the network into the ratings leader in Australia. Packer went on to become Australia's richest man. Despite his personal affection for the Nine Network, Packer had sold Channel Nine to Alan Bond for $1 billion in 1987 and purchased it back three years later for $250 million. He was also a compulsive television viewer. He would watch television late into the night, presumably channel surfing, but with a particularly keen and critical eye for Channel Nine content. Well-known for ringing up Channel Nine executives and expressing his point of view,[9] this time his call was to the Channel Nine lawyers demanding that they 'Stop these f**kers stealing my material'. The catalyst for this demand is believed to have been the

---

5 *TCN Channel Nine Pty Ltd v Network Ten Pty Ltd (No. 2)* (2005) 65 IPR 571.
6 *Network Ten Pty Ltd v TCN Channel Nine Pty Ltd* [2005] HCA Trans 842 (7 October 2005).
7 This chapter is concerned with the cultural background to and significance of the case. For a more detailed analysis of the technical nature of copyright in television broadcasts and its legislative history, see D Brennan 'Australian Television Broadcasts as Copyright Property' in F Macmillan and K Bowrey (eds.), *New Directions in Copyright Law, Vol. 3*, Edward Elgar, Cheltenham, UK, 2006.
8 *The Panel* was broadcast on Channel Ten on Wednesday evenings at 9.30 pm, running for 60–90 minutes. The show was live to air, and featured a panel of regulars and special guests, discussing the week's events, news and media. The program was produced by Working Dog Pty Ltd, which was not a party to the action, as the case concerned broadcast copyright. The program was broadcast regularly from 1998 to 2004, with Christmas specials only being produced during 2005–07. See further discussion below.
9 See G Stone, *Compulsive Viewing, The Inside Story of Packer's Nine Network*, Viking, Melbourne, 2000, pp. 104–5. Stone describes Packer ringing then TCN Managing Director David Leckie in September 1992 and demanding that he take *Australia's Naughtiest Home Videos* off air, five minutes into the screening. Leckie refused, on the grounds that it had been passed by the censor and he did not want to disrupt scheduled programming. Packer persisted with repeated phone calls. Stone continues: "'You fucking do as I say or I'll fucking well do it myself.'" Packer finally tells him. Which he does, phoning directly to the station's on-air co-ordinator. She can still see the mushroom cloud rising from the earpiece as she turns in catatonic shock to cue in a laugh-filled edition of *Cheers*.'

THE *PANEL* CASE   253

re-broadcast by *The Panel* of a notorious piece of footage that had harmed the reputation of one of Packer's closest friends, former cricketer turned Channel Nine commentator, Tony Greig. It may also have had something to do with the fact that *The Panel* was perceived by some at Channel Nine as singling Nine out for ridicule, although there was no evidence at the time that Nine was targeted any more frequently than other networks. *The Panel* was very popular, rating highly and attracting spin-offs in Ireland and New Zealand.[10] That in itself may have been enough to earn Packer's wrath.

Tony Greig had been friends with Packer since the World Series Cricket days.[11] Greig had taken a risk by signing up as the captain of the World XI, losing the captaincy of England and gaining the ire of the traditional cricketing fraternity. So taken with the concept of World Series Cricket was Greig that he acted as a recruiting agent for Packer, with whom he formed a life-long friendship, and become a star of the Channel Nine cricket commentary team.[12] It was as a commentator that Greig was to fall under the critical gaze of the team at *The Panel*.

In 1999, during a quiet moment in a one-day match between New South Wales and Victoria at the North Sydney Oval, the camera panned outside the oval to St Mary's Church where a happy couple happened to be leaving. The bride, then Marlene Case, was of Asian appearance, born in the Philippines, and the groom, Mark Zorn, was caucasian. Greig was in the commentary box with former Australian captain Mark Taylor. Adding some flavour to the footage on a slow day, Greig commented: 'Lovely little bouquet there and have a look at the carnation in his lapel.' Unfortunately, unable to resist the opportunity to make a joke at the bride's expense, he lowered the microphone, wrongly believing his next comment would be inaudible to the audience, and asked 'Do you think she's been flown in?' referring to the practice of 'mail order brides'.[13] This comment was heard by the viewers and later by the bride. Importantly, two viewers also brought the footage to the attention of *The Panel*, who re-broadcast the comments

---

10 The Panel, *Wikipedia*, available at http://en.wikipedia.org/wiki/The_Panel.
11 World Series Cricket involved not only a radical restructure of the game, with four new teams – Australia, the West Indies, Pakistan and the World XI (consisting of players from India, England and South Africa) – but also a drastically new approach to packaging, presenting and televising the game. Taking advantage of colour television and advances in camera technology, World Series Cricket introduced coloured uniforms, games under lights and improved coverage, with more angles, slow motion replays and the 'snick-o-meter'. The breakaway competition was prompted by Packer's frustration at not being able to secure the exclusive rights to televise cricket, despite offering $500 000 a season (well above the $70 000 paid by the ABC). The competition ran for three years, after which Packer and the Australian Cricket Board reached a settlement, brokered through Sir Donald Bradman, with Packer obtaining exclusive rights to televise the game for 10 years, as well as lucrative marketing and merchandise rights. The outcome included significantly higher pay for the players and has been hailed as bringing a whole new generation of fans to the sport of cricket. See further Stone, op. cit. n. 9, pp. 130–57.
12 G Haigh, 'Greig, a Limited Edition', *Age*, 3 January 2004, available at http://www.theage.com.au/articles/2004/01/02/1072908905386.html.
13 A 'mail order bride' is the disparaging colloquial term for a woman (usually from a developing country such as the Philippines) who marries an Australian man after meeting through an introduction agency. See *The Macquarie Dictionary*: 'a woman who comes from another country to marry a man after arrangements by correspondence, often through an agency.' *The Macquarie Dictionary Online* (2008), available at http://www.macquarieonline.com.au/dictionary.html.

254 LANDMARKS IN AUSTRALIAN IP LAW

and footage in October 1999.[14] Following this re-broadcast the incident became the subject of intense media scrutiny, leading to Greig's temporary suspension from the Channel Nine commentary team.[15]

Sport and television

At the time the *Panel* litigation was instituted, a dispute between Nine and Ten had long been brewing over the reuse of sporting content on Channel Ten's nightly sports wrap up, *Sports Tonight*. According to industry insiders, David Leckie, then Chief Executive Officer at Channel Nine, would regularly ring Channel Ten to complain about reuse of Channel Nine footage on *Sports Tonight*. *Sports Tonight* repackaged highlights from a range of sports and, as a half-hour sports show, went beyond what the networks have traditionally permitted one another to use in terms of sports highlights. Australian television broadcasters have traditionally worked upon the '3×3×3 rule', an unwritten 'gentleman's agreement' understood by industry members to allow the re-broadcast of three minutes of highlights, three times during a 24-hour period. In order to fill its half-hour timeslot, *Sports Tonight* frequently pushed Ten beyond the usage permitted under this gentleman's agreement, and a writ had been expected by industry players for some time.

Sporting content is an essential feature of Australian television. It is extremely popular[16] and, compared to drama and other content, cheap to produce. The cost to the networks comes, of course, in the price of exclusive access. Sport has had a significant impact on television; television in turn has impacted on how sport is played and organised.[17] The uptake of telecommunications facilities to provide nationwide broadcasts was driven largely by demand for access to sporting events.[18] Significantly, Kerry Packer himself shaped the future of cricket with the breakaway World Series Cricket competition. Not only did World Series Cricket change the players' uniforms, the format of the game and time of day at which matches were played, it also led to the design and construction of the light towers, which could turn night to day for the benefit of the cameras.[19]

---

14 L Hannan, 'How Tony Greig Ruined My Wedding', *Sun Herald*, 17 October 1999.
15 'Nine Gags Sport Commentators', *Australian*, 23 October 1999.
16 So popular, in fact, that the *Broadcasting Services Act 1992* (Cth) contains anti-siphoning provisions intended to ensure that specified sporting events are not 'siphoned' off to subscription broadcasters. The minister is empowered by s 115 of the Act to list sporting events 'the televising of which should, in the opinion of the minister, be available free to the general public', to which free-to-air broadcasters essentially have a right of first refusal. Such events include the Melbourne Cup, the AFL and NRL Premiership competition games (including finals), and all Australian test cricket matches and all one-day matches involving Australia.
17 For example, the delay in Australian Rules Football after a goal has been scored before the ball is bounced to restart play in order to allow for an ad break, and the playing of key tennis matches at night time during the Australian Open. See S Cunningham and T Miller, with D Rowe, *Contemporary Australian Television*, UNSW Press, Sydney, 1994, pp. 64–72.
18 T O'Regan, *Australian Television Culture*, Allen & Unwin, Sydney, 1993, p. 6.
19 G Stone, *Who Killed Channel 9?* Pan Macmillan Australia, Sydney, 2007, pp. 152–3.

During the 1990s, in addition to straight broadcast of sporting competitions, a number of what Cunningham and Miller have called 'inter-textual, post-modern sports shows'[20] emerged. These included HG Nelson and 'Rampaging' Roy Slaven's *This Sporting Life*, and *Live & Sweaty*, first hosted by Andrew Denton and later Elle McFeast. These shows facilitated 'critique and parody'[21] of the frequent banality, sexism, racism and jingoism of sports commentary, and *The Panel* was, in part, an inheritor of the mantle of this type of show, although its focus was on media more generally rather than sports alone.

At the time the action commenced, Channel Nine was the industry leader and had a strong reputation as a sports rights holder. Channel Ten on the other hand targeted a different market, the lucrative 18–35s, and could therefore have been perceived, through programs such as *The Panel*, as exploiting or free-riding on the content created by others such as Channel Nine.[22] As noted above, Kerry Packer characterised what Ten was doing as 'stealing his content'; this was echoed in argument by counsel for Channel Nine at first instance:

- ... We invest a lot of money in it. Have they got a commercial interest in being able to present TV using footage without having to pay for it, yes, where that does but help their bottom line. Do we have a commercial interest which competes with that, yes, plainly we do;
- ... Are they using our footage in a way which competes with us and hurts us – plainly they are;
- ... our commercial interest is winning the rating battle. Do they harm our commercial interest by pursuing a precisely competitive personal interest by means of filling up their program in part with [our] footage, yes.[23]

It is also interesting to observe that this case fits into a string of copyright cases brought by Channel Nine, including *Nine Network Australia v Australian Broadcasting Corporation*,[24] *Nine Films Television v Ninox Television*[25] and *Nine Network Australia v IceTV*.[26] Kerry Packer was regarded as a prodigious litigator, with respect to both his newspaper and television interests,[27] and these cases have, in turn, shaped the nature of copyright in Australia. Channel Nine is itself perceived in the industry as aggressive and prepared to push the boundaries in order to maintain its ratings position.[28]

---

20 Cunningham and Miller, op. cit., p. 70.
21 ibid., p. 87.
22 Channel Ten claimed that *The Panel* was the highest rating program in the 16–39 age demographic produced in Australia. See (2001) 50 IPR 335, 338.
23 ibid., p. 357.
24 *Nine Network Australia Pty Ltd v Australian Broadcasting Corporation* (1999) 48 IPR 333.
25 *Nine Films Television v Ninox Television Ltd* (2005) 67 IPR 46.
26 *Nine Network Australia Pty Ltd v IceTV Pty Ltd* (2007) 73 IPR 99.
27 D Salter, *The Media We Deserve*, Melbourne University Press, Melbourne, 2007, p. 269.
28 A more recent example of this attitude can be seen in the decision to produce *Underbelly*, a drama series based on Melbourne's gangland war. A suppression order was placed on transmission, publication, broadcast and exhibition of the series in Victoria on 15 February 2008, on the grounds that the Director of Public Prosecutions was concerned that the series would prejudice an upcoming murder trial.

256   LANDMARKS IN AUSTRALIAN IP LAW

The battle commences

Channel Nine commenced its action against Channel Ten by filing a statement of claim on 9 February 2000, seeking declaratory and injunctive relief and damages for infringement with respect to re-broadcast of Channel Nine material in breach of s 87(c) of the *Copyright Act*. A further amended statement of claim was filed, claiming additional damages relating to re-broadcasts made by *The Panel* after the original statement of claim had been filed.[29] During the hearing, Channel Nine sought leave to amend its statement of claim to include a claim that in recording the footage prior to broadcast, Channel Ten had also authorised an infringement of s 87(a) ('to make a cinematograph film of the broadcast, or a copy of such a film').[30] Conti J dealt with this issue in a later judgment.

The action related to 20 segments broadcast between 10 August 1999 and 28 June 2000.[31] As it transpired, the footage of Tony Greig's misfired joke that so enraged Kerry Packer was dropped from the action, most likely because Channel Nine's lawyers considered that it would most easily satisfy the test of being a fair dealing for the purposes of criticism or review[32] or the reporting of news.[33] The extracts the subject of the litigation covered a range of programs and subject-matter, including footage of the then Prime Minister John Howard getting up to shake hands with cricketer Glenn McGrath after he had won the Allan Border Medal and being overlooked by the cricketer; extracts from *A Current Affair* interviews with people who had visited a brothel believing it to be an introduction agency, used by *The Panel* to highlight the poor disguises employed; Prime Minister Howard singing 'Happy Birthday' to Sir Donald Bradman on *Midday*; and extracts from *Days of Our Lives* which drew attention to its bizarre storylines.

The arrival of the writs was met with some surprise by Channel Ten and its lawyers, who, as noted above, may well have been expecting such a claim with respect to *Sports Tonight* but not *The Panel*. Both parties probably assumed that the battle would be fought on the question of fair dealing, but as it soon transpired the arrow fired by Channel Nine across the bow of Channel Ten was to take a totally different trajectory, and one that would have significant repercussions for the industry as a whole.

---

29 (2001) 50 IPR 335, 338.
30 The videotaping of the extract was a necessary step in re-broadcasting the extract in the context of the discussion. Consideration of this issue arose from the testimony of Michael Hirsh during the hearing. See [2001] FCA 841, para. 4.
31 See the appendix at the end of this chapter for a complete list of programs and broadcast dates.
32 *Copyright Act 1968* (Cth) s 103A: 'A fair dealing with an audio-visual item does not constitute an infringement of the copyright in the item or in any work or other audio-visual item included in the item if it is for the purpose of criticism or review, whether of the first-mentioned audio-visual item, another audio-visual item or a work, and a sufficient acknowledgement of the first-mentioned audio-visual item is made.'
33 *Copyright Act 1968* (Cth) s 103B: 'A fair dealing with an audio-visual item does not constitute an infringement of the copyright in the item or in any work or other audio-visual item included in the item if: . . . (b) it is for the purpose of, or is associated with, the reporting of news by means of broadcasting or in a cinematograph film.'

The hearing of the matter commenced on 13 November 2000. Conti J was a little bemused by the basis of the claim, asking on the first day, 'Well isn't this just a clear case of parody or satire?' At that time, there was no fair dealing defence for the purposes of parody or satire, although one was introduced in the amendments to the *Copyright Act* in 2006.[34] The outcome in this case contributed to that reform by highlighting the need for such a defence. Conti J struggled with the need to fit the fair dealing defence either in the category of reporting of news or criticism or review, given the nature of *The Panel* as a humorous review of weekly events, combining sport, satire, current affairs, social commentary and chat.

The Panel was first broadcast in 1998. A weekly program broadcast live on Wednesday evenings at 9.30pm, *The Panel* featured a panel of regulars and guests discussing news, sport and current events in a humorous, unscripted chat style. Footage was selected from all Australian free-to-air networks, pay TV and other sources (such as films, advertisements and overseas material). As indicated above, material was often suggested by viewers who would send in video tapes with the relevant extracts. Frequently, the original broadcaster would provide the producers with better quality tape when informed by Channel Ten that their footage was to be used on *The Panel*. In fact, Channel Nine was still doing this during the course of the legal proceedings.[35]

Channel Nine claimed that each of the segments (originally broadcast on Channel Nine) were re-broadcast by Channel Ten, infringing Nine's broadcast copyright. 'Television broadcast' is defined by the *Copyright Act* as 'visual images broadcast by way of television, together with any sounds broadcast for reception along with those images.'[36] Notably, the definition does not refer to the scope of a broadcast and makes no reference to linking the broadcast copyright to a particular program or segment. At the relevant time, copyright in a television broadcast was defined in s 87 as follows:

> For the purposes of this Act, unless the contrary intention appears, copyright, in relation to a television broadcast or sound broadcast, is the exclusive right:
>
> (a) in the case of a television broadcast in so far as it consists of visual images – to make a
>
> (b) cinematograph film of the broadcast, or a copy of such a film; and
>
> (c) ...
>
> (d) in the case of a television broadcast or of a sound broadcast – to re-broadcast it.

---

34 The *Copyright Amendment Act 2006* introduced ss 41 A and 103 AA into the *Copyright Act*. Section 103AA provides: 'A fair dealing with an audiovisual item does not constitute an infringement of the copyright in the item or in any work or other audiovisual item included in the item if it is for the purpose of parody or satire.' The meaning of the words 'parody or satire' is not further defined. See further M de Zwart, 'The Copyright Amendment Act 2006: The New Copyright Exceptions' (2007) 25 *Copyright Reporter* 4.
35 Michael Hirsh, interview with Damien Carrick, *The Law Report*, ABC Radio National, 16 March 2004, available at http://www.abc.net.au/rn/talks/8.30/lawrpt/stories/s1065842.htm.
36 *Copyright Act 1968* (Cth) s 10(1). See also the definitions of 'broadcast' and 'wireless telegraphy', later amended by the *Copyright Amendment (Digital Agenda) Act 2000*.

258 LANDMARKS IN AUSTRALIAN IP LAW

Channel Nine claimed that each of the segments re-broadcast by Channel Ten constituted a 'substantial part' of its broadcast copyright.[37] Channel Ten rejected that the broadcasts of the excerpts constituted a substantial part of the original broadcasts, and even if they did, such re-broadcast was justified on the basis of fair dealing for the purposes of criticism or review or the reporting of news. In support of its argument, Channel Nine relied upon s 25(4)(a) of the *Copyright Act* as promoting an interpretation that a copy of 'any of the visual images comprised in a broadcast' is an infringement, each image which is broadcast constituting 'a television broadcast'. Alternatively, Channel Nine argued that the calculation of a substantial part of a television broadcast related to the program or, where a program was broken into segments, such as a news or current affairs program, the relevant segment. Channel Ten argued, at the opposite end of the spectrum, that the definition of broadcast required transmission to the public and hence, as the signal is transmitted 24 hours a day, the relevant period of broadcast was either one day or seven days, representing the weekly schedule.

Conti J held that Channel Ten had not broadcast a substantial part of any of the Channel Nine broadcasts. In doing so, he rejected both extremes contended for by the parties. He concluded that a broadcast must consist of a program or a segment of a program 'if a program is susceptible to subdivision by reason of self-contained themes'.[38] The issue of substantiality was to be determined by reference to quantity and quality of what had been taken, as well as in certain cases 'the object or purpose of taking'.[39] Thus if the re-broadcast images are used for a different purpose than the original broadcast, even if there is a commercial advantage, that use may not constitute an infringement. Conti J provided the following example:

> in particular circumstances, the taking of a relatively miniscule segment of a competitor's television broadcast for the object or purpose for instance of satire comedy or light entertainment, particularly in the wider context of a free and democratic society, may well in particular circumstances fall within '. . . the Tribunal's sense of fairness' . . . rather than constitute 'pirating'.[40]

This conclusion is based upon Conti J's understanding that copyright in television broadcasts was granted primarily to prevent signal piracy,[41] such protection being granted to protect the broadcaster's commercial interest.[42]

In writing his decision, Conti J was well aware that both parties thought the matters in dispute were important enough to be fought to the bitter end. He knew his decision, whichever way it went, would be appealed all the way up to the High Court. For this reason, he undertook a full consideration of whether each

---

37 See *Copyright Act 1968* (Cth) s 14(1)(a): 'a reference to the doing of an act in relation to a work or other subject-matter shall be read as including a reference to the doing of that act in relation to a substantial part of the work or other subject-matter'.
38 (2001) 50 IPR 335, 369.
39 ibid., pp. 370–1.
40 ibid., p. 371 (citations omitted).
41 ibid., pp. 354–5, 368.
42 ibid., p. 381.

THE *PANEL* CASE   259

of the extracts could be justified as a fair dealing, despite the fact that this was not necessary as he had found that there was no infringement of a substantial part of any of the original broadcasts. He began by establishing a list of principles regarding fair dealing[43] and then applied these principles to each of the extracts. Conti J reached a variety of conclusions. He found that fair dealing would have excused 11 out of the 20 segments on either the basis of fair dealing for the purposes of reporting of news or criticism or review. For example, with respect to the footage of Prime Minister John Howard singing 'Happy Birthday' to Sir Donald Bradman, Conti J would have rejected the use of footage on the basis of 'criticism or review' on the grounds that the purpose of the use of the extract was 'to satirise aspects of Ms Kennerley's performance as presenter of *Midday* and certain supposed personality traits and political allegiances' rather than a critique of *Midday* itself.[44] Similarly, Conti J rejected that use of the footage could be justified as the 'reporting of news' as the footage had already been shown on Channel Nine: 'Ten's purpose in re-broadcasting the event was rather to satirise the Prime Minister's already well-known admiration for Sir Donald Bradman.'[45]

Conti J issued a separate judgment with respect to the question of infringement with reference to s 87(a) which provides:

> For the purposes of this Act, unless the contrary intention appears, copyright, in relation to a television or sound broadcast, is the exclusive right:
> a) in the case of a television broadcast in so far as it consists of visual images – to make a cinematograph film of the broadcast, or a copy of such a film.

Channel Nine again relied upon s 25(4) as extending this definition to include making a cinematograph film of 'any of the visual images comprised in the broadcast', meaning that each image of the Nine broadcast copied by Channel Ten was the subject of television broadcast copyright. Conti J concluded that there was no basis for concluding that s 87(a) should be interpreted to apply television broadcast copyright to each single image of the broadcast[46] and that the relevant test should be applied to a television program or identifiable segment, as with respect to s 87(c).

Channel Ten had argued in the alternative that it had an implied licence to tape the Channel Nine programs 'based upon trade practice and usage in Australia'.[47] Evidence was presented to the court that it was common practice for broadcasters to tape material put to air by other broadcasters, with or without permission.[48] However, reviewing the more specific evidence presented by Channel Nine, Conti J concluded:

---

43 ibid., pp. 380–1.
44 ibid., p. 388.
45 ibid.
46 [2001] FCA 841 (4 July 2001), para. 18.
47 ibid., para. 21.
48 ibid., paras. 12–16.

There does not exist in Australia, at least among the major television broadcasters, such as those the subject of the present proceedings, any established trade practice or custom constituting a mutually implied license to the effect that a television broadcaster is entitled to make a video tape of a programme, or an excerpt of a programme, previously broadcast by another television broadcaster, for any purpose, and that the second-mentioned television broadcaster would consider itself uninhibited from making complaint or seeking redress, unconstrained by any supposed existence of any custom or usage to the contrary, by such processes as it may judge to be appropriate in the circumstances of the case, where the infringement of copyright has occurred in circumstances outside what it may consider to be the perceptibly justifiable protection of applicable fair dealing defences.[49]

On appeal, the Full Federal Court rejected Conti J's findings regarding what constituted a television broadcast and therefore the calculation of a substantial part, holding that by making videotapes of the relevant segments, Channel Ten had infringed s 87(a) of the *Copyright Act*, and the re-broadcast of those segments on *The Panel* was an infringement of ss 87(c) and 101 of the Act.[50] Hely J, delivering the majority judgment, held that copyright subsisted in the 'visual images and accompanying sounds' and that by broadcasting those images and sounds, Channel Ten had infringed the broadcast. The court was then required to apply the fair dealing defences to determine infringement. The court held that there was infringement with respect to 11 of the extracts. There was little consensus between the judges, however, regarding the application of the particular fair dealing defences to the various segments.[51] For example, with respect to the re-broadcast of the footage of the then Prime Minister singing 'Happy Birthday' to Sir Donald Bradman, Sundberg J held that this was neither for the purposes of criticism or review of *Midday* nor the reporting of news.[52] Finkelstein J on the other hand, held that fair dealing was made out on both grounds: the discussion of Ms Kennerley related to her 'talents as the program's host' and was therefore criticism or review, and 'an incident where the prime minister of a country has behaved in a way which some might call "silly" is certainly newsworthy.'[53]

During this time, *The Panel* continued to go to air and continued to use footage originally broadcast on others stations, including Channel Nine. As Michael Hirsh told *The Law Report*, however, the producers of the program were told to be more careful and deliberate in the way in which they introduced and presented the material, making it clear that the material was being used within the scope of fair dealing.[54]

---

49 ibid., para. 27.
50 (2002) 55 IPR 112.
51 For an analysis of these decisions, see further M de Zwart 'Seriously Entertaining: *The Panel* and the Future of Fair Dealing' (2003) 8 *Media & Arts Law Review* 1; M Handler 'The *Panel* Case and Television Broadcast Copyright' (2003) 25 *Sydney Law Review* 391; and M Handler and D Rolph '"A Real Pea Souper": The *Panel Case* and the Development of the Fair Dealing Defences to Copyright Infringement in Australia' (2003) 27 *Melbourne University Law Review* 381.
52 (2002) 55 IPR 112, 113–14.
53 ibid., p. 118.
54 See n. 35 above.

THE *PANEL* CASE   261

Before the High Court: the meaning of substantial part of a broadcast

The two issues on appeal before the High Court were the questions of what constitutes a television broadcast for the purposes of the *Copyright Act* and what is a substantial part of such a broadcast.[55] The Full Federal Court had held that a single image would qualify as a broadcast, leaving little scope for re-broadcast without permission of the original broadcaster.

Ultimately, the High Court did very little to assist with the resolution of this question. The majority (McHugh ACJ, Gummow and Hayne JJ) stated:

> There can be no absolute precision as to what in any of an infinite possibility of circumstances will constitute 'a television broadcast'. However, the programmes which Nine identified in pars 5.1–5.11 of its pleading as the Nine Programs, and which are listed with their dates of broadcast in the reasons of Conti J, answer that description. These broadcasts were put out to the public, the object of the activity of broadcasting, as discrete periods of broadcasting identified and promoted by a title, such as *The Today Show, Nightline, Wide World of Sports,* and the like, which would attract the attention of the public.[56]

This of course left open the question of whether anything less than a complete program (other than advertisements) could constitute a broadcast, and this question remains to be determined as a question of fact in later cases.

Kirby and Callinan JJ, in separate dissenting judgments, held that each visual image capable of being observed as a separate image on a television screen and the accompanying sounds is a 'television broadcast'. Kirby J adopted a strict approach to the wording of the legislation, concluding that parliament intended to create a form of copyright appropriate to the visual medium of television. Callinan J based his reasoning in the commercial nature of the interest being protected, concluding: '[I]n recognising the validity of the respondents' copyright in excerpts from their programmes, the court would not be denying access to the general public of the golden words of a new Shakespeare.'[57]

The matter was remitted back to the Full Federal Court.

The return leg: back to the Full Federal Court

All that remained for the Full Federal Court to do was to apply the High Court majority's test of substantiality with respect to the taping and the re-broadcasts.[58]

---

55 As counsel noted, this is the 'only case which has been decided on television broadcast copyright in the whole of the common law world': [2005] HCA Trans 842 (7 October 2005) (Ireland QC). For further analysis of the High Court decision see M de Zwart 'Copyright in Television Broadcasts: *Network Ten v TCN Channel Nine* – "A Case Which Can Excite Emotions' (2004) 9 *Media & Arts Law Review* 277.
56 (2004) 59 IPR 1, 21 (footnote omitted).
57 ibid., p. 39.
58 (2005) 65 IPR 571. For further analysis of this decision, see M de Zwart, '*TCN Channel Nine v Network Ten (No. 2)* (2005) 10 *Media & Arts Law Review* 249, upon which this section is based.

262   LANDMARKS IN AUSTRALIAN IP LAW

All three judges concluded that Channel Ten had taken a substantial part of several of the Channel Nine broadcasts. They disagreed yet again, however, about which ones. Finkelstein J (with whom Sundberg J concurred) held that infringement had occurred with respect to the extracts from the *Inaugural Allan Border Medal Dinner*, *Midday* (Prime Minister John Howard singing 'Happy Birthday'), *Wide World of Sports* (Grand Final celebration), *Australia's Most Wanted* (re-enactment of stabbing), *Pick Your Face* (Kerri-Anne Kennerley) and *The Today Show* (child yawning). Hely J would have found infringement with respect only to the extracts from *Midday*, *Australia's Most Wanted* and *Pick Your Face*.

In his assessment of what constitutes a substantial part with respect to broadcast copyright, Finkelstein J incorporated concepts such as the economic significance of the part which has been copied and the use to which the defendant puts the copied portion of the work.[59] He identified that the key question which needs to be asked in determining substantiality is: 'Does what has been taken amount to "essentially the heart" of the copyrighted work?'[60] If the answer is yes, then a substantial part may have been taken, even if the extract is very short. For example, Finkelstein J held that the footage showing a child yawning during an interview, although constituting only nine seconds out of a much longer program, was substantial on the basis that '[i]t [wa]s a memorable part of the interview'.[61] Hely J reached a completely different conclusion, stating:

> The part taken is fleeting in nature and on the periphery of the original broadcast, making little, if any, contribution to the subject matter of that broadcast. The footage taken is only incidental to the source broadcast, and is trivial, inconsequential or insignificant in terms of that broadcast.[62]

The end of the game

The matter was to have its final hearing in a special leave application by Channel Ten before McHugh and Kirby JJ on 7 October 2005. By this time, the broadcasting landscape had changed considerably. *The Panel* was no longer a regular feature at Channel Ten, Working Dog moving on to the highly successful format of *Thank God You're Here*. Kerry Packer was gravely ill and was to die on Boxing Day of 2005, his empire left in the hands of those who would spend the next year tearing it apart.[63]

The last outing for the case was an argument put by John Ireland QC that the High Court should grant leave to appeal on the question of substantial part.[64] He argued that the majority in the Full Federal Court had developed 'a new and racy approach to the legal test to be applied [to determine substantiality]' based upon

---

59 (2005) 65 IPR 571, 575, paras. 11 and 13.
60 ibid., p. 580, para. 27.
61 ibid., p. 582, para. 37.
62 ibid., p. 590, para. 65.
63 See Gerald Stone, op. cit. n. 19, pp. 1–14.
64 [2005] HCA Trans 842 (7 October 2005).

a series of 'catchphrases' drawn largely from US authority. McHugh J rejected this argument stating that the test is a factual one only and these are merely descriptions of the process of reasoning:

> Even if this was a unanimous judgment of the Full Court and these statements were contained in it, they would be binding on nobody. The most junior judge in the nation would be entitled to disregard them. They are questions of fact, that is all they are. They stand for nothing. The only legal test is substantiality.

Kirby J too had a swipe at counsel:

> KIRBY J: . . . Lawyers do not like statutes. We have found that over and over again.
> MR IRELAND: We work with them every day, your Honour.
> KIRBY J: The Bar table hates statutes: they love the words of the judges. We understand this affection but ultimately the duty is to the statute.

At one point, however, Kirby J did seem to be willing to grant special leave:

> Is there a danger if this judgment stands that some of these American expressions in paragraph 27, for example, of Finkelstein J's reasons will get the standard of holy writ and that instead of statute these American endeavours to explain the idea in our state will become elevated into so-called legal test? This is a bit of a worry if this would be the result of what Finkelstein J has done.

Counsel for Channel Nine, Bannon SC, however, argued that the test proposed by Finkelstein J is merely a restatement of the application of the statutory test, rather than a deviation from it. Ultimately the High Court judges were persuaded and special leave was refused, with a warning that courts should avoid turning factual synonyms into legal tests.[65]

Conclusion: what lessons can we draw from this story?

As one leading practitioner in this area stated, the outcome of the case has made it a lot more difficult to advise clients regarding the concepts of substantiality and fair dealing. Every judge who heard the case came to a different conclusion regarding the legitimacy of the use of the extracts, resulting in less certainty. Less predictability in outcomes inevitably raises the risk and hence the costs of production. The next case to arise in this area will be a difficult and fraught process. It is likely, of course, that the next case will also consider the new parody and satire fair dealing defences.

Further, this case raises issues about postmodern concepts of creativity, or as one person interviewed for this article put it, 'The Panel as a mash up'. What scope does the decision leave for the reuse and repackaging of existing material in a different context? The tests proposed by Finkelstein J would appear to leave very little scope, even for creative reuse.

---

65 ibid. per McHugh J: 'The synonyms or descriptions used by Finkelstein J are factual synonyms. In other cases, they will no doubt be entitled to respect but they do not bind as a matter of law.'

Watching the excerpts in the context of their re-broadcast as part of *The Panel* discussion, it is difficult to believe that they became the subject of an infringement action. For example, the extracts from *Wide World of Sport* were brief and divorced almost entirely from the broader context of their original broadcast. They conveyed little about the standard of the game or the players' involvement or performance in that game, and much more about society's attitudes to male bonding. Hely J suggested that the fact that Glenn Lazarus was playing his last game transformed the eight-second footage of him turning a cartwheel into something substantial.[66] The influence of sports on television and in turn upon the copyright protection of the investment in that medium is an extensive one. The stakes are likely to increase with the expansion of high definition television, which is more expensive to produce.

The case, and the fact that it was run at all, tells us something about the history and nature of the Australian broadcasting industry. Channel Nine was at the time of the action the clear ratings leader, Kerry Packer was on top of his game and Channel Ten was seen as the upstart. Much has changed since then. Channel Nine has ended its reign as ratings winner, losing to Channel Seven in 2007 after a number of years in decline.[67] The result will be of little comfort to Channel Nine in seeking to explore new models of production and program formats. The uncertain outcome of the case leaves the door open for further litigation on issues of user creativity and creative re-use.[68]

---

66 (2005) 65 IPR 571, 582.
67 See L Sinclair, 'Nine Losing its Grip on Advertising', *Australian*, 10 May 2005; D Enker, 'The Stars of 2007', *Age*, 13 December 2007, available at http://www.theage. com.au/news/tv-radio/the-stars-of-2007/2007/12/12/1197135533655.html.
68 Perhaps in the context of television content being repackaged on the internet or perhaps vice versa: see, for example, Channel Ten's *Friday Night Download*, which repackages material from the internet.

Appendix

Channel Nine Program Title	Date of Broadcast by Nine (Chronological Sequence)	Date of Re-broadcast by Ten of Excerpts from Nine Broadcast	Duration of Nine Program	Duration of Nine Segment (if applicable)	Duration of Ten Re-broadcast (i.e., *Panel* Segments)
The Today Show (Boris Yeltsin)	10 August 1999	11 August 1999	90 mins & 2 secs	1 min & 24 secs	13 secs
Midday (Prime Minister singing)	26 August 1999	9 September 1999	67 mins & 34 secs	15 mins & 5 secs	17 secs
Wide World of Sports (Grand Final Celebration)	26 September 1999	29 September 1999	4 hrs 57 mins & 30 secs	8 mins & 16 secs	8 secs
A Current Affair (Masquerade as Introduction Agency)	19 October 1999	20 October 1999	22 mins & 51 secs	6 mins & 39 secs	9 secs
Australia's Most Wanted (ARIA Award)	11 October 1999	13 October 1999	43 mins & 2 secs	8 mins & 55 secs	20 secs
Pick Your Face (Kerri-Anne Kennerley)	20 August 1999	1 September 1999	22 mins & 32 secs	7 mins & 23 secs	28 secs
Crocodile Hunter (Scuba Diving)	21 August 1999	25 August 1999	42 mins & 50 secs	7 mins & 23 secs	28 secs
Days of Our Lives (Marlena Standing)	19 August 1999	26 August 1999	40 mins & 5 secs	3 mins & 42 secs	21 secs
Days of Our Lives (Marlena Levitating)	20 August 1999	26 August 1999	38 mins & 9 secs	6 mins & 52 secs	25 secs

(cont.)

Channel Nine Program Title	Date of Broadcast by Nine (Chronological Sequence)	Date of Re-broadcast by Ten of Excerpts from Nine Broadcast	Duration of Nine Program	Duration of Nine Segment (if applicable)	Duration of Ten Re-broadcast (i.e., *Panel* Segments)
Simply the Best (Ray Martin)	19 October 1999	20 October 1999	49 mins & 48 secs	3 mins & 10 secs	17 secs
'The Inaugural Allan Border Medal Dinner' (Prime Minister Embarrassed)	31 January 2000	8 March 2000	2 hrs 11 mins & 44 secs	42 mins & 17 secs (or at best 5 mins & 50 secs)	10 secs
Sunday (Drugs at Olympics)	19 March 2000	29 March 2000	1 hr 32 mins & 1 sec (alternatively 42 mins & 17 secs)	5 mins & 50 secs	36 secs
The 72nd Academy Awards (Artificial Fog)	27 March 2000	29 March 2000	3 hrs 26 mins & 32 secs	11 mins & 39 secs	25 secs
Sale of the New Century (Lighting Switched Off)	4 April 2000	5 April 2000	21 mins & 47 secs	8 mins & 11 secs	16 secs
The Today Show (Prasad Interview)	4 April 2000	5 April 2000	1 hr 29 mins & 56 secs	5 mins & 9 secs	42 secs
The Today Show (Opera House)	5 May 2000	10 May 2000	1 hr 29 mins & 59 secs	4 mins & 50 secs	27 secs
Nightline (Gosper Interview)	15 May 2000	24 May 2000	25 mins & 50 secs	3 mins	10 secs
Newsbreak (Technical Glitch)	22 May 2000	24 May 2000	40 secs	22 secs	13 secs
Who Wants to be a Millionaire (Ingredients of Xmas Pudding)	29 May 2000	7 June 2000	43 mins & 21 secs	10 mins & 18 secs	20 secs
The Today Show (Child Yawning)	28 June 2000	28 June 2000	1 hr 30 mins & 30 secs	4 mins & 33 secs	9 secs

Source: *TCN Channel Nine Pty Ltd v Network Ten Ltd* [2001] FCA 108 (20 February 2001).

Index

2,4-D (2,4-dichlorophenoxyacetic acid) 75–7

Aboriginal art
  bark painting 194
  cases xx, 191–208
  communal ownership and collective protection 203–7
  growing market 191
  recognition of private and communal rights 192
  religious significance 194–6
  unauthorised reproduction 191–2, 195
Aboriginal artists
  and fiduciary relationship with clan group 205–7
  and originality for copyright protection 197–200
  ownership rights 194
Aboriginal Arts Board 118
Aboriginal customary rights 110
Aboriginal folklore
  cases xx, 110–25, 191–208
  protection of 197–200
Aboriginal Sacred Sites Protection Authority 120
act of state doctrine 7–8, 13
Adams, Phillip 162
Administrative Appeals Tribunal (AAT) 210, 218–22
Advisory Council on Industrial Property 156–8
Advisory Council on Intellectual Property 245
agricultural and horticultural processes 92–4
Aickin, Keith 83
Amalgamated Society of Engineers v Adelaide Steamship Co Ltd 33
American Law Institute, principles for cross-border property adjudication 12
Angus & Robertson 99, 101

anthropology
  and cultural privacy 110
  emergence as academic discipline 111–16
  relationship between lawyers and anthrolopists 121–2
  role of anthropologist as expert 121
appellations of origin 213
Associated Racing Clubs (ARC) 56
Association for the Protection of Copyright in Sports (ACPS) 64
Association of Northern and Central Australian Aboriginal Artists 192
At the Waterhole (painting) 191–2, 194
Attorney-General of NSW v Brewery Employees' Union xx, xxiii
  constitutional challenge 22–4
  High Court decision 24–34
  implications of decision 34–6
  majority judgments 24–7
  minority judgments 27–32
Australasian Mechanical Copyright Owners Society (AMCOS) 182
Australasian Performing Right Society (APRA) 101
Australian Consolidated Press 252
Australian Constitution
  relationship between states 3–5
  s 51 3, 16, 19, 25, 30, 32–5
  s 92 3
  s 118 3
Australian Copyright Council (ACC) 99–101, 107
Australian Film Commission 161
Australian Jockey Club 56
Australian Law Reform Commission (ALRC), review of *Designs Act 1906* 152–7
Australian Music Publishers Association 182
Australian Record Industry Association 182
Australian Vice-Chancellors Committee (AVCC) 99

267

268 INDEX

Australian Wine and Brandy
Corporation 214
Authors' Right Act (Germany) 181–2

Banki, Peter 99, 107
Banks, Glenn 226
Barton, Edmund 7, 17, 22, 24, 32, 41
Barwick, Garfield 105, 134
Beaumont J 166, 167
*Beringer Blass v Geographical Indications
Committee* xx, xxii, 210
background – AAT decision 218–22
the case 218–25
discourse on evolution of geographical
indications 210–12
full court of the Federal Court 222–5
significance and influence of decision
225
Berndt, Catherine 114–15
Berndt, Ronald 115, 121–2
Berne Convention xx, 177, 180, 185, 189,
190, 203
Beveridge Committee into Broadcasting 64
BHP 6
Billy Tea 247–8
Boosey & Hawkes 182
Bowen, Nigel 184
Bowrey, Kathy 211
Bradman, Donald 243–4, 256, 259–60
Brandeis J 58, 60
Brennan CJ xxi, 206
Brennan, Paul 101
Brewery Employees Union of New South
Wales 15, 16, 22
registered mark 16, 21, 27
British Broadcasting Corporation (BBC) 64
broadcast rights 58
and the internet 65–6
in sporting spectacles 65–6
broadcasting industry 251–2
sport and television 254–5
Brown, Michael 122, 123
Brussels I Regulation 9–10
Buchanan, Alexander 184
Buckmaster, Lord 79–81
Bulun Bulun, John 191–2, 195–6, 198–200,
204–5
Bulun Bulun v R & T Textiles xx, xxii, 124
background 191–2
the case 193–6
direct infringement and copying 200
issues arising from the case 203–7
originality of artworks 196–200
trade practices issues 202–3

Burchett J 168
business name registration 133–4

Cadbury Schweppes 126–7, 133–4, 136,
137, 139
Cadbury Schweppes v Pub Squash xx
ancillary matters 133–4
appeal to Privy Council 134–6
the first instance decision 130–4
impact of case 138–40
initial Solo campaign 127–30
jurisdiction issue 134
unfair competition and passing off
131–2
Caenegem, William van 210
Calabresi, Guido xxiv
Callinan J 69–70, 123, 261
Carl Orff foundation 175
Carmina Burana cantata 171–5
Caruana, Wally 199
Case, Marlene 253
Catterns, David 99, 184
Central Land Council 120
Channel Nine 252, 255
Channel Ten 254–5
Chaplin, Charlie 161
cinema industry, in Australia 160–3
Coca-Cola 126–7
Codex Buranus 173
Colossal Records of Australia 182
common law, development of 73, 93, 94
Commonwealth trade mark 19
competition law 59
goals of 51
interaction with intellectual property
law 50–2
practical operation of 51–2
tension with intellectual property law 37
compulsory licencing provisions *see* statutory
and compulsory licencing provisions
confidential information, equitable doctrine
of 111, 116
public interest defence 119–20
constitutional interpretation
approach of Higgins 30–1
divisions over proper approach to 33
Conti J 251, 256–60
Cooke, Peter 198
Coonawarra case *see Beringer Blass v
Geographical Indications Committee*
Coonawarra Grape Growers Association
Inc 210, 218, 222
Coonawarra Vignerons Association Inc 210,
218, 222

Coonawarra wine label case
  see Beringer Blass v Geographical
    Indications Committee
Coonawarra wine region 209
  dispute over boundaries 210, 218–22
Copyright Agency Limited (CAL) 107–8
copyright law
  adaptation of works which are common
    property 197
  and communal ownership and collective
    protection 203–7
  compilations and raw data 61–4
  dealing with effects of new technology 97
  direct infringement and copying 200
  and education xix–xx
  in events 64–6
  liability of intermediaries for copyright
    infringement 97
  the meaning of 'substantial part of a
    broadcast' 261
  and originality 196–200
  player statistics 62
Copyright Tribunal 107
Cornell, John 163
Cowan, Marie 247–8
Crean, Simon 213–14
Crennan, Susan 139
Crocodile Dundee (film) xx, xxiii, 161–4
cross-border disputes, in a federation 1, 3–5
cross-border property adjudication,
  principles for 12
cross-vesting legislation 5, 12
Cullen, Sir William Portus 24
cultural icons 238, 239
  protection of 243–9
cultural privacy 110, 123
  and breach of confidence 117, 119, 124
  indigenous knowledge and cultural
    secrecy 122–5
  public interest defence 119–20
  and secret-sacred material and
    ceremonies 114–17

Dawson, Darryl xxi
Days of Our Lives (TV program) 256
Deakin Coalition Government 18
Deakin Liberal Government 17
Deane, William xx, xxii, 66
debasement
  meaning of 187–8
  in parliamentary debate 184
Delprat, Guillaume 2
Delprat–Potter process 3–5
Denton, Andrew 255

Derham, David 99
designs law
  ALRC recommendations relating to
    registered designs 153–6
  broader reform issues 157
  definition of 'design' 151
  definition of 'visual feature' 153
  infringement provisions 153–6
  protection of function 156–7
Designs Law Review Committee (DLRC) 151
Diplock, Lord 90
Dixon, Owen xxii, 58, 66, 90, 93, 94, 140, 143
Downe J 227–9
Dowsett J 229
Drahos, Peter 54
Drayton, Trevor 230
Duffy, Charles Gavan 24

economic rights 180
Edison, Thomas Alva 37
Edison phonograph 37
Edmond, Gary 211, 226
Elkin, AP 113–14
Enderby, Kip 45
English common law 3–9
  rules of private international law 3–5
epistemic things 81
European Community–Australian Wine
  Agreement 1994 210, 212–15
European Community–Australian Wine
  Agreement 2007 231–2
European Convention for the Protection of
  Human Rights and Fundamental
  Freedoms 69, 71, 123
European law 9–10
Evatt, HV 53, 57, 59–61, 68
Evershed J 88

federal politics, post-federation 16–19
federation 3
  founding fathers 17, 35
Finkelstein J 260, 262–3
Firmagroup Australia Pty Ltd 148
Firmagroup Australia Pty Ltd v Byrne &
    Davidson Doors (Vic) Pty Ltd xx–xxiii,
    142
  analysis and impact of case 142, 150–2
  background to case 142–4
  the case 146–50
  relevant designs law 144–6
Firmagroup designs case
  see Firmagroup Australia Pty Ltd v Byrne &
    Davidson Doors (Vic) Pty Ltd
Flash Screenprinters 192

270 INDEX

flotation process 2
Foale, Max 226–30
foreign intellectual property rights 3, 9–12
  current relevance of *Potter*
    principle 12–14
Foster v Mountford & Rigby xx, xxi, xxiii, 203
  significance then and now 110, 116–22
  social and political background of
    case 111–16
  and wider debate on indigenous
    knowledge and cultural secrecy 122–5
Frankfurter J 84, 85
Franki Committee 107–8

Gaudron J xxi, 123
geographical indications 43–4, 210–12, 214,
  226, 231–2
Geographical Indications Committee
  (GIC) 210, 216–20, 227, 229–30
Gibbs, Sir Harry xxi, 105, 134, 197
Gibson, Mel 161, 163
Gleeson, Anthony Murray 70
Glynn, Patrick 23
Godjuwa, Charles 198–9
Gould, Richard 115
Gregory Committee 64
Greig, Tony 253, 256
Griffith CJ 7, 9, 22, 24, 25, 32, 41–2
Grosby spoof advertisement 163–5
Grosset, Jeffrey 212
guild marks 29
Gummow J 70, 122, 123, 165–7, 261

Hack, Barton xviii
Hall, DR 23
Hall, Lynn 203
Hannah, Rell 225
Hardie, Martin 192
Hayne J 70, 122, 123, 261
Heath J 87
Hely J 260, 262
Hepworth, Cyril 161
Higgins J xxi, 17, 21–2, 24, 28–33, 35, 41
High Court
  approach on principle in *Menck* case 41
  composition of 22–3
  creation of 3
  judges and conflicts of interest 105
Hill J 186–7
Hilmer Committee 50
Hitchcock, Alfred 161
Hogan, Paul 161–3
Holman, WA 23
Hong Kong cases, *Esquel Enterprises v Tal
  Apparel* 10–11

Hooke, Huon 226–7
Howard, John 243, 256, 259–60
Hunter Valley wine region 230
Hutley JA 99, 102–5

indigenous cultural property
  doctrines of equity 123–4
  protection of 124–5
indigenous knowledge, and cultural
  secrecy 122–5
indigenous secrecy, violations of 110,
  111
innovation patent 158
Institut National des Appellations de
  Origine 213–14, 230
instrumentalism 54
integrity right 177, 185
Intellectual Property and Competition
  Review Committee (IPCRC) 50, 52
intellectual property law
  first appeal to Privy Council 39
  interaction with competition law 50–2
  and jurisdictional problems 6–14
  and objects of cultural heritage 243–9
  practical operation of 51–2
  symmetry across jurisdictions xix
  tension with competition law 37
  territoriality of jurisdiction xxiv
  universal tensions within xix
intellectual property rights 52
  interplay with property rights 211–12
intellectual property system, goals of 51
International Olympic Committee 65
IP Australia 159
Ireland, John 262
Isaacs, Isaac 17–19, 22–4, 27–8, 31, 33, 38,
  41, 45

Jacobs J 105, 106
Janke, Terri 212
Joint Committee of the Coonawarra Grape
  Growers Association Inc and the
  Coonawarra Vignerons Association
  Inc 210, 218
judges
  attitude to role xxi–xxii
  challenges for xxii
judicial activism, Mason era xxi

Keating, Paul 238
Kennedy J 42, 46
King J 148–9
King Valley 227–9
Kirby J 123, 261–3
Kraus, Ezra 75–6

land law 61
Latham CJ xxi, 57
law and geography movement 211
Leckie, David 254
Lees, Meg 214–15
legal obsolescence xxiv
Limestone Coast wine region 225–7
Lindgren J 186–8
Live & Sweaty (TV program) 255
Lloyd-Jacob J 88, 91
Lockhart J 145
Lomas, Brenda 239
Lomas v Winton Shire Council xx, xxii, 234
  the case 239–42
  significance of decision 234, 243–9

McFeast, Elle 255
McHugh J 261, 262
McMullan, Bob 214
McTiernan J 57, 105
Mad Max films 161–3
Maeder v Busch 90, 94
Magpie Geese and Waterlilies at the Waterhole (painting) 193
Manjimup Wine Region Association 230
Mansfield, 222
Margaret River wine region 229
Mason, Anthony xxi, 105, 119
Menck, Walter T 37, 39–40, 45
Menzies, Douglas 105
meta-litigation 218–25
Midday (TV program) 256, 259, 260
misappropriation 67
misrepresentation 169, 170
Mitchell, Edward 23
Mocambique rule 7, 12, 13
Moorhouse, Frank 97, 98, 101–2
moral rights xx, 172
  link to compulsory licensing 181–2
  protection in Australia 180, 183, 186, 189–90
  protection in Europe 176–7
  UK provisions 185
Morton J 88, 93, 94
Morton's rules 88, 89, 91
Mountford, Charles 110–14, 118
Muirhead J 117, 119–20
Murphy, Lionel 107
musical debasement 172, 183–4
Myers, Rupert 100, 104

national identity 238, 243–9
National Phonograph Co v Menck xx–xxiii, 37
  background 37–8
  case against Menck 38–44

the contract case 39–41
legacy of case 44–50
the patent case 41
US v English authority 41–2
National Phonograph Company of Australia 38–40, 44
National Research Development Corporation v Commissioner of Patents xix, xxii, xxiii
  background to case 74–9
  claims in patent application 78–9
  doctrinal issues 73
  impact of decision 73, 79, 95–6
  manner of manufacture 85–92
  new use claims 79–85
native title disputes 211, 225
Nelson, HG 255
New South Wales Law Reform Commission
  enforcement of foreign intellectual property rights 12–13
  privacy 69
New Zealand cases, *KK Sony Computer Entertainment v Van Veen* 10–11
nuisance 57–61

O Fortuna chorus xx, 172, 173–4
  Dutch litigation 178–9
  FCB remix 182–3
  litigation by Schott in Europe 178–9
O'Connor, Richard Edward 7, 17–19, 22, 24, 32–4, 220–2
O'Donnell, Gus 99, 104, 107
O'Loughlin J 222
Orff, Carl 171–5

Pacific Dunlop v Hogan xx, 136
  background to case 160–3
  facts 163–5
  judgments 165–6, 168
  limited remedy 170
  witness evidence and affidavits 166–8
Packer, Kerry 252–6, 262
Panel case
  see *TCN Channel Nine v Network Ten*
The Panel (TV program) xxiii, 252–7, 260, 262
passing off 131–4, 169
patent law
  agricultural and horticultural processes 92–4
  emergence and development of modern law 73, 79, 95–6
  innovation patent 158
  invention v discovery in biological science 83–5

272 INDEX

patent law (*cont.*)
  manufacture and performative nature of invention 91
  meaning of 'invention' 73, 80, 82
  meaning of 'manufacture' 85–7
  meaning and role of 'vendible product' 85–92
  purposive interpretation of patent claims 90
  role of High Court over scope of patentable subject matter 90–1
patents
  and agricultural and horticultural methods 79, 95–6
  earliest granted by Commonwealth 37
  federal legislation 3
  granting in Australian colonies xviii
  High Court approach on principle in *Menck* case 41
  as immovable property 7
  petty patent system 156–8
Paterson, Banjo 235, 245, 247
Pearce, George 17–18
Pemberton Wine Region Association 230
Peterson J 197
petty patent system 156–8
photocopying 97–8
Pickford, Mary 160
Pink, Olive 114
Pitjantjara Council 110, 117, 119–20
plant hormones and herbicides 74–9
Posner J 49
Potter, Charles Vincent 2, 6
Potter v BHP xx, xxiii
  current relevance in Australian law 12–14
  the decision 6
  factual background 1–2
  impact 1, 3
  intellectual property and jurisdiction 6–14
  jurisdictional problem 3
  legal landscape 3–5
  state patent laws 3
Powell J 128, 131–2, 139
privacy 68–72, 122, 123
  see also cultural privacy
Privy Council
  appeals from High Court 37, 39, 134–6
  appeals from states 127
  composition of board 39
  final appeals 127
  Menck case 43–4
product placement 248

professional sports industry, and player statistics in fantasy league games 62–3
property rights
  differing views on nature of 59
  infringement of 57
  interplay with intellectual property rights 211–12
  utilitarian approach to 59
proprietarianism 54
proprietary interest, recognition of new form of 56
Protection of National Icons (report) 245
Pub Squash 129–30, 133–4

quasi-property 57–9
Queensland Patent No.1, 1860 xviii

racing industry 55–6
Registrar of Trade Marks 234
Reid Government 17, 18
Reilly, Alexander 211, 225–7
resale price maintenance (RPM) 38
  changing attitudes to 45–6
  and the Chicago School 49–50
  current law 46
  deadweight loss under 49
  demand and supply in equilibrium 48
  legislative prohibitions on 44
  and mainstream economic theory 47–9
  and the retailer 46
  and the supplier 46–7
Rich J 57, 61, 68
Rigby 110, 118
Roch LJ 10
royalties 181

Sackville J 120, 218
Sacred Waterholes Surrounded by Totemic Animals of the Artist's Clan (painting) 192
Schott music publisher 175–6
  Dutch litigation 178–9
  legal action in Australia 180, 182–8
  O Fortuna litigation in Europe 178–9
Schott Musik v Colossal Records xx, xxiii, 172
  the appeal 186–8
  arguments on behalf of Schott 184–6
  background to legal action 176–7
  the case 182–4
  place in Australian law 188–9
  Tamberlin J's reasoning at first instance 186
Sedley LJ 70–1
service marks 31, 34

INDEX 273

Sharpe, Scott 226
Sheffield Cutlers' marks 19, 29, 31
Sheppard J 166–7
Sherman, Brad 210
Six Million Dollar Man 129
Slaven, Roy 255
Smith, Derek 226
Smith, James Joynton 56
social conditions, relationship with law xviii
soft drink market 126–7
Solo 126–7, 139
  the image before the product 129
  initial advertising campaign 127–30
  recent advertising campaigns 137–8
  revival of the Solo man 136
Somervell LJ 200
special events legislation 64
Spender J 234, 241–2, 244
Spicer Committee 62, 64
sport, and television 254–5
Sports Tonight (TV program) 254, 256
state patent laws, post-federation 3
states
  cross-vesting legisation 5, 12
  relationship between 3–5
states' rights xxi
statutory and compulsory licensing
    provisions
  limits on 181–2
  link to moral rights 181–2
  loss of power of authors 180–1
statutory and compulsory licensing
    provisions, debasement control 188–9
Steinberg, Kerry 199
Strehlow, TGH 114
strict legalism 93, 94
Sundberg J 262
Supreme Court of New South Wales 60
Supreme Court of Victoria 2, 6
Synerholm, Martin 77

Tailoresses Union of New South Wales 15, 22
Tamberlin J 186
TCN Channel Nine v Network Ten xx, xxii, 251
  on appeal 260–1
  hearing 256–60
  meaning of 'substantial part of a
    broadcast' 261
  re-broadcasts of Nine footage on Ten 266
  significance of case 263
  test of substantiality 261–3
terroir 212, 217
This Sporting Life (TV program) 255

Thomas A Edison Ltd 44
trade mark law
  and business registation 133–4
  importance of image over product 129
  national identity and cultural icons 235
  settled principles 234
trade marks law 15–16
  constitutional challenge over worker's
    marks 22–34
  meaning of 'trade mark' 25, 27–30
  proper function of trade mark
    protection 33–4
  provisions for workers' marks 15–16,
    19–21
trade unions, and trade marks 25
TRIPS Agreement 231

unfair competition 66–8
  appropriateness of a general tort 137
  and passing off 131–4
Union Label case
  *see Attorney-General of NSW v Brewery
    Employees' Union*
universities, and potential infringement of
    copyright law xix–xx, 99–100, 104,
    108–9
University of New South Wales 100–1,
    103–4, 106
*University of New South Wales v
    Moorhouse* xx, xxiii
  aftermath of case 107–9
  background to case 97–9
  High Court decision 105–6
  impact of decision 105–6
  legacy of 97
  mounting of an appeal 104–5
  public policy issues 102
  relevance of case 109
  scope of possible relief 102–4
  setting up a test case 99–101

vendible product test 87
Victoria Park Racing and Recreation
    Ground 53, 56
Victoria Park Racing v Taylor xx–xxiii, 140
  background to case 53, 55–6
  legacy of case 53–4, 61–8
  legal analysis 56–61
von Doussa J 123, 205–7, 222
Voyce, Malcolm 211

Wain, Ralph Louis 74, 77–9, 81–2
'Waltzing Matilda' (song) 235–9, 244–5,
    247–8

274 INDEX

Waltzing Matilda case
  see *Lomas v Winton Shire Council*
Waltzing Matilda Centre 234, 239
WALTZING MATILDA trademark 239
Watson, John Christian 17
Watson Government 17, 22
Went, Frits 74
West, Margaret 194–5, 198, 201–2
Whitlam Government 98, 99, 127, 134
Wilcox J 186–7
Williams, Sir Bruce 99
Williams, Terry 239
Wills J 42

Wilson J xxi
Winton Shire Council 234, 239
workers' marks
  origins of provisions 16–19
  provisions for 15–16
  statutory protection 31
World Intellectual Property Organisation
  (WIPO) 124–5
World Series Cricket 253, 254
Wright, Judith 98

Zimmerman, Percy 77
Zinc Corporation 2

For EU product safety concerns, contact us at Calle de José Abascal, 56–1°,
28003 Madrid, Spain or eugpsr@cambridge.org.

www.ingramcontent.com/pod-product-compliance
Ingram Content Group UK Ltd.
Pitfield, Milton Keynes, MK11 3LW, UK
UKHW020405060825
461487UK00009B/810